Война

1981.

BY JOVE, BIGGLES!
The Life of Captain W. E. Johns

BY JOVE, BIGGLES!

The Life of Captain W. E. Johns

Peter Berresford Ellis
and
Piers Williams

For Barry
With warmest good wishes
& soft landings!

Jenny Schofield
(Piers Williams)

W. H. ALLEN · LONDON
A Howard & Wyndham Company
1981

Typeset by Computacomp (UK) Ltd,
Fort William, Scotland

Printed and bound in Great Britain by
Mackays of Chatham Ltd, Kent

for the Publishers, W. H. Allen & Co. Ltd,
44 Hill Street, London W1X 8LB

ISBN 0 491 02775 3

*This book is affectionately dedicated to
Catriona Cardiff and the countless Biggles
fans, young and old alike.
Soft landings and no dud engines!*

W. E. JOHNS' PHILOSOPHY

Of two things, one thing is certain:
Either you are on the ground or in the air.
If you are on the ground there is no need to worry.

If you are in the air, one of two things is certain:
Either you are flying straight or you are turning over.
If you are flying straight there is no need to worry.

If you are turning over, one of two things is certain:
Either you will crash or you will not crash.
If you do not crash there is no need to worry.

If you do crash, one of two things is certain:
Either you will be injured or you will not be injured.
If you are not injured there is no need to worry.

If you are injured, one of two things is certain:
Either you will recover or you will die.
If you recover there is no need to worry.
If you die you CAN'T worry![1]

CONTENTS

	Acknowledgments	xi
	Introduction	1
1	An Ambition to be a Soldier	11
2	In the Trenches	19
3	The Flying Instructor	33
4	No. 55 Squadron, France	50
5	War Flying	72
6	Johns 'Fails to Return'	83
7	Prisoner of War	90
8	The Recruiting Officer	104
9	Artist to Editor	120
10	Biggles is Born	131
11	The Militant Pacifist	144
12	Voices Prophesying War	163
13	For the Duration	175
14	Years of Fame	198
15	Successful Juvenile Fiction	217
16	The Attacks	230
17	Biggles Lives!	244
	Source Notes	253
	Bibliography	273
	Index	299

ACKNOWLEDGMENTS

It is unfortunate that W. E. Johns never wrote a full-length autobiography. His style and wry humour would have created a story about his early flying days which would have ranked equally with his best air adventure fiction. The authors are well aware of their limitations in this respect, and when and where possible they have sought to let Johns' own descriptions speak for themselves.

It is a tragedy that, as the authors discovered while researching for this biography, Johns' personal papers and extensive library, including cuttings, books and albums of aviation photographs, have not been preserved. This proved to be a major stumbling block in piecing together the jigsaw of his life. Johns' own accounts, in numerous articles published in a wide variety of magazines but mostly in *Popular Flying*, *Flying* and *The Modern Boy*, are often undated and sometimes contradictory. Johns, of course, was not writing with a biography in mind but merely giving random reminiscences to entertain his readers. A great deal of our research was concerned with comparing and dating these accounts and contrasting them with other authoritative sources.

We would like to register our gratitude and thanks to the many people who offered their help, advice and encouragement during our researches for this work. In particular, special thanks must go to Mrs Marjorie Ellis and her husband, Squadron Leader Teddy Ellis; Mr and Mrs James Broom; Mrs Margaret Collins (herself currently preparing a memoir about her uncle W. E. Johns); Mrs Sabena Johns and Mrs Kathleen King; Michael Horniman of A. P. Watt Ltd, Johns' literary agent, who is also chairman of W. E. Johns (Publications) Ltd; J. W. Bell of Hope Agar & Co, Johns' accountant; and to A. E. Cormack of the Department of Aviation Records, RAF Museum, Hendon, for his enthusiastic advice and practical help. Thanks should also go to the above for much of the photographic material used in this work and also to

Roy Bateman, of Canton Studios, London NW5, for carrying out reproduction and studio work.

We should also like to thank Doctors Heyl and Braun of the Bayerisches Hauptstaatarchiv (Kriegsarchiv) of Munich; the staffs of the Imperial War Museum, the British Museum and Public Record Office; D. F. Jack MA (headmaster of the Robert Hale School, Hertford); Geoffrey Trease; Eric Leyland; Jack Cox (former editor of *The Boys' Own Paper*); Daniel Kirkpatrick (author of *Children's Writers*, St James Press); John Kirby (of the Adelaide *Sunday Mail*); Keith MacDonald (the Australian actor who played Biggles on radio); Philip Geeves (archivist of Amalgamated Wireless (Australia) Ltd); former Oxford University Press editors Charles Hadfield, Frank Eyre and John Bell; Miss Challice B. Reed (assistant programme information officer at the BBC); John H. Boag (former OC, Norfolk Yeomanry); M. Claude Nielsen and Mme Janine Freret of Les Presses De La Cité; Don Aitkin of Macquarie University and Sue Elderton of the University of Sydney; Mrs Elizabeth Lewisohn, Chris Lowder, Robert Polendine, Ian Fryer, John Carson and James Smith; the librarians of Express Newspapers, Mirror Newspapers and Associated Newspapers; Miss Yvonne Seeley (former publicity manager of Hodder & Stoughton); and also A. W. Lawrence and Jonathan Cape Ltd for permission to quote from *The Mint* by T. E. Lawrence.

In making these acknowledgments we hasten to add that all interpretations are our own and that any errors that may occur are the responsibility of nobody save ourselves.

Peter Berresford Ellis and
Piers Williams

INTRODUCTION

It is September 1918.

The young pilot looks nervously behind him. Behind and below he can make out seven black shapes, closing fast with his machine. They grow larger and he can identify them as Fokker DVIIs – enemy interceptors. He peers around desperately. His heavy bomber has been hit by anti-aircraft gunfire, petrol is swilling all over the cockpit and he has had to drop out of formation, away from the protection of the other aircraft of his squadron. His comrades fly on in the distance as if indifferent to his fate. The German fighter-aircraft are closing in for the kill.

Machine-gun fire rakes his lumbering bomber. A bullet sears painfully across his thigh; another smashes his goggles, causing the glass to fragment in his face and blood to gush into his eyes, obscuring his vision. In the rear cockpit his observer/gunner slumps to the floor – dead. As more bullets smash into his engine, the young pilot snaps off the switches and braces himself for the inevitable fire.

Within the past month – or is it a year? It seems so long – he has seen many of his comrades go down in flames. He feels strangely detached from the situation, as if observing everything in slow motion. Is this how it feels to become a 'flamer'? Now his aircraft begins to spin down out of control from a height of 20,000 feet; down towards the brown autumn fields of Germany. The fighters follow the stricken machine, still firing ...

This is not a scene from a Biggles book, with the intrepid air-hero fighting against tremendous odds. It is an event which happened on Monday, 16 September 1918 to Captain W. E. Johns, one of the hair-raising incidents in his own exciting life which were to form the basis for the adventures of his hero in nearly 100 air adventure books.

That W. E. Johns is a writer of some significance there can be little doubt. His name, coupled with that of Biggles, has been a magical one to generations of young readers from Britain to Australia, from Iceland to Malaya. He was the author of 168 books, but it is his Biggles series, consisting of 96 titles, which has made him one of the best-loved children's writers of the twentieth century. Few other writers in this genre can claim a sustained popularity spanning, to date, five decades. As a writer Johns was certainly prolific and his works have been translated into over a dozen languages. They have been the subject of radio and television dramatisations and serials in Britain, Australia, South Africa and New Zealand. His airman hero has also appeared as a comic-strip character as well as having comics devoted especially to him. Biggles has been 'sent up' by Monty Python and parodied in *Punch*. In the Edinburgh Festival of 1980 he was the hero of a successful fringe revue written by two Edinburgh University graduates, in which he was affectionately portrayed as an indomitable ass.[1] There has been a Biggles card game and actor Simon Ward recently made a commercial recording of excerpts from one of the books. Several film companies have taken out options on film rights, though to date no company has reached the stage of completing a Biggles film. At the time of writing, Yellowbill Productions Ltd with Walt Disney Inc. are funding the production of a screenplay. It is hoped the film will be released in 1982.

Biggles has become a synonym for any adventurous or would-be pilot. Scanning newspapers in recent years, one finds many examples of how deeply engrained in the language of flying the name has become. On 16 July 1979 the *Daily Mirror*, reporting how a former RAF pilot, John Churchill, had to ditch in the sea off the Isle of Wight, headlined their story 'Biggles is Down!' When the Prince of Wales flew a 1930s Tiger Moth, the *Daily Mail* used the headline 'HRH Biggles takes the air'.[2] The same day even the usually sober *Daily Telegraph* reported that the Prince wore 'a Biggles-style flying outfit'. When the staff of British Airways received an order from their chief executive, Roy Watts, to the effect that they should smile when on duty, the *Daily Mail* devoted a leader column to a comment on the affair, written in an attempted parody of Johns' style and headlined 'Biggles flies into the teeth of a storm'.[3] A letter on aviation matters published in the *New Statesman* was couched in Johns' style and referred to his characters, as did the reply.[4] The word Biggles has passed into the English language. There can be few people in the United Kingdom under the age of sixty who, even if they have not read a Biggles book at some time, have not heard of Johns' dauntless hero. Recently a clothes store, selling mainly RAF surplus uniforms and equipment opened in North London, calling itself Biggles.

Yet popularity has brought notoriety, for Johns, like several other children's writers of his generation, has been increasingly attacked in recent years as a jingoist, racialist, sexist and chauvinist; a writer who advocated blind patriotism and who glorified war. Since the early 1960s many libraries, both in the UK and Australia, have refused to allow Johns' books on their shelves.

In subsequent chapters we shall be examining these attacks and their validity in detail. By and large, most of the criticism would appear to be derived from a superficial reading of a selected few of Johns' titles, with quotations taken out of context. This is not totally to absolve Johns from criticism. There are many valid points to be made and answered, but in their eagerness to 'savage' Johns, most critics have failed to make a careful and scholarly study of all his works.

In no way did Johns ever preach that war was glorious; in fact, the very reverse was true. He made his views on the subject very clear in *Flying*.

War may be a fine thing to read about, to hear about and to talk about, but when you get down to the thing itself it is a pathetic business, the crowning infamy of the slavery of man to the masters, who, in his folly, he sets up over him.[5]

The latter part of that remark is also hardly consistent with the accusation that Johns taught 'blind patriotism'. In fact, it was Johns' vehement attacks on British Government attitudes, such as its failure to support the legitimate government of the Spanish Republic in its attempt to suppress Franco's Fascist uprising, that caused Johns to be removed in 1939 from his position as editor of *Popular Flying* and *Flying*. Throughout the Biggles books, Biggles displays a healthy scepticism, a mocking suspicion, about the political intentions of all governments and the abilities of 'brass hats'. It was an attitude that Johns derived from his experience of having fought in Britain's costliest and biggest political and military blunder – the Gallipoli campaign of 1915.

Johns' loathing of war was clearly mirrored in the early Biggles books. In *The Rescue Flight* (1939) – later retitled *Biggles and the Rescue Flight* – there is a passage which is most untypical of the average 'blood and thunder' boys' adventures of the time. One of Johns' characters, a young pilot, is flying his fighter over the lines on the Western Front:

> For the first time he began to perceive what war really meant: he felt the relentlessness of it – the ruthlessness, the waste, the cruelty, the incredible folly of it. It gave him a shock to realize that he did not really know what everybody was fighting for. Something about Belgium ...

When Japan launched her invasion of China in 1937, Johns wrote a very significant passage stating that war

> ... is just wholesale carnage, the turning of a town into a vast slaughter-house. What have these poor devils of Chinese done, whose mangled remains I saw being forked into carts like so much manure? It is a pity the Japanese bomber pilots cannot be shown what they did, but that, I fancy, is the last thing the Japanese Government would permit. *Nor, for that matter, would our Government allow our bomber pilots to see it.* [authors' italics]
>
> I'll tell you this. Conscription or no conscription, I shall never drop another bomb – unless it be on the Japanese warlords' headquarters. And that I would do so, at this moment, with the greatest possible satisfaction, for even now, when I close my eyes, I can still see that dreadful picture of Shanghai.
>
> They go on talking at Geneva, talking, talking, always talking, while a lot of blood-thirsty barbarians massacre one of the oldest and most cultured peoples on earth. Very pretty. First Abyssinia now China. Who are going to be the next poor devils to be splashed and de-gutted over the ruins of their homes?[6]

That is not to say that Johns was a pacifist – far from it. But he understood the nature of war and hated it. Perhaps 'militant pacifist' would be a fitting description of his attitudes. During the 1930s he stood prophetically against the British Government's appeasement of Fascism and, in particular, its lagging air policy. He did so not because he wanted war but because he saw war was inevitable; that sooner or later the world would have to stand up in military opposition to the new Fascist empires. As early as 1934 he wrote: 'Our recent editorials, it seems, have led one or two people to believe that we, or I, personally want war. What utter nonsense. No one in his right mind wants war. Paradoxical, though it may seem, it is my fear of war that makes me plead for more aeroplanes.'[7] Again, in 1936, he stated: 'That I have supported armaments – or, rather, the policy of re-armament – is true, because it is my firm conviction that only by a fair balance of power can peace be maintained.'[8]

Johns summed up his attitude to war when he said that he wanted 'the barbaric custom of war condemned to the limbo of such things as witchcraft, torture and feudalism.'[9]

Some critics of Johns' works have seized on the fact that women play little part in his Biggles adventures to infer that Johns was a sexist. One critic went so far as to state, 'Biggles and his associates rarely seem to think about women at all, let alone to have relationships with them. The members of Biggles' team receive their emotional gratification from their relationships with one another.' This criticism has arisen again from a superficial reading of the Biggles books. In the very first Biggles book, *The Camels Are Coming* (1932), Biggles fell heart-rendingly in love with a beautiful woman, Marie Janis, who turned out to be a German spy. Johns explained:

When the affair began he was young and carefree.

Shock left him bitter and disillusioned. He never really got over it. He couldn't forget it. Or perhaps he wouldn't allow himself to forget it. Algy knew about it. So did Air Commodore Raymond, now his chief. But it was never mentioned.[10]

Johns brought Marie and Biggles together again in *Biggles Looks Back* (1965) in a tale in which Biggles goes to Czechoslovakia and rescues Marie from imprisonment. 'You're not by any chance thinking of carrying on from where you left off in France?' his friend Ginger asks suspiciously, but is reassured by Biggles' answer: 'At my age? Don't be ridiculous.' According to Johns' chronology, Biggles was by this time sixty-four years old. This passage, amongst others, refutes another frequently made criticism that Biggles remained ageless. But between *The Camels Are Coming* and *Biggles Looks Back* it is true that Biggles, apart from his fervent admiration for Princess Marietta in *Biggles 'Fails to Return'* (1943), remained faithful to the memory of Marie Janis. As for Biggles' companions, Algy appears as something of a ladykiller in *Biggles Flies Again* (1934) – in fact, after he and Biggles have rescued the daughter of the President of Bolivia from a brigand, Biggles feels constrained to say, 'Algy, old son, you can't go on flirting with Consuelo unless you intend to marry her.' Ginger becomes fast friends with a Polynesian girl called Full Moon in *Biggles in the South Seas* (1940), which would seem to strike a double blow against those who have attacked Johns for sexism and racialism. He then fell passionately in love in *Biggles 'Fails to Return'*, this time with a girl called Jeanette in Monaco.

Johns later told interviewers that he received so many protests from children thinking that the Biggles books were 'going soft' that he purposely stopped including a love interest in the later titles.

In his Worrals books – about Flight Officer Joan Worralson, WAAF – his heroine is an embryonic feminist who is quick to resent any paternalistic behaviour on the part of her male colleagues. In the books about her, Worrals is always the leader and the men play subordinate roles. Even Johns' critics have been forced to admit: 'Given Johns' ready acceptance of the prevailing values of his time, it is surprising to find that he does, in one respect, challenge the traditional conceptions of the capabilities of women and their proper place in society'. As early as 1934 Johns was advocating the training of more women pilots and their greater participation in the air services. At this time he was a friend of many famous women flyers, among them Amy Johnson.

Perhaps the most devastating criticism of Johns' works, however, concerns the racist remarks they contain. There is no denying that there are some comments in his books which can only be interpreted as racialist. One of the most blatant examples occurs in *Biggles Forms A Syndicate* (1961):

'... I didn't care much for the chap. He was a shifty-eyed oily-looking type.'
'I see. He wasn't British?'

While no defence can be made of such remarks, one has to bear in mind the attitudes that prevailed among his contemporaries. The charge of racialism can be made with very few exceptions against all writers of popular literature of Johns' times. Even Jack London (1876–1916), a Marxist, and America's foremost adventure writer, was not above making the most astonishing racialist remarks. This is not to absolve Johns but to put him in context.

And as for Johns himself, when he lapses in this respect his lapses are usually very mild compared with those of his contemporaries. Ironically, in 1933 he was advocating cheap air travel as a means of overcoming racial prejudice by getting people to go to other countries and meet each other. 'By becoming accustomed to foreign travel they will forsake the beaten paths so often sown with prejudice and suspicion and see the people of the country as *they are* ...'[11] For a 'racialist', even his earlier books contain some remarkable passages. In *Biggles Flies Again* Johns appears to be making fun of authors who create racial stereotypes. In a story entitled 'The Oriental Touch' Biggles and Algy come to the aid of a naked, unconscious Chinese man whom they find afloat on a raft in the Indian Ocean. Aboard their flying-boat they bring him round with brandy.

'Thanks,' gasped the rescued man.
Biggles raised his eyebrows. 'Speakee English, eh?'
'Not that sort,' replied the exhausted man in a cultured voice, with a ghost of a smile ...

He had been at Oxford.

Humour is an essential ingredient of Johns' books. Johns had a wry, Puck-like humour: he was always ready to 'send up' everything and everybody, including himself. So subtle is his laughter that one wonders whether even such an apparently blatant piece of racialism as that suggested in the quotation above (from *Biggles Forms a Syndicate*) is to be taken at face value. In *Biggles and the Plot that Failed*, published a few years later in 1965, a Brigadier was describing a man who 'claimed to be an Egyptian':

'I hope I'm not doing the fellow an injustice when I say that in my opinion he could have been anything from a Turk to an Indian.'
'I gather you didn't like him,' said Biggles.
'There was really nothing you could put a finger on, but I wouldn't

have trusted him a yard out of my sight. He was a bit too suave, too oily, if you know what I mean.'

Biggles nodded. 'I know the type. Are you sure this wasn't colour prejudice?'

In several of his books Johns underscores the point that 'savages' are no more savage than their 'civilised' Western counterparts, and often causes his young readers to question the benefits of empire. As early as *Biggles in the South Seas* (1940) one of his characters, Sandy, tells Ginger:

'A hundred years ago there were more than a thousand people on this island; now there aren't more than two hundred. The rest have died from the diseases white men have brought ...'

In *Biggles' Chinese Puzzle* (1955) the air-hero is asked to fetch some clay with special properties from an islet in mid-Pacific, but his chief, Air Commodore Raymond, says the operation is not as simple as it seems:

'The snag is the question of ownership. The group happens to be one of those to which, in these days of radio and aircraft refuelling stations, several countries now lay claim. If it were known that one of the islands had a particular value, and we had made a raid on it, there might be an international rumpus, and we don't want that.'

'I would have said that the people who have most right to the islands are those who live there,' asserted Biggles ...

Biggles and the Leopards of Zinn (1960) begins with an introduction roundly condemning the white man's imperialism in Africa.

Then came a time, and this not very long ago, when small parties of men, dissatisfied with conditions in their own country, or perhaps seeking wealth, would set out for some new land that took their fancy and establish themselves there regardless of how the native inhabitants might feel about it. As the new arrivals were usually armed with guns, and the local people had only bows and arrows, argument was one-sided, and more often than not the invaders stayed.

Let us admit it. The conquerors generally came from Europe, and their victims were the coloured races that occupied most of the great land masses of the earth. This has sometimes been called 'The Age of Discovery'.

This sort of thing, this casual seizure of other people's property, came to an end less than a century ago, and the coloured races, those that have managed to survive the disastrous habits and disease introduced by the white men, are now reminding us of certain sinister facts that cannot be denied.

This passage surely leaves a young mind in no doubt of the immorality of empire and its disastrous results.

Admittedly, at times Johns can be accused of being slightly paternalist in his defence of native peoples. *The Boy Biggles* (1968) is a series of tales about how young James Bigglesworth spent his boyhood growing up in a jungle area of India where his father was a commissioner. A white man verbally attacks an Indian.

'He's only an ignorant native!'
This annoyed James. He bridled. 'These people may be ignorant according to university standards but they know all there is to know about conditions where they live; and that's as much as they need to know for their own good, which is more than can be said for some white men,' he retorted.

Also, in the posthumously published *Biggles and the Little Green God* (1969), which is undoubtedly one of Johns' worst efforts, we find Biggles and his friends about to be attacked by primitive Indians in a jungle region of Chile. Pepe, a Chilean, advises Biggles to shoot them in order to scare them off:

Biggles looked shocked. 'That's pretty good, coming from you, a Chilean. These people may be Indian, but it doesn't alter the fact that they're Chilean subjects just as much as you are. The colour of their skins doesn't alter that. I've no more right to kill one of them than shoot a white man in Santiago.'

At the time of his death Johns had completed twelve chapters of a new Biggles tale called *Biggles Does Some Homework*. In this book Biggles is finally contemplating the idea of retirement from the Air Police. In an interview with Air Commodore Raymond, Biggles talks about training a successor. New blood has to be brought into the Air Police, for when Biggles retires so also will Algy, Ginger and Bertie. Raymond has a likely candidate, a former RAF officer. The man who may one day take over Biggles' job enters:

A hush fell. No one spoke. Everyone was staring. Biggles had been prophetic when he remarked the world was full of surprises, for the man now standing before them bore no resemblance to the type that had been expected.

He was small and slight in stature. His features were finely cut, as if they had been intended for the opposite sex. His eyes were dark under black brows. His hair, as could be seen when he took off his cap, was straight, brushed well back and as black as the plumage of a crow. But what had probably taken everyone aback was the colour of his skin. It was the pale brown tint of heather honey.

We learn that Biggles' successor is not only coloured but is, to use the parlance of the 1930s, 'a half-caste Indian'. In subsequent chapters the young man proves his worth and becomes part of Biggles' team and a worthy successor to take over as head of the Air Police. It was Johns' greatest joke against those who not only accused him of racialism but claimed, with obvious lack of knowledge of his work, that practically all his villains were half-castes! It is a shame that Johns died before he had completed the book and that his literary agent has steadfastly refused to allow the book to be finished by another writer and published. The reason given is that it is untypical of Johns' work, yet a reading of the manuscript shows it to be far better, even in embryonic form, than many of his later books.

And when all the criticisms have been made, all the attacks levelled, will it make Biggles any less a part of our cultural heritage? Not our's alone either, for Biggles is considered a hero in many countries, even in Iceland, where his name is unpronounceable and therefore translated as Benni, and in Malaya, where Biggles books are also tremendously popular. Captain W. E. Johns' Biggles books are still avidly devoured by countless children throughout the world; they still, in spite of their age, hold some magical attraction. Perhaps the *Guardian* critic Stanley Reynolds put his finger on it when he wrote:

… the appeal is that Biggles is a flyer, and Captain Johns writes wondrously about flying. Even diving through that old cliché, a hole in a cloud, comes alive in an amazing fashion. The writing is so vivid that it sticks in your mind and years after you remember it, but forget where you read it.

It comes as a surprise to remember that it was only in Biggles. Only in Biggles? By Jove!

1

AN AMBITION TO BE A SOLDIER

William Earl Johns was born at a time when the average boy entertained an ambition to become a soldier. He was no exception. 'It is impossible for a boy of today to realise the enthusiasm the boys of 1900 had for anything military,' wrote Johns in later years.[1] 'Soldiers were gods. Mind you, in those days a soldier in full dress uniform was something to look at. When troops went overseas they did not creep away furtively, for security reasons, in the middle of the night. They marched through cheering crowds in broad daylight, bands playing, colours flying, flowers in their caps. We boys, decorated with as much red, white and blue ribbon as we could afford to buy, marched with them to the railway station and yelled our heads off as the train steamed out, whistle screaming and fog signals thundering under the wheels.'

Johns was born on 5 February 1893 at Mole Wood Road, Bengeo, a suburb of Hertford. His father, Richard Eastman Johns, was a tailor, as his father had been before him. His mother was Elizabeth Johns, formerly Elizabeth Earl, the daughter of a master butcher. Richard Eastman Johns had come with his father to Hertford from Devonshire. Johns once told Jack Cox, the editor of *The Boys' Own Paper*, that he had traced his family back to soldiers who had seen service in the Peninsular War.[2] Certainly, there was a Devonshire family called Johns which had the same Christian names as the author's own family. A William Johns was adjutant of the Cornwall Militia and died in 1834. His son, Richard Johns, was a major in the Royal Marines and died at Stoneham, Devonshire, in 1851. This Richard Johns wrote half a dozen books – volumes of poetry and books on naval and military battles.

William Earl was the elder son. A second boy, Russell Ernest, was born on 24 October 1895. According to Mrs Margaret Collins, Russell Johns' daughter,[3] 'the family was a very happy one. My father's parents were devoted to each other. According to relatives, Richard was the most delightful of men and was adored by the whole family. Of course, I did not know him. He was certainly not a strict disciplinarian. My grandmother, of course, I knew very well indeed. She was a great character. My uncle [W. E. Johns] went his own way but liked her to approve. He was always in touch with her and respected her advice.' The closeness which Johns felt for his mother is shown in an article he wrote in *My Garden* (August 1938) in which he said: 'Yesterday, my mother came to see me ... she ... smells faintly of lavender. Perhaps that is why I, too, am a little *triste* today and why I grow lavender in my garden. And why I caress it with my hand in passing ...'

Johns also remembered his grandmother. 'I remember her quite well. She was dressed in black. Black unrelieved except for that queer shining stuff called jet ... She was growing old and was always a little sad but unafraid – with her always went the faint perfume of lavender.'[4] He also recalled 'my grandfather telling me when I was a small child that for years he grew [tomatoes] and took first prize at the local flower show. Then he threw them away.'[5] Gardening, in fact, was to feature prominently in Johns' life, but it was an interest which he did not develop until after the First World War. In later years he recalled that it was an uncle who had sown the first seeds of that interest.

When I was a small boy my uncle Harry gave my mother some crocus bulbs, which, after discussion, were planted under the tulip tree at the end of the lawn. I can see my father planting them now, awkwardly, for he was no gardener. Did he but know it, he was planting a living spirit in that garden for, before the year was out, my uncle was no longer with us. He was killed in the Boer War. But in the Spring we were cheered by 'Uncle Harry's bulbs' which, as you may suppose, had acquired a new significance. Now observe the joy of such a gift and the wisdom of the giver, for that same pleasure was repeated every Spring for nearly thirty years. Every March we would say, one to another, 'Have you seen Uncle Harry's bulbs'? I never saw him again, the years rolled on, and his face became a hazy memory (so soon does youth forget) but he lived with us always in that simple gift.

At first the bulbs occupied perhaps a foot of ground; the last time I saw them they were a gleaming carpet, covering many yards.[6]

Johns and his brother both attended a local school in Bengeo before Johns was admitted to Hertford Grammar School[7] on 26 January 1905. Russell was to follow him to the school in September 1907. The headmaster, from 1905 to 1928, was Major G. W. Kinman MA. According to the present headmaster, D. F. Jack MA:

Kinman was something of a character, very military in manner, as indeed one would have expected from his keeping his army title long after he had left the army. Right to the end of his time he used to arrive at school on horseback each morning and, at least in his earlier days, he used to use his horse to provide a simulated 'cavalry charge' during cadet force exercises. To the boys he was a holy terror, and even to his youngest staff. But one old boy told me that when he returned to Hertford after a year in the Air Force, Kinman greeted him in a most friendly way and showed great interest in his career, seeming an altogether more human person than he was to boys in the school.[8]

According to Jack Cox: 'Johns has written no autobiography so far, but *Biggles at School* [sic], a reminiscent tale of Biggles as a schoolboy in Edwardian Hertfordshire [sic], is based very frankly on his own experiences at Hertford Grammar School.'[9] Cox is obviously referring to *Biggles Goes to School* in which Biggles is at school in Edwardian Norfolk.

Major Kinman certainly sounds remarkably similar to Colonel Horace Chase MA, headmaster of Malton House School in the Biggles story. The school's cadet corps was Colonel Chase's pride and joy; he lectured the whole school on the art of war on Saturday mornings, and there were weekly drill parades that 'Biggles suffered in silence as part of the price he had to pay for his education'. There was general scepticism about the cadet corps:

The Head took it seriously but few of the boys shared his enthusiasm. To most of them it was a silly game played for the Head's amusement ...

However, Johns goes on to point out:

None could guess that within a few years most of them would be doing these things in grim earnest on the war-stricken fields of Flanders; or that before the First World War was over nearly a third of them were to die on that same battlefield ...

Johns frankly admitted that he was not much good at school work. 'It may be some consolation to readers of my books, who have failed their examinations, to know that I have never passed an examination in my life; yet I have managed to get all the things I coveted, although some of them appeared as remote as the moon.'[10] In subjects such as English, history and geography, Johns could hold his own, but at anything to do with figures he was 'a dead loss'.[11] When the examination results were pinned to the notice board, he did not read down from the top like other boys but up from the bottom. 'I never had far to go'. He could never understand why it was necessary to prove that X equalled Y or that two triangles of the same size placed one upon the other would be found to be equal. The maths master did his best. 'Breathing heavily over my shoulder he would go through an equation with infinite pains. At the end he would say: "Now do you understand?" All I could do was hang my head and whisper, "No". Making funny noises in his throat he would walk away like a man going to the scaffold. Wretched fellow. I must have put years on his life.'

To Johns, anything mechanical was a devilish contrivance to be avoided at all costs. 'I have never been able to make, or even mend, an article of wood, metal or anything else,' he confessed. It was not a promising outlook for one who was to become a war pilot. 'I have never been able to knock a nail in straight. On the rare occasions when I have been forced to try, it was usually my thumb that came under the hammer. As a small boy I once tried to fix the mast of a toy boat. It was too long. Fetching the carving knife I hit it a smart crack – and away went half the tip of the finger of my left hand. There is a simple answer to this handicap. Get someone else to do it.'

One thing Johns could do well – he could hit a bull's eye nine times out of ten at 1,000 yards with a .303 rifle. This stood him in good stead: 'In 1914 the crossed guns on the arm of a cavalry trooper was worth sixpence a day; and that meant sausage and mash in the canteen instead of hard tack and stew.' The school army cadet corps had twelve obsolete rifles and when Major Kinman took the boys out to drill there was a scramble to get one. Johns admitted that, at this time, he had 'a depraved taste' for weapons and 'collected a small armoury of swords, guns and pistols'.[12] According to Johns' son, Jack:

No gun was too big or dangerous for him. He was using his father's twelve-bore gun at an age when the 'kick' half spun him round every time he fired. Many a rabbit has he dispatched to its 'Happy Lettuce Beds' with an old horse pistol loaded with black powder and nails. He was an expert at smashing clay pigeons; one record of later days which he remembers being twelve pigeons with as many shots.[13]

Although Johns' first ambition was to be a soldier, he also had a burning desire to become a conjurer. 'I saved my pocket money for months to buy a conjuring outfit. I could turn a red handkerchief into a black one and push a nail through my finger without hurting myself – and things like that.'[14] However, when young Johns tried out these party tricks in front of audiences something inevitably went wrong. He also wanted to be a ventriloquist and, as a first exercise, he would go round making a noise like 'a hysterical bee' and driving everyone mad. He never seemed to get beyond the first exercise.

Johns' son, Jack, writing for young readers of his father's books, revealed that, whilst at school, Johns had been vice-president of a mysterious society, known as the Secret Seven. It baffled those in authority, 'licked prefects to a frazzle, terrified all masters and generally bossed the show'.[15] Johns was certainly an adventurous and active boy. He broke his nose twice playing rugger and cracked a kneecap playing ice hockey.[16] 'When I was a lad we skated and tobogganed. Not having much sense I was usually one of the first to test the ice. I ought to have been drowned more than once.'[17] He was fond of animals and had a passion for pet mice;[18] he was attacked by a stoat, chased by a cow, knocked down by a ram, tossed by a donkey and chased by a bull many times.[19]

Johns' schooldays came to an end in the summer of 1907. He was to revisit Hertford Grammar School once, just after the 1914–18 War:

I sat with the Head (that stern man) in his study, that same awful room into which, ten years earlier, as a trembling schoolboy I had more than once gone to take my 'medicine'. The big bundle of canes no longer stood in the corner. With tears in his eyes he told me the names of the boys of my time who had gone to the war and would not be coming back.

I never saw him again: but I know now how much I owe to him.[20]

Years later, when the storm clouds of war were threatening for a second time, Johns reflected on the boys with whom he had been at school and who had been killed in the First World War. It was on a June Sunday afternoon in 1938 that he lay under an old apple tree on his lawn and recalled the days

... when I often lay like this beside a brook with form-mates who I shall see no more. Pip, with his merry laugh, silent for ever, lies somewhere in the chalky soil beside the Somme. Cyril, who loved to chase butterflies, fell early, while poppies yet grew wild in Flanders. Peter, with whom I smoked so daringly my first cigarette, is a pinch of fat earth in the sterile sand of Mesopotamia. Somewhere in the silent depth of the grey North Sea is a handful of lime that once was Nigel. Happy days! How little we knew ...[21]

On leaving school, Johns still had dreams of a military career but at this time the thought of flying had never entered his head. 'I was playing fives when the first aeroplane went over. I watched it with awe. How could I have known that for many years I would be flying one myself? A university can't teach you what's waiting round the corner.'[22] Asked what he wanted to do now that he had left school, Johns had no hesitation about opting for the army, but: 'My father had other ideas about my career. I arrived home one day to be introduced to a county municipal surveyor to whom I was to be articled for the next four years. So I went to work. My pocket money was sixpence a week. This taught me the value of money.'[23]

At the same time as working his indentures to the municipal surveyor, Johns studied music under a piano teacher for three evenings a week and for a further three evenings a week he attended the local art school from six o'clock to nine o'clock. His proficiency in music and art proved useful accomplishments. Before the advent of the 'talkies', Johns found he could raise extra cash by playing the piano in the local cinema, and by doing this he was not only able to see the picture show free but was able to save up for his first motorbike. Later in life his artistic talent led him to a career as an aviation artist.

Towards the end of 1912, having completed his apprenticeship with the municipal surveyor, Johns set out to find work, and was appointed as a sanitary inspector in the little market town of Swaffham, in Norfolk. Soon after he left home, his father, who had been ill for some time, died of tuberculosis at the age of forty-seven. Johns' brother, Russell, who had hoped to go on to university to read chemistry, gave up his education and took a job to support Mrs Elizabeth Johns. 'Savings had been swallowed up by three years' of doctor's bills and sanitorium fees'.[24]

Johns' move to Swaffham had important consequences. According to Mrs Kathleen King:

Soon after Captain Johns' arrival in Norfolk he was performing (he was musical) at a concert and my sisters were in the audience, sitting in the second row. After the concert was over he enquired who the pretty girls were. Having obtained the necessary information, the following Sunday he came to evening service at my father's church.[25]

The 'pretty girls' were Maude, Ruby, Dorothy and Kathleen, the daughters of the Reverend John Hunt, vicar of St Margaret's, Little Dunham, near Swaffham. Reverend Hunt, who had received his ordination at Tuam, Ireland, in 1884, had become vicar at Little Dunham in 1900, having had various livings in Ireland, London and Sussex.[26]

When the service was over he [Johns] introduced himself as a newcomer to the district and my father with his usual charm invited the young man in for supper at the rectory.

That is how it all began.

In those days there was no radio or television and young people organised their own entertainment. We were all keen on amateur dramatics, producing plays etc. The Captain (Johns) was very versatile and my sister Maude was a gifted pianist so they had much in common. Father had a beautiful tenor voice so there were many, many musical evenings. We spent such happy times together with lots of fun and laughter − during the summer there were tennis parties with other outdoor activities including the parish, with fund-raising efforts for the church.

My parents became devoted to Captain Johns and looked on him as a son ...

Johns and the Reverend Hunt's eldest daughter, Maude Penelope, were often in each other's company. Although Maude was eleven years older than Johns, an attraction grew between them. By the end of 1913 it was generally accepted by the Hunt family that Maude and Bill Johns were 'walking out together'.

Working as a sanitary inspector at Swaffham was not exactly Johns' ideal role in life and, although he was also studying to become a qualified surveyor, he decided to take a step towards fulfilling his boyhood ambition. On 4 October 1913, he joined the Territorial Army and was attested as Private No. 74451 in the King's Own Royal Regiment (Norfolk Yeomanry). He spent weekends and holidays training with the Yeomanry, which was commanded by Lieutenant Colonel A. F. Morse. The Yeomanry was a cavalry regiment and Johns had his own horse, called Pistol. He hardly found time to return on visits to Hertford, 'spending my holidays in barracks with the 9th Lancers'.[27]

He had been in the Norfolk Yeomanry less than a year when, in August 1914, Great Britain went to war with Germany, an event that was profoundly to alter his life, along with the lives of millions of other men whether or not they had ever cherished an ambition to be a soldier.

2

IN THE TRENCHES

To many, August 4th, 1914, was to be a parting of the ways: almost as abrupt as the closing of a door; the end of one life and the beginning of a new. We did not know it then. We only perceive it now by looking down the vista of the years, route-marked by the mocking milestones of what-might-have-been.

I little dreamed, on that fateful morning when I put away my compasses and T-square (I was trying to be a surveyor), that I should never take them out again. When I said goodbye to the men and boys whom I had known since childhood, many of them friends of schoolboy days, not for one moment did it occur to me that I was bidding most of them farewell for ever − or I might have said, like Brutus:
'Fare thee well, and if for ever
Still for ever fare thee well.'
A yeoman, I led my mare from the stables, and, slashing with my sword at imaginary foes, galloped down the drive to what, in my youthful folly, I supposed was going to be death or glory. I had yet to learn that in war there is plenty of death but little glory; that in war only death is real; that the glory is simply gilt and tinsel to wrap around the other so that it looks less like what it really is.[1]

Thus, in later years, Johns reflected on the event that was to change his life. The King's Own Royal Regiment (Norfolk Yeomanry) were mobilised on 4 August as a cavalry regiment. For the next three years Johns was to serve in the army, fighting in the trenches in two theatres of war. In later life he hardly ever mentioned these years of military service, although he would recall numerous experiences from his career in the Royal Flying Corps and Royal Air Force. That his period in the trenches left a deep impact on Johns' sensibilities is evident from the few comments he did make and his firm anti-war stance.

Within a week of his mobilisation, on 11 August, the Norfolk Yeomanry were moved to the village of Great Bealings in Suffolk, between Ipswich and Woodbridge. They were to form part of the 1st Eastern Mounted Division, whose duties were to keep watch on coastal defences and to undertake training for eventual posting overseas.[2]

Like so many other couples at the time, faced with the prospect of an uncertain future, at least of long separation, Bill Johns and Maude Hunt decided to get married. It seemed there were no objections from Reverend and Mrs Hunt, in spite of the fact that Johns was eleven years younger than his bride. The marriage actually took place at Reverend Hunt's parish church on 6 October 1914, and was performed by the curate, A. C. Manston. Johns' brother, Russell, came from Hertford to be his best man and Johns, entering his profession in the register, wrote 'sanitary inspector' rather than 'soldier'. There followed a brief leave before Johns rejoined his regiment which, on 1 November, moved to Rendelsham Park, four miles northeast of Woodbridge, where they were to remain in training and home defence duties for nearly a year. It was not until September 1915 that the regiment received embarkation orders for duty overseas. It was a hard parting for young Johns, particularly as Maude had discovered that she was pregnant. However, such leave-takings were the order of the day.

It was at this time that Johns had his first taste of the realities of war.

I remember clearly the first man whom I saw die. It was in 1915. His name was George Bellingham. We were amateur soldiers in the amateur cavalry (sometimes called yeomanry) and we had gone to the rifle range at Colchester to do our firing practice. For a time I sat on a pile of horse-blankets behind the firing point, talking to George, who was standing up. He was telling me, I remember, about a mare he had at home. He was not to know, of course, that he was never going home. At that moment there was nothing to indicate that in precisely one minute of time he would be a dead man.

I got up – I don't really know why, unless it was to stretch my legs. Anyway, if there was a reason, I've forgotten it. George sat down. As he did so there was a sharp bang somewhere near at hand, and almost simultaneously a sort of dull *phut*. Looking up to see what it was I became aware of a curious silence. The troops were all staring at me – or rather, at my feet. I looked down. I did more than that. I stared fascinated by what I saw. George was on his back, twitching.

The silence was broken by a man who started repeating, with parrot-like monotony, 'I didn't know it was loaded ... I didn't know it was loaded ...' They marched him away.

The date, I recall, was September 16th.[3]

On 25 September the regiment was ordered to entrain for Liverpool for embarkation on the SS *Olympic*. The popular rumour among the troops was that their destination was France. It was not; it was Gallipoli. The British and French had determined that the strategic passage between the Mediterranean and the Black Sea, the Dardanelles, should be opened to Allied shipping. A naval attack on 18 March 1915 had failed to accomplish this and it was decided a land campaign would achieve the aim. An expeditionary force under General Sir Ian Hamilton landed on 25 April, making two amphibious assaults on the northern side of the Gallipoli Peninsula, which flanked the Dardanelles. The Turks and Germans had known an attack was imminent and General Otto Liman von Sanders had deployed his Fifth Army of 60,000 men around the entrances to the channel. So fierce was resistance that, by the end of the first day, the Allied troops were still unable to move off their beach-heads, on which they were firmly pinned down. Within two weeks Hamilton lost one third of his 75,000 troops, but failed to capture the heights from which the Turks and Germans could shell the beaches with impunity. Rather than withdraw, it was decided to strengthen the expeditionary force with three British divisions, two French divisions and three ANZAC (Australian-New Zealand Army Corps) divisions.

It was as part of these reinforcements that Johns' regiment, the Norfolk Yeomanry, commanded by Lieutenant Colonel A. F. Morse, sailed. They had a rough passage through the Bay of Biscay and in the Mediterranean, on 30 September, the *Olympic*, with great risk to itself, stopped to pick up survivors from a French collier which had been sunk by a submarine. Later a periscope was seen and fired at and the *Olympic*, with a great deal of zigzagging, got away safely. The ship reached Mudros on 2 October and the regiment remained on board until 8 October, when they were transferred onto a smaller ship, the *Abbasieh*, for landing on the Gallipoli beach-heads. But as they were entering Anzac Bay, a storm blew up, making a landing impossible, and the *Abbasieh* had to lie hove-to in Imbros for two days before a successful landing could be effected on the evening of 10 October. The following day the Norfolk Yeomanry marched three miles to a place called Dixon's Gully and spent the day digging in. On 14 October two squadrons were sent to the front line to learn the work in the trenches and immediately came under artillery fire. For Private Johns and the Norfolk Yeomanry the war had begun in earnest.

The regiment now formed part of the 54th East Anglian Division, temporarily commanded by Brigadier H. W. Hodgson CVO, doomed to spend its time in irksome and monotonous trench warfare. More losses were suffered from disease than from enemy fire. When the regiment withdrew from Gallipoli on 20 December only 13 officers and 221 other ranks were fit for duty, out of a complement of 26 officers and 504 other ranks. Of that number only 6 had been killed and 20 wounded by enemy action; the rest had succumbed to dysentry and other diseases, and the terrible trials of exposure, especially in the blizzards at the end of November.

Johns wrote only one article about his memories of trench warfare, but he put a good deal into it.

In fact, if there is one thing calculated to give an ordinary human being the screaming willies, it is crawling about in the pitch-dark, catching your chin on barbed wire, and sliding into water-logged shell-craters. When, added to these pleasantries, you remember (and you never forget it) that there is a chance that at any moment you may trip over a land-mine, walk into a line of bullets discharged by a windy machine-gunner, or bump into a thug with a dagger in one hand and a life-preserver in the other, you'll see what I mean about a patrol not being all fun and games.

By the time you've dodged out of the way of a lunatic who is amusing himself by broadcasting grenades, and lain in a few puddles while another maniac blazes away with star shells, you don't know whether you're coming or going. Even if you do remember, you're likely to have forgotten the password, in which case you'll probably be greeted at the firestep by a poke in the eye from a bayonet. If you've got the password on the tip of your tongue, you might strike a pal who forgets to ask for it before he pulls the trigger.

These guys who moan because the only news they get is 'our night patrols were active' ought to do one. Just one. This is the way it goes.

Six of you, or maybe a dozen, crawl out of the trench into a wilderness that goes by the cheerful name of No-Man's Land. Now don't get the idea that all you have to do is stroll to the nearest shell-hole and sit there for an hour before going back with the glad news that everything is O.K. Oh no, it isn't as easy as that. You always have to do something. Maybe your job is to catch a prisoner and bring him home alive. It needs no great imagination to perceive that this is likely to be an exhilerating pastime besides which the stalking of a mad tiger with your bare hands would be a tame pursuit. Germans don't stand about waiting to come clean. Most of them object to your invitations and they back up their protests in a most unfriendly manner.

If your job isn't to find a prisoner, you may be given the engaging little task of crawling up to the enemy's front line trench and there doing a spot of eavesdropping. This again is rarely taken kindly by gents who sport coal-scuttle titfers. To induce you to mind your own business they throw things at you, things that disintegrate with considerable noise. To make sure they don't miss you they fill the air with lights which enable you to appreciate to the full the sort of place you are in.

Another little job that may come your way is to cut holes with blunt wire cutters through the enemy's wire — which may be anything up to forty feet wide. To make this as disagreeable as possible you will find (if you haven't done the job before) that German barbed wire has things like pointed razor blades sticking out of it. On the wire, too, may hang little bells that tinkle merrily the moment you touch it, and inform the bloke who is standing by a trench mortar just where you are. Occasionally a piece of wire will be found to be carrying a few thousand volts of electricity, all of which gives the business a nice element of anticipation every time you stretch out your hand.

To enliven the whole proceedings, the enemy are playing exactly the same game, so that at any moment you are likely to encounter a party of playboys in grey suits. In the intervals of this dull sport you pretend to be a corpse while parachute flares and searchlights flood the scene with a nasty white light, in the rays of which you feel as conspicuous as an elephant in a parlour. This usually happens when you are half-way across a mud lake, and a wet seat does nothing to enhance your comfort.

All the time you are out, vague sounds assail your ears. These sounds may be quite different, but they have one thing in common — they are all sinister A foot being dragged out of the slush somewhere near at hand gives you a tingling sensation at the nape of the neck. A grunted oath a few paces away makes you hold your breath while a line of vague shadows goes past. The hollow groans of some poor devil who has collided with a piece of hot metal travelling in the opposite direction makes your blood run cold.

Just as you reach the stage when you feel you can't bear it any longer, or it is time you went home, anyway, somebody decides to start a war. Probably it is quite unofficial. It just happens — starting with ordinary bullets and ending in a barrage from the 'heavies' of both sides. And you're in the middle of it.[4]

Only by viewing their world with the type of 'black humour' that Johns displays in this article could men hope to retain their sanity amid the horrors of the trenches.

In November, General Sir Charles Monro replaced Hamilton as GOC, and it was finally decided to withdraw from Gallipoli. The debacle had cost the lives of 250,000 Allied troops and its architect, Winston Churchill, was dropped from the War Cabinet. The Norfolk Yeomanry were among the last to be evacuated. The regiment was divided into three sections and the smallest section, consisting of twenty-one men, remained in the trenches, firing as if they were fully manned until 1.40 am on 20 December. This section then made its way to Suvla Bay and Anzac Cove and were the last men of the Gallipoli expeditionary force to be evacuated. The Allied force on nearby Cape Hellas were evacuated on 9 January without loss of lives.

The Norfolk Yeomanry arrived at Alexandria, in Egypt, at 8.00 am on Christmas Day. After disembarking, they marched through the town to the tram station, from which they were taken to a temporary camp at Sidi Bishr, five miles from the city. On the following day they were transported to a permanent camp nearby. They now became part of the 1/1st Eastern Mounted Brigade. The regiment was re-equipped and sent to Crewe's Post, an outpost of the Suez Canal defences, deep in the desert.

It was here that Johns learnt that he had become a father. On 18 March 1916 Maude had given birth to a son at Little Dunham. Mother and child were well and the boy was named William Earl Carmichael Johns.

In May the Norfolk Yeomanry were posted to El Kubri, where they remained working on the Suez Canal defences, training, route-marching and practising musketry. Johns appears to have received training as a machine gunner about this time. At the end of June the regiment removed to El Ferdan, where they were similarly employed, and on 27 July returned to Sidi Bishr. They were now grouped as part of the Western Coastal Force watching Senussi, with their headquarters at Sollum on the Mediterranean coast, some 250 miles west of Alexandria. It was at this time Johns left the Norfolk Yeomanry, for his machine-gun training meant that he was badly needed elsewhere. Men with knowledge of machine guns were being seconded to a new force, founded on 15 October 1915 – the Machine Gun Corps. Johns received his formal attachment to the Corps on 1 September 1916, and was promoted to lance corporal.

He returned to England in September for leave before embarkation to a new battlefront. Most of his time he spent at Little Dunham with Maude and his young son, who was nicknamed Jack to differentiate him from his father. In mid-September came orders for embarkation, and Johns, writing from the YMCA at Wivenhoe, near Colchester, sent a letter to Maude's mother, Mrs Hunt, with whom he had developed a fond relationship, addressing her as 'mater'.

Now that the time has actually come that I must go and do my bit, I feel I must write and try to say what is in my heart to say.

Not being a Shakespeare or Byron I'm afraid I can't sort of put it, to let you understand of course I want to thank you for the kindness and love you have always showed me in a thousand different ways. To write in cold black and white 'thank you' seems to me to be more or less ridiculous in the light of what I actually do feel. I want you to realise, mater, that, although perhaps I have not always shown you that I appreciate what you have done nevertheless I *do* appreciate it. I know in your own unselfish way you have been satisfied with helping me – thinking perhaps it had been unnoticed by me. Don't make a mistake – no one knows more than I what you have done for me – and Maude.

It is not often, however, that I say anything – but that's my way. I *try* to be unemotional – in fact, I won't permit myself to be and that is the chief reason I seldom say as much as 'thank you'. Perhaps I haven't trusted myself to speak. This I know – and say – that no one on this earth – even had it been my own mother – could have been kinder, truer and more loving than you – and this I know – and can only say 'thank you'.

You, however, do not know that it is one of the dreams of my life to be able to do something big for you – some sacrifice – to show my appreciation.

It has not been my luck yet – but perhaps one day it will and then I trust I shall not be found wanting.

I could not go away without letting you know this.

So I write now while I still may, for the voyage I am about to go on, as you know, is not without its dangers. I am not getting morbid – but anything may happen. Never fear, I shall come back, I know it, and many happy times we shall have yet together. The darkest hour is always before morn, and the darkest hour has commenced for Maude and I. It is unnecessary for me to say 'take care of her'. I know too well you need no telling or asking to do that.

But now *au revoir.*

I have said – badly I know – that which I wanted to say, so must close now. Goodbye, Mater dear, for a little while.

Keep a brave heart – dawn is not far away!

All my fondest love to you,

from Bill.

PS. I found the little Testament in my bag. I think I can guess who put it there. Anyway, where I go, that goes from now on. B.[5]

Johns thought he was destined for France. A week confined on a troopship dispelled that notion. As the troopship steamed into its destination, Lance Corporal Johns looked out on a picturesque, romantic-looking city with white houses, domes, minarets and battlemented walls, set off by the foliage of elms, cypress and mulberry trees. The city rose gradually from the shoreline of a bay to heights on which an old castle stood. It was Salonika, the northern port of Greece.

When Bulgaria mobilised on the German side in September 1915, and, together with German and Austro-Hungarian troops, attacked Serbia, the Allies had rushed a British and French army of 40,000 men to Salonika. It was a vital seaport. The force, commanded by the French general Maurice Sarrail, began marching to Serbia's aid, but they were too late. The Bulgarian Second Army had driven southward, cutting the railway from Salonika and deflecting the Allied advance. Sarrail, and his Armée d'Orient, fell back to Lake Dorian, on the Greek border. Here, they dug in, reinforced by two more French divisions and another British division.

King Constantine of Greece, a close relative of the German Kaiser, had thrown Greece into turmoil by making pro-German statements and calling for an Allied withdrawal from Greek territory. This, coupled with pressure from the Bulgarian army, forced the Allies to fall back on Salonika. Civil war seemed to loom in Greece between pro-German royalists and the supporters of the Allies. Eventually Venizelos, the Prime Minister, kept Greece from declaring for Germany, although it was not until 11 June 1917 that Constantine was forced to abdicate in favour of his son Alexander. The new king and Venizelos together represented a united Greece committed to the Allies.

In the summer of 1916 Sarrail began an advance towards the

Macedonian frontier of Greece, meeting strong counterattacks from the German Eleventh Army on the west and the Bulgarian First and Fourth armies aligned eastward. A front was established on 27 August. Rumania entered the war on the Allied side and helped Sarrail launch an offensive against Monastir. In this attack the Allies suffered 50,000 casualties, while the Central powers lost 60,000. But it was malaria which was a prime cause of casualties during that summer. Of the 35,122 French hospital cases only 672 were combat casualties, and there were no less than 481,000 British malaria cases compared with 18,000 combat casualties.

When Johns arrived at the Salonika front in October 1916, the British trenches ran for twenty-five miles from Lake Dorian following the Jumeaux Ravine through a series of foothills in a southwest direction ending at the river Verdar. The British troops gave their own names to these hills, such as Horseshoe Hill, One Tree Hill, Tortoise Hill and Machine Gun Hill. According to Jack Cox: 'There are old soldiers who can still recall the famous battles for Tortoise Hill and Machine Gun Hill. Bill Johns fought in both.'[6]

To the rear of the lines were countless deserted villages. Before them were the Bulgars, whose positions had been reinforced under the direction of German military engineers. From their strongholds on Grand Couronne, Petit Couronne and Pip Ridge, they took a daily toll of life by bombardments with 5.9-inch guns.

The British troops were commanded by General Sir George Milne, known to his troops as Uncle George. Troops served eight days in and eight days out of the trenches. As Johns moved up to the front, beyond the village of Oriovika, 'which was the last point of civilization I touched before disappearing into the wilderness'[7], the British were engaged in an offensive during which they managed to capture three villages southwest of Seres, but, because there were no reserve divisions, they were unable to follow up their advantage and their casualties were severe. However, the French managed to take Monastir, an important military objective, on 19 November.

Johns recalled that he was in 'a cavalry machine-gun squadron' and that, on his way to the front lines, escorting a mule carrying 500 rounds of ammunition, he ran into trouble when the mule would not step across a plank bridge spanning a trench.[8] It was not his only trouble with mules.

Once under fire ... I was sent to fetch a team of gun-mules which had been tethered to a venerable fig tree. I do not often give way to unprintable invective but on this occasion I did, for those satanic quadrupeds must have spent the night running round the tree in circles. The tethering chains made one big knot in the middle, against which each head was firmly anchored. Of course they were frightened. But not so frightened as I was.[9]

Johns also recalled that, 'high in a lonely pass in Macedonia', he was ordered to chop down a tree for firewood. Not yet having developed a knowledge of trees he tried to cut down a species of acacia. Other soldiers tried to help him. 'The tree won.'[10] It was impossible to cut down because of the hardness of the wood. He also recalled having to wear a gas mask for seven hours in a temperature of 100 degrees in the shade.[11] His subsequent horror of quicksand developed from an incident which happened at Stavros when he stepped into one and was caught. 'I thought someone was gripping my ankles. I fell down, but managed to roll clear, not a little frightened.'[12] He used the incident to good effect in *Biggles – Air Commodore* (1937).

It was obvious that Johns' war in the trenches was a bitter one, judging from the few reminiscences he put down concerning Salonika.

Take ten million men at random from between those man-made boundaries which we call frontiers, and ask them if they want to leave their homes to fight, perhaps die. Not one will answer 'Yes'. Yet when the time comes they will go, straining to be at the throats of other poor fools as helpless as themselves. Why will they go? They will go because the handful of men who control their destinies will, by the subtle means at their disposal, by lies and lies, and still more lies, make it impossible for them to stay at home without appearing contemptible cravens. Being one of the fools, I shall probably go myself, and presently find myself destroying the home of a man who has done no more harm to me than I to him. Oh no; I have no delusions left about war. When you have seen such sights as I have, you won't either.

I once discussed this very point with a dying German on the Oriovika Road. A lad of perhaps eighteen, he had been thrown off a GS Wagon for dead, but when I came upon him he was still alive. He asked me for a drink. I gave him one. We talked. He knew he was going to die, and wept at the thought of it. Not for himself, I think, but for his mother to whom he sent, by me, a rosary that hung around his neck. She never received it because a nurse stole it from me in Salonika – as a souvenir. A souvenir! Turn that over in your mind, and ask yourself, a souvenir of what? When you rub off the gilt and tinsel you will find that it was a souvenir of the agony of two poor souls who probably did no one any harm. Well, that's war.[13]

Speaking his mind about politicians and generals in 1935, Johns wrote:

… they cost the hundred thousand or more trusting lads who now lie between Calais and Kut, their lives. I helped to shovel eighteen hundred of them into pits (without the blankets for which their next-of-kin were probably charged) including sixty-seven of my own machine-gun squadron of seventy-five, in front of Horseshoe Hill in Greek Macedonia. We were sent to take the hill without big guns. Oh yes, they sent guns out to us, but when they got to Salonika there wasn't any tackle big enough to lift them out of the ships. At least, that's what we were told. Later, when we took the hill, and the guns afterwards appeared, there wasn't any tackle powerful enough to haul them up the hill. So back we came again. They sent us boats, too – to patrol that fever-ridden sewer called Lake Dorain [sic] – sent them out as deck cargo to the eastern Mediterranean under the mid-summer sun, so that their shoddy timbers warped and when we put them on the water they sank. So to square the deal they sent us an overdue cigarette ration – in cardboard boxes, during the rains, so that each man got a nice packet of green mildew to smoke …[14]

During the winter of 1916–17 a stalemate had set in between the two armies firmly entrenched against each other. With temperatures of 1 degree Fahrenheit and fever raging along the front, a heavy toll of casualties was suffered.

In January it was rumoured that the German air ace Baron Manfred von Richthofen and his squadron had moved up to reinforce the Bulgars. Certainly, a German bomber squadron did make an appearance and carry out three devastating raids, including one on the British 12th Corps headquarters at the Yanesh Hotel in Salonika on 27 February. A witness to the raid, Captain H. C. Day, wrote:

To meet this massed attack, our local air force – consisting of a few old-time open fuselage de Havilland machines, which had nothing like the climbing powers of the enemy machines – was wholly inadequate. The more modern types of machines were all required in France. As a result our really indomitable fighters of the 47th and 105th Squadrons were vastly handicapped. On this particular occasion it was impossible for them to give the enemy battle, and all they could do was to 'take off' with every aeroplane from the aerodrome, in order to save their machines. It would have taken them nearly twenty minutes to get to the height of the raiders, and in that time the enemy would have accomplished their purpose.[15]

A spring offensive was ordered and the British divisions were to advance. On 21 April the preparatory bombardment started, lasting for three days, and then on 24 April wire-cutting patrols were sent out. The 22nd Division moved forward the next day and captured Mamelon Hill, holding off five counterattacks with a loss of only 100 men. Johns and the 26th Division found themselves facing a stiffer resistance from the Bulgars; the division lost 80 officers and 2,000 men. According to Captain Day, the Bulgars humanely allowed British stretcher-bearers to search no-man's-land for the dead, wounded and dying for a few days after this abortive attack. 'In consequence of this generous consideration on the part of the enemy, a great number of lives were spared, many wounded being rescued and brought back into our lines after long periods of exposure and starvation.'[16]

Johns recalled:

I remember particularly one early morning. Dawn had just broken, and the newly risen sun was streaking the sky with all the colours of a madman's palette. I was standing just outside my machine-gun emplacement in the front line, drinking from a mess tin, tea which I had culled from war-scarred dixies. I was talking to Harry Barnes who was also having an early morning cup. We spoke in whispers, for the breathless hush of dawn hung in the air and the Bulgars were close. It was not because we were afraid but because it seemed sacrilege to break a silence so profound. Nothing moved. The war seemed far away.

We were not talking about death or glory, as writers of epic poetry or prose would have you believe; we were talking about partridges in stubble, and the smell of damp earth on an autumn morning ... and things like that. Harry told me that when he got back he was going to put down a field of mustard for his birds, for cover. It seemed a good idea. I knew the field well, and could visualise it, gleaming yellow amid the surrounding green – which is one of the things you do not miss until you have lost it. Actually, he was due to die in fifteen seconds, but there was little reason to suspect it. As I have said, everything was quiet, that morning on the Eastern Front.

I forget who it was who came drowsily out of the emplacement murmuring for a cup of tea. On the way to the dixies he glanced casually into the periscope with which our bay was fitted. Instantly he stiffened. 'My God!' he whispered tersely. 'I can see that b——sniper.'

Harry handed me his tea and grabbed his rifle. 'Where?' he said, and peered over the sandbags.

He stood like that for perhaps a second. It might have been less. I swear it wasn't more. There was a crisp *snick*. That was all. All as far as Harry was concerned. Very slowly, like a wet sack slipping from a peg, he collapsed into the firestep. There was a crimsoned-edge hole exactly between his eyes. There he lay, with me still holding his steaming tea in my left hand. The sergeant ran up, breathing unprintable obscenity. That's how it happens in war. Death is always handy – but glory is not so easily attained.[17]

Another offensive was started on 8 May and spearheaded by the 77th (Scottish) Infantry Brigade. It was met with a fierce Bulgar counterattack and by 20 May another stalemate had been reached. The lines remained unchanged until the armistice of 1918. The endless routine of trench warfare, sniping and coping with disease became a way of life. According to Captain Day, the war on this front became

... chiefly a campaign against our worst enemy – malaria. Preventative and curative treatments were experimented with in hospitals, while a number of sanitary precautions, including the spreading of oil on water surfaces, to discourage the mosquitoes, were adopted. Of the many safeguards attempted, the most satisfactory proved to be the removal of troops, wherever possible, from the lower fever-struck ground to higher and healthier ground. This was carried out with the best results on the Syrzma front, where at the beginning of the summer most of our forces were withdrawn to the hills, only a small number being kept on the plain to man a few fortified bridgeheads. The Bulgars followed a similar plan, leaving a message in our lines: 'You are going to the hills – so are we!'

Despite these precautions, thousands of troops fell sick from malaria – including Lance Corporal Johns. 'I went down with malaria – as everyone did sooner or later, in that disease smitten pesthole ...'[18] Years later he wryly recalled that the mosquitoes nearly slew him.[19] He was sent to hospital in Salonika and it was there that he made what was to be the most important decision of his life. He put in for a transfer to the Royal Flying Corps. 'I was learning something about war, and it seemed to me that there was no point in dying standing up in squalor if one could do so sitting down in clean air.'[20] On 25 September 1917, Lance Corporal W. E. Johns (No. 74451) was discharged on appointment to a commission and on 26 September he was granted a temporary commission as 2nd Lieutenant (No. 74534) on the General List of the Royal Flying Corps. The London *Gazette* carried the notice of his appointment on 23 October. He was going home to England to learn to fly.

3

THE FLYING INSTRUCTOR

On 26 September 1917, 2nd Lieutenant W. E. Johns was instructed to proceed to the School for Officer Cadets at Oxford. A short course instructed those commissioned from the ranks in the mysteries of being 'officers and gentlemen'. A month later, on Friday, 26 October 1917, Johns arrived at No. 1 School of Aeronautics at Reading, where he was to learn the art of flying. The headquarters of No. 1 School were at 14 London Road, where Lieutenant Colonel G. C. St P. de Dombasle commanded. The chief flying instructor at the school was Major S. McClure and Johns' immediate instructor was a Captain Ashton. The actual art of flying was only one of the intensive courses which Johns had to go through. He had to attend the Yeomanry Hall to learn about aircraft rigging, go to the Reading Tramsheds to explore the dangerous intricacies of bombs, and sweat in University College over the mysteries of aeroplane instruments. To obtain a thorough knowledge of aeroplane engines, aerial navigation, aerial observation, signalling and aerial gunnery, a great deal of time was taken up before the eager 2nd Lieutenant was allowed to go to the school's aerodrome at Coley Park and report to Captain Ashton for flying instruction.

'I learnt to fly in an old Rumpity,' Johns recalled, 'which would as soon go one way as another. You had to use both hands, both feet, and your teeth to keep it going where you wanted to go!'[1] The 'Rumpity' was the Maurice Farman Shorthorn, which was also affectionately known as a birdcage because of the vast number of wires securing the wings. In the Biggles' story 'First Time Up', Biggles' instructor tells him: 'The easiest way to find out if all the wires are in their place is to put a canary between the wings; if the bird gets out, you know there is a wire missing somewhere.' This tale, along with others in the collection *Biggles Learns to Fly* (1935) has a strong autobiographical element.

Johns discovered that he had an aptitude for flying and was

soon allowed to go solo. The flight was a disaster. The entry in his logbook is short: 'Time: 8.30 am. Pilot: self. Type and number of machine: MFSH 2113. Passenger: none. Time in air: five seconds. Height: 30 feet. Remarks: crashed taking off.' He later admitted: 'There is no story attached to it. I simply stalled taking off.'[2] Captain Ashton obviously did not believe in allowing his trainee pilots to brood on their crashes because the next day Johns was allowed to make another attempt. This time he took to the air without mishap. 'Tickled to death with myself I soared, in ever increasing circles, until I lost my way and finally returned home – more by luck than judgement – after having been in the air for ninety minutes. Which must be pretty well a record for a first solo. I was told not to be more than ten minutes.'[3] It was dark when Johns finally found Coley Park aerodrome and he admitted that he was frightened.[4] The story of this first successful solo flight was retold by him as 'First Time Up' in *Biggles Learns to Fly*.

Having made a solo flight the new pilot had to perfect his skills – he had already learnt to adopt a laconic attitude towards the prospect of sudden death.

I learned to fly sharing a cabin with a fellow out of the Royal Scots who had seen his brother die at Arras and couldn't get the picture from his mind. We called him Tony. I forget his other name. Apart from using the same quarters we shared the same machine: an R.E.8. Usually there was an argument as to who was to have it first. Sometimes we tossed for it, when, being lucky at that sort of thing, I usually won. One day I lost. Tony took the machine up. At 2,000 feet it shed a wing and spun into the carpet with all the ferocity the type could display when it was out of humour. It took the mechanics most of the day to dig Tony out, so I heard.[5]

Johns' early aptitude became overshadowed by a run of bad luck. 'I had three forced landings in three days when I was learning to fly.'[6] Today it is rare for trainee pilots to break their machines. In those early days of flying the reverse was true. According to Johns:

I don't suppose there is a pilot in the world who could claim never to have broken anything ... it may surprise you to know that some of our best pilots had bad reputations for crashing in their early days. The leading war aces were not exempt, either. Mind you, I'm not talking about serious crashes. An aeroplane isn't a difficult thing to break, and every year hundreds are smashed that you never hear of – usually the result of bad landings or collisions on the ground, sometimes with machines and sometimes with hangars. I've seen a sudden gust of wind throw seven or eight aeroplanes over on their backs.[7]

It was not an uncommon occurrence for aeroplanes to become 'runaways'. In those days, unless chocks were placed under the wheels to prevent the aircraft from moving, any attempt to start it by swinging the propeller would result in the machine moving forward and gathering speed. According to the regulations, the propeller was only to be swung if the pilot was in his seat, but this rule was not always observed. Johns, like many an inexperienced pilot before him, found himself the cause of a spectacular crash by allowing his aircraft to become a runaway.

I had not been flying very long at the time, and having done a short flip, I finished up with a nice landing on the far side of the aerodrome. Unfortunately, I lost my prop. This doesn't mean that it fell off. To 'lose your prop.' in flying parlance, means that it stops. If the engine timing is correct it shouldn't stop, nevertheless it does sometimes.

Well, I didn't want to drag mechanics all the way across the aerodrome to start it for me, so I decided to swing it myself. It didn't seem to be a very difficult thing to do, so, with this object in view, I got out to turn the propeller round a few times to get some gas in the cylinders of the engine. So far so good.

I put the switch on 'contact' and went back to the prop. and swung. I swung until I was blue in the face but couldn't get so much as a buzz out of it. Panting from the exertion and the heat – I was all wrapped up in my flying kit – I did about the craziest thing I could have done. I opened the throttle a little way.

Nothing doing! After a ten minutes' catch-as-catch-can wrestling bout with the confounded thing I gave it up and lay down under the wing to get my breath back. Then I opened the throttle a little wider and sailed in for the next round.

Bang! My hand hardly seemed to touch that prop. before I was flat on my back.

I was soon on my feet again staring in horrified dismay at a rapidly retreating aeroplane, already half-way to the sheds, leaping and prancing like an old crow with rheumatism in his wing joints.

I set off after it like a stag, yelling like fury, not that there was any need for me to strain my vocal cords. A bunch of air mechanics had already seen the old bird and were racing out to meet her.

At a distance of twenty yards or so most of them changed their minds about grabbing her, and flung themselves flat to get out of the way of the churning prop. One fellow grabbed a wing tip and hung on long enough to point her nose in my direction, sending up a cloud of dust from her skidding wheels. Then he fell off.

All this time I had been running after the thing, but as she put her nose down and charged at me, I, too, changed my mind and started putting my feet down one after the other the way I had come as rapidly as possible. I'm no bullfighter!

Just when I had abandoned all hope of escape the brute evidently got the breeze on her tail, for she swung round again and made for the sheds, while I, panting and gasping for breath, watched her in impotent fury. To think that she should turn on me like that!

At this moment what should happen but a poor unlucky hoot of a pupil, no doubt breathing a sigh of relief at having done ten minutes' flying without busting anything, decided to land. He sat down right in the path of the fiendish machine running amok.

My heart went out to him at that moment, but that didn't help him. He scarcely had time to realise what was happening before there was a splintering crash and he sat gazing in stupefied surprise – as if he couldn't believe his eyes – at the place where, a moment before, his lower port plane had been.

But my late aerial conveyance was by no means out of action. Oh no, sir! She just swung her nose round towards the CO's office and off she went again as if she was thoroughly enjoying herself.

There must have been a crowd of close on two hundred people chasing her by this time. Airmen, officers, cooks, mess orderlies and goodness knows who else, all in full cry after the culprit. The din sounded like the baying of a pack of hounds.

I am not going into all the sad details of what the machine did but among other things she 'wrote off' a 'Tinside (Martinside Scout), an R.E.8 and a little 'Ack.W.' (Armstrong-Whitworth) before she tried to climb over the CO's office.

The place looked as though it had been bombed by a squadron of enemy bombers and casualties came limping in from all sides of the aerodrome. I brought up the rear, the cynosure of all eyes.

The CO was waiting for me. His expression was not that of a father welcoming a long-lost son.

'Did you do that?' he asked, breathing heavily and pointing at the tangled remains of what, ten minutes earlier, had been a perfectly good aeroplane. The mangled remains piled up against the squadron office were not pretty to look at.

'Yes sir,' I replied, sadly bracing myself for the worst.

The CO gulped, swallowed once or twice, shook his head like a man who finds it difficult to express his thoughts in mere words, turned on his heel and strode away.[8]

Such incidents were not altogether unusual and, a few days after Johns' spectacular runaway, a similar incident took place when another runaway slewed into a line of machines lined up for inspection on the tarmac and, within seconds, 'wrote off' five of them, wheeled into a hangar and smashed several more, setting the hangar on fire.

Crashes were not always confined to pupils either. While at Coley Park, Johns recalled:

I was doing some gunnery practice at a nice steady speed, shooting at an old worn-out plane, on the far side of the aerodrome, which we used as a target. Satisfied with my work, I landed and got an awful shock.

A senior instructor came across and told me what he thought about my flying. The things he said made me blush but not with pleasure. He had rather an unpleasant way of talking to pupils, making you feel as if you were about as much use as a bad headache.

'Now,' he said, after his red-hot speech, preparing to get into the cockpit I had just vacated. 'I'll show you the way to do it. Dive at the target, not glide at it. Hold your fire until the last second – say twenty or thirty feet – then zoom up over the target. Watch me!'

I watched. He took off, climbed to a thousand feet, put his nose down nearly vertically and streaked like a shooting star at the target, guns spitting tracer bullets.

That part of it was pretty to watch but what followed was not so pleasant. It seemed to me that he pulled out of his dive just about a tenth of a second too late. There was a crash of splintered wood, a cloud of dust rose in the air and then silence.

'Well,' I said to a pal who was standing watching the performance. 'That's that. It may be his idea of how to shoot up a target, but it isn't mine.'[9]

Johns was given his 'wings' towards the end of the year but remained at Reading waiting for a posting. He was a competent but not a brilliant pilot. 'I was never in the masterpiece class or I might now be an Air Marshal. Perhaps! I always knew my limitations as a flying man and while that is nothing much to boast about, it probably accounts for the fact that I am still alive to tell my tale!'[10] But limited or not, Johns could rise to the occasion under pressure as his subsequent service record showed.

While waiting at Reading, Johns was detailed to help the instructors at No. 1 School, and ferry machines from the manufacturers to the aerodrome and vice versa. Once he recalled being asked by an instructor to bring back a machine that had force-landed in a very small field which was bordered by trees. The machine had been repaired, so Johns was told, but as he took off the engine cut out. Ahead was an even smaller field and Johns made 'what was probably the best landing of my life'.[11] He spent some time trying to mend the engine and finally took off again. It was nearly dark and he became hopelessly lost. Finally, with fingers crossed, he set the machine down in pitch-dark conditions, making a perfect landing. To his astonishment he found himself in a field separated from Coley Park aerodrome by a hedge.

On 20 January 1918 Johns received his first posting to No. 25 Flying Training School at Thetford, close by Little Dunham. It was a lucky posting because it meant that Johns could spend time with his wife Maude and young Jack. No. 25 FTS Squadron had been formed on 22 May 1916 at Thetford and remained there until it was disbanded the year after the war ended. Thetford was crowded in those days, as hundreds of pilots passed rapidly through to receive minimal instruction in aerial warfare before being posted directly to a front line squadron. The overspill of training flights was handled at an aerodrome at Narborough, some twenty miles away. Johns, expecting to be sent to France, found, to his surprise, that his flying proficiency had resulted in a posting as a flying instructor. He never recorded whether he was unhappy with a Home Establishment posting, though this was not without its dangers, as he soon found out.

Early in 1918, when I was stationed at Narborough, in Norfolk, at least one or two spies were tampering with our machines – half-sawing through joysticks, so that they snapped off short in the air, cutting through control wires and the like. Machines broke up in the air every day. I leave you to guess what it was like, flying an aeroplane that was liable to shed its wings at any moment. In one month no less than three officers were killed, including my best friend.[12]

Johns' best friend at this time was Arch Farmer and one night as they walked across the aerodrome to their quarters, Farmer said to him: 'Bill, somebody's cutting the wires on these machines. I have a feeling my turn is about due.'

'Rot!' Johns replied.

The next morning both airmen were down for early flying. They were sharing the same machine. Farmer was up just before Johns and pulled a sweater over his pyjamas. 'I'll take her up first. You shave,' he called out cheerfully. 'I'll be back by the time you are up at the sheds.'

From the window, as he shaved, Johns saw Farmer taxi out and take off. At about 2,000 feet he started to turn. There was a crash and the port wing of the aircraft went up like a sunshade blown inside out. In horror, Johns saw the aircraft dive towards the ground and Farmer's figure climb out of the cockpit and jump. Parachutes were rare in those days and hardly ever worn by pilots. Johns later reflected: 'God knows why he jumped – unless it was because he had a horror of fire. He had always told me that he would jump if ...'[13]

The next day Johns helped to carry Farmer's coffin to the local churchyard. Farmer's girlfriend was there. 'She didn't cry, but I can still see her face. She kept asking me if I thought he had been killed outright.'

The day following Farmer's funeral two more machines – DH4s – went to pieces and two pilots named Lee and Shaw were killed. According to Johns, no less than thirteen pilots and observers were burnt to death in crashes in as many days, and the local village blacksmith, who had been a juryman on all the inquests, committed suicide, overcome by the horror of the situation.

There were a number of American mechanics and crew stationed at Narborough who were apparently of German descent. Suspicions ran high among British airmen when it was pointed out that some of the Americans had names like Schmidt and Guggenheimer. Johns recalled that it was a 'big fellow by the name of Hazell' who, having seen his observer burnt to death, suddenly refused to fly any more. 'It ended in a general strike, perhaps the only case on record when a hundred British officers refused to obey orders. Nobody would fly.'[14]

A major from the Air Board was sent down to investigate and all aircraft were locked in the hangars with a company of infantry placed over them as guards. The major confessed that there was probably a German agent among the American airmen, but if anything was done without proof America, Britain's new ally against Germany, would become outraged. He also told the officers that the sabotage might be part of a plan to create friction between British pilots and American personnel. 'Finally,' says Johns, 'every machine was subjected to a thorough inspection and an infantry soldier placed on guard over it. Thus, all day and all night, while the machine was on the ground, it was being guarded. That ended the trouble ...'[15]

Sudden death in the air by accident was a common occurrence. One Sunday evening, when Johns was Orderly Officer of the day, he was sitting smoking a cigarette outside the hangars at Thetford. The aerodrome was deserted, most of the personnel having gone into the nearest town. Johns' reverie was interrupted by a strange single-seater scout making a landing on the aerodrome. It was a type which he had not seen before. The pilot made a neat landing and taxied towards the spot where Johns was sitting. Leaving his prop ticking over, he clambered out and exchanged a greeting. He was from Harling Road, a nearby station.

'What's that?' asked Johns, nodding towards the strange machine.

'An SE5,' the pilot replied scornfully.

'Pretty useful?' asked Johns.

'Useful?' replied the pilot. 'Useful! I should say she is. She'll loop off the ground.'

Johns' expression must have betrayed his incredulity, for the pilot muttered, 'Watch me!' and climbed back into his machine. The SE5 took off and soared in a circle, swinging over the top and coming down. The SE5 hit the ground at about 300 mph. Johns did not move. He could not. When the ambulance took away the pilot's remains and the air mechanics started to pick up the pieces, Johns noticed he was still smoking the same cigarette as when the SE5 had first landed.

Now up to that moment the height of my ambition had been to loop off the ground; it was a brand new stunt then. It was far more spectacular than just flying under the telegraph wires like Warley used to, before he hit the wires, or flying between hangars like Brisbane did, until he went through two wrong hangars and hit the watch tower. As I sat and pondered the cloud of dust, it slowly dawned on my ordinary intelligence that looping off the floor was a thing to be avoided at all costs. Presently, still thinking of what I had seen, it occurred to me that doing things with an aeroplane near the ground was a selfish pastime. It was unfair for other officers to be detailed for a burying party after they had no doubt made other arrangements for the day.[16]

No. 25 Squadron was possessed of a 'bad aeroplane', although the cause of her badness was a mystery. She was rather like the ship described by Joseph Conrad in 'The Brute', but to start with she appeared to be stupid rather than malicious. She was 20 mph slower than any other machine in the squadron, the controls were 'sticky' and she was hard to fly, yet to all intents and purposes she was exactly the same as the rest. Fitters, riggers and mechanics had done their best to find the trouble, but without success. No one wanted to fly her, but she had to be used because she was on the squadron's strength. If the machine could be 'written off' a replacement could be ordered, but whereas other machines were smashed, nothing ever happened to the jinxed aircraft.

Finally, after a pilot had nearly lost his life flying her, the CO of No. 25 went to the sheds with a purposeful look on his face. 'I think we all guessed what he was going to do,' recalled Johns.[17] The machine was wheeled out onto the tarmac, the prop was swung. The CO stood beside the fuselage and opened the throttle wide, then jumped clear. The machine was pointed towards the barbed wire fencing in the perimeter of the aerodrome. She started to move forward, but then, for no apparent reason, swung round towards the CO. The officer bolted. The aircraft began to smash her way across the aerodrome, and Johns watched, fascinated, as the CO dashed into his office and reappeared with a Very pistol. The maverick had just struck the corner of a hangar and was trundling off towards the far side of the airfield when the CO let drive at her. The blazing flare of the cartridge did the trick. A stream of flame shot out of the petrol tank and the next minute Johns and his fellow pilots watched the machine, wrapped in fire and smoke, streaking across the grass.

'Of course, as soon as the fabric coverings were burnt off it came to a standstill, and blazed out its existence in solitary state. Later we sprayed it with fire extinguishers and dragged the metal skeleton to the rubbish pile where, for all I know, it still remains.'[18]

While at Narborough, Johns undertook a course of 'blind flying', an art which was very much in its infancy. His logbook carried the laconic statement that he undertook a 'compass test course' with a navigation specialist, Lieutenant David, in an Armstrong-Whitworth, No. 9626. The test was to prove a pilot's ability to fly in cloud or fog. Johns and David worked out a compass course from Narborough to Sedgeford and took off, climbing to 3,000 feet, where a thick blanket of cloud stretched from horizon to horizon. Johns flew watching his compass for twenty minutes before David patted him on the shoulder and motioned downwards. 'Good!' shouted the lieutenant. 'Now go down and you will see that we are exactly over Sedgeford aerodrome.' They were not. In all directions, as far as the eye could see, stretched the cold, briny ocean. Johns, without waiting for instructions, turned due west while Lieutenant David puzzled over his compass readings. A few minutes later the navigation expert shouted into Johns' ear: 'It's all right. I've discovered the error. Keep on your course and in fifteen minutes you will see Skegness straight ahead.' Two minutes later Johns spotted Cromer. Lieutenant David seemed to be losing his confidence. 'Let us try and make Cranwell, we ought to do it in about twenty-five minutes,' he suggested. Johns acknowledged the man's compass reading and twenty-five minutes later they found themselves over an aerodrome. It was Narborough.

When I pointed out this detail to the compass expert, instead of being pleased to be back home, he seemed really peeved about it and started slating the compass. As I told him at the time, it had brought us safely back home – what more could a compass do?[19]

At Narborough, Johns had a spectacular crash. He was flying an RE8 at 4,000 feet in the vicinity of the aerodrome, holding the machine in an almost vertical bank, and was about to pull out when he discovered that his lateral controls would not function. The result was that he could not get out of the turn. 'I was pretty badly scared,' confessed Johns, 'and tried to work out what was to be done about it. I dared not switch my engine off because I was almost certain to go into a spin if I did.'[20] Indeed, if Johns had spun, the machine might have come out of its own accord – but it might not. He decided that his prime task was to get the machine back on an even keel, but with his stick malfunctioning it was hard to see how this was to be managed.

He had to get down somehow so he set about what seemed the

only way of doing so. He drew back his throttle and let his nose dip a little. The moment it went too low and the risk of spinning became imminent he opened up again. By this means he lost two or three hundred feet, still circling on his side. By repetition of the movement he came closer to the ground. Twenty feet from the ground he cut his switches to lessen the risk of fire and curled his knees into his stomach, folded his arms over his face and waited for the impact. His wing tip struck the ground first and broke most of the shock. The machine scattered itself over the landscape, but the main fuselage, with Johns in it, was flung into a hedge. 'I wasn't hurt. Not even a scratch,' he recalled later.[21]

Johns just missed going nose first into the ground not long afterwards. He was practising with a new bomb-sight, which was a lens fitted into the floor of the cockpit. He was flying along with his head well down between his knees, eyes glued to the lens. As he did so he unconsciously moved his stick to obtain a better view. Suddenly he noticed that the ground below was at an irregular angle. He jerked his head up just as the aircraft stalled and the controls went 'sloppy' in his hands. To his horror he found that he was only 100 feet from the ground. The nose of the aircraft went over and it began to plunge straight downward. Johns snapped off his switches and pulled the stick right back with all his strength. The aircraft managed to pull out of it – but only just. 'People who saw the show declare that my wheels actually brushed the grass.'[22]

Thetford and Narborough were so close to Little Dunham that Johns was unable to resist the temptation of flying over the rectory and giving his wife, son and in-laws a free aerobatic display. One day a sergeant asked Johns if he would test a two-seater machine which had just been re-serviced. Johns climbed in and took off. 'Then I slipped along to a house where a particularly pretty girl I knew lived, and gave her a short exhibition of my idea of super airmanship. It was while I was holding the machine in a vertical bank, the more easily to see the garden below me and in order not to miss any of the applause, that I saw a hand clutching the side of the rear cockpit!'[23] Johns put the aircraft back on an even keel and peered behind. There was no hand. For a moment he felt a slight shiver run down his spine. He stopped his display, went back to Narborough and landed. Cautiously, he peered into the back cockpit. 'On the floor was two-pennyworth of warmed-up death.' It was a young fitter who had climbed into the cockpit for a quiet smoke. The boy had never been in the air before and, by his looks, Johns felt, never wanted to again. The fitter was turned over to the sergeant who had been wondering where the lad had disappeared to.

On 1 April 1918 the Royal Flying Corps and Royal Naval Air Service became one new service – the Royal Air Force. Johns was confirmed as 2nd Lieutenant, on probation, in the new service and he also received a posting to No. 2 School of Air Fighting at Marske-on-Sea, Yorkshire. Marske-on-Sea stands on the bleak Yorkshire coastline just outside Saltburn. The CO, said Johns, was a Major Champion who was nicknamed Gimlet, a nickname Johns was to make popular in his series of Gimlet commando books. According to Johns, Major Champion was credited with shooting down 28 German aircraft.[24] It has been impossible to establish the real identity of the CO at Marske. According to the Department of Aviation Records of the RAF Museum: 'We have been quite unable to find anyone with the name of Champion who had a score of 28 to his credit. It obviously is a pseudonym although quite why Johns should think it necessary to have one I really don't know.'[25]

As a flying instructor, Johns seems to have started off his new posting with another run of bad luck. 'I once had three forced landings in three days at Marske-on-Sea – an aerodrome which has since been abandoned – from engine failure.'[26] The first of these was while he was flying a Sopwith Camel fighter. He had to ditch it in the sea about one hundred yards from the shore and was picked up by a boat. The next day, while flying a Dolphin, the Hispano-Suiza engine cut out dead in almost the same place. This time Johns reached the shore, but could not clear the sand-dunes. His wheels struck the top of them and only the soft sand saved him from serious injury as the aircraft cartwheeled. He injured his knee and fractured his nose. However, he was up again the following day and this time the engine of his Avro cut out when he was taking off. 'I made an unceremonious entry into a brother officer's house on the edge of the aerodrome, through the back door. I broke the door and bent the Avro but escaped with no more than a slight shaking.'[27]

Bad luck continued to dog No. 2 Squadron's new flying instructor. He was coming in to land a 'Harry Tate' (RE8) and flattened out for a perfect landing. The only trouble was that he was twenty feet too high. The machine fell to the tarmac with a sickening thump. 'When I walked back dejectedly to the sheds I was greeted with ringing cheers from the pupils I had been giving instruction on it. One of them took a snapshot of the poor old Harry Tate ... standing on its nose in the middle of the aerodrome.' However, a few minutes later one of Johns' pupils came in to make a perfect landing in a DH4. The only thing wrong with the pupil's landing was that he made it upside down. Johns borrowed the camera to take a snapshot of the machine, which years later he published as an illustration to an article on plane crashes.[28]

Johns made very few references to his pupils, mainly preferring to tell of his own mistakes in flying. He did, however, devote an entire article to one pupil – an officer called Smell, who soon won the prefix Smasher.[29] Johns gave him instruction on a 'Rumpity' but, after long hours of patient teaching, he came to the realisation that the man was 'ham-fisted'. 'Alone in the air he had about as much chance of surviving as a rabbit in a wild beast show.' During his course of instruction Smasher destroyed eight machines, but somehow Johns managed to push him through the course and he was sent to France. When Johns went to France himself and was waiting at Couban aerodrome, a DH9a crashed in the centre of the airfield and a smiling Smasher Smell emerged from the wreckage. Smell survived the war.

Another of Johns' pupils was called Grafton Harmey, who was immediately nicknamed Barmy. When the young man reported to Johns at Marske, Johns asked him: 'Ever been up?'

'No. But I know all about it.'

Johns gave a hollow laugh, but Barmy proceeded to tell Johns how to fly.

'Stop!' roared Johns. 'Who told you all this?'

'I got it out of a book,' replied the young man modestly.

Grimly, Johns took him up into the air, and after half an hour he had to admit that the lad was right. Whether the book had helped or not, Barmy was perfectly capable of flying the machine and went solo after another half-hour. Johns met him later in France, and when Johns was shot down, Barmy wrote a letter of condolence to Johns' family.[30]

On the other hand, another of Johns' pupils who told him he

could fly, this time though 'instinct', flew straight into the side of a building on his first solo attempt. Luckily the building turned out to be a hospital.

There seem to have been several self-confident would-be aviators about. 'One of the worst pupils I ever had started off by telling me where, theoretically, I was wrong. It took me twenty hard hours to teach him enough to trust him with an aeroplane – then he took off and at once flew straight into a tower, but he had beginner's luck and only broke a leg. A good pilot would have broken his neck!'[31] Yet another raw pilot could fly well enough but was hopeless at aerial gunnery. He could not hit the targets set up on the aerodrome perimeter. The pupil told Johns that it must be a matter of the gun-sights being inaccurate. Unbeknown to his instructor, the enterprising young man then altered the sights and shot up the aerodrome bath-houses.

In those early days of flying, every flight had its complement of surprises. Recalling one incident, Johns wrote: 'This took place at No. 2 School of Fighting, early in 1918, and it all came about by Boyle losing an undercarriage wheel just as he left the ground. This was by no means an uncommon occurrence and we laughed as the wheel went bowling along gaily across the aerodrome.'[32] But, of course, the comedy of the situation was likely to turn to tragedy when the hapless pilot tried to land, not knowing he only had one wheel. One of the instructors, an officer named Hicks, took Boyle's wheel and took off in his aircraft, determined to catch up with Boyle and indicate he only had one wheel. As Hicks took off, however, his own wheel came off. Now there were two pilots in the air, neither knowing he had only half an undercarriage! As Hicks tried to signal Boyle by showing him the wheel, Boyle thought that Hicks was pointing out that his own undercarriage was adrift. Comedy turned to absolute farce when two more officers clambered into a DH9a, the observer holding Hicks' wheel aloft to join in the signalling contest. At last the DH9a's crew managed to indicate to both Boyle and Hicks that they were without undercarriages.

Both crippled planes made excellent side-wind one-wheel landings and just piled up quietly on their noses at the end of the one-wheel run, when the axle stumps, of course, caught the ground. Neither pilot was hurt and could therefore enjoy the joke.[33]

Sometime later Johns was leading a formation of three aircraft along the north Yorkshire coast on a training flight. Crossing the mouth of the Tees, a sea fog suddenly swirled up. Within moments Johns had lost contact with his two wing men and had to come down almost to sea level to find out where he was. 'I still held north expecting to strike Hartlepool and turn to follow the coast line,' he recalled. 'Buzzing along at about ten feet I suddenly saw a great grey mass loom up in front of me and I'll wager that machine never did a quicker turn in its life. I had an instant's vision of towering cliffs grazing my undercarriage wheels, a flash of screaming gulls, and I was doubling my course.'[34]

The next day he flew an Armstrong-Whitworth down to Norfolk to see his wife. On the return journey he began to feel ill. Feeling unable to carry on flying, he spotted a large field and made a good landing, climbed out and lay down under his wing. He dozed off, hoping the sickness would pass. A short time later he awoke to find a curious crowd of people standing around him and, feeling embarrassed, decided to continue his journey back to Marske. One of the crowd said, 'You look ill. You shouldn't try to fly.' However, Johns, like Biggles, who in similar circumstances was to mutter, 'While I'm conscious I can fly', insisted that it would be all right. He took off, becoming uncomfortably aware that the ground was rising towards him and then receding in an extraordinary way. The spectators scattered in all directions. 'Badly scared, for I had no idea I was so low, I made for home.'

After an interminable age, Johns sighted Marske and came down for a landing. The sheds on the field, one moment far away, suddenly rushed to meet him. He crashed into the wind indicator pole, ripping it out of the ground, and careered onto a hangar roof, running over it and then onto the top of a machine standing on the tarmac. His wheels caught the top-plane and ripped it off. This impeded the forward motion of the Armstrong-Whitworth and it tipped violently into the ground. 'Actually,' he explained later, 'it was almost excusable as, although I was unaware of it, I was suffering from 'flu. My temperature when I was carried into hospital was 103.'[35]

From the hospital window that afternoon, 'I saw one of the most remarkable crashes I have ever seen in my life.' An officer named Ludgate stalled his machine about 200 feet over the aerodrome. The aircraft, an RE8, went nose first into the ground.

By the law of averages the pilot should have been killed. However, by some miracle, the nose dive was into the thickest part of a large hedge. The machine bounded into the springy foliage and came to rest with its tail in the air. Ludgate climbed out, shaken but unhurt. Someone on the station took a snapshot which Johns afterwards stuck into his photograph album.

Johns recovered from his flu and his injuries, and was soon back on flying duties. Not long afterwards he was flying an RE8 when the top of the engine cowling blew off and went into the centre section bracing, where it stuck fast. It made Johns jump and for a moment he could not think what on earth had happened. It blocked his forward view. When he realised what was wrong, he became frightened. The thought that the large sheet of metal might burst through the wires into his face caused him to land immediately in the first available field. Then came another forced landing when he was taking a machine back to the makers for reconditioning. Flying at 5,000 feet, he discovered to his horror that two rear centre section struts were not bolted down. There was a fair chance of the whole thing, including the top-planes, coming adrift. He landed immediately.[36]

One of Johns' most hair-raising moments occurred soon after, when he shot his own propeller off because the synchronisation gear had not been set properly. 'It was my own fault,' he admitted ruefully. 'It gave me a rare fright, I can tell you. I thought my gun had burst. The noise as the engine raced was frightful. I had to come down, of course.'[37] He managed to glide back to the aerodrome and later picked up one of the splintered blades, which he kept for some time as a souvenir.[38]

By modern standards, from the number of crashes Johns had, it would appear that he was more of a liability than an asset to the Allied cause. Had the Allied aircraft he destroyed been German, he would certainly have qualified for the designation 'ace'. However, it must be remembered that in those days flying was still a very hit-and-miss affair and many top pilots had reputations of being 'plane smashers'. Even aces such as 'Billy' Bishop, 'Jimmy' McCudden, 'Mick' Mannock and 'Don' MacLaren could claim their fair share of crashes. Johns was always to remember the day he heard of the death of one of these legendary airmen.

On July 9, 1918, I was climbing out of my machine when my fitter made a remark that brought me down with a jerk.

'Major McCudden's gone west, sir,' he said.

'Good God!' I replied, as shaken as if he had said the Kaiser was in Paris.

Walking from the mess, I saw the CO, Major Champion, just leaving the bath-house.

'I hear Jimmy McCudden's gone topside,' I said.

'Good God!' he cried, staring at me aghast.

At that moment the same words were no doubt on a thousand lips.[39]

Major James T. B. McCudden VC, credited with shooting down 57 enemy aircraft in combat, was Britain's fourth top-scoring ace of the war. He had been on his way to take command of No. 60 Squadron in France when he was killed in a flying accident on 9 July. While Britain did not like, nor officially recognise, the ace designation, public morale was boosted by the publicity given to the deeds of men like Major 'Mick' Mannock, with 73 victories, Lieutenant Colonel 'Billy' Bishop, with 72 victories, Major McCudden, Captain Albert Ball and others. The publicity also had a reverse effect, for when Mannock, McCudden and Ball were killed, it hit the public, and their fellow pilots, hard, as Johns indicates.

On 20 July 1918 Johns received notification that he had finally been confirmed in his rank as 2nd Lieutenant with pilot proficiency on aeroplanes and seaplanes. Soon after, Major Champion sent for him and told him to report to Air House in London for instructions; he was being posted to the front in France.[40] The next weeks were to be the most adventurous and dangerous of his entire life.

4

No. 55 SQUADRON, FRANCE

Johns' method of joining No. 55 (Day) Bombing Squadron in France was, to say the least, somewhat unusual, though by no means unheard of in those confused days of war. He literally posted himself to it.

Johns travelled by train from Yorkshire, and reported at the Hotel Cecil in London. He was given a warrant to go to Lympne airfield in Kent, where he would, he was told, find a DH4 which he was to ferry to France. He was assured that Lympne would have his further travel instructions and destination. The CO at Lympne, a man Johns recalls as being named McKay, had heard nothing of him and had no DH4 ready for ferrying to France.

Johns hung about Lympne for three days, waiting for his orders and aircraft to show up. 'Life became boring, so I butted into a Canadian poker school. Two hours later I got up from the table, not only broke, but having distributed my next month's pay in IOUs.'[1] Disconsolate, he was in the officers' mess when a man in flying gear looked in.

'Well, I'm just off.'

'Where?' asked Johns.

'France in an H. Pip.' (A Handley Page).

On impulse Johns asked for a lift. The pilot agreed so Johns 'paid my mess bill with a cheque I hoped Cox's' [the bankers] 'would meet but was afraid they wouldn't, fetched my valise, threw it into the Handley and crawled into the front seat.'

It was cold and Johns was not wearing flying gear – in subsequent years of flying it was a mistake he never repeated. The machine landed at Marquise, where he had a drink with the pilot. He made an unsuccessful attempt to get some money from the station cashier and decided to make his way to the RAF pilots' pool at St Omer. He had little luck in hitching a lift. Finally, he managed to secure transport in a machine going to Bourget, near Paris. The passenger seat was already occupied, 'so I climbed into the carcase. There was nothing to sit on except the floor, so I sat on it, with my legs hanging through the bomb holes.' Johns knocked out his pipe on the edge of one of the holes. They had barely been in the air five minutes when the main petrol tank burst, and he went cold with fear as the petrol geyser hit him. The pilot circled back to land safely at Marquise, where he picked up another aircraft, and this time conveyed his passengers to Bourget without incident.

At Bourget Johns made another unsuccessful attempt to raise some cash from the station cashier. His erstwhile pilot offered to cheer him up by showing him Paris, adding that he had a car at the aerodrome. Johns decided to let fate take its course. He accompanied the officer to a hotel in the city where they dumped their overnight kit, bathed and spruced up and proceeded to the Follies, at which point Johns lost his companion and guide. 'I came out about one in the morning and remembered I had forgotten to ask him the name of the hotel. I had never been in Paris before and it all looked alike to me. I cruised about a bit in a taxi, calling at hotels to see if I was staying there, but finally I had to make the driver take me to Bourget in order to get the money to pay him. I never saw my pilot again.'

The next morning a rather dejected 2nd Lieutenant, missing his overnight kit and 'finding I was unpopular with the mess secretary', found a pilot who was ferrying a brand new DH9a to Couban. He offered to give Johns a lift. Johns had no idea where Couban was, but hoped it was near St Omer. 'The lad who was flying stalled at a hundred feet coming in, and threw me and my valise out on to the aerodrome. He killed himself doing it ...'[2]

Johns was shaken but unhurt. There was nothing to be gained by staying at Couban. His odyssey continued when the CO fixed him up with a lift in a Handley Page going to Xaffervilliers.

It seemed as good as anywhere, wherever it was, so I went. I sat next to the pilot who soon lost his way, with the result that we arrived after dark, and not being expected, no lights were put out. We hit the ground before I knew we were near it, and, I suspect, before my pilot knew it. The HP spread itself over the landscape; my valise burst and I lost more kit.[3]

It was at Xaffervilliers that the station's Record Officer, getting details from Johns of who he was and where he should be, mentioned that No. 55 Squadron were crying out for replacement pilots and observers. He offered to fix Johns up with a tender to take him to their base at Azelot first thing in the morning. Just then a solitary German aircraft, attracted by the lights and activity around the crashed Handley Page began bombing the aerodrome. It was Johns' official welcome to war in the air.

'I slept the night on my valise in an empty room. In the morning I won nine hundred francs and his revolver from a delivery pilot at two-handed pontoon.' A tender took Johns to Azelot where he reported to the commanding officer of No. 55 Squadron – Major Alec Gray MC (later to be Group Captain). Johns assured the slightly bewildered Gray that he had been posted to the squadron, but his papers had 'gone missing'. This was a frequent occurrence in those days and Gray did not look the gift-horse in the mouth. He had just lost five machines and their crews. The paperwork could be sorted out later. In fact, Johns was officially posted to the squadron on 21 August.[4]

No. 55 Squadron had been formed at Castle Bromwich, Warwickshire, on 27 April 1916, from a nucleus provided by No. 5 Reserve Squadron and No. 34 Squadron. It was originally a training unit, but was then mobilised for active service in mid-January 1917, crossing to France in March as the first squadron to be equipped with De Havilland DH4 heavy bombers with 275 hp Rolls-Royce Eagle engines. Its main tasks were bombing, photography and reconnaissance. It had a reputation for expertise at long-distance raids into enemy territory. On 17 June when the squadron raided Ingelmunster, six of its heavy DH4s had to fight ten enemy fighters the whole way there and back. Each side lost one aircraft, but the target was attacked successfully.

In October 1917 the squadron had moved to Ochey and joined the 41st Wing of the Independent Force, commanded by Major-General H. ('Boomer') Trenchard – later Air Chief Marshal of the RAF. The squadron was ordered to carry out special bombing raids on strategic targets within Germany and became the first British squadron to bomb Mannheim on 24 December 1917; Mainz on 9 March 1918; Coblenz on 12 March 1918 and Duren on 1 August 1918. In June the squadron moved to Azelot, where they shared an airfield with No. 99 Squadron (commanded by Major L. A. Pattinson) and No. 104 Squadron (commanded by Major J. C. Quinnell). Azelot was not far from Nancy, a tiny hamlet with a population of only 160 people. It was part of the cantonment of St Nicolas-du-Port in the department of Meurthe-et-Moselle and situated close to the front line trenches which formed part of the St Mihiel Salient, occupied, on the Allied side, mainly by American troops.

The DH4s with which the squadron was equipped had the sinister soubriquet of 'flaming coffin'. The reason for this nickname among pilots was the fact that the main petrol tank on the aircraft was set between the pilot and his observer – a likely place for the bullets of an attacking enemy machine to strike. Johns recalled:

According to current rumour at the time a DH4, when shot down, invariably became a 'flamer' and records do in fact show that a 'flaming coffin' awaited many DH4 pilots who were unlucky enough to be defeated in an air battle. Not unnaturally the DH4 was at one time an unpopular machine, as fire was, and is, the greatest dread of an airman, and nothing could ruin the reputation of a machine faster than a tendency to burn in the air.

Many pilots swore by them, however. I did, and I put in several hundred hours in them. I will go further and say that the DH4 was one of the finest machines that ever went to France. Records also show that many enemy pilots regarded it with the greatest respect, as well they might, for the old 'Four' took deadly toll during its career.

In its earliest form it was fitted with a 230 horse power BHP engine which was replaced in 1917 with a Rolls-Royce 275 hp Eagle VII engine. Later, in 1918, it had the 375 hp Eagle VIII. At the time of its introduction, no faster machine flew in France, and it was not until 1918 that the enemy produced fighters which surpassed it in speed and climb. It marked a new era in two-seater planes, and it may well be called the direct ancestor of the latest day-bombers. It was one of the few machines that dared operate on long-distance shows without an escort, and its manoeuvrability was on a par with many single-seater fighters of the period.[f]

Major Alec Gray gave his new recruit some advice about war flying in a short, crisp lecture; advice that, according to Johns, was tattooed into his mind during the following month with Spandau needles.[6] Major Gray's advice was reiterated when Johns was introduced to No. 55 Squadron's four flight commanders – Captain B. J. Silly MC, DFC (later Squadron Leader); Captain D. R. G. Mackay MC; Captain J. R. Bell DFC and Captain Fox MC. Later in the month, Captain Mackay was to become Johns' regular flight commander. In his foreword to *The Camels Are Coming*, Johns recalled: 'Captain "Jock" Mackay of my squadron survived three years of air warfare only to be killed by "archie" [anti-aircraft gunfire] an hour before the Armistice was signed.' This was not strictly accurate. Mackay, with his observer, 2nd Lieutenant H. G. T. Gompertz, was shot down the day before the Armistice was signed during a raid on the Ehrang railway sidings. A combat report said they were 'last seen between Thionville and Metz gliding down under control.'[7] Mackay was killed, but Gompertz managed to land the machine. Johns does not state whether he was at all awed by the fact that most of the pilots and observers in the squadron sported the ribbons of the Military Cross or the new RAF equivalent, the Distinguished Flying Cross – indications of the 'crack' status of the squadron.

Though by now Johns was an experienced pilot, and in spite of the advice from the veterans of No. 55 Squadron, his first reaction to aerial warfare was one of bewilderment.

The first dog fight I was ever in, it seemed to me that one minute we – that is, my formation – were sailing along all merry and bright, and the next minute the air was full of machines, darting all over the place. I didn't see where they came from or where they went. I didn't see where my formation went either.

By the time I had grasped the fact that the fight had started and I was looking to see who the dickens was perforating my plane, the show was all over. Two machines lay smoking on the ground and everybody else had disappeared.

While I was considering what the dickens I should do I suddenly discovered that I was flying back in formation again! The fellows had come back to pick me up and formed up around me. I didn't even see where they came from.[8]

Extending this story in another version, Johns recalled that, having missed his formation after the brief encounter with enemy machines, he looked around for them. 'A bunch of enemy scouts had appeared from nowhere and placed themselves between me and the other machines of my flight with the obvious intention of frustrating my plan [to rejoin them].'

I looked around nervously at my gunner but he was an old hand and merely gave me a pitying glance as if to say, 'You poor boob!' Then he sent a stream of tracers in the direction of the rapidly approaching scouts, to let them know he was ready for them.

What would have happened if at that moment our second formation had not arrived is too unpleasant to think about. As it was, in my panic, I barged into them with such a rush that they had to open out to avoid a collision, and the result was a pretty mess.

There was about five minutes of frantic tail chasing, and then somehow we got back into position again. The leader gave the signal for the bombs to be dropped, and we turned for home. I knew I should get it in the neck when we got back for behaving so foolishly – and I did.[9]

On one of his first flights with No. 55, Johns managed to repeat his performance of shooting off his own propeller.

Approaching the trenches one day, I thought I would fire a short burst through my forward gun to see if it was all in order. I fired, and shot my propeller into about a thousand pieces. I thought the end of the world had come. The engine raced and nearly jumped off its bearings before I could switch off. Some silly ass had timed the synchronizing gear all wrong, and instead of the bullets passing between the blades of the propeller, they hit them and cut them clean off instantly. There were plenty of fields handy, so there was no difficulty about getting down. I've shot my propeller off twice, curiously enough, for it is a very rare accident.[10]

Johns was teamed with 2nd Lieutenant F. N. Coxhill, who became his regular 'sandbag' – observer/gunner. On one of his first major raids deep into enemy territory, an incident took place which nearly ended his flying career. The details of this raid as given by Johns seem to fit in with combat records of a raid on Coblenz, carried out by six aircraft of No. 55 Squadron commanded by Captain Silly, on 31 July. The British aircraft were homeward bound and over Bobigen when fifteen enemy scouts attacked them. In close formation, the DH4s fought them off, but more came up southeast of Strasbourg. John recalls that 2nd Lieutenant J. T. L. Attwood (who was to be shot down and killed on 25 September) managed to get one of the enemy aircraft, which apparently discouraged the rest.

Johns, after his previous 'ticking off' for losing his formation, had his eyes glued to Silly's machine. Suddenly he was aware that his flight commander was flying rather close to him. Then he saw the nose of Silly's aircraft creep up, which he thought was unusual. The leading edge of his centre section prevented him from seeing above, even if he had been looking. Then, from Silly's forward machine gun, he saw tracer for an instant before Silly's machine moved back into its original position.

It was then that Johns became aware of the Albatross scout for the first time, and saw its yellow, shark-shaped belly. It was in front and slightly above them. As it went by, climbing slightly, it turned, as if the pilot had dragged the stick back into his right thigh without using the rudder. The movement held, became a tight crazy loop, and then the machine roared straight down towards the British formation, out of control. Johns was sure that it was going to hit one of them – the six British machines were too close together for it to go through. The British pilots 'skidded', loosening their formation, and to everyone's surprise the Albatross passed through on its back. Johns could see the German spinning. 'We were at nineteen thousand. I didn't see the end but the gunners said he crashed into a wood.'[11]

Towards the beginning of August, 'Boomer' Trenchard's Independent Force had been creating such havoc in the Rhineland towns that the German High Command began to move interceptor squadrons into the area. 'They started by sending down some really brisk squadrons from up north to stop us,' recalled Johns. 'They did not inform us of this but we were not slow to discover it.'[12] The German fighters still failed to keep the DH4s of No. 55 from penetrating deep into the Rhineland. On 1 August the squadron bombed Duren, a week later they carried out a special raid on a factory at Rombas, while on 11 August Captain Mackay and Captain Bell led an assault on Buhl.

Johns recalled a raid on Frankfurt on 'August 10' which 'became a nightmare' when thirty-five enemy fighters pounced on No. 55's formations.[13] It seems that Johns misremembered the date, because most of the aircraft of the squadron were grounded on that day because of adverse weather conditions. Only two reconnaissance patrols took off; a machine piloted by Captain Silly, with 2nd Lieutenant T. F. L. Myring as his observer, flew towards Strasbourg, while Lieutenant W. J. Pace DFC, with Lieutenant D. W. Steward as his observer, flew towards Saarburg. Both patrols were washed out due to heavy cloud.

Combat reports stated that 'all country to north covered with cloud.' Pace and Steward, however, managed to find their way to Metz and dropped a bomb from 15,000 feet behind cloud cover.[14]

The raid on Frankfurt actually took place on 12 August. Johns, in fact, correctly recalled the date when writing in *Wings* (1931). The official record states: 'On August 12, 1918, a daylight bombing raid was carried out on Frankfurt by twelve DH4s without escort. On the return journey they were attacked by over forty Pfalz, Albatross and Fokker Scouts which they engaged. They returned to their aerodrome without the loss of a single machine.' Writing in *Wings*, Johns says: 'I was on that show and it was one to be remembered, believe me.' No. 55 Squadron had sent out two formations to Frankfurt. The first was led by Captain Silly, while Captain Mackay commanded the second. According to Johns the enemy aircraft began their attack east of Saarburg. He recalled that an observer, 2nd Lieutenant C. W. Clutson, managed to send one German machine down in flames. Another German pilot Johns remembers as 'a stout lad'; he dived to attack Silly's aircraft on his own. 'Silly brought us back with only one casualty. Stewart, Bridgeland's observer, was killed.' This was 2nd Lieutenant E. R. Stewart DFC, who was, indeed, killed in this combat on 12 August. According to Captain Silly's laconic combat report, the enemy machines 'did not press their attack with much vigour owing to our excellent formation.'[15]

The next day Captain Mackay and Captain Bell led twelve aircraft to raid Buhl. There was another casualty. A sergeant named Lewis was killed. On 14 August Captain Mackay led six DH4s to bomb the railway sidings at Offenburg. Although 2nd Lieutenant J. B. Dunn and his observer, 2nd Lieutenant A. S. Papworth, were shot down, they managed to bring their machine down on the British side of the lines at Saulcy-sur-Meurthe.

'We had a bad show on August 16, losing Campbell, Fox, Brownhill, Madge, McIntyre and Bracher,' Johns remembered. 'Roberts was wounded but managed to get down.'[16] Official records state that on 16 August Captain Silly led a bombing raid on the railways at Darmstadt. Missing in action were 2nd Lieutenants J. Campbell, J. R. Fox, E. A. Brownhill, W. T. Madge, J. B. McIntyre and H. H. Bracher, while 2nd Lieutenants A. C. Roberts and W. Wallace were listed as wounded.[17] During that month of August, No. 55 Squadron lost 15 aircrew killed, 5 wounded and 5 missing. The spectre of death caused the pilots to live in an artificial atmosphere of gaiety and youthful high spirits. For example, as Johns reports:

It happened in France. A party of flying officers off-duty were out looking for fun. We came upon two steam-rollers, their funnels smoking gently while the drivers had their tea. In a brace of shakes two officers had climbed aboard, and away went the steam-rollers down a hill, of all things. What a sight! One finished on its side in a ditch, minus its funnel. The other one hit a tree. No one was hurt ...[18]

Card-playing, drinking, playing schoolboy tricks and making trips into the nearby town of Nancy to visit a hotel called the Liégeois, a spot popular with Allied officers, helped to relieve the daily tensions and fears. The strain under which the pilots of a squadron such as No. 55 lived was tremendous and release could only be found in such seemingly light-hearted behaviour. Death was always a constant companion – one had to become immune to the abruptness of it.

One of the most vivid pictures I see is a DH4 silhouetted against an unbroken background of blue sky. It is flying level, quite close, perhaps thirty feet away. From it, a long trail of jet black smoke swirls away aft in a dead straight line. The pilot is a friend of mine; I had taught him to fly. I was flying number 3 in the formation and he was flying 5. I looked across at him, as I had done a hundred times, and saw the smoke. He was, at that instant, unaware of the fate that had already claimed him, and was even now overtaking his gunner. He saw me staring. I pointed. He looked. His nose went down and he was gone. We were at twenty thousand. For half an hour or more I could see the smoke trail to the ground.[19]

Even what was euphemistically called 'a routine patrol' was highly hazardous, perhaps more hazardous than a full-scale raid, where six or more aircraft, flying in formation, could offer protection to one another. A single aircraft on reconnaissance was a very different matter. Towards the end of August, Johns' logbook recorded a 'normal' photographic reconnaissance: 'Reconnoitred aerodromes 37, 11, 48 and 78. Height 15,000–19,500 feet. Dept. 5.15 a.m. Crossed lines S.W. Chateau Salins, route via Dieuze, Biedesdorf, Lanterfingen, Beusdorf, Morhange and Chateau Salins. Ret. 9.55 a.m. Exposed 12 plates.'

The realities of the laconic logbook statement were every bit as exciting as the tales Johns was to weave around his air-hero, Biggles.[20]

The day began for Johns at 4.30 am when his batman shook him awake. 'Time to get up, sir. You're on the early show. Mr Coxhill is dressing.'

Johns lay listening intently, hoping to hear the sweet music of raindrops falling on the roof of the hut, that would cancel the flight and enable him to have an extra hour's sleep, which seemed desirable at that hour of the morning.

'How's the weather doing?' he muttered.

'Fine morning, sir − lovely,' was the cheerful reply.

'Lovely be damned!' replied Johns, as he took the proffered cup of tea and crawled out of bed. Outside the stars were still twinkling in the sky, but there was a pale flush in the east, which told of the approaching day. He shivered as he pulled on a thick woollen sweater, for the August morning air was still keen. With his flying suit over his arm, he made his way to the mess hut, where a dozen fellow officers were drinking hot tea or coffee by the dim light of candles. They were due to go on a raid coinciding with Johns' reconnaissance mission. Johns sought out his observer, 2nd Lieutenant F. N. Coxhill, who grinned in greeting: 'You coming to Nancy tonight?'

'You'll be lucky if you ever see Nancy again,' growled Johns. 'I'd like to lay hands on the chap who started this confounded war. What an hour to be hauled out. I never could get up in the morning.'

'Get a move on, misery,' mocked Coxhill. 'I'm going along to have a look at the guns.'

'Push off; go and shoot yourself,' retorted Johns, in mock anger.

Coxhill was a happy young man and, according to Johns, 'as good a gunner as ever pulled the cocking handle of a Lewis'. Johns joined him a few minutes later, feeling somewhat mellowed as a result of plenty of hot coffee. The squadron's main raiding party had just taken off and were circling for height. Johns and Coxhill watched them for a few minutes until they turned and headed towards the lines.

'I hope they collect all the Huns,' commented Johns as they climbed into their DH4.

'Switch off, petrol on, suck in,' called a ginger-haired mechanic.

'Switches off, suck in,' echoed Johns.

'Contact!'

'Contact!'

There was a sharp explosion, a tongue of scarlet flame from the exhaust, and the Rolls-Royce Eagle engine settled down to a steady, deep-throated, rhythmic roar. Johns glanced around the cockpit to ensure everything was in its place: Very pistol, maps, writing pad ...

The staccato rattle of the rear gun caused Johns to glance round. Coxhill was testing it by firing a few rounds into the ground. He gave the thumbs-up sign. Johns eased forward on the throttle and taxied onto the runway. The needle of his thermometer wavered on the red line; the DH4 was warm enough for take-off.

The mechanics gave the all clear signal and Johns opened the throttle and the ponderous bomber was away, climbing steadily for height. Azelot passed below them, the inhabitants no doubt cursing the noisy *Anglais* who disturbed their sleep. Charmes loomed hazily ahead through the morning mist. The altimeter crept slowly upwards as Johns climbed: 5,000, 6,000, 7,000 ... When it reached 10,000, he swung round in a wide curve and headed towards the lines. He swung back over Azelot and could see the long white poplar-bordered road which led to Nancy. Further on were the wooded slopes of the Vosges. Little summer clouds, pink-flecked, and soon to be dispersed by the rising sun, floated by him, and he could even see, far over to his right, the glittering icy minarets of the Swiss Alps.

He examined the sky ahead of him with watchful eyes, for he was getting near the lines now and there was always danger of attack by enemy scouts. Far away in front, he could pick out the gleaming silvery thread of the Rhine. It was 60 miles or more away but Johns was now at 15,000 feet and from that height one could see a fair distance.

Suddenly his eyes caught what at first glance appeared to be a little string of white beads. Anti-aircraft fire – 'archie'! He could tell by the white smoke it came from Allied guns, for German 'archie' gave off black smoke. It meant only one thing: an enemy aircraft was in the vicinity. He shifted his course a trifle and watched intently for the black speck, or specks, which he knew must soon emerge. He was not worried, for he was still within easy reach of Azelot in case of bad trouble.

There! The spot came into view. Coxhill gave the dual control stick a shake to attract his attention and pointed to make sure Johns had seen it. Johns saw Coxhill's fingers were crossed.

The enemy aircraft was a Halberstadt two-seater, probably engaged on a similar reconnaissance patrol. 'I shan't worry him if he doesn't worry me,' Johns decided. 'I've something else to do besides fighting. I've got to get some photographs and bring them home. There will no doubt be plenty of fighting later on.' The DH4 passed within a hundred yards of the Halberstadt. The German pilot and his observer raised their hands in salute. However, Johns gave a swift look around to make sure this was not a signal to some lurking enemy fighters. 'No – they are honest-to-goodness airmen all right. We give them an answering wave and pass, like ships in the night.'

Now the DH4 ran into flashes of crimson and black smoke. German anti-aircraft batteries were opening up as the British machine passed over the lines. Once over, Johns turned towards the German aerodrome designated as No. 37 on his map. It was his first objective and the furthest he had to go into enemy territory. At a height of 16,000 feet he reached the aerodrome without incident and began to take a series of photographs, while Coxhill watched the sky for any signs of trouble. Below him, Johns could see enemy machines standing on the field and some taking off. They reminded him of tiny dragonflies. He had exposed three plates when Coxhill signalled and started to fire his Lewis gun. Johns flung the DH4 round in a swift bank, knowing that this meant an enemy aircraft within range.

Seven Pfalz DIIIs screamed past him, their guns snarling and spitting.

He pulled his machine round again, hoping to give Coxhill a chance to bring his gun to bear, and then, without waiting to see what the enemy were doing, he turned and opened his throttle wide for home. He was 50 miles over the lines and was therefore in no position to take on seven enemy fighters.

The Pfalz came out of their dive in a climbing turn and came at the DH4 again. The speed they had picked up on their dive brought them within 200 yards behind Johns, and they were now flying at about the same height and speed. Over the next twenty gruelling minutes the German fighters tried to close the gap, shooting straight from behind. Every now and then, one would put his nose down and dive in an effort to zoom up from below. Coxhill was using his ammunition sparingly, only giving the Germans a short burst now and then.

As the DH4 neared the lines, the Germans sheered off and soon disappeared. Johns' job was only half done and so, once again, he turned in an arc and headed for his second objective: aerodrome 11. He took his photographs, this time without incident, and went on to his third objective: aerodrome 48. He had not reached it when, 2,000 feet below, he saw a formation of three DH9s bearing the squadron markings of No. 99 Squadron. Hard on their heels were a squadron of Albatross DVs. Johns automatically moved into the sun hoping that he would pass by unobserved, but one of the enemy fighters spotted him and left the pursuit of the DH9s to climb after him. His comrades, seeing the 'cold meat', began to follow. 'I don't mind admitting that I was badly scared,' Johns reflected, 'for the air seemed to be suddenly full of them and Coxhill's gun started stammering good and hard.'

A row of holes appeared in his top-plane not a foot from his head. Johns put his nose down after the three DH9s and managed to reach their protective formation. For the next fifteen minutes the Germans attacked the British machines without success. They reached the lines in safety, and the enemy aircraft, minus two of their number, one of whom had gone down in flames and the other out of control, abandoned the pursuit.

Having only photographed two of his four objectives, Johns did not feel much like continuing. He passed a message back to Coxhill to see what he thought, but his observer jabbed a finger east, into German territory, and then upwards. With a sigh, Johns climbed to 20,000 feet and once more headed into enemy territory. Within minutes they encountered a Fokker DVII who appeared to be doing an altitude test. The German hung about their tail for a while, but apparently did not have the nerve to come in close. He finally broke away and disappeared.

Over aerodrome 48 Johns exposed three more plates and then turned for his final objective, aerodrome 78. At last the job was over and he could heave a sigh of relief. It was premature; the

DH4's engine coughed, spluttered and faded out. Guessing his main fuel tank was empty, Johns casually switched to his extra tank. There was no response. It had been holed by a bullet in one of the encounters. He felt a moment of panic. Then he switched to the emergency gravity tank and started to fly nose down for the lines. The gravity tank did not contain much petrol and he knew that it was a toss-up whether they would make it back or not.

A Hanoverana appeared, causing the pilot to make a detour, and while his eyes were on the heavy German bomber there came the chatter of a gun. A beautifully painted Fokker DVII came at them in a straight dive with both guns yammering. 'How we weren't killed in that lightning charge I shall never know. A double pencil of tracers streamed towards us and bullets seemed to be hitting us everywhere.' Johns and Coxhill had been caught napping.

Coxhill turned his Lewis gun towards the enemy machine and let out a raking burst as it swept by. It flicked into a loop and came round again. Johns, with his fuel in such a precarious state, could not afford to indulge in aerobatics, and could only hold the ponderous DH4 in a straight line. The German's bullets thudded into his starboard plane and smashed an aileron hinge.

Then, by a stroke of luck, Coxhill's answering fire apparently hit the German's engine for the Fokker stalled at the top of its zoom and went into a spin. Coxhill afterwards told Johns that the German had managed to pull out of it and land in a field.

Two miles from the lines the DH4's engine failed entirely. Johns was now losing height fast and he glided in fairly low across the lines. 'It seemed to me that every gun of every calibre had been brought to bear on us. Flaming onions [orange blobs of anti-aircraft fire] whizzed by us, smoke, black, yellow and white swirled about us. Twisting and turning like an eel I shot across the line.' Johns glanced behind to see Coxhill standing up calmly, blazing away with what was left of his ammunition into the enemy trenches as they passed over.

Still gliding, Johns managed to turn over Azelot and start coming in over the sheds of No. 104 Squadron, cross-wind. He almost scraped the top of the sheds with his wheels. He held the heavy machine off for as long as he could and suddenly pancaked her onto the tarmac in front of the squadron office. The DH4 would obviously never fly again. Johns extracted himself unhurt, while Coxhill climbed out 'calmly as if he was used to landing like that'.

Major J. C. Quinnell, the CO of No. 104, came storming out of the squadron office and eyed Johns grimly. 'You stalled that aeroplane,' he accused. Johns was about to explain, but the major interrupted. 'Don't argue. I distinctly saw you stall her.'

Johns sighed. 'As I slowly made my way across the aerodrome towards my own squadron office to make my report I could not help pondering on the ingratitude of commanding officers.' For the pilots of No. 55 Squadron, such a flight was marked up as 'a routine patrol'.

Another incident which took place early in August had a great effect on Johns. He was to use it as the basis for one of his Biggles tales. It started one morning when, half an hour before Johns and Coxhill were due for early morning reconnaissance, Coxhill reported that he had a toothache and, on the advice of the Medical Officer, was sent down to Charmes to have the tooth extracted. Johns reported to Major Gray. By coincidence, some replacement observers were just arriving from the St Omer pool at that very moment. Gray suggested that Johns pick one of these new airmen and take him up immediately. Johns chose what he thought to be 'a likely lad'.[21] He was 'a big awkward, fair-haired kid in his 'teens, wearing a spotless new uniform.' When he recalled this incident, Johns called him Seeley, withholding his real name for obvious reasons. The boy expressed his willingness to do the show right away and drew a Sidcot flying suit from the stores.

Johns flew across the lines, dodging the anti-aircraft fire and, east of Metz, he started to turn for home. There was apparently 'nothing out of the ordinary about the show'. It was then that seven Albatross DVs, flying at Johns' altitude, appeared between his aircraft and Azelot. Johns rocked his machine to attract his gunner's attention. 'I went at them like a bull at a gate, trusting him to fight them off my tail if we got through. We had thirty red-hot seconds and the enemy closed in behind us, but after one short burst from Seeley's gun it stopped and I looked round for the reason.'

He was on the floor of his cockpit, the muzzles of his guns pointing to high heaven, telling the tale as plainly to the enemy as it did to me. The lad was down. It was my lucky day and somehow I got back, dropped a red Very light for the ambulance as I sideslipped in over the trees and taxied tail-up to meet the 'bloodwagon'.

As the machine ran to a standstill I turned to help lift him out, but to my amazement he was standing up, pale, it is true, but untouched. He jumped out. I choked back the curse that rose to my lips, but my face must have asked an unspoken question.[22]

'My guns jammed,' faltered the observer.

'Guns!' yelled Johns to the gunnery officer. 'Come here.'

Climbing into the observer's cockpit, Johns shook the drum, pointed the muzzles into the ground and pulled the trigger. A stream of lead poured into the earth of the aerodrome. The gunnery officer also checked them. 'Nothing wrong with that.'

'What the hell do you think I took you for — to see the sights?' growled Johns sarcastically.

Seeley turned white, hung his head down and walked away. Johns went into the mess to get a drink. He was still there when the boy came in and admitted that he had 'funked it'.

'I want you to give me another chance,' he said, on the verge of tears.

Johns relented. 'Okay, but if you let me down again, God help you when we get back.'

The next day Captain Silly led six machines on a raid on Stuttgart. Coxhill was still recovering from his extraction and Johns took Seeley. All went well until they were on their way home, above Hagenau. A bunch of Pfalz scouts had been trailing them, but were too far behind to cause them any worry. However, ten Fokker DVIIs were waiting for the formation and came down to the attack from 20,000 feet. One DH4, piloted by an officer named Hickes, went down in flames. One of the enemy machines, Johns noticed it was painted yellow and black, swung low under Johns' elevators and raked the DH4 with two streams of yellow phosphorus bullets. Risking a collision with the DH4 flying alongside him, Johns swung his tailplane in order to give his observer a 'sitter' at point-blank range. The boy fumbled with his gun and then dived to the floor of the cockpit. 'I came home sweating with fright,' Johns commented.

The boy was transferred to Home Establishment.

It was some weeks later that Johns went to Neufchateau to see a comrade called Warley, who was in hospital, having been wounded. Outside the hospital he ran into Major Lloyd Evans, the commander of an SE5 squadron, whom Johns knew slightly. The major told Johns he had come to see one of his men, a boy named Seeley. Curious, Johns asked for further details. There was no doubt that it was his former observer. The boy had somehow got his pilot's wings, had joined Evans' squadron and that very day had been on his first trip over the lines. Now he lay dying with an explosive bullet in his back.

Johns went in to see the boy. Seeley recognized him and told him that Major Gray's report sending him to Home Establishment for lack of moral fibre had gone missing. Seeley pretended that his return home was due to his having volunteered for pilot training. The RAF were desperate for pilots. After a minimal ten hours' solo, he had been sent out to France again. Johns asked Major Evans what had happened.

'I was showing two new lads the line – Smithson and Seeley.

'We were cruising at 15,000 when a Hanoverana came beetling over at 6,000. Smithson, the damn young fool, in spite of my orders and all I had told him, goes down after it. Of course, the air was full of Fokkers in a second, piling up on him.

'I didn't go down because I didn't want to be chauffeur to my own funeral, and – well you know how it is – I couldn't have done any good anyway. It wouldn't have been a fight, just plain suicide. Seeley nearly rammed me trying to point, thinking I hadn't seen the mess Smithson was in, and without waiting for me, down he goes into the middle of it.

'I had to go down, too, then. By the time we got down, Smithson's machine was smoking on the ground, and I made a break for home. Twice I got out and had to go back for Seeley because he must stay and fight the whole damn bunch. First time over the line too.

'I don't know how we got home, but we did, scraping our wheels on the barbed wire. My God, that kid had guts! If he'd lived long enough to learn sense he'd have made a name. His sort don't come up from the pool every day.[23]

Before Johns left Seeley's bedside the dying boy whispered: 'I know I funked it with you, but I thought I could get over it in time ... If only I could, I'd be satisfied.' That the incident had a profound effect on Johns is shown by the fact that he used it as the basis for the Biggles tale 'The Funk' (*Biggles of the Camel Squadron*, 1935).

During August the squadrons of the 41st Wing were ordered to use incendiary bombs. These early incendiaries were almost entirely without safety devices and after one or two observers had accidentally dropped them in their own cockpits, RAF enthusiasm for their use waned. Many pilots simply refused to carry them at all. Some pilots, however, took them up in large quantities and, according to Johns, played a sort of dart game with them as they passed over enemy territory. When No. 55 Squadron received the bombs, they were ordered to try to set enemy cornfields on fire. 'The snag was, the cornfields would not burn,' recalled Johns. 'There was a little, round, burnt-out spot where the bomb fell; but a good crop of corn, being damp at the bottom, soon brought the fire to an end. This was disappointing, so we tried to set fire to a still bigger target.'[24] The 'still bigger target' was no less than the Black Forest. Hundreds of incendiaries were dropped with little result. One fire did start which lasted for three weeks but eventually died out, leaving an ugly scar. The results were not considered worth pursuing and so incendiary bombing was forgotten.

The pilots of No. 55 made reconnaissance flights pretty frequently, interspersed with long-distance raids. On 22 August eight DH4s raided the railways and factories at Coblenz. The following day the railway station at Trèves and the barracks and railways at Cologne were bombed. The same day 2nd Lieutenant Don J. Waterous DFC and his observer 2nd Lieutenant C. L. 'Pip' Rayment DFC, made a lone patrol and were attacked by Pfalz scouts. Rayment was slightly wounded, but returned to duty within a day. On 25 August the squadron bombed Mohrange aerodrome. This was done by a formation commanded by Captain Mackay at 1.15 pm, while a second formation, commanded by Captain Bell, attacked the railways in Luxembourg at about the same time. Bell's formation was unlucky, for one of his pilots, 2nd Lieutenant J. A. Lee, was killed, and Lee's observer, a Sergeant Allan, was wounded.

Johns recalls that about this time a flight of the squadron were returning from a raid on Offenburg when they were pounced upon by enemy fighters. Second Lieutenant J. B. Dunn's machine was so badly shot up that he had to force-land near La Matacuelle, just within the British lines. The victorious German pilot was so excited that he was apparently unaware he had crossed into enemy territory. He tried to land beside Dunn to take the British pilot and his observer prisoners, and in doing so hit a hedge and hurt himself. He managed to extricate himself, then to his utmost chagrin found himself facing a platoon of French troops doubling across the field. 'He was taken prisoner, and was so sick with himself that he refused to eat, drink or speak ...'[25]

On 28 and 29 August the weather was bad and the scheduled raids and reconnaissance patrols had to be abandoned. But the Germans were making an all-out effort to try to destroy the bombing squadrons, seeking out their bases and attacking them. One evening the pilots of No. 55 were in the mess having a sing-song. Abruptly someone shouted: 'Come and look at this.' They ran to the door and saw a magnificent parachute flare floating down, illuminating the aerodrome. They watched for a moment, not understanding what it portended. Then all hell broke loose. Bombs began to whistle down. There was nothing to do but take cover. One bomb fell right beside the mess building and had it gone off most of the pilots would have been killed or wounded. Luckily, it was a dud. The next morning someone (Johns thought it was probably Waterous) dug out the bomb. Some curious fool put a match to the explosive to see what would happen. The material did not explode but caught fire. The acrid black smoke poured into the mess where the CO, Major Gray, was at breakfast, causing him to storm out cursing.

No. 55 had suffered no casualties in this raid, but No. 104 had several of its personnel killed. 'The same sort of thing happened several times afterwards,' says Johns, 'but we were never caught napping again: at the first warning we used to sprint up the road to the archie battery and watch the fun from there.'[26] Second Lieutenant 'Pip' Rayment was convinced that there was a spy at work and several of No. 55's officers recalled seeing a car driving across the airfield with its headlights on just before the German air raid started. It was decided to investigate this and Johns remembered that the next night a group of officers lay in wait with a Lewis gun. When a car approached, one of them jumped out and called on it to stop, but the driver appeared to go faster. The officer manning the Lewis gun fired at the car.

Where the shots went I don't know, but they didn't stop the car, although the driver must have had a nasty moment. The fellow behind the gun was cursed up hill and down dale for missing, and the next night everyone who fancied his chance took a gun. If the car had come along, the driver would have thought he'd run into the front line by mistake, but it didn't. Nor did we ever see it again.[27]

On 30 August the weather lifted and the squadron conducted a raid on the Thionville railway sidings at Cologne and sustained their heaviest casualty toll. Johns misremembered the date when he recalled the occasion in 1935: 'One of the worst blows suffered by the squadron was on 27 August. The previous evening I was one of a poker school of six. By lunch time the next day I was the only survivor, and that because I wasn't on the show.'[28] The squadron's records list 2nd Lieutenants P. J. Cunningham, J. G. Quinton, C. E. Thorpe, R. I. A. Hicks, T. A. Jones, T. H. Laing and T. F. L. Myring as killed in action. Lieutenants W. E. Tanney and S. L. Dowswell, 2nd Lieutenants H. H. Doehler (an American), A. S. Papworth, H. C. T. Gompertz and A. J. G. Gormley were listed as missing.[29] Gormley was later reported to be a prisoner of war. A day or two previously he had taken a snapshot of Johns in flying kit before the squadron office, and had only received the prints on the day he was shot down. Johns was later to receive a copy of that snapshot in rather unusual circumstances. Dowswell and Gompertz also turned up, having managed to bring their machine down on the Allied side of the lines.

In recalling the disastrous raid, Johns wrote:

Bell took a formation of six machines over and came back alone after fighting twenty-seven EA [enemy aircraft] for the best part of an hour. Dowswell brought his machine back over the lines, but force landed at Pont St. Vincent. Gompertz was his gunner. He got two EA but what a mess he was in when the tender brought him home! This was due to the fact that Dowswell had an aileron shot off and could only fly dead straight. Gompertz's sidcot hung on him in ribbons; it had been literally shot off his back; and those who read this who saw him will confirm that this is no exaggeration. One bullet only hit him – in the shoulder. He didn't seem in the least upset. He just sat in the door of his hut, with the rags still hanging on him, and laughed.[30]

The combat report of the incident confirms Johns' account. According to Dowswell's report: 'I, myself, witnessed my observer, 2nd Lieutenant Gompertz, bring down two Enemy Aircraft which were out of control. I might also say it was due to my observer that I got back this side of the lines, as I could only fly in a straight line on account of the left-hand aileron control being shot away.'[31] Two more enemy aircraft had been shot down by 2nd Lieutenant 'Pip' Rayment and 2nd Lieutenant W. R. Patey DFC.

From Johns' reminiscences, it seems that Gompertz was quite a 'character' in the squadron. In one dogfight Johns witnessed, the observer ran out of ammunition after being attacked by a Fokker. In exasperation, Gompertz lifted his Lewis gun from its Scarff ring-mounting and flung the heavy weapon at the enemy fighter, as it passed under his DH4 at the end of its dive. The missile missed the German machine and actually fell into the main square of Nancy, which led to a strong complaint from the mayor, who objected to aircraft unloading their superfluous equipment over the town.[32]

The heavy casualties suffered by No. 55 Squadron on 30 August underscored, if such underscoring was needed, the brutality of war. Fourteen years later, in 1932, as the editor of *Popular Flying*, Johns was reflecting on the current demand for war-in-the-air stories. He considered that with the passage of years, those who had taken part in the war had discovered, in retrospect, there was a certain romance to war flying.

To the younger male generation these stories satisfy the healthy natural craving for the thrills which were once supplied by stories of redskins, pirates and man versus beast. They know that the redskin and pirate have gone for ever, and the wild beast nearly so; but the aeroplane lives. So hero-worshipping youth turns his eyes upwards and visualizes himself in the cockpit of the fighting plane that wings its way across the sky. The glorious romance of air fighting probably stands out far more clearly on the printed page than ever it did in actual practice.[33]

Johns sought to dissuade his readers from seeing romance in aerial combat. He reflected that life in August 1918 had resolved itself for airmen into a simple, vicious struggle for existence. There were endless days of struggling out of bed before daylight, almost too tired to gulp down the cup of tea brought in by a persistent batman with his eternal 'Early morning show, sir. Fine morning, sir'. Pilots would make their way, half-dazed, half-dressed and unshaven to the sheds; flying in all weathers; flying at all hours; flying when they were ill but would not say so because the squadron had lost men on the previous day and was short-handed; flying with their souls sick at seeing their friends go down in flames; flying on days when the rattle of guns turned their lips dry because they had a feeling that their turn had come.

Only politicians saw the romance in it then, with their beautiful speeches about 'our boys' – 'to be an immortal, undying symbol – a wonderful spirit of self-sacrifice – the unquenchable fire which must bring us glorious victory' – and so on – you know the stuff. Glorious victory, my hat. With most of us the war was a personal matter. Another fellow shot at you and you shot back; you shot at another fellow and he shot back; and it jolly well served you right. That's all there was to it.

The war-time pilot fought the war in his own way. If the authorities wanted to drag a lot of infantry into the affair, well, that was nothing to do with him. He spoke a language of his own, understandable only to his own kind. If he was hurt, he complained solely because it meant leaving the Squadron; if he was killed his friends drank themselves unconscious and never mentioned his name again.[34]

Recently, Johns has been accused of glorifying war and war flying, but as a young man he had seen and experienced too much to ever turn away from the reality. Far from glorifying war, whoever turns the pages of the early Biggles stories will find that Johns presents a grim picture of aerial warfare from 1917 to 1918. It is understated, true, but by that very understatement, by not dwelling on the deaths of countless young pilots, English and German alike, often still in their teens, Johns evokes in his readers a realisation of the true nature of war. The boy who identifies with Biggles, the daring air-fighter, will also find himself identifying with him in his bitterness as he surveys the carnage. 'There were moments when he loathed war and everything concerned with it with a whole-hearted hatred ...' As Biggles flew his single-seater fighter over a world lost in a well of purple shadows, 'Around, above and below, was a scene of peace and unutterable loveliness. It was hard to believe that within a few miles thousands of men were entrenched, waiting for the coming dawn to leap at each other's throats. War! He was sick of it, weary of flying, and the incredible folly of fighting men that he did not know ...'[35] Biggles, like Johns, makes his view of war abundantly clear; there is no glorifying 'the relentlessness of it – the ruthlessness, the waste, the cruelty.'

5

WAR FLYING

'The weather conditions generally throughout the month have been unsatisfactory,' states a secret report on the operations carried out by Trenchard's Independent Force during September 1918.[1] 'During the period of the useful phases of the moon, conditions for night flying were particularly bad. Strong winds, low clouds, and much rain prevented many of the long-distance objectives being reached. On nineteen days and eighteen nights no operations were carried out owing to adverse weather conditions ...'

However, on Monday, 2 September the weather was clear enough for ten DH4s of No. 55 Squadron to raid Buhl aerodrome. An early reconnaissance had been carried out during the day by two machines piloted by Lieutenant W. J. Pace DFC, with Lieutenant D. W. Steward as his observer, and Lieutenant P. E. Welchman MC, DFC, with Lieutenant J. Parke as his observer. They reported favourable conditions for the main mission and the squadron took off from Azelot at 9.20 am, with Captain Mackay in command and leading the first formation. Johns, with Coxhill as his observer, flew in the number 4 position in Mackay's group. The second formation was commanded by Captain Bell.

The squadron was lucky. Anti-aircraft fire was moderate and they encountered no enemy machines. They reached their target at 10.40 am and dropped sixteen 112-pound bombs and a 230-pound bomb. The pilots and their observers reported several hits and 23 photographic plates were exposed. They returned to Azelot without any casualties – but it was very nearly Johns' last mission. As Captain Mackay signalled that they were over the target, 'somehow or other I got under another chap or he got over me, I don't know which, and he just touched my top-plane.'[2] The other pilot was 2nd Lieutenant Don Waterous, who was flying with 'Pip' Rayment as his observer. Their aircraft was positioned number 3 in the formation. As Waterous's DH4 scraped across Johns' top-plane, Rayment, not noticing Johns' aircraft, but seeing Mackay's green Very signal to commence the attack, released his 112-pound bombs, which hurtled past Johns' machine, missing it only by feet.

Back on the ground, the pilots of No. 55 relaxed over lunch and had a brief rest before a second attack on Buhl was ordered. This time eleven aircraft took off at 3.20 pm, with Major Gray in command, but flying at the head of the second formation. Johns and Coxhill flew in number 4 position in the first formation again. As with the morning's raid, anti-aircraft fire was slight and no enemy aircraft appeared to challenge them. The attack began at 4.40 pm, with nineteen 112-pound bombs and one 230-pound bomb being dropped. The combat report comments that a broken wire prevented the release of one of the 112-pound bombs.[3] The unlucky pilot was Johns.

Recalling the incident some years later, Johns thought that the objective on that raid had been Stuttgart, though he corrected it to Buhl in another reminiscence.

I had been on a raid carrying two 112 lb bombs. One I dropped on Stuttgart and the other I tried to drop on the same place but the confounded thing stuck in its rack. This, by the way, happened occasionally. I got very worried because I'd pulled the toggle and there was nothing to keep the bomb in place. It had been wedged in rather hard and had simply stuck, but the slightest jar would probably be sufficient to cause it to fall off. The jar would come, without a doubt, when I landed. And I'd got to come down sometime. There was no doubt about that.

Well, I got back to the aerodrome with the wretched bomb still hanging on, and started to glide in to land. I need hardly tell you that I was flying very, very carefully, but, by a bit of bad luck, the direction of the wind was such that I had to come in over 99 Squadron's sheds. I got a very bad 'bump'. The bump was, of course, caused by the shed itself – or rather the wind striking the shed and being deflected upwards, causing an up-current.

Flying gingerly, at only a fraction above stalling speed, I hadn't a chance. The machine gave a nasty sort of lurch. Instantly, I jammed the throttle wide open to try to get off again, but it was no use, and I hit 99's tarmac a frightful bang. The bomb flew off, but by a stroke of luck did not explode. Not only was it lucky for me, but for most of the fellows in 99 Squadron who dashed out to see what all the noise was about.

Naturally, they didn't know I had a bomb on board.

Actually, it had a fifteen second 'delay' fuse, but I didn't wait to see if it was going to explode. I extricated myself from the pieces with all possible speed and made off up the tarmac like a scalded cat.[4]

The next day, 3 September, dawned with fair weather. The squadron made another raid on Buhl and also one on Karlsruhe. Then for a few days the weather turned bad and it was not until Sunday, 7 September that Waterous and Rayment flew out on a reconnaissance patrol. They were lucky to return alive, for they were attacked by seven enemy aircraft over Saarburg. The enemy, they reported, consisted of six Fokker DVIIs and possibly a Hanoverana. They had to fight their way back to Azelot, finally observing one of their attackers go down out of control and the rest sheer off. Major Gray, reporting on the condition of Waterous's DH4, wrote in his report: 'Machine is very badly damaged, probable.'[5] A further patrol went out later over the Saar valley, but did not encounter any opposition, while Captain Mackay led a raid on Ehrang.

When the pilots and observers of No. 55 Squadron were not flying, there were plenty of stories, gossip and strange tales to keep them occupied, as they sat in the mess waiting for the weather to lift. Some of these tales, comic or tragic, were remembered by Johns and used in later years for the early adventures of his air-hero Biggles, but there was one incident that occurred at this time that he never included in any work of fiction. A white-faced pilot came into the mess, where Johns was alone, and confessed that he had just shot down a compatriot.

It was 'H', a tall South African SE pilot, who came in white-faced and told me that he had just shot down a Camel by mistake. It was the Camel pilot's fault. He playfully zoomed over the SE, apparently out of sheer light-heartedness. 'H' told me that he started shooting when he only saw the shadow; he turned and saw the red, white, and blue circles, but it was too late. He had already gripped the Bowden control and fired a burst of not more than five rounds. He had fired hundreds of rounds at enemy aircraft without hitting one, but the Camel fell in flames. He asked me if he should report it, and I, rightly or wrongly, said no, for nothing could bring the Camel back. 'H' went west soon afterwards.[6]

Even with the weather restricting long-distance raids, the pace of life was hectic and nerves were fraying. In later years, Johns, in an editorial in *Popular Flying*, defended RAF officers from charges of excessive drinking levelled at them by members of the House of Commons, but admitted that drinking had gone on in wartime messes.

I should be the last one to deny that. A lot of fellows started the day on a stiff whisky, and, by thunder, they needed it. If they were lucky they ended the day with a dose of the same medicine. Again, by thunder, they needed it. By September, 1918, when the Huns were as thick as midges over a midden on a summer's evening, I started the day with a half-bottle of champagne. We were in the champagne country, and it cost next to nothing, chiefly because there was a chance of the Huns breaking through, in which case the French vintners would have got nix for it. It got the old arteries moving again. And don't anybody who has not done any war flying write to me and say that I was a naughty boy.[7]

Some recent critics of Biggles – those who have mistakenly concluded that Johns devised a cardboard, stereotyped hero with no flaws – may be surprised to learn that after his tragic affair with Marie Janis, Biggles begins to drink heavily. Mahoney, his flight commander, speaks to the CO:

'Biggles is finished unless he takes a rest,' he said. 'He's drinking whisky for breakfast, and you know what that means – he's going fast. He drank half a bottle of whisky yesterday morning before daylight, and he walked up to the sheds as sober as I was. A fellow doesn't get drunk when he's in the state Biggles is in.'[8]

As mid-September approached a thick mist was hanging over the aerodrome at Azelot, lying close at 500 feet and effectually washing out any flying by the squadron. 'While we were lounging about outside the officers' mess, the sound of an aeroplane with the engine cut off became audible overhead. All eyes were turned upwards, naturally expecting to see a British machine appear. There was a wild stampede for machine-guns as a Boche machine, with beautiful black crosses painted under the wings, came gliding down, evidently intending to land!'[9]

The anti-aircraft batteries at the edge of the aerodrome, evidently thinking the machine was about to bomb the airfield, opened up. The German pilot, realising his mistake, raced for the cloud cover. But as he zoomed back into the mist, it suddenly rolled away in the wind which had abruptly arisen – a freak weather condition. The anti-aircraft guns opened up on the machine for all they were worth. The German pilot seemed hopelessly lost and had no idea where the lines were (he confessed as much to the officers of No. 55 Squadron afterwards when they entertained him in their mess). Suddenly the anti-aircraft fire died away. A flight of French scout planes, Spad VII single-seaters, were closing in on the German machine. The leading Spad pilot, who turned out to be the commanding officer of the squadron, dived on the German almost vertically. The German observer fired a long burst and the French machine dived straight into the ground just beyond the aerodrome – its pilot shot through the head. But by this time the German pilot, realising the hopelessness of his situation, had glided down and made a neat landing on Azelot airfield. He was unharmed, but his observer had been slightly wounded by shrapnel from the anti-aircraft gunfire. 'So,' recalled Johns, 'we had a nice new German aeroplane to play with for the rest of the day. The French afterwards exhibited it in Nancy.'[10]

On Thursday, 12 September the weather conditions had improved enough to send off a reconnaissance patrol. It was the same day that the squadron CO, Major Alec Gray MC, went off on a long-overdue leave and left Captain Silly in command. Silly was to be promoted to major on 25 September. The patrol returned to report that weather conditions over prospective long-distance targets were not good. The patrol consisted of Lieutenant P. E. Welchman MC, DFC, flying with 2nd Lieutenant Patey DFC. They also flew over the St Mihiel Salient to Pont-à-Mousson. They reported seeing 'very many Spads on and over the lines, and very few EA [enemy aircraft].'[11] The following day a further patrol reported no improvement in conditions for long-range raids, but the squadron was ordered to bomb short-range targets in support of a new Allied offensive.

On 13 September the Americans began an offensive in the St Mihiel sector along a forty-mile stretch of the front. Some 1,481 Allied aircraft, commanded by Brigadier General 'Billy' Mitchell, the largest air armada ever assembled at that time, supplied air cover. On 14 September, according to the American commander General John Pershing, the Americans had erased the Mihiel

Salient and liberated 150 square miles of French territory from the Germans. The German counterattack was not long in coming and began to roll the American advance back to its former entrenchment. Johns recalled the event.

Early in September the American First Army marched across the aerodrome into the St. Mihiel Salient. When they halted, officers used to come into the mess for a drink, and they talked of the War as if it was a joke, referring to the line as the 'shooting gallery' and so on. They were 'going to show us, and the Frogs'. I got fed up with this one day and started to say something, but 'Jock' Mackay said, 'Shut up, the poor B's don't know what they're talking about.' And that was about the truth of it. They knew in a day or two, though. We supported their show by bombing back areas. By midday it looked as if the US lads had made about nine kilometres, but by nightfall they were back pretty well where they started from, having suffered terrible losses. Poor beggars; how could they know what the War was like? Two or three American pilots joined us about this time, and I must say they were very good chaps, quiet and unassuming, quite different from the article that is presented in fiction.[12]

On Saturday, 14 September two early-morning patrols reported improved conditions and it was decided to send the entire squadron, consisting of twelve DH4s, to raid Ehrang. Johns was allocated a new observer, 2nd Lieutenant A. E. Amey, who had just arrived as a replacement and had not seen action before. Johns and Amey flew in the second formation. The squadron took off at 10.55 am; anti-aircraft fire was slight and no enemy aircraft appeared. They went into attack at Ehrang at 12.55 pm. The squadron returned to Azelot with two casualties: 2nd Lieutenant G. P. Dymond and his observer, 2nd Lieutenant A. C. Keyes, had to make a forced landing, while 2nd Lieutenant J. B. Dunn, with Sergeant Adams as his observer, crashed as he made his landing approach.

Sunday, 15 September was still fair for flying and patrols were sent towards Speyerdorf, Karlsruhe, Frescarty and Bersdorf. At 7.20 am twelve DH4s from No. 55 Squadron prepared to take off for a raid on the great industrial centre at Stuttgart, a heavily defended target. Captain Silly was in command, leading the first formation in which Johns flew in number 4 position. Captain Mackay led the second formation. Johns was to write a vivid account of this raid.

The first stream of dawn in the eastern sky reveals a dozen pilots standing chatting and laughing outside the hangars. A cloud of cigarette smoke curls mistily about them and rises slowly into the still morning air.

It is our last cigarette for five hours at least, perhaps longer — perhaps much longer.

An air mechanic seated on an upturned chock [wheel block] vacantly contemplates the crows who are persuading themselves they are looking for the early worm on the sun-baked aerodrome. Another mechanic breaks off from the idle survey of the wind stocking to yawn mightily. Another, unshaven, with tousled hair, listlessly supports the hangar door as, with sleepy eyes, he gazes moodily at the group of officers responsible for his early rising. No one feels his best …

'Start up!' The CO's voice, keen and alert, cuts through the air like a knife as he steps out of the map room followed by the skipper who is leading the show.

The dozing air mechanics spring to life and jump to it. Others, hitherto unseen, appear staggering under the weight of 112 lb high explosive khaki-coloured bombs.

Where a moment before all was still and quiet, swift motion dominates the scene as the DH4s are wheeled out and, one after the other, six Rolls-Royce Eagle engines commence the deep-throated roar which they will, we hope, keep up without a break for the next few hours.

The skipper waves to the CO and walks across to us and names our destination.

One long, last draw at our cigarettes and we climb into our seats. Rat-at-at-at-at-ratatat, spit the Lewis guns harmlessly into the ground as our observers, already in their places in the back seats, test the weapons upon which our lives will shortly depend.

I slip a piece of chewing gum into my mouth and turn to have a last word with my observer as the engine warms up.[13]

The take-off of No. 55 Squadron was observed by a high-flying enemy machine which, in spite of fire from nearby anti-aircraft batteries, including the one from Azelot, turned and sped back for the German lines. The smoke from the archie bursts were watched with interest by Johns and his fellow pilots, for by this means they were able to gauge wind drift, Johns estimating that the wind was blowing 30 to 35 mph at 10,000 feet, which meant a tough haul. Captain Silly's aircraft taxied forward and took off. Soon all twelve aircraft were climbing steadily — 8,000, 10,000, 12,000, 14,000 feet. Below them lay St Nicholas, Nancy, Pont-à-

Mousson, and the trenches curving in a wide arc to Verdun. Little jabs of flame and patches of black smoke marked the opening barrage from the German anti-aircraft batteries as they crossed the lines at 15,000 feet.

A flash of flame and a cloud of putrid black smoke swirled swiftly about Johns' aircraft and was gone. It was close. 'I test all controls quickly, glance into the reflector and see my observer swing his thumbs – the OK signal – then grimace at the battery below as a sign of contempt.'[14] There was another explosion and a little jagged hole appeared near the trailing edge of his lower port plane. Johns chewed a little harder on his Spearmint. Then the anti-aircraft fire suddenly stopped. To the experienced war pilot it could only mean one thing, and Johns swiftly scanned the sky. His observer, Amey, was pointing: enemy aircraft – Pfalz Scouts. They began shooting at 300 yards, much too far off to do any damage. The observers of No. 55 held their fire. They had only ten drums of ammunition to last them at least five hours and they could not afford to waste a round. Johns, keeping one eye on his place in the formation, and the other on the German machines, saw the enemy aircraft draw near, and then the observers opened up. The Pfalz Scouts swerved away from the concentrated fire, diving away beneath the British formation. Johns watched them pull out 500 feet below and then try to climb back, guns still chattering.

Amey signalled Johns and pointed ahead. The pilot made out a string of dots growing larger – Fokkers. 'The sun flashes on them and I recognise the yellow-and-blue striped lads from Metz.'[15]

I slip another piece of gum into my mouth and chew hard. There will be no swerving away from these boys! There they go, round into the sun – eight of them. They waste no time. Down go their noses towards us, and I crouch a little closer in the 'office' watching them over my shoulder.

Three hundred feet, two hundred, a hundred and fifty, a hundred, and still no one fires. I don't like it a bit! Great Scott! They are coming right in. In a second the air is full of the black and white sparks of tracer bullets.

I watch the lad who has honoured me with his particular attention. Flames spurt from his guns and his bullets trace a neat pattern in my lower starboard plane, a foot from the fuselage.

I move my stick a fraction of an inch and watch the seeking tracers stream between the planes. There is the sound of a dozen rattles as my observer's gun spits out a series of short sharp bursts.

The EA holds on to the last second, lurches, swings, and dives past us, gun still going, turning on his back as he goes and missing my tail by ten feet. I see the pilot's face, and touch stick and rudder bar to let my observer rake him with his gun as he goes past. He spins.[16]

Johns discovered that every British machine was still in formation and that there was another enemy aircraft spinning. Johns recalls that 2nd Lieutenant Gompertz, in the back seat of number 5 aircraft, waved to him and held up his thumb, pointing to the falling Fokker.[17]

An hour later Stuttgart lies below us. The skipper turns slowly, without banking, and fires a green light. All ready! His bombs go off. I pull my toggle [bomb release handle] and glance down to make sure that both my hundred-and-twelve pound bombs have gone for, should one stick, I should be unable to get to the height of the others on the return journey.

It happened to me once, on a short show to Buhl, and I never want a repetition of that performance.[18]

Captain Silly gave the signal for the attack at 9.40 am. The anti-aircraft fire over the target was heavy, but, with the job completed, the aircraft turned for their own lines. Now more squadrons of German fighters were diving at them.

I glance behind and see my gunner still shooting. A dozen or so enemy machines, oblivious of the flying lead, are right on our tails. I touch the rudder bar very slightly – left and right – to spoil their aim and crouch a little lower in the cockpit.

Something snatches at my sleeve, my rev. counter flies to fragments, and I nearly swallow my chewing gum ...[19]

The aircraft of No. 55 Squadron bunched a little closer to reap the benefit from each observer's fire as they strove to protect each other. According to Johns, one of the DH4s slipped out of formation and stalled. He thought the pilot had been hit and that the observer was trying to get the aircraft down. The Germans appeared to have left this machine alone. ('Jolly sporting of them!' commented Johns. 'But they don't all do that.'[20]) However, if Johns' reminiscence is correct, the pilot and observer managed to make it back to Azelot for there was no report of a casualty on this mission.

The squadron were now flying in such tight formation that Johns was worried about a collision with number 3 aircraft in the formation. Later, he was also to remember 'Pip' Rayment throwing him a kiss from the observer's seat of number 2 aircraft. However, Rayment was flying in number 3 aircraft, while number 2 was flown by Attwood (who was to be shot down and killed on 25 September) with Turner as his observer.

Captain Silly climbed to 21,000 feet and Johns found himself lagging behind.

A bunch of EA come in on me and every observer's gun swings round to drive them off. I get back into place, sweating with fright. Gompertz, another observer, hurls an empty [ammunition] drum, which misses by a yard, at an EA.

Another hour passes slowly and my engine coughs – coughs again. Frantically I switch over to a new tank and breathe again as she picks up. The rattle of guns is incessant. My observer is only using his when the enemy come right in on us, and I know the reason.

He looks at me and holds up a drum – his last, and an hour to go.[21]

The enemy fighters did not have the ability to climb to the height of the DH4s, which was why Silly had taken the squadron up to 21,000 feet. All the while the British aircraft maintained their height they were safe from the waiting Germans. Then Johns saw Don Waterous begin to slide down out of formation. Apparently he was able to elude the enemy fighters and make the British lines safely.

The last ten minutes is warm work as the enemy make their final effort. A burst of fire rips the side of my instrument board and I look round to see whence it came. A scarlet Fokker is on my tail and I swing violently to spoil his aim.

'Pip' Rayment sees my plight and puts his last few rounds into him. He jerks up, hard hit, and bursts into flame.[22] The skipper puts his nose down and dives for home, the rest of us streaking after him. A smother of 'archie' plasters us as we cross the line.

A green light – that's the washout signal. I sit back, push up my goggles and raise my arms. My observer sees, and takes the spare stick. It's the only chance he gets to practise flying and he might have to bring me down some day.

I laugh as we stagger about the sky. Ordinary flying seems a puerile business after the last five hours.

I land, taxi-in and switch off, feeling suddenly tired.[23]

Johns and Amey clambered out of the DH4 and walked to the squadron office to write their report. A tender took them to their quarters, where Johns threw himself onto his bed and tried to get the singing out of his ears. Five hours with the constant roar of an aero-engine creates headaches and tension in all aircrew.

The official account of the raid states that the two formations of No. 55 Squadron, six aircraft to each formation, encountered considerable but inaccurate anti-aircraft fire and twenty enemy aircraft while en route to the target, after the squadron had crossed the lines at 15,000 feet by way of St Die, Strasbourg and Baden. The return journey followed the same route, though slightly to the south. Fifteen enemy aircraft were seen to leave the ground at Bobigen, but they could not catch up with the British formation. However, several more enemy aircraft attacked the squadron southeast of Strasbourg. Second Lieutenant J. T. Attwood, with his observer Lieutenant C. Turner, flying in number 2 position in Johns' formation, were credited with shooting down one machine. 'One EA coming under my tail,' reported Attwood, 'I fired a few bursts and the machine went down in a spinning nose dive and was seen to crash into a wood.'[24] Captain Silly claimed another machine. 'On the return journey,' he reported, 'I saw the EA approaching me from the front; I held my fire until he was within 100 yards and then fired a burst. The EA passed very close over my right wing, stalled and spun. I was unable to see the result.'[25]

By evening Johns had recovered from the raid and was able to join his comrades, with a group of aircrew from Nos 99 and 104 Squadrons, who were taking a tender into Nancy to spend the evening at the Hotel Liégeois. Captain Silly, seeing them off, warned them not to be late back for there was a 'show' scheduled for the morning. Little did Johns know, as he joined the singing, laughing pilots, rolling into Nancy, that it would be his last 'show'.

6

JOHNS 'FAILS TO RETURN'

The Liégeois in Nancy was a gay spectacle in the latter days of 1918. The hotel was filled with Allied officers in uniforms of all sorts, from be-medalled French officers, *pilots de chasse*, to RAF officers from local bombing squadrons Nos 55, 99, 104 and the specialist night bombing squadrons Nos 100 and 112. Among the Allied officers, according to Johns, 'fluttered ladies of considerable charm and persuasion'.[1] Had the uniforms been changed to sombreros and leather chaps, Johns felt it might have been mistaken for a frontier saloon in the nineteenth-century American West.

Everyone was happy. The proprietor would cash cheques for any reasonable amount, and Cox's was far away. The occasional roar of a bomb in the street was greeted with cries of derision. Indeed, Nancy was a fine example of the futility of incessant bombing. Admittedly the best people had departed long ago, but after four years of daily hate, bombs were accepted as a matter of course – even as they are today by the Afridi – and only caused comment when some well-known establishment was fanned down.[2]

Midnight, that Sunday, 15 September, found Johns waiting outside the *hôtel de ville* for a fellow officer who had promised to give him a lift back to Azelot in his car. The tender had departed long since. In the quiet hush of the sleeping city Johns could hear the rumble of guns near Pont-à-Mousson, and here and there a string of orange blobs of anti-aircraft fire, 'flaming onions', floated upwards. He could hear the purr of a Beardmore engine and see the dark silhouette of an FE approaching low over the city. A searchlight flashed the password letters of the night and a glowing ball of green, changing slowly to red, shot from the aeroplane – the answering colour code. The searchlight faded and the aircraft continued into the darkness. It was now growing late and Johns became worried. The officer had apparently forgotten about him and departed homewards. Johns knew he was scheduled for the raid the next day. Azelot was too far to walk.

While he was wondering what to do, an American ambulance rumbled round the corner heading for the road to St Nicholas. Johns hailed it eagerly.

'Going anywhere near Azelot?' he called.

'Nope,' returned the driver.

'Anyone inside?' pressed Johns.

'Nope,' was the reply.

'Wait!' cried Johns, 'would fifty francs pay for the petrol?'

'Nope,' responded the garrulous driver. 'I guess I'm tired.'

Desperate to get back to the aerodrome, Johns offered the man 100 francs, but still the answer was in the negative. Johns pleaded that he was on an early show and this, apparently, moved the driver to allow him to climb aboard. He had no idea where Azelot was and Johns gave general directions before falling asleep with exhaustion.

Some time later he was awoken by a shout. The ambulance was stationary. In front of it were two French military police, rifles pointing, faces regarding the American and his passenger with suspicion.

'Where the hell have you got to?' demanded Johns. 'Are we lost?'

'I guess,' yawned the American.

The French soldiers hustled them into a nearby cottage which, it turned out, was being used as a military command post. An officer eyed them with disapproval.

'You speak French?' he asked Johns.

'Yes.'

'Your friend?'

'It will only be one word if he does,' Johns assured the Frenchman.

'*Qu'est ce que c'est?*'

'Nope,' said the American.

'*Comment?*'

'Aw hell!'

The French officer seemed convinced that Johns and his companion were spies. He spent twenty minutes on the telephone checking their identities before he would allow them to proceed. Johns had no idea where they were and told the driver to stop at the next house so that he could get directions.

Conversation languished after that and I dozed again, but opened my eyes at the grinding of brakes. We had pulled up before a massive pair of iron gates. They were locked. However, the matter was urgent, so climbing the wall I made my way up an overgrown drive of interminable length before it opened onto a space of grass. Looming ghost-like in the moonlight, stood a big rambling white house. Not a light showed anywhere which was not surprising, considering the hour.[3]

It was 3 am.

Johns pulled on the bell chain and set up a frightful clamour. After a while a light showed at one of the windows and voices were audible from within. 'Bolts were drawn, the door opened a few inches, and the flickering light of a candle disclosed a face which looked like something off Notre Dame. Behind this horror I saw another face – the face of a girl. If the old crone had the face of a gargoyle then this girl had the face of an angel.'[4]

'Mille pardons, madame, je me suis perdu la route. Pouvez-vous me dire quelle est la direction pour Azelot?' mumbled Johns.

The old woman muttered something but the young girl came forward.

'Mais attendez, monsieur; reposez-vous; peux-je vous offre un petit verre?'

Johns stepped into the hall and felt that he had been transported into a Rafael Sabatini novel. Portraits of men and women in the fashions of a previous age stared disapprovingly down at him. The dying embers of a fire still glowed eerily in the grate. The girl returned with a dusty bottle and poured Johns a drink. The crone was studying his uniform curiously.

'You are an *aviateur?*' she asked at length.

'Oui, madame.'

'My husband was killed in the war of 1870,' the old woman went on. Had she said that he had been killed in the battle of Hastings Johns felt he would have believed her without question. The girl – Marcelle, the old woman called her – told Johns that her father had been killed in the war. Her companion seemed to be her grandmother.

'Et maman?' asked Johns.

'Maman est morte aussi.'

Johns sat talking to the girl and sipping his wine by the red light of the dying fire. The crone fell asleep in her chair. He felt he could have stayed for an eternity, but dawn was in the sky and he could hear the sound of an aero-engine. He glanced at his watch. It was already 3.30 am.

'Azelot, m'amoiselle, how far is it?'

'*Vingt kilomètres.*'

Johns made for the door, but lingered for a moment 'I shall come back, Marcelle.'

'*Oui, monsieur.*'

'*À demain,*' he added.

'*Mais non,*' she replied, pointing to the pale sky in the east. '*À tout à l'heure.*'

'*À tout à l'heure.*'

He did not return. A few hours later he was standing by his wrecked aircraft, behind German lines, trying to pull his dead observer out of the machine before it caught fire.

He never saw Marcelle again, but she remained in his memory to be recreated as Marie Janis, the beautiful young German spy with whom Biggles fell in love in *The Camels Are Coming*.

On Monday, 16 September twelve DH4s of No. 55 Squadron took off at 12.20 pm. They flew in two formations; the first was commanded by Captain Mackay and the second by Captain Fox. Johns, with his observer Amey, was flying in position number 5 in Mackay's formation. Coxhill, who had been Johns' regular observer during August, was now flying with 2nd Lieutenant G. Gorrill in position number 5 in Captain Fox's formation. The target was the Lanz Works and railway yards at Mannheim. Fox's formation failed to rendezvous with Mackay and returned to Azelot without reaching the target. Mackay's six aircraft crossed the lines at Raon l'Etape and proceeded over Saverne, west of Hagenau, then by Landau to Mannheim. They attacked their targets, meeting moderate but accurate anti-aircraft fire and six enemy aircraft. Four 112-pound bombs and three 230-pound bombs were dropped and eighteen photographic plates were exposed. But of the six aircraft, only five reached the target and returned to Azelot safely at 4.40 pm. According to the War Diary/Intelligence Summary of the day, 'one machine failed to return'. The pilot of the missing aircraft was Johns. The squadron's combat report states: '2/lt WE Johns and 2/lt AE

Amey not yet returned. Fell out of formation near Hagenau after firing green light.'[5]

'The trouble,' Johns remembered, 'began near Saverne.'

I was watching a string of what appeared to be gaudy butterflies crawling along the ground; now and then the sun flashed on their wings. It was a full squadron of Fokker DVIIs trailing us and climbing fast. There was a bit of 'archie' about, nothing to worry us, but the odd chance came off. There was a terrific explosion almost in my face, and a blast of air and smoke nearly turned my machine over. I tried the controls anxiously and all seemed well but a stink of petrol filled my nostrils and I glanced down; my cockpit was swimming with the stuff.[6]

Johns switched over to his reserve tank, but it was empty. Amey passed over a scribbled note. 'Main tank gone.'[7] Johns glanced around. The German aircraft were about two miles behind and some 4,000 feet below. Johns' altimeter registered 19,500 feet and he was sixty miles from home. The situation was grim. He pulled his bomb toggle and sent his bombs on their last journey. Relieved of their weight he tried to climb for the sun as Amey fired a green Very light to let Mackay know they were in trouble and leaving the formation. Afterwards Johns wondered why the flash from the Very pistol had not set the petrol-soaked machine on fire.

Five minutes later Amey's Lewis gun was in action as the leading Fokkers approached. Adjusting his compensator, which cut fuel and speed but also extended range, Johns tried to climb to 21,000 to get beyond the German fighters' height capabilities.

The leader came in with a rush and I touched the rudder-bar to let his tracer go by. A bunch of them came up under my elevators and I kicked out my foot, slewing Amey round without losing height, to bring his guns to bear. The Fokkers came right in and I give them credit for facing Amey's music. One turned over, a second spun out of it, but another came right in to point-blank range; Amey raked him fore and aft without stopping him. Others came down on us from above.[8]

Johns' windscreen shattered and the instrument board shed glass and wood splinters. A bullet ripped his goggles off while another seared his hip painfully. Wiping the blood out of his eyes, Johns peered round in time to see Amey sinking slowly to the floor of his cockpit.

Sick with fright and fury, I looked around for help, but from horizon
to horizon stretched the unbroken blue of a summer sky. Bullets were
striking the machine all the time like whip-lashes, so I put her in a steep
bank and held her there while I considered the position. For perhaps five
minutes we tore round and round, the enemy getting in a burst now and
then and me 'browning' the whole bunch of them, but I could not go on
indefinitely. My ammunition was running low and I was still over forty
miles from home ... Things looked bad. To try to make forty miles
against ten or a dozen enemy machines (several others were joining in
the fun) was going to be difficult. In fact, I strongly suspected that my
time had come.[9]

Strangely enough, at this desperate moment Johns became
aware of another British aircraft not far away. A second drama
similar to his own was taking place as a solitary DH9 put up a
stubborn fight against a swarm of enemy machines. It was
obviously impossible for Johns to give support and after heroic
resistance the DH9 fell in flames. 'Later, I asked the German
pilots for the names of these brave men, but they did not know
because the bodies had been burned beyond identification.'[10] In
another account of this incident, Johns says that all the Germans
could tell him was the fact that the pilot and observer had been
sergeants.[11]

Johns now shot off at a tangent, but before he had gone a mile
the German machines were after him, shooting his lumbering
DH4 to pieces. Johns recalls, in his fear, yanking his machine
round as if it had been a fighting scout and going for the Germans
like a mad dog. How the bomber held together he did not know.
Wires trailed loose behind him, fabric stripped off and a centre
section strut splintered at the fuselage junction.

He was at 6,000 feet when a striped Fokker sent a stream of
bullets over his shoulder into his engine. It cut dead, a cloud of
white petrol vapour drifted aft and Johns braced himself for the
inevitable flames.

I had seen the vapour and what followed it before. That was my
worst moment. I switched off and literally flung the machine into a
vertical sideslip, but she still smoked as the petrol ran over the hot
engine. Suddenly the joystick went loose in my hand as the controls
broke somewhere; we spun, half came out and spun again.[12]

Mercifully, the flames held off. With his left hand Johns tried to wipe the blood and broken goggles from his eyes in an effort to see where he was going, while with his right hand he fought to get the machine under control.

Even in this state, he could observe, with dispassionate detachment, the figure of a man who had been ploughing a field below. The man was running in one direction while his horse was galloping in another, as bullets from the machine firing at Johns kicked up the dust around them.

Every detail of that field is stamped on my memory with vivid clarity. I knew I was going to crash, but curiously enough I do not think I was afraid: (I have been much more scared on other occasions). I hadn't time to be scared. My brain was whirling at full revs. – should I jump as we hit the ground – should I unfasten my belt – and so on, and all the time I was automatically trying to get the machine on an even keel. Twice her nose nearly came up of her own accord as she tried to right herself, and it was in that position that we struck.[13]

A clump of trees on the edge of the field seemed to race towards him. He kicked out his foot instinctively, lifting his knees to his chin and covering his eyes. There was a crash like the end of the world, then utter blackness.

7

PRISONER OF WAR

Johns' first recollection on regaining consciousness was of madly fighting to get out of the wreck before it caught fire. Somehow he managed to scramble from the fuselage of the splintered aeroplane, poised vertically above the ground. He leant for a moment against the wreckage and began to pick pieces of glass from the instrument panel out of his face. The cuts were beginning to sting uncomfortably and he was bleeding pretty badly. He later discovered that his nose was broken and his lips were badly lacerated. His safety belt had come apart and he had smashed his face against the Vickers gun butt. The force of the crash had thrust his feet through the soles of his flying boots, and his safety belt had ripped the clothing and the skin off his stomach as cleanly as if it had been cut with a razor.

Suddenly he was aware of a Fokker diving at the field and he heard the rattle of a machine gun. Bullets began to kick up the earth around him. The German pilot afterwards told him that he had fired warning shots in order to drive him away from the machine in case he was about to set fire to it.

His next thoughts were for his observer, but when he turned to pull him out of the crash his worst fears were confirmed; Amey was obviously dead. Johns made an attempt to heave his body from the wreckage, but the task of extricating it was too difficult. Johns had his Very pistol in the knee-pocket of his Sidcot flying suit, but now there was no chance of setting fire to his machine. A long line of grey-coated soldiers led by an officer was racing across the field and was almost upon him. Johns sighed. For him the war was apparently over. Beginning to feel the aches of his badly bruised body – it was some days before he could stand upright comfortably – he leant back against the fuselage and continued to pick instrument glass out of his face and mop up the blood as best he could.

A German NCO reached Johns first and, without warning, the

man smashed his fist into Johns' face. What Johns did not know was that some days before a DH4 had dropped bombs onto a nearby village, Ettendorf, hitting the Sunday school and killing many children. Several others had been killed while taking part in a religious feast-day procession in the streets. The Germans claimed that the DH4 belonged to No. 55 Squadron. The local people were incensed against RAF personnel.

Johns, in blind reaction, made a rush at the NCO, but several soldiers caught hold of him and half-dragged, half-carried him to Ettendorf. He was taken to the schoolhouse, where, moments later, German soldiers carried in the corpse of Amey and placed it on the floor. After what seemed a painfully long interval, the door opened and an officer wearing a spiked *Pickelhaube* helmet came in. He wore an Iron Cross on his chest. He looked at Amey's body and then, punctiliously, he clicked his heels together and saluted. He turned to Johns and snapped, 'So, you will be shot for throwing bombs!'[1]

With that the man left. Johns was still digesting his words, unaware of the incident involving the Ettendorf children, when a cheerful and friendly crowd of German pilots entered the room. 'The chief object of their visit,' recalled Johns later, 'appeared to be to find out if I knew the colour of the machine that had actually fired the fatal shot.' He went on: 'as if I knew, when there were nearly a score of them at it.'[2] However, in another early reminiscence concerning this incident, he remembers his reaction to the pilots' questions differently. He records his feelings when he was brought face to face with the man who was credited with bringing him down.

I realised that hitherto I had regarded him only in the abstract. With something like a mild shock it slowly dawned upon my numbed brain that the fellow who had been in the red nosed, black crossed machine was an ordinary mortal like myself. Before, the aircraft and the occupant had been one, a hideous instrument – creature, if you like – bent on my destruction; the individual had never entered into my calculations. But there he was, saluting with the inimitable little German bow, his keen grey eyes smiling whimsically in a clean-cut face. He wore a perfectly streamlined blue-grey tunic of fine material, relieved only by a beautiful enamel cross at his throat which, I later learned, was the *Pour-le-Mérite* [the Blue Max] – and a nifty little dagger on his hip.

'Well,' he said in French, 'you've had a bit of bad luck – but it might have been worse, eh?' He picked up a slip of paper from the things that had been taken from my pockets; it was a pass to Paris. He tipped me a knowing wink — what he said doesn't matter.

Again I felt that something was wrong somewhere. It was all very unreal. Far from hating the man, it would have been churlish not to have responded to the obvious friendly spirit with which he made arrangements for my immediate comfort. Trouble followed later, but as far as he and the officers of his staffel were concerned I must give them their due, they were as cheery a crowd as I should have met had I gone down over my own side of the lines.[3]

After the German pilots had left, a doctor came and removed the remaining glass from Johns' face and bound up his wounds, which — in spite of the blood — were only of a superficial nature. The doctor also discovered that a bullet had chipped a piece off his right hip and another had scored his scalp. Eventually Johns was taken down to the cellar below the Ettendorf schoolhouse, where he spent an uncomfortable night with Amey's body. The children of the village, whose friends had been killed by the British bomber the previous week, gathered outside and chanted 'Schweinhund Englander!' and other taunts.

Later Johns came to believe that the Fokker DVIIs that had attacked him were from Metz and were therefore part of Jagdstaffel 4 commanded by the German air ace Ernst Udet. Jagdstaffel 4 had been one of the Staffel which formed the Jagdgeschwader commanded by Baron Manfred von Richthofen, the famous 'Red Baron', who had been shot down on 21 April, after having been accredited with 80 'kills'. In later life Johns became attached to the idea that it was Udet who had personally shot him down. He told Frank Entwistle of the Evening Standard: 'Ernst Udet ... shot me down, too. He landed nearby, saluted my dead gunner, got me to a doctor in the village and said — "Bad luck. My turn tomorrow." Poor fellow shot himself years later because he didn't like Hitler.'[4] The story was repeated until it was accepted without question, and was used in Johns' obituary in The Times.[5] However, it is certain that Udet was not even at Metz at this time, although Jagdstaffel 4, commanded by Hauptman Hermann Göring, was. Udet had gone on a month's leave only returning on 26 September, when he shot down his 61st and 62nd enemy aircraft, which were his last victories of the war. Rather than machines from Udet's Staffel, it seems far more likely that the aircraft which brought Johns down were part of a Fokker DVII Jagdstaffel from Hagenau aerodrome, which was situated close by Ettendorf.

Johns' comment on Udet's suicide, 'because he didn't like Hitler', was a little too simplistic. Udet had supported the rise to power of the Nazi Party and rose to be Chief of the Technical Department of the German Air Ministry, now in the hands of his former subordinate from Jagdstaffel 4 – Hermann Göring. He was a fun-loving bachelor and while helping Leni Riefenstahl make some flying films in the 1930s began an affair with her. Hitler soon afterwards became attracted to her, but when he discovered about her relationship with Udet he dropped her and began harassing the former air ace. After the war started, Hitler continually blamed the inability of the Luftwaffe to stop enemy bombers and fighters on Udet's failure to supply new types of aircraft. Udet's health began to fail and he lost his happy-go-lucky manner. He began drinking heavily, became depressed and took pep pills. On 17 November 1941 he shot himself through the head. Göring threatened Leni Riefenstahl with arrest if she revealed the truth about his death. It was then announced that Udet had died in an aircraft accident and a spectacular state funeral was held, attended by Hitler.[6]

The day after he was taken prisoner, Johns, together with his dead observer, was placed in a cart and transported to Zaburn, where there was a German army headquarters. At Zaburn, Amey's body was taken away – Johns later presumed it was buried there. He was left waiting for some time before being taken into an office for interrogation. The German officer who rose to greet him appeared friendly enough, but his first words came as a shock.

'Hello, Johns. Who's commanding 55 now Major Gray's on leave?'

I was so completely taken aback by this question that I could only stare. Actually, the Hun overreached himself, for my astonishment was so genuine that I fancy it bore out my assertion that I didn't know what he was talking about, and I saw a glimmer of doubt creep into his eyes.[7]

As Johns well knew, Major Alec Gray had gone on leave on 12 September, although he was unaware that the CO had returned on the 16th, after the squadron had taken off for Mannheim, and had later signed the bomb reports. The shocks did not end there for the German officer then produced a snapshot of Johns taken at Azelot aerodrome. Johns was at a loss to know how such a photograph could have come into the man's possession and he could not even recall posing for it. Actually, it was the snap taken by his fellow pilot 2nd Lieutenant A. J. G. Gormley, and it had fallen into German hands when the airman had been shot down on 30 August.

Johns controlled his feelings and gave only his name, rank and number. The German officer then started to pump Johns for information about the machine he had been flying, asking what horsepower his engine was. Johns replied that an examination of the wreckage would provide that information. The officer smiled and said he already knew that it was a 275 hp Rolls-Royce Eagle VII engine. The statement was comforting to the prisoner – his interrogators were not all-powerful and all-knowing. Johns had, in fact, been flying one of the new 375 hp Eagle VIII engines, probably the first of its kind to be shot down. He congratulated the German on his knowledge, hoping that the officer would take the type of engine for granted instead of examining it closely and discovering the differences between the two Eagle engines.

His interrogator said that if Johns would 'co-operate' in answering questions he would be sent to a *Sonderlager*, a 'special camp' for 'good boys'. Johns tersely replied that there was 'nothing doing'. The officer pressed him further, bringing forth a series of photographs of Allied aerodromes and watching intently as Johns looked through them. The latter pretended to stare hard at an aerodrome he had never seen before, noting with satisfaction the German's reaction. Finally, the 'send a letter home' trick was tried; Johns was invited to send a letter to let his relatives know that he was alive and well and a prisoner of war. Johns simply wrote on the card provided: 'Prisoner-of-War 16.9.18. Johns 2/Lt.' and addressed it to The Air Board, London, England. The interrogator had been hoping that Johns would fall for the trick and address it to his squadron. When he saw the address, the German berated Johns and some harsh words were exchanged. The card, incidentally, was either never sent or, if so, never delivered, for Johns was officially recorded as missing in action. Only when he arrived on his own doorstep in Little

Dunham after the war did his family know that he was alive.

The session was over until the next day. When it started again, different officers questioned Johns. Interrogations lasted a further two to three days. Towards the end Johns was asked what he thought of the new Snipe and he replied truthfully that he did not know what the questioner was talking about. He had never heard of the latest Sopwith Snipe fighter which, according to *Janes' Aircraft* for 1918, was first used in France by No. 43 Squadron on 23 September. To Johns' surprise the interrogator took out a complete set of photographs and design drawings of the aircraft, and showed them to him.

At the end of the final interrogation Johns received his greatest shock. He was, the Germans told him, a *Terrorflieger*; the very man who had dropped bombs on Ettendorf and massacred the children in Sunday school. Johns protested his innocence. The Germans told him he would be taken to Strasbourg Civilian Gaol to await a court martial. After the transfer there followed long, dreary and nerve-racking days. Johns tried to keep his spirits up by reminding himself of his rights as a prisoner of war, but he remembered cases such as the pamphleteers of No. 11 Squadron, who only just escaped execution for dropping propaganda leaflets, and the case of Captain Fryatts, who had perished in front of an execution squad for a similar offence.[8]

The day came when Johns went through a ceremony in which a number of officers sat at a table, while one officer talked volubly and at length on one side of the room and was answered by another officer on the other side. At the end of these proceedings Johns was asked to stand. He was told that he had undergone a trial by court martial, had been found guilty of bombing undefended German towns and was therefore sentenced to death by shooting.

... to this day I do not know whether the whole thing was a farce to intimidate me into talking, or whether it was really meant. Actually, it was not so bad as it sounds, because by that time I was so utterly sick, and so Bolshie, that I didn't care much whether I was shot or not. Sometimes the Hun rather overdid it.[9]

The days went by, each morning Johns fully expecting to be taken for the promised 'dawn walk', but after a while it became evident that the Germans were not in a hurry to carry out the sentence. In the light of subsequent research it seems likely that the court martial was a charade designed to get Johns to talk – as he himself suspected. To the German Intelligence officers, even a 2nd Lieutenant was a potential source of information. If he had recently arrived in France, he might know something useful about events in England. If he had been in France for some time and could be persuaded or tricked into talking about his experiences, even the most trivial detail could be used by Intelligence staff, in the task of building up a comprehensive picture of the Allied Forces. Facts that were harmless in themselves might be used to glean more valuable facts later on. An Air Intelligence Officer liked to be able to surprise a prisoner by showing an intimate knowledge of the personnel of his own squadron, hoping that the captured airman would see no harm in talking when his interrogator knew so much already.[10]

However, whether Johns was actually court-martialled or not remains an open question; Dr Heyl, Archivdirektor of the Kriegsarchiv of the Bayerisches Hauptstaatsarchiv, could find no reference to such a proceeding at Strasbourg and states that, in view of the circumstances, such a court martial 'does not seem very likely to us'.[11]

At this time in Strasbourg Gaol there were a number of war prisoners awaiting transfer to a proper *Kriegsgefangenenlager* (prisoner-of-war camp). Johns recalled meeting a man named Harley there, 'a crazy South African SE5 pilot who cursed the Huns to all eternity in low Dutch on every possible occasion'. Every morning Johns was led out of his cell into the courtyard for exercise. The exercise was supervised by a German NCO. 'My God!' Johns wrote. 'He was a swine ...!' In fact, in his cell, 'the only thing I had to read was a notice scribbled on the wall by a former prisoner. It read – "the Sergeant Major is a pig". The fellow who wrote it was right. The Sergeant-Major was a pig!'[12]

As the days passed, Johns' thoughts turned to escape. 'When I became a prisoner it was only natural that I should think of them [escapers] and their deeds. Often I would tell myself that Casanova got out of a more difficult place than the one I was in; then I would grip the bars of my window and wonder how on earth it was going to be done'.[13] The answer came from an unexpected source. Among the prisoners taking morning exercise were a dozen American soldiers. One morning an American sergeant sidled up to Johns and asked him, *sotto voce*, whether he wanted to escape. Johns assured the sergeant, whose name he never learnt, that it was his dearest wish. The sergeant then asked whether Johns could fly him back to the Allied lines if he succeeded in getting him out and if they could find an aerodrome. 'This "pinching an aeroplane" idea was first and foremost in every airman prisoner's mind, but I don't think it was ever done', noted Johns.[14]

At the time Johns agreed enthusiastically. The American told him that when the prisoners were ordered back to their cells he was to run straight down the corridor, past his cell, to the lavatory at the end. The American would do the rest. Johns knew the lavatory well, for during the ten days he had spent in Strasbourg Gaol, his only source of recreation had been to hammer on his cell door and demand to be taken to it whether it was necessary or not, simply to relieve the monotony of his existence. Like the rest of the building, it was stone-built and had an iron-barred window.

According to the American sergeant, one of the bars was made to slide up and down in order to permit the entry of a hosepipe that was used to empty the lavatory. Normally the bar was locked in place, but somehow the American had managed to break the lock. Outside the window there was a drop of twelve feet into a yard which was patrolled by a single sentry. On the far side there was a high wooden fence surmounted by barbed wire, and beyond that there was a river. It is doubtful whether Johns or the enterprising American sergeant knew this when they made their bid for freedom.

After a while the German NCO gave the command for the prisoners to return to their cells. Johns walked to the corridor closely followed by his guard. As soon as he reached his cell door he sprinted forward. A guard called on him to halt. Johns glanced over his shoulder and saw the American push the man aside and race after him. They reached the lavatory and slammed the door shut. The American knocked off the window bar and pushed it up. 'Out you go!' he snapped to Johns, who needed no urging. He started to wriggle through, but, unfortunately, he was fairly stocky and halfway through he stuck fast. At that precise moment a sentry came round the corner of the building and gaped in astonishment; then recovering his wits he let out a yell and dashed to the window, making a pass at Johns with his bayonet. Behind him the American, knowing nothing of the sentry outside, began to push Johns, while outside the lavatory door the German guards were bellowing as they tried to smash it in. Then it was all over. The door burst open and the guards seized the American. They took Johns by the legs and hauled him backwards with a wrench that nearly pulled him apart. He landed on the stone floor none too gently and saw the American being dragged outside, struggling with the guards. He never saw his companion again. Later he reflected that the attempt was 'a most desperate and foolish affair. Looking back on the incident I realise that we both must have been crazy'.[15]

Johns was informed that he would suffer ten days' solitary confinement for the attempt. Now he had no contact at all with his fellow prisoners and not even interrogations to break the long, dreary days.

Day after day I sat on my bed, consisting of three planks, in a tiny stone cell. It was cold and damp. But the worst thing was having absolutely nothing to do. I didn't know the time. I hardly knew if it was day or night. Hour after hour I just sat and stared at the opposite wall. The solitude was broken twice in twenty-four hours. At twelve noon a warder brought me a plate of soup and some water. He did the same at 6 p.m. From 6 p.m. until twelve the next day seemed a life time. Only those who have been through it can form the slightest conception of how slowly time can go.[16]

Seven days later a guard abruptly told Johns to be ready to go on a journey. He was sent north to Karlsruhe, which was a general clearing house for officer prisoners. Johns was only a few days there, when, with Harley, the 'crazy South African SE5 pilot', he was sent to a regular POW camp at Landshut. Harley had not lost his habit of cursing Germans in Afrikaans and on the train to Landshut Johns recalled that a German booted the South African in the ribs for 'speaking out of his turn ... it was a brutal kick and curled him up for some time.'[17]

Landshut POW camp was situated on an island in the river Isar just outside the town from which it took its name, some thirty miles or so east of Munich. Here Johns found many Air Force prisoners.

... one shares quarters with the other fellows, and that is not bad. The talk is all of one thing – escape. I must have spent more than half the hours I was a prisoner talking about ways and means of escape. It isn't easy. The knowledge that guards are standing around with loaded rifles is distinctly discouraging.[18]

Discouraging or not, Johns immediately threw himself into escape activity. There was an escape committee and elaborate codes were drawn up as a means of communication. A letter or note was written but with the words of the message left unjoined. For example, to transmit the message 'go now' one would write 'He had some g o. But n o w things have changed.'[19]

The officers at Landshut were allowed to have batmen to do menial work. These were enlisted men, mainly Italians: Johns came to know one such Italian, who served his hut as an orderly, and who had been one of the 100,000 troops who had surrendered to the Germans at Piave. He told Johns that the Germans had no time for them and allowed them to die of plague in hundreds.

Prisoners were allowed prison money – 10 Pfennig notes were paid out to prisoners but were clearly marked *Inspektion der Kriegsgefangenenlager*. With his money Johns was able to buy some German ersatz leather boots, but when it rained they turned to mush.[20] To smarten himself up he also made a purchase of a hat for the equivalent of £5. The Germans also sold him a German-style pipe, but no tobacco, which was in short supply.

Among his fellow prisoners there was a young boy who had run away from school to join the Royal Naval Air Service as a pilot. The boy had been shot down and was celebrating his seventeenth birthday in the camp.[21] After the war, Johns recalled that the boy went back to his school to finish his education. Johns also became friendly with an RNAS officer named Carter, who described to him what had happened on his last flight.

He was a Camel pilot then and was so tickled to death one day at finding a column of enemy troops on the march that he could not tear himself away from them.

He amused himself for a time by unloading his 20lb Cooper bombs on them, and when this began to pall he came lower and sprayed them with his gun. So fascinating did this pastime become, and so vastly entertaining were the antics of the warriors below in their frantic haste to remove themselves from the locality, that he quite failed to notice the telegraph wires which, as so often happens, accompanied the road on its winding course. He hit the wires at the bottom of a zoom and took them together with a snapped off post or two, for a short joyride. It was a pity he could not have given the troops a treat by taking them all the way home, but the Camel, not being designed for such work, gave up the ghost and spread itself over the landscape.

The tables now being somewhat turned, his erstwhile victims proceeded to amuse themselves by battering him to pulp with their rifle butts, a comparatively tame pursuit from which they were only compelled to desist by the arrival of a senior officer.

Carter was taken to the same hospital as the men he had wounded, where a state of affairs prevailed for the next week or so that can be better imagined than described.[22]

However, Carter survived all vicissitudes and, according to Johns, went on to command the Iraqi Air Force after the war.

Also confined in Landshut were two Canadians, Pat Manley and a man called Swayze.

Pat Manley and Swayze were friends who joined the infantry and came over with the Canadian contingent. They were hit on the same day, went to different hospitals and completely lost touch with each other. A year later Pat, beetling over the line in a Bristol Fighter, saw another Bristol going down under a cloud of enemy aircraft. He throttled back and put his nose down in a steep dive to join the party: but he was too late and saw the other Bristol crash in a field. Perceiving that no good purpose could be served by hanging around, Pat was about to make for a healthier quarter of the sky, when ... he lost his propeller. Being very low he was unable to dive to get it back so he landed beside the crash, just in time to see Swayze crawl out. Thus, they were both taken prisoner within one minute of each other on the same field in France.[23]

Towards the end of October Johns made a successful solo escape bid from Landshut, managing to get outside the wire enclosure and across the river Isar.[24] For three days he kept trekking in what he considered a westerly direction. He could not find anything to eat and not much to drink. Reminiscing to Robert Pitman of the *Sunday Express*, Johns recalled: 'I escaped and wandered about for five days. It was awful. I was cold and hungry and it was at the beginning of November. I think I was glad when a farmer with a shotgun finally caught me in his orchard.'[25] In an earlier reminiscence, Johns said that it was at dawn on the *fourth* day when, half-starving, dirty and ill-clad, he came to an orchard by a Bavarian farmhouse. Johns stole into the orchard and was just reaching for an apple when he heard a dog bark and, a moment later, a sound behind him. He turned and found himself looking into the muzzles of a twelve-bore shotgun held in the unwavering hands of a burly German farmer. The man was only ten yards away and so Johns did the obvious thing – he raised his hands and shrugged.[26]

Back at Landshut he received ten days' solitary confinement. Then, on 7 November, he was transferred to a *Straflager*, a punishment camp for 'bad boys' who persisted in escape attempts. The camp was Fort Ten, one of a series of fortresses, built after 1872, surrounding the town of Ingolstadt and situated a few kilometres southeast of it. The camp served as a POW camp for British, French, Russian and Belgian officers who made a habit of attempting to escape. It was, said the Germans, 'escape proof', with the same reputation that Colditz Castle (*Offizierlager IVC*) was to enjoy in the Second World War. In fact, only thirty or so British officers made successful escapes from German prison camps during the entire period of the war. Johns reflected:

Prison camps differed a good deal. Once you had tried to escape, it usually meant that you were sent to a punishment camp where conditions were bad. One just had to put up with it. Guards were changed frequently, so that you never got to know one well enough to risk offering a bribe for assistance in an escape. The eternal barbed wire and fixed bayonets had a depressing effect on one, particularly if one's vitality was lowered through bad and indifferent food. Some fellows just became ill and died under the strain of it. Luckily I was never ill, but I lost a lot of weight. I went in weighing eleven stone and came home weighing seven! One developed rather a nasty smell through under-nourishment. This was helped by one's clothes, which, of course, got very dirty.[27]

For Johns, 'when I was twiddling my thumbs in a cell, the thought of spending Christmas there became a nightmare'. But on Monday, 11 November there was sudden jubilation in the camp. The war was over! An armistice had been signed after four long and bloody years of conflict. But this did not mean an immediate return home. Johns, with other prisoners, fretted and fumed in

Fort Ten until 20 November when they were told to get ready to be moved. Optimism at being returned home soon collapsed when they were informed that they were merely being transferred to Fort Five, or Fort Orff, a similar type of POW camp a few kilometres northwest of Ingolstadt near the village of Heppberg. This camp had housed British, French and Belgian officers and had been known by its inmates as 'Fort-Orf-ful'. Now it was being used as a clearing camp for prisoners being repatriated. Between 20 November and 30 November, when he left the camp, it is recorded that Johns was paid the sum of 60 Marks, according to the camp's pay register.[28] His trousers were badly torn, but a French prisoner, a man named Boulenger of the Battalion d'Afrique who had been in the camp since 1914, gave Johns a pair of red French cavalry breeches so that he might return home decently clad.

On 30 November, Johns and other prisoners were loaded into trucks and driven to Strasbourg and then across the lines near Nancy. There was a period of delay while he was debriefed. Then, on 23 December, he embarked at Calais for Dover.

After crossing the Channel in a terrific gale, I arrived home on Christmas Day, causing a small sensation, for although I did not know it, I had simply been reported 'missing' and given up for dead. When I walked in at the back door, dressed in odd bits of old French uniform, the parlourmaid who first saw me let out a yell, dropped the saucepan of potatoes she was just lifting off the range, and flopped down in a faint. I must have looked an odd sort of ghost, if that's what she took me for. Anyway, having been nearly starved to death, for months, I certainly tucked away some pudding that day …[29]

The Reverend John Hunt did not let the return of his 'war hero' son-in-law pass without some form of celebration. He invited all the children of Little Dunham to a firework display in the rectory garden to celebrate Johns' return. But the display did not go off as expected. A spark inadvertently exploded all the fireworks before the display, with Johns trying his best to stamp them out.[30]

To Johns, now with a wife and a two-year-old son to support, the peace was somewhat bewildering. It was his own attitude that he described when writing an introduction to his serial 'Winged

Menace', which was retitled in book form *The Cruise of the Condor*.

To officers of Biggles' type the Declaration of Peace – the end of the Great War – came as a curious shock. Their first reaction was a sense of emptiness and unreality. It seemed that everything, their own lives and the world in which they moved, had stopped suddenly.

For months, or even years, they had lived at high tension, every organ of their bodies working at full pressure. They lived entirely in the present with no thought of the future, which was, of course, the only possible way to face the grim conditions of air warfare.

At 11 a.m. on November 11, 1918, the only life they had known since they had left school (in many cases) ceased abruptly, and a new era opened before them. To expect them to settle down to the humdrum routine of a peace-time existence was out of the question.

Their tired nerves craved for action, and they sought it anywhere and everywhere that it might be found.[31]

But for Bill Johns where was that excitement to be found?

8

THE RECRUITING OFFICER

The war over, many sailors, soldiers and airmen were pressing for early demobilisation to get home. Bill Johns, however, was reluctant to return to a job as sanitary inspector and resume his studies to become a surveyor. Although he had hated the horrors of war, service life had shown him an alternative, more exciting life style. He wanted to remain in the Royal Air Force. But all the armed forces were now being run down to peacetime establishments and No. 55 Squadron in January 1919 had already been reduced to a cadre and was to be disbanded within the year.

Within a few weeks Johns had managed to get a posting to 59 Wing, a training unit forming part of 12 Training Group, which was comprised of Training Depot Stations Nos 56, 57 and 58; No. 59 Training Squadron; three squadron cadres Nos 209, 210 and 213; and an Engine and Aeroplane Repair Section. In mid-January 2nd Lieutenant Johns reported to 59 Wing's headquarters at Cranwell as a flying instructor and his career as a pilot seemed to have come full circle. Life at Cranwell was fairly quiet after the hazards of war, but flying was never without its dangers. Remembering his own crashes and others he had witnessed, Johns wrote, years later:

... to this day I can 'feel' the horrible silence that suddenly descends on the tarmac, or in the officers' mess, when it happens.

I think the worst thing of that sort I ever saw was at Cranwell, some years ago, when a Bristol Fighter with an instructor and pupil on board got into difficulties at a high altitude. With a lot of other fellows I was on the tarmac, and the first intimation we had of the impending tragedy was when a dreadful sound like a distant moan was borne to our ears. Looking up, we saw a Bristol coming down almost vertically, engine full on. We knew at once that something was wrong, for only a madman would dive a machine at such colossal speed. I expected its wings to tear off at any moment; yet, curiously enough, they hung on. The moan became a howl as the machine neared the earth, and it must have been travelling in the region of five hundred miles an hour when it hit the ground. Never for an instant did it look like coming out of its dive. There was a sound like a forest of trees falling together; then silence. What happened to cause such a shocking crash will never be known.[1]

There were a number of Japanese pupil pilots training there to form the nucleus of the Japanese air service. Johns did not think much of their capabilities as fighter-pilots. 'I can't say just what was wrong with them, but I can never imagine them being first class air fighters.'[2] During the Second World War he was to change his mind.

Johns' posting at Cranwell only lasted until 11 April 1919. No. 59 Wing was to be disbanded in the autumn. He was then transferred to the Unemployed List. It was tantamount to demobilisation − there was simply no job in the Royal Air Force that he could be given. The Air Ministry Weekly Orders for 1919 states: 'Officers who are placed on the Unemployed List have no claim to pay and allowances, nor have they any service liability other than recall in the event of a national emergency.' Johns returned to Little Dunham to live at the vicarage with Maude and Jack in a very depressed mood. He now spent most of his days painting, having taken up his hobby for the first time since the outbreak of war. His subjects were mostly aeroplanes.

Johns' unemployment added to the tensions already existing at the Little Dunham vicarage. His marriage was breaking down. Since the birth of their son, Maude had never been well, and now continuous aches and pains had developed into acute arthritis. Jack, too, was a delicate and even sickly child. Maude was thirty-seven and Johns was only twenty-six − illness and age were creating a barrier between them. More importantly, like so many other young men, Johns had been changed by his wartime experiences. Besides giving him a new maturity and toughness, the war had widened his horizons and he could no longer be content to settle down to become a provincial surveyor. It seemed as if his longing to do something with his life would only be satisfied by an RAF career. Now it seemed that was denied him and he was morose and moody. The months he spent at Little Dunham painting or caring for his pets were not happy. His son, Jack, wrote:

... he spent most of his time in taming birds. In a special loft he kept jackdaws, hawks and owls, of all sizes and tempers, some of them remarkably tame. One owl, named Algy, actually went free outside, but came on hearing a particular call from his owner.

When he returned to the Royal Air Force he was obliged to allow all these pets to become wild again, which they did, all expect the tamest jackdaw, who came to a sudden end in the jaws of Tango. I heard a lot about Tango. A nice little terrier, but he developed a bad habit of biting people, and in the end was 'bumped off' by an infuriated gamekeeper.[3]

Between painting and attending to his pets, Johns continued to press the Air Force for re-employment, but it was not until twenty months later, on 23 November 1920, that he was informed that he would be reinstated on the Active List for a Short Service Commission of three years and promoted to the new RAF rank of flying officer, the equivalent of a full lieutenant. His posting was a non-flying one – he was to join the Inspectorate of Recruiting based at 4 Henrietta Street in London's Covent Garden. Filled with hope for the future, Johns – with Maude and Jack – took a flat at Lancaster Gate.[4] Although delighted to be back in the RAF, he later recalled: 'When, one day, at the Air Ministry, Colonel Blomfield, Inspector of Recruiting, grabbed me for his Interviewing Officer, I said farewell to life and prepared for a lingering death from sheer boredom. As a flying officer with little imagination, I could think of no worse fate.'[5]

Johns found that his work gave him insight into the economic realities of the time, with mass unemployment of former servicemen. Within a week of taking up his appointment at the Henrietta Street depot, he had recruited a former colonel and a brigade major into the ranks. A friend from the past, whom Johns calls Captain B of No. 110 Squadron, walked into the depot. Johns had known him as a POW in Germany. The ex-pilot was in a bad way; for six days he had existed on a penny-bun a day and had been sleeping in St Martin's Crypt. Unfortunately, there was a rigid rule forbidding the enlistment of former officers of the RAF, RFC or RNAS into the ranks of the RAF – although former army and naval officers could be so enlisted. Johns gave the man some money from his own pocket, but it was a practice he eventually had to stop. 'There were far too many hard luck stories, so I just had to harden my heart like a bank manager and learn how to say "no".'[6]

But the fate of those ex-servicemen was something he could not forget or forgive. Later he made the hero of his first full-length story, *Mossyface*, a penniless ex-officer, and when he wrote a series of novels about another former RFC pilot, Steeley Delaroy, he made his hero embark on a career of crime in order to give away the proceeds to the poor and needy, especially to men who had fought in France and their dependants. Steeley defended his actions to his friend Tubby, maintaining that those who had actually done the 'dirty work' on the battle fronts had been treated shamefully by the Government. When he instanced his own case, he was speaking for them all:

'Tubby, without any false modesty, I did all that was in my power to do in France, did I not? Day after day I put my life in the hands of Fate, regardless of whether it was taken or spared.'
'You did.'
'Yet those who did not lift a finger would have seen me starve to death in the gutters of London without one moment's regret or care. Indeed, I did very nearly starve to death. Yet all I asked for was work, a means of earning a livelihood in any capacity in the country I had done my little bit to save. It was denied me. Is *that* fair?'[7]

Steeley, like Captain B, had been reduced to eating one roll a day and sleeping in St Martin's Crypt.

'One day,' Johns recalled, 'a thin, pale-faced chap walked in. There was something so off-hand about his manner, almost amounting to insolence, that I took an instinctive dislike to him. I had got to know the type. He was "different" from the other recruits and he was letting me know.'[8] The man gave his name as John Hume Ross but in reality he was Thomas Edward Lawrence – Lawrence of Arabia. The date was 28 August 1922.

The history of the enlistment of T. E. Lawrence in the RAF as Aircraftsman Ross (No. 352087) is well known, mainly through Lawrence's own version of it given in his book *The Mint*. According to him, and to subsequent biographies based on his account, he was down on his luck and joined the RAF under the name of Ross. His true identity was not discovered until he was spotted by an observant officer and discharged in January 1923. Two and a half years later, he was allowed to re-enlist as Shaw, a name under which he had served in the Tank Corps in the intervening period. Lawrence was killed in a motorcycle accident on 19 May 1935, and as early as July 1935 Johns put the record straight about what really happened to Ross/Lawrence. '... More rubbish has been written about that than anything else I know. The old story of how Lawrence was recognised by a particularly observant officer some time after he had joined the service has been told so many times that it has become legendary. Don't believe a word of it.'[9]

Lawrence gives a vivid and moving account of his experiences at the Recruiting Office in *The Mint*:

God, this is awful. Hesitating for two hours up and down a filthy street, lips and hands and knees tremulously out of control, my heart pounding in fear of that little door through which I must go to join up. Try sitting a moment in the churchyard? That's caused it. The nearest lavatory, now. Oh yes, of course, under the church. What was Baker's story about the cornice?

A penny; which leaves me fifteen. Buck up, old seat-wiper; I can't tip you and I'm urgent. Won by a short head. My right shoe is burst along the welt and my trousers are growing fringes. One reason that taught me I wasn't a man of action was this routine melting of the bowels before a crisis. However, now we end it. I'm going straight up and in.

All smooth so far. They are gentle-spoken to us, almost sorry. Won't you walk into my parlour? Wait upstairs for medical exam? 'Righto!' This sodden pyramid of clothes upon the floor is a sign of a dirtier man than me in front. My go next? Everything off? (Naked we come into the RAF). Ross? 'Yes, that's me.'

Officers, two of them ...

'D'you smoke?'

Not much, Sir.

'Well, cut it out. See?'

Six months back, it was, my last cigarette. However, no use giving myself away.

'Nerves like a rabbit.' The Scotch-voiced doctor's hard fingers go hammer, hammer, hammer over the loud box of my ribs. I must be pretty hollow.

'Turn over: get up; stand under here; make yourself as tall as you can: he'll just do five feet six, Mac: chest – say 34. Expansion – by Jove, 38. That'll do. Now jump: higher: lift your right leg: hold it there: cough: all right: on your toes: arms straight in front of you: open your fingers wide: hold them so: turn around: bend over. Hullo, what the hell's those marks? Punishment?' 'No Sir, more like persuasion, Sir, I think.' Face, neck, chest, getting hot.

'H ... m ... m ... that would account for the nerves.' His voice sounds softer. 'Don't put that down, Mac. Say *Two parallel scars on ribs.* What were they, boy?'

Superficial wounds, Sir.

'Answer my questions.'

A barbed-wire tear, over a fence.

'H ... m ... m ... and how long have you been short of food?'

(O Lord, I never thought he'd spot that. Since April I've been taking off my friends what meals I dared and that my shame would let me take. I'd haunt the Duke of York steps at lunch-time, so as to turn back with someone to his club for the food whose necessity nearly choked me. Put a good face on it; better.)

Gone a bit short the last three months, Sir. How my throat burns!

'More like six' ... came back the growl. The worst of telling lies naked is that the red shows all the way down. A long pause, me shivering in disgrace. He stares so gravely, and my eyes are watering. (Oh, it hurts: I wish I hadn't taken this job on.)

At last. 'All right: get back into your clothes. You aren't as good as we want but after a few weeks at the Depot you'll pull up all right.' Thank you very much, Sir. 'Best of luck, boy,' from Mac. Grunt from the kinder-spoken one. Here's the vegetable market again, not changed. I'm still shaking everyway, but anyhow I've done it. Isn't there a Fuller's down the street? I've half a mind to blow my shilling on a coffee. Seven years now before I need think of winning a meal.[10]

What actually happened was rather different.

Sergeant Major Gee, who was assisting Johns, showed in Ross, but signalled to him that the man seemed a suspicious character. Johns surreptitiously went through the photographs of criminals, who, it was thought, might try to hide in the services. Ross had no identity papers on him so Johns told him to go away and obtain a birth certificate and three character references. Ross volunteered details of his birth and then went off to obtain the necessary credentials. While he was away Johns contacted Somerset House (then the headquarters of the Registrar of Births, Deaths and Marriages) and quickly learnt that the details were false. Sometime later, Ross returned with the required references – but Johns soon discovered that these were false too. He challenged Ross, who admitted that they were fakes, and consequently Johns turned him out of the Recruiting Depot.

Within the hour, the would-be aircraftsman was back again, this time accompanied by an Air Ministry messenger, who handed Johns an order requesting Ross's immediate enlistment.

'The signature at the foot of the minute sheet was quite enough ...' Johns wrote.[11] Ross was despatched to the medical examination room with his forms marked 'special case'. However, a few minutes later the medical officer – Squadron Leader Valerie – buzzed Johns on the intercom and asked him to go to the examination room. '... there stood Ross in his birthday suit. One glance at his scarred back ... Ross was turned down on medical grounds.'[12] Ross began to throw his weight about, but to no avail – 'the doctors refused to pass as fit a man who was not up to the medical standard laid down.'[13] At last the Air Ministry sent a special doctor to sign Ross's medical form, and the new aircraftsman was finally accepted. By this time, however, Johns, as Recruiting Officer, felt really angry about the whole affair and went to protest about it to his Commanding Officer. The latter looked him in the eye and said, 'Watch your step. This man is Lawrence of Arabia. Get him in, or you'll get your bowler hat!'[14] Colonel Lawrence's identity was no secret in the RAF.

By this time everyone on the station knew who Ross was. Certainly Lawrence knew that I knew, because I had a long talk with him while he was waiting for the train to take him to Uxbridge. When he went he left me with the memory of a cold, clammy handshake.

I then rang up Flight Lieutenant Nelson, my opposite number at Uxbridge, to warn him of who was on the way, for by this time Lawrence was making it clear that he had no time for junior officers. Lawrence himself soon saw to it that everyone knew who he was.[15]

Even before Johns had contacted him, Nelson had been wary of Ross; he complained bitterly to Johns on the telephone about the new recruit, 'who's not only teaching me my job, but is telling me where I'll step off if I'm not careful.' Johns duly uttered his warning, 'Watch your step, laddie; it's Lawrence of Arabia,' and that warning continued to echo round the service:

Lawrence went on, and wherever he went word of who he was preceded him: for officers are officers and, I hope, gentlemen, and no one was going to let down a comrade by failing to put him wise as to the real identity of the aircraftsman 2nd class who spent weekends with Cabinet Ministers.[16]

Johns retold this story to Phillip Knightly and Colin Simpson while they were researching for their book *The Secret Lives of*

Lawrence of Arabia. They gave a final twist to the tale by being the first to reveal the extent of Lawrence's involvement in secret service work. They showed that no less a person than Sir Hugh Trenchard, then Chief of Air Staff, knew of Lawrence's plan to enlist and had delegated the job of overseeing it to his assistant, Air Vice-Marshal Sir Oliver Swann. It was Swann who chose the name of Ross, suggested the faked references and wrote to Lawrence to instruct him where he should go to enlist. A copy of Swann's top secret instructions were sent to the Henrietta Street Recruiting Depot five days before Lawrence was due to arrive. Johns denied failing to carry out these instructions and it seems that, because of some administrative failure, Swann's orders were not passed on to him.[17]

Johns ran into similar trouble on another occasion, this time when 'the son of a gardener of a Very Important Person'[18] came into the depot. 'His references were weighed down with coats-of-arms and what-nots. The signatures were those of princes and peers.' The potential recruit was so impossible, however, that Johns rejected him. 'Within the hour I thought the end of the world had come. Air-Commodores and Air Vice-Marshals poured into the Depot from the Air Ministry. In short, there was hell to pay. This youth had apparently gone straight back to his palace and reported me. I was told to hold myself ready for arrest.'[19] The recruit duly passed on to Uxbridge where, according to Johns, observing a dose of 'square bashing', the young man broke ranks and fled. 'We never saw him again. Which, I fancy, was just as well for everyone concerned.'

From time to time, the Recruiting Depot was supplied with details of men who might try to enlist under false names to hide from the police. On one occasion Johns spotted a wanted man and sent him to the medical examination room. While he was there, Johns rang the police. Two detectives arrived. The man came back into Johns' office.

The wretched victim, all unconscious of what was waiting for him, marched up to my desk. He was smiling. Then the 'tecs stepped forward. One of them tapped him on the shoulder in the approved style. The smile faded. The blood drained out of his face, leaving it grey. He looked at me with that hurt look in his eyes of a dog that has just been kicked. Then he smiled again and walked away. I reckon I felt worse than he did. That was the last time I gave a man in charge. Occasionally, if things were quiet, I'd tell a fellow his real name. That would be quite enough. Once in a while, if there was nobody about, they'd linger for a few minutes and tell me about it.[20]

One man, wanted for assault, explained why he had committed his crime. Johns felt so strongly that the man was in the right that he gave him some money and told him to go back and finish the job. 'It was talking to fellows like this that first gave me the idea that the law might well be leavened with a little spice of humanity. No law will ever alter human reactions to primary emotions. At least, I hope not. The human race will be a lot of poor saps if and when that time comes.'[21]

But life was not all serious at the London Recruiting Depot. A large number of people used to call in with collecting boxes for various charities and philanthropic causes, always assured of obtaining a few shillings from the officers on duty. Johns decided that such donations were making inroads into everyone's pay and gave orders to the NCOs to refuse to admit anyone except service personnel or bona fide recruits. One day two Sisters of Mercy called and were not easily disposed of. They waited until the NCO's back was turned and slipped in and upstairs. The first room they entered was the medical waiting room in which a score of naked recruits were waiting to be examined.

The first thing I knew about this was a wild scream of – well, I don't know what. Surprise, perhaps. No matter. There was a scream. Dashing to the stairs I was in time to witness the unusual spectacle of an elderly lady coming down four at a time. The other one had swooned on the threshold, causing the troops-to-be no small entertainment – they not knowing whether to go to her assistance or bolt. There was a row. The ladies complained. I was blamed, of course, for the whole thing.[22]

Johns says that during this period he was also able to do some flying. Although a highly unusual proceeding, according to the RAF Records Department, Johns says he flew in the Hendon Air Display. He claimed that he had 'taken part in the display several times',[23] and certainly he was on the organising committee for 1927. Johns says it was while practising for the display that he had his last crash.

... I have only had one crash worth talking about since. That was in a

DH9A practising for the RAF Display. The squadron was doing formation flying, in line abreast, that is, in a straight line across the sky, wing-tip to wing-tip. I was at the left hand end of the line.

The trouble started when the leader commenced to turn to the left. Now, when this manoeuvre is performed, it stands to reason that if the machines are to keep in line the outside flank man must fly a lot faster than the inside man. In the infantry the inside man marks time while the outside man has to double round in order to keep the line straight. That's all very well on the ground, but an aeroplane can't mark time − a fact that was quickly brought to my notice. I flew as slowly as I could, but there came a time when I couldn't fly any slower, and I was left to choose between stalling and ramming the fellow next on my right. I stalled, and *nearly* had sufficient height to come out of it.

But not quite.

In flying, a few inches can make a lot of difference, and this case provides a good example. A few inches more altitude and I should have got away with it; a few inches less and it would have been − well, goodbye. As it was, my wheels actually touched the ground as I came out. For perhaps two seconds the undercart stood up to the strain, but it wasn't designed for that sort of treatment, and announced its displeasure by spreading itself over the landscape. The machine followed suit. So did I.

I woke up about three days later with the world all rosy red. Talking about 'looking at the world through rose-coloured glasses'! I didn't need any glasses. I damaged the blood vessels behind my eyes, or something of the sort − so they told me − so that I seemed to live in a perpetual sunset. And it wasn't so good as it sounds, believe me! I've hated sunsets ever since.[24]

Johns also states that during part of 1924 he was posted on operational duties in Iraq and India. This is not confirmed by the RAF. 'Although a thorough search of the records has been made, there is no indication in Flying Officer Johns' records that he served in either India or the Middle East between 1921 and 1925. According to his records, he was stationed in the UK for that period.'[25] Yet Johns is very specific. 'When the Waziristan operations were going on along the North-West Frontier of India in 1924, I drifted into the Frontier Aerodrome at Miranshah ...'[26] He adds: '... we dropped a few bombs on the tribesmen who were kicking up all the trouble in the hills ...' In an account of 'The Air Patrol of the North-West Frontier' he described a disaster that occurred 'during my flying days in India'. Two machines flew into a hillside in a mist, near the RAF station of Dardini.[27] Other references are casually scattered amongst his writings.

When I was in India in 1924, a Bristol Fighter pilot was attacked [by a bird of prey]. The gunner fired at the eagle, or vulture – I forget which it was – but was unable to hit the swiftly wheeling mark. The bird finally swooped into the prop. no doubt thinking it was attacking its adversary's head. The bird was killed instantly and the pilot, forced to land in mountainous country, was uninjured.[28]

He also recalls:

Once flying in India over some of the worst country in the world my engine cut out dead. Just when a crash seemed inevitable, it picked up again and I got a bit nearer my destination. Then it cut out again.[29]

The engine kept cutting out due to magneto trouble, but Johns eventually reached his destination.

Johns mentions memories of being stationed in Iraq, describing how he stood on mounds of earth that were once Nibeah – now Mosut.

When one sees the massive bricks and stones of which these old cities were built, one cannot help wondering how long it would take our cities to fall to pieces if there was a great calamity.[30]

He felt:

Iraq is, I think, the most depressing place on earth. There is something inspiring, even about the breathtaking infinity of the Sahara and the stupendous grandeur of the Himalayas, but in the barren land of Departed Greatness one only feels an overwhelming sadness, an aching sympathy, as one always must for beauty that is no more.[31]

In another article Johns mentions in passing that he was stationed in Baghdad,[32] and when Johns' story 'The Raid' was published in *Wings*, a John Hamilton magazine,[33] the editor introduced it by saying that the tale was set in Iraq, a country Johns 'knows well', and that after the war 'he was posted to Iraq, where he served for some years'! Although this is impossible, and some of Johns' dating may well be suspect, on balance it seems

likely that the RAF records have failed to record these postings of
Johns. A number of his paintings from this period are of India
and Iraq, a fact which gives further support to his statements.
Some of these pictures were reproduced in the *Illustrated London
News* such as 'Flying in the East: Iraq and the Indian Frontier' in
the 1 January 1927 issue; and 'Aircraft on Empire Outposts:
Indian Frontier and Iraq Machines' in the 18 June 1927 issue.
Certainly, there were several postings missing from Johns' earlier
RAF record which have had to be confirmed by other sources.

Johns had originally been accepted back into the RAF on a
three-year short service commission in November 1920. In 1923
he was informed that he had been selected for an extension of
four years' service on the Active List and he was ordered to open
an RAF Recruiting Depot in Birmingham. One of his new duties
was to tour round the Midland towns with an NCO putting up
recruiting posters. The NCO was 'Navvy' Johnson, who had
been a boxing champion in a Guards regiment before transferring
to the RAF. On one occasion they went to Luton in a Crossley
tender. Johns sat in the tender while Johnson, with ladder and
paste, proceeded to stick up a recruiting poster.

A crowd collected. Just as Johnson got the first poster nicely in
position, a man walked under the ladder and stripped it off. Johnson
looked pained but, without speaking, took out another poster and pasted
it up. Whereupon the same man, encouraged by the titter from his
companions, repeated his tearing-off act. The crowd roared. I saw
Johnson change colour. His jaw stuck out like a door knocker, and I
knew that Something Was Going to Happen. Very slowly and
deliberately he took out yet another poster, and very carefully pasted it in
place. The joker moved forward.

Now there is an old saying about 'third time lucky'. But this was the
exception that proved the rule. Johnson was ready. As the joker's hand
made contact with the corner of the poster, Johnson's paste-brush (a big
professional looking instrument) well loaded with paste, flew round like
a back-firing prop and caught the culprit square across the face with a
smack that sounded like a bullet going through a spar. The recipient did
a sharp flick roll and finished on his back in the gutter. That did it.
Pandemonium broke loose. Somehow I managed to get Johnson into the
car, and away we went, carving a way through the crowd. This little
affair, and the enquiry that followed it, caused me a lot of trouble.[34]

Johns spent over a year in Birmingham and it was while he

was there that he met and fell in love with Doris Leigh. After Johns had rejoined the Air Force, his fragile relationship with Maude had finally broken down. A last attempt to live together as a family in London had failed, and Maude and Jack had returned to her father's vicarage at Little Dunham. Johns had asked Maude for a divorce but, according to her sister Kathleen, it was the Reverend John Hunt who would not hear of this.

> In those days for a man to leave his wife and child was beyond the pale, and when folk married it really was 'till death us do part.'
>
> My father was a Victorian – stern – but gentle disciplinarian and quite intolerant of anything which did not fit in with his code of conduct. A narrow outlook, of course, but that is how it was in his generation.
>
> Divorce for his daughter was unthinkable and my sister (they were devoted to one another) would never go against his wishes. She and her son returned from London to live at the Rectory and she remained the Captain's legal wife until her death in 1961.[35]

Johns had moved into a private hotel in Hackney Road, Edgbaston, next door to a large house where a family called Leigh lived. Mrs Florence Beatrice Leigh was a widow, whose husband Alfred Broughton Leigh, a cotton merchant, had died at the beginning of the war. Shortly after his death, Mrs Leigh had moved her family from King's Norton, Worcester, to Edgbaston. She had four children: Doris Mary, born on 6 September 1900; Marjorie, born on 4 February 1906; Stanley Howard, born on 16 July 1909 and Elsa, born on 6 January 1910. Johns used to play tennis on a court at the back of the hotel and would often see the Leigh family in the garden of their house. He was especially attracted by the pretty, 24-year-old Doris. Trying to think of a way of meeting the girl, Johns came up with the idea of hitting a tennis ball into the Leigh's garden and then knocking at the door to ask for it back. His ruse worked. The door was opened by Doris. 'They were immediately attracted to each other,' recalled Marjorie, her sister. 'It was love at first sight. Thereafter, Bill proceeded to knock many tennis balls into the garden to continue his meetings with Doris. When things became serious between them he explained that he was married but separated from his wife. He was scrupulously honest in this. My mother was upset by the fact that he could not obtain a divorce but accepted matters because Doris and Bill were simply made for each other.'[36]

In late December 1924 Johns received a new posting to open another RAF Recruiting Depot at Ellison Place, Newcastle – the depot was later moved to New Bridge Street. 'I found myself outside a big, empty, rambling old barrack of a place that had once been a lunatic asylum or a nursing home, I forget which.'[37] Johns had not arranged for alternative accommodation that New Year's Eve, and so he installed himself on a camp bed. He was awoken by the noise of rats! 'These rats sounded to me as if they were dancing with clogs on; occasionally stopping to tear lumps out of the floor!' The bed collapsed and he had run out of matches. He had to spend the rest of the night on the floor in the dark with rats crawling about. His assistant, Sergeant Sullivan, arrived the next day and took charge of clearing out the rats.

Johns and Doris Leigh had reached a decision about their future before Johns left Birmingham for Newcastle. As there was no prospect of his obtaining a divorce, nor of ever being reconciled with his wife, they decided to wait no longer before starting life together. Doris – Dol, as Johns always called her – joined him in Newcastle and they set up home in Whitley Bay. Until Maude's death in 1961, Johns continued to pay for his wife's upkeep and, due to her continuing illness, the employment of two nurses.[38] He maintained friendly relations with Maude's sister Kathleen and saw his son occasionally. In 1924 Jack was still a weak child, suffering from diabetes, although he was now able to attend school at Beacondale in Norwich.

On 1 August 1925 Johns left the Inspectorate of Recruiting and on 5 October 1925 was posted to the Record Office at Ruislip. During this time Doris opened a guest house at Gerrard's Cross to help supplement their income. On 3 September 1926 Johns was transferred to the Headquarters Air Defence (Great Britain). During this time he began to paint seriously, specialising in aviation illustrations, and as early as 1924 he had begun to try his hand at writing articles. In March 1924 he produced a piece about racing entitled 'Lincoln – 1924 by a Punter', signing it William Earl, a pseudonym he was later to change to William Earle. Whether he managed to sell this effort is uncertain; it was his artwork that was beginning to find a ready market.

Captain Bruce S. Ingram OBE, MC was editor of the *Illustrated London News*, one of a group of illustrated papers which included the *Sketch*, *Graphic*, *Bystander*, *Sphere*, *Tatler*, *Eve* and others.

He began to buy aviation illustrations from Johns on a regular basis, and by the issue for 2 July 1927 he was describing the artist as 'our specialist W. E. Johns'. Johns' first big spread of pictures, four full-colour prints covering pages 9–10, appeared in the *Illustrated London News*, 1 January 1927.

Johns left the Air Defence Headquarters on 3 March 1927. He was approaching the end of his seven-year commission, but the prospect was not daunting, for in selling paintings and aviation illustrations, Johns had discovered an alternative and agreeable way of making a living. With Doris giving him her wholehearted support, he determined to become a specialist aviation artist, selling material to magazines.

The eighth Royal Air Force Air Display was to be held at Hendon on Saturday, 2 July and Flying Officer Johns was invited to serve on the organising committee. He was commissioned to design a poster for the display that would also appear on the front of the official programme, and his especial task as one of the organisers was to attempt to assemble a parade of fighting aircraft from the First World War.

Some years ago, while acting on the Committee of the Royal Air Force Display, I endeavoured to locate as many 'veterans' as possible, with a view to arranging a display of them at Hendon on Display Day, for comparison with the latest types. Alas! I was reluctantly compelled to admit that with one or two exceptions, they did not exist. There are a few, very few, scattered about; perhaps ten all told. There is a Camel, an SE5 or two (Major Savage uses them for skywriting), a B.E. and strangely enough an old Bristol Scout that I discovered in a motor wrecker's yard. There are, I am told, about half-a-dozen war machines in a hangar at Cardington, but I have not seen them so I cannot say what they are. I understand that they belong to the Trustees of the Imperial War Museum, who have placed them there for safe storage. Perhaps they will one day find a home in a British aeronautical museum.[39]

As well as carrying out his official duties in connection with the display, Johns found time to sell three pages of sepia and full-colour illustrations to the *Illustrated London News* for the 2 July issue on the display. He also wrote long captions to his pictures, pointing out the main features of the entertainment: two squadrons of bombers (DH9s, Hyderabads and Vimys) endeavour to attack London and 'after a thrilling battle are turned back by fighters of Nos 19 and 29 Squadron (Grebes) which form part of the air defences of Great Britain. Casualties occur on both sides: machines spin down out of control and one bursts into flames, the crew escaping by parachute (that is, if weather permits) ... the action begins with the approach of the "enemy" machines, flying in squadron formation from the direction of Chipping Barnet, while some of the defenders (No. 29 Squadron) arrive from the south. Heavy anti-aircraft fire opens on the enemy.'

The air display provided a happy climax at the end of his RAF career. On 15 October 1927 Flying Officer Johns relinquished his commission on completion of his service and was transferred to the RAF Reserve Class 'C', being allowed to retain his rank. He and Doris had rented a small cottage at Lingfield, Sussex, and it was here that Johns planned to establish his studio and begin his new career, at the age of thirty-four, as an aviation illustrator.

9

ARTIST TO EDITOR

Johns could not have picked a better time to establish himself as an authority on aviation. Public interest in the subject had never been so great. The year that Johns left the RAF was the year that Charles Lindbergh crossed the Atlantic single-handed in a one-engine monoplane. It was the year when Britain won the coveted Schneider Trophy, the pilot being Flight Lieutenant S. M. Kinkead DSO, DSC, DFC, flying a Gloucester Napier. He was killed six months later while attempting a new speed record. Another member of the British Schneider Trophy team that year was Harry Schofield, later co-author with Johns of a popular flying manual. The public's imagination was also captured at this time by the developments in passenger-carrying airships, and it was in 1928 that the ill-fated R101 took to the skies. It was supposed to offer the most luxurious form of air travel, but when Johns went aboard the airship he felt troubled. 'In spite of its size I got no feeling of security,' he wrote.[1]

Near the cottage Johns had rented in Lingfield was a larger one which had been occupied by a retired colonel who had recently died. Johns decided to move into the larger cottage and establish his studio there, and he invited Doris's family, then living in Hove, to move into the one he and Doris had vacated. Doris's young brother, Howard Leigh, now eighteen years old, had just left school and was passionately interested in art. Johns allowed him to join him in his studio, encouraging the boy to become an aviation artist. Howard received no formal training at art school, only the advice and encouragement of Johns during those early days at the Lingfield cottage studio. Yet during the 1930s Howard Leigh was a much sought-after specialist in aviation illustration and he is still highly regarded. Readers of Johns' early Biggles books, published by John Hamilton and the Oxford University Press, will know his accurate and graceful frontispieces in these volumes.[2]

According to Johns' son, Jack, who was a frequent visitor, the cottage at Lingfield was delightful. It was 400 years old and thatched, with low eaves. It had an extensive garden, and Johns was a keen and knowledgeable gardener. He had started to gather his formidable expertise after the war.

Early in 1919, when I returned home after four years of war, I found the gardener still digging away. Not for some time did I learn that he had been to the war, and been wounded several times. He had served in France, Gallipoli and India. He had been at the battle of Goza and had chased Sennusi in Upper Egypt. He knew nothing about these places except the outlandish plants he saw growing there ... I still carry in my mind a picture of an incredible carpet of flowers coming up through the melting snow at a wild spot on the borders of Albania and Serbia, about forty miles in front of a little village called Oriovika, in Macedonia, which was the last point of civilisation I touched before disappearing into the wilderness. Alas! I knew nothing about gardening until after the war, so all I brought back with me was malaria.[3]

Now his stocky figure in French corduroy trousers, Canadian shirt and Basque beret could be seen working away at all hours and seasons. He was especially enthusiastic about his Alpine rockery. He loved old-fashioned, sweet-scented flowers, and had doubts about hybrids. After service life, a garden had its own excitements – the enemies were sparrows, ferociously slashing his polyanthus, or the rabbit on the gentian bed, 'its jaws working ominously'. Johns grabbed a gun and fired, but his aim had deteriorated over the years and it was his best rake, propped against a plum tree, that flew in halves. Doris was not very sympathetic when Johns leapt out of bed in the early dawn to chase a cow away that had strayed into a border and was eating his best delphiniums.[4]

Life at Lingfield meant that pets could be part of the household, and with a place of his own Johns could start to build up his invaluable collection of aviation material. Jack wrote:

Imagine an air museum in a small, beautifully furnished library, add a few stacks of papers and lots of letters, a big office chair, piles of press photographs, and a typewriter, and you have a picture of my uncle's study. Here he works, surrounded by air and travel books of every age and description. From the walls, portraits of famous English, French and

German war aces gaze gravely down; in between these hang maps showing every air-line in the world.

One rarely enters this fascinating study without meeting the Faithful Three. In a chair beside him, or occupying the arms of his own chair, or sitting cheekily on the desk as he writes, are three beautiful little Sealyhams – Susan, Bert and Chump, his constant companions through thick and thin. Wherever he goes, whatever he does, they will try to be with him. They enjoy more privileges than most people but then they are not always asking questions.[5]

But dogs could present their own problems. One autumn morning Johns was horrified to see that every white label naming a plant had been pulled up and scattered over the lawn.

No need to seek the culprit. She was there, even now throwing another with the rest. It was Dinah, my wife's new Scottie pup.

At the roar that left my lips my own three Sealyhams fled, tails down. But not Miss Dinah ...[6]

Johns had already established himself with Illustrated Newspapers with his *Illustrated London News* illustrations, and articles on aviation in its sister paper *The Graphic*. But new markets were opening up for aviation illustrations and articles, especially among publications for children and adolescents. In particular, the Amalgamated Press had a group of juvenile publications which greatly favoured articles and stories with aviation themes. On 11 February 1928 Amalgamated Press launched *The Modern Boy*, a 2d weekly for older boys, which gave very significant coverage to aviation, with the famous pioneer aviator and writer Sir Alan Cobham writing a serial from the first issue onwards. Johns began to sell his aviation illustrations to the magazine in 1929 and soon short, chatty articles were appearing by the 'air expert'; by the end of 1930 'our air expert' was named as Flying Officer W. E. Johns.

From the 27 December 1930 issue Johns began to contribute a regular aircraft spotter's column entitled 'What Plane Was That?' It started as a weekly column, but eventually became irregular, finally finishing with the 3 March 1932 issue. By this time he was also writing full-length articles for the magazine, consisting mainly of flying reminiscences, which began with a piece entitled 'The Plane Smashers' in the 6 December 1930 issue. This article was billed as being 'by a flying man who is also a well-known artist'.

The work provided Johns with a steady and respectable income and he found he could still indulge in holidays abroad. Since the war he had become enamoured of foreign travel, and he and Doris had been frequent visitors to France during his leave periods. In 1929, however, Doris and Bill Johns decided to undertake a trip to Africa. They went to what was then French Algeria. Years later Johns still recalled the trip with pleasure, especially a week at Sidi Feruch.

In February and March of 1929 my wife and I were vagabonding along the coast under an azure sky, striding along the broad untrodden sands that sweep round in a magnificent *coup d'oeil* to Tipasa forty kilometres distant. We stopped at the tavern, the Hotel de la Plage, for food. It was so good that I can only make animal noises now when I think of it. And there was wine, a vin rosé – but let us not talk of that. We stopped. Time, too, stopped, while we lay in the sun and slept, and ate, and drank, and dived in the sea for strange shells and again lay in the sun, and ate, and slept ... The dream ended, as all dreams must. It ended because I was down to my last fifty francs in the world, and could not bring myself to abuse the hospitality of friends who would have us stay. M. Velesid, a Greek doctor who had grown weary of trying to keep in step with a crazy world, and had retired with his charming Irish wife to Sidi Feruch. Where is he now, I wonder? And Emile, Parisian *apache*, and a murderer to boot. But, after all, he had only killed the man who made a pass at his wife, which is at least as pardonable as killing people one does not know. Emile, with *Fatalité* tattooed across his forehead. Where is he now? And M. le Maire, Monsieur Smith, an Englishman who had stopped at Sidi Feruch forty years before and had forgotten to go on ... What friends! What fun! *Mot de Cambronne!* What a life![7]

The memories of the holiday became sharper when Johns learnt that it was in this area that Anglo-American forces, commanded by American general Charles Ryder, made an amphibious assault on Vichy territory in October 1942. Of Emile, the ex-Parisian *apache* who had murdered his wife's lover, Johns said he was 'one of the most charming men I ever met'.[8] He had served for five years in the French penal regiment – the Battalion d'Afrique. 'With him I walked about North Africa'.

Returning to England, articles began to pour from his pen at an incredible rate. Even so, Johns still regarded himself as primarily an artist. From 7 March 1931 he was illustrating a serial by Percy F. Westerman, one of the major air fiction writers of the period. He was also doing several front covers for *The Modern Boy* and contributing illustrations for another Amalgamated Press publication, *Ranger*. Full-colour pictures of aircraft by Johns were given away in this magazine on 7 March and 14 March 1931.

Johns' protégé Howard Leigh was also achieving success with his aviation illustrations. His work was accepted for the front cover illustration of *The Modern Boy*'s 29 June 1931 issue, and he supplied another front cover a month later.

The young readers of *The Modern Boy* were certainly air-minded, and when the magazine's editors decided to produce *The Modern Boys' Book of Aircraft* they naturally turned to their own expert. Johns edited the book, also contributing seven signed articles and many unsigned pieces. Among the other contributors he used was Christopher St John Sprigg, a young writer who was beginning to attract attention, whose thrillers were to be highly acclaimed, and who would end his short career fighting for the Republicans in Spain a few years later. Johns also contributed three full-colour illustrations, including the frontispiece, and several black-and-white illustrations. By the time the volume came out in August 1931 he had edited an anthology of flying stories, both fiction and non-fiction, entitled *Wings: A Book of Flying Adventures*, in which he included two of his own articles. *Wings* was also published in August 1931 by John Hamilton, a company which had been established in 1925 by Charles H. Daniels and his wife, Mary. They had been directors of Brentanos Ltd, a British subsidiary of the American publishers and booksellers. John Hamilton, seeing the new enthusiasm for aviation, had begun to specialise in books with air subjects, and in the 1930s the company was established as the leading publisher of aviation books. Johns illustrated many of their titles, such as Covington Clark's *Desert Night* (1935).

Encouraged by his success as an author, Johns now tried his hand at a work of fiction, a 'penny-dreadful' type of thriller. He used a pseudonym – William Earle – and was successful in selling his manuscript to Mellifont Press Ltd, a firm which specialised in producing popular literature in paperback form. Johns' tale was called *Mossyface*. His hero, Captain James Margerson (nicknamed

Mossyface), is an ex-RAF officer who finds himself down on his luck after demobilisation at the end of the war. He is fortunately on the spot to save the lives of Professor Graham and his beautiful daughter, Mary, who are besieged in their country house by a gang of murderous crooks. The professor has a secret document showing the whereabouts of a ruined temple of ancient Egypt, somewhere in the Nubian desert, and the crooks are determined to get possession of it. Mossyface enters the service of the professor and proposes to search for the temple by aeroplane. It is a situation and an opening that Johns appears to have a particular fondness for, because he used it in three other books: *The Cruise of the Condor* (1933), *Biggles Hits the Trail* (1935) and *The Man Who Lost His Way* (1960). *Mossyface* was a competent piece of pulp literature, full of a succession of thrilling incidents and daring adventures told at a breathless pace. The tale, however, was too short for the usual Mellifont paperback format, taking up only 128 pages, so the publishers added another short story entitled *Hobson's Choice* by Esther Miller, bringing the book to 160 pages. With its publication in 1932 Johns could consider himself a writer of fiction as well as non-fiction.

Now that Johns had discovered his talent for writing, there was no holding back. Through 1931 he was contributing at least one article a week to *The Modern Boy* and, as their 'air expert', undertaking special trips on the magazine's behalf. In September of that year he went on a flight in a new type of passenger aircraft called a Hannibal. It was then the height of luxury for a civil aircraft and Johns headed his piece 'A Trip in a Flying Hotel'.[9] Johns had breakfast at his home in Lingfield at 7.30 am, was on the tarmac at Croydon at 9.15 am, and was at Le Bourget at 11.15 am watching a French air display. In those days it was the last word in fast travel and, Johns noted, the return fare was only £7 19s 6d.

Johns seemed to be bursting with ideas. He asked Flight Lieutenant Harry Schofield, who had flown as part of the winning 1927 British Schneider Trophy team and who was then the instructor of the Oxford University Air Squadron, to write a book with him. Johns' idea was to take advantage of the popular interest in aviation by producing a simplified flying course with illustrations. The result was *The Pictorial Flying Course* by Flt. Lt. H. M. Schofield and F/O W. E. Johns, which John Hamilton produced in May 1932. All the illustrations were by Johns. *The Field* called it 'a most ingenious book' and the *Popular Flying* reviewer said it was 'clear, concise and amazingly interesting'.[10] Certainly the public thought so, for during the 1930s the book was constantly in print as the bible of student pilots. A few months later, in November 1932, John Hamilton produced a companion volume to the book – this time written solely by Johns – *Fighting Planes and Aces*. It was illustrated by Howard Leigh, and gave accounts of First World War aircraft and the aces on both sides. 'The book not only makes intensely fascinating reading but also has historical value', commented the *Morning Post*.[11]

Surprisingly, in spite of all this literary output, Johns continued to produce paintings and illustrations. His work for John Hamilton included designing bookjackets as well as illustrating books, and he continued to sell material to magazines. However, as an illustrator, Johns was now being overshadowed by the young Howard Leigh, whose work was in constant demand by editors. Within the next year, Johns' career as an artist came virtually to an end, making way for his even more successful and far more lucrative career as a writer.

The year 1932 was an important one for Johns for two reasons: firstly, John Hamilton decided to launch a new aviation magazine, *Popular Flying*, aimed at the adult market, and asked Johns to edit it; secondly, it was the year when he wrote the first stories about Biggles, the most famous character he ever created.

According to Mrs Marjorie Ellis, it was Miss Glenda Graham who originally suggested that Johns should become involved in John Hamilton's plans to produce an aviation magazine.[12] Glenda Graham was an aviation enthusiast and ardent air traveller. In 1934 she was to marry Captain Hugh 'Tony' Spooner, a younger brother of a pioneer airwoman, Winifred Spooner, who had been killed in a crash. Captain Spooner, manager of flying operations at Misr-Airwork, Cairo, and a former chief instructor at the Montreal Light Aeroplane Club, was also killed in an aircraft accident a few months after the wedding. Glenda Graham became business and general manager of the new magazine. According to Johns, '... much of the success of *Popular Flying* has been due to her untiring efforts.'[13]

The first issue of *Popular Flying* took off on Wednesday, 16

March 1932, dated April, and published from Hamilton's offices at 32 Bloomsbury Street, London WC1. It was an instant and overwhelming success. In the second issue of the magazine, Johns wrote:

Before going to press with the first number of *Popular Flying*, we tried hard to find out just how much it would mean to people in the aeronautical world, and how ready the public were for a non-technical journal devoted entirely to aviation. We went to some pains to enquire what was most needed, likely to be of service to the industry and of interest to the ordinary reader. The question of how much space to devote to current events, pure fiction, civil and Service flying, and so on, presented difficulties which may work themselves out as we proceed.

Broadly speaking, *Popular Flying* will cover the whole field of aviation without necessarily segregating each section into separate departments. So far as current events are concerned we may find it impossible to publish in detail the mass of indiscriminate information which reaches us daily. If so, we shall select such items as appear to be of lasting significance and set them down with any general relevant information or appropriate historical background; this should be sufficient to give the regular reader a clear idea of how aviation is progressing. Those who wish to learn more about flying generally will find it presented in a new form which we believe will be more digestible than the old.

Popular Flying will leave no stone unturned to banish the notions which have done so much to retard the progress of civil aviation, notions which confine aviation to a chosen few, either wealthy, or possessed of a physique beyond ordinary standards. These matters are too involved to be covered in a single editorial, but we shall return to them from time to time.

Flying is now within the reach of everybody. Individually, sooner or later, everybody will fly, because it is the quickest, easiest and most pleasant form of transportation yet discovered. Collectively, as a nation, we must fly because the nation which does not fly will be left behind.[14]

The day following publication of the first issue, Hamilton was inundated with orders and by Friday afternoon the magazine had sold out. 'On Saturday morning,' wrote Johns, 'the manager wanted one of my two copies back.'[15] The publishers had hoped to reach a circulation of 12,000 a month but by the following year the magazine's audited circulation stood at 22,576 copies a month, and within a few years it was selling at 32,667 copies.

Within the first year Hamilton had made the magazine into an independent subsidiary registered as Popular Flying Ltd with offices at 34/5 Southampton Street, WC2.

In spite of his limited journalistic experience, Johns proved to have a natural flair for editorship. His editorials – characteristically written from 'The Editor's Cockpit' – were crisp, chatty, informative and often highly controversial. He was never afraid to be outspoken, especially on political matters, although his views brought him criticism and even pressure from government sources. Under Johns' robust guidance *Popular Flying* established itself within a few short months not only as the leading popular aviation magazine in Britain but a magazine with a strong following in America. Johns' choice of articles and stories, with their literate standards and controversial content, caused the circulation to increase by leaps and bounds. Even Hermann Göring contributed an article: 'My Most Thrilling Combat'.[16] Göring, of course, had been in Baron von Richthofen's famous 'Flying Circus' and was an accredited ace, having shot down 22 enemy machines in combat. Johns pointed out in the issue: 'The publication of this article does not necessarily mean that we agree with Captain Göring's present political activities; we are concerned only with his career as an airman.'

From the first, Johns used Howard Leigh as an illustrator and with the third issue Leigh began to do regular front covers for the magazine. At the age of twenty-two he was considered the foremost aviation illustrator in the country.

Popular Flying was born partly because no such magazine existed in Britain to meet a potentially huge market, and partly because America was flooding that market with her own 'aviation pulps'. In fact, most of the literature about flying, both fiction and non-fiction, emanated from America. In the fourth issue of his magazine, Johns attacked the flood of Hollywood films with wartime flying backgrounds. Citing one example where a gorgeous blonde heroine is apparently, together with the hero, at an aerodrome 'somewhere in France', Johns comments: 'Those of us who were in France wonder vaguely where the aerodrome was and kick ourselves for missing the boat. The only females we had at Azelot were more like bargees than women.' In the film, 'she then goes back to the CO and tells him in lisping, broken English how and when her beautiful *aviateur* shall fly. I should like to have seen anybody, man or woman, trying that on with Alec Gray.' Johns detested inaccuracy in aviation films – in which, for example, 'Every bomb hits its objective ... If anybody in my squadron hit the town in which the objective was situated it was reckoned to be pretty good going.'[17]

Johns's criticisms were not confined to fictional accounts of flying. After attending the Hendon Air Display of 1932 and observing combat items, he wrote: 'A small minority who were concerned with aviation during the Big Fuss probably went home wondering if all the lessons of war had really been forgotten ...'[18] Johns goes on to write about some methods of air combat which had been used in the First World War – methods that pilots were being told in the 1930s were outdated due to the greater speeds of modern aircraft. When the Second World War started, the new generation of fighter pilots quickly learnt that the old methods, upheld by Johns in his magazine, were the only ones. The famous legless air ace Douglas Bader encountered stubborn resistance from the RAF hierarchy when he attacked the new methods and insisted war flying had not altered since the First World War. 'The boys in the last war knew,' said Bader. 'The basic idea is the same as now.' He felt certain that 'Bishop and McCudden and the others were right.'[19] The point was proved in British skies during the grim days of 1940–1.

Johns' task was to justify the title of his magazine and make flying popular. He attacked the press for making the public afraid of flying by always writing of crashes in lurid detail.[20] He wanted to see people able to afford to run aeroplanes as they did motor cars. 'The world will suddenly realise that there is nothing either clever or heroic in being able to fly. Flying will become common place. A few carefully balanced halos will slip off, and some of the snobbery which has ulcerated the otherwise healthy bodies of certain flying clubs will either have to heal up or find itself under the knife. Aviation will become a real business and the hardworking people who fought their way through the lean times will reap their reward.'[21] To emphasise how popular flying could become, Johns wrote a story for the November 1932 issue, under his pseudonym William Earle, entitled 'A Flying Start'. This was a rather mawkish romance about a couple who have a flying honeymoon – a novel idea at the time.

Johns' energy and the amount of work he produced in 1932 was phenomenal. Despite the busy full-time job of editing and writing for *Popular Flying*, he did not desert *The Modern Boy* and continued to contribute two or three articles for it a month. It was in the midst of all this activity that he wrote a series of short stories for *Popular Flying* about a teenage Royal Flying Corps pilot, James Bigglesworth. Johns had no idea at the time that his hero's career would last for the rest of his own life, or that 'Biggles' would become a British institution.

10

BIGGLES IS BORN

Biggles was born for a reason as practical and matter of fact as the airman himself. 'I was the editor of an aviation magazine,' wrote Johns, 'and needed an air story to counterblast some of the war-flying nonsense that was being imported in the cheap papers.'[1] Johns was well aware that people had to turn to American sources for tales of aerial warfare, to American pulp magazines such as *War Birds*, *Flying Aces*, *Sky Birds* and *G-2 Battle Aces*, and, according to him, some of these journals were crediting to others exploits that had been performed by British airmen.[2] Johns wanted to give his readers fiction that would portray the realities of fighting in the air and present a true picture of the kind of officer who had served in the First World War in the Royal Flying Corps, Royal Naval Air Service and the Royal Air Force. Needing a story and unable to find one, he took the obvious course. The first Biggles story entitled 'The White Fokker' and written by 'William Earle', appeared in *Popular Flying* (Vol. I, No. 1) in April 1932. Six more Biggles stories were published in the magazine in the following months, and, together with eleven more, the tales came out in book form as *The Camels Are Coming*, published by John Hamilton in August 1932.

The immediate success of the stories showed how well Johns had achieved his aims. His picture of aerial warfare had the stamp of authenticity. As well as writing from personal experience, he included the deeds of other officers in Biggles' adventures.

> ... the exploits with which he has been credited have nearly all been built on a foundation of truth, although needless to say they were not all the efforts of a single individual. Students of air-war history may have no difficulty in recognising the actual incidents and the names of the officers associated with them ...[3]

Other countries had had official ace systems during the war; if a French pilot shot down five enemy machines or a German shot down ten, he was acclaimed as an ace and made a public hero. The British authorities did not acknowledge aces, frowning on personal publicity. Johns was still on the Reserve List of RAF officers, and under the orders of the Air Ministry.[4] He considered that the only way out of his difficulty was to use a fictitious name and setting for his stories and Biggles was his tribute to all those British pilots 'who daily performed deeds of heroism yet whose names are unknown'.[5] In the foreword to *The Camels Are Coming* Johns wrote:

Captain James Bigglesworth is a fictitious character, yet he could have been found in any RFC mess during those great days of 1917 and 1918 when air combat had become the order of the day and air duelling was a fine art ...

Later, he added:

... he developed under the stress of war into the sort of man most men would like to be; fearless but modest, efficient and resolute in what he undertook ...[6]

Biggles was to represent the spirit of the RFC, and with this daunting blueprint it was amazing that Johns' young airman should prove to be anything other than a lifeless stereotype, bloodless brother of Bulldog Drummond and James Bond, complete with stiff upper lip and steely blue eyes. Fortunately, the born writer in Johns took charge; he created a hero who was far from flawless. From the first story, Biggles is represented as a sensitive and nervous human being.

Bigglesworth, commonly called Biggles, a fair-haired good-looking lad still in his 'teens, but an acting Flight-Commander, was talking; not of wine or women, as novelists would have us believe, but of a new fuse spring for a Vickers gun which would speed it up another hundred rounds a minute.

His deep-set hazel eyes were never still and held a glint of yellow fire that somehow seemed out of place in a pale face upon which the strain of war, and sight of sudden death, had already graven little lines. His hands, small and delicate as a girl's, fidgeted continually with the tunic fastening at his throat. He had killed a man not six hours before. He had killed six men during the past month – or was it a year? – he had forgotten. Time had became curiously telescoped lately. What did it matter anyway? He knew he had to die some time and had long ago ceased to worry about it. His careless attitude told one story, but the irritating little falsetto laugh which continually punctuated his tale told another ...[7]

The strains of war flying are much in evidence in *The Camels Are Coming* and their effects on the youthful airman are carefully observed. Courageous as he is, Biggles is frequently keyed up to near hysteria, although it is not until he believes his girl has been killed in an air raid that he begins to drink whisky for breakfast. Like his real-life counterparts, however, he finds relief from tension in schoolboy humour. Johns never made Biggles challenge anybody to a race in steamrollers, or paint RFC roundels on the ducks in a nearby farmyard as Billy Bishop and his fellow officers did,[8] but, in the stories, accounts of battles and sudden death are interleaved with authentic interludes in which boyish high spirits find an outlet, often in practical jokes.

Five further RFC Biggles stories appeared in *Popular Flying* from January to May 1933, and were then published with another eight tales as *Biggles of the Camel Squadron* in March 1934. Meanwhile, the stories which comprised *The Camels Are Coming* had been sold for second serial rights to *The Modern Boy* and were published from January 1933 onwards, followed by some of the *Camel Squadron* stories. No further RFC tales were printed in *Popular Flying*, but new ones continued to appear in *The Modern Boy* from April 1934, onwards. The first collection of these, entitled *Biggles Learns to Fly*, appeared in 1935, in paperback only, in The Boys' Friend Complete Library, priced 4d. It was not issued as a hardback until a revised edition was published in 1955 by Brockhampton Press. Johns explained some of the background to *Biggles Learns to Fly*:

Biggles' meagre instruction was precisely the experience of hundreds of pilots – including mine. Many officers went overseas with less than ten hours flying experience, knowing that they might find themselves opposed to pilots who had been flying for months, or even years.

Every incident that occurs in these stories runs parallel with fact and the methods employed by the various squadrons and individuals were those actually employed in France during the Great War.[9]

Further RFC stories printed in *The Modern Boy* became

another Boys' Friend Complete Library paperback, *Biggles in France*, issued in July 1935, and never republished in its original form. Some of the stories from it were brought out as *Biggles of 266*, published by the Thames Publishing Company in 1956, Johns himself updating others for inclusion in *Spitfire Parade*, published by Oxford University Press in 1941.

Johns' First World War stories are consistent with his wholehearted condemnation of war. His memories would not allow him to paint a picture of total misery – he described the unique comradeship created by the daily sharing of danger, and he writes frankly of the excitement and exultation felt by pilots engaged in aerial combat. Like Billy Bishop and Mick Mannock, the top-scoring British VCs, Biggles feels a fierce elation in the heat of battle, but is often sickened when he sees his enemy go down in flames. Johns does not moralise, but presents the facts, and it is because he does not distort to reinforce his message that the horrors of war and its tragic waste are so apparent. There are moments of obvious emotion in the stories, as when Biggles sees his friends shot down beside him or holds a dying pilot in his arms, but usually the point is made laconically. Biggles and his observer are shot down themselves and flounder in the obscene mud of no-man's-land:

'I can't stand much more of this!' growled Biggles. 'It's giving me the creeps. I've just crawled over somebody – or something that was somebody.'[10]

A short life-expectancy is taken for granted. Biggles tells two new young pilots in his flight who have just arrived fresh from England:

'You can't last for ever at this game, but it's up to you to last as long as you can. If you can get just one man before you go, you break even with the enemy – you've done your bit and it's all square. If you can get two Huns – Germans – before you go, you're one up on the enemy and you've helped to win the war for England ...'[11]

Biggles was a representative young officer, but did Johns base him on anyone in particular? He once stated that Bigglesworth was something like the name of the officer he had in mind.[12] According to Mrs Marjorie Ellis that officer was Air Commodore

C. G. Wigglesworth CB, AFC (1893–1961), whose long and distinguished career included serving during the First World War in the RNAS and the RAF.[13] A portrait of Biggles painted by Johns, which he used to illustrate the story 'The Balloonatics' in the July 1932 issue of *Popular Flying*, is said by Marjorie Ellis to resemble Howard Leigh and she believes that Biggles was given some of her brother's characteristics. Certainly every fictional character must owe something to real people and inevitably the personality of the author must be considered in this respect. Was Biggles the kind of man Johns was or would have liked to have been? Johns thought that Biggles had been in his mind for a long time before he wrote the tales.

... a shadowy figure created by my admiration for the courage and resource displayed by some of the men with whom it was my good fortune to spend several years of my life. Having had some experience of air warfare, and knowing my own limitations, I was better able to appreciate what these fellows did ...[14]

'In a way,' admitted Johns during an interview, 'he is myself.'[15]

A review of *Biggles of the Camel Squadron* in *Popular Flying* in June 1934 stated:

Here is the second series of Biggles war time stories, four or five of which have appeared in *Popular Flying*. They have now been touched up to make them suitable for the younger generation.

The touching-up process had already begun when the Biggles stories started to appear in *The Modern Boy*. The story from *The Camels Are Coming* entitled '*Affaire de Coeur*' was renamed 'Biggles Falls in Love!'

Biggles was no longer allowed to take his girlfriend in his arms and kissing was cut out. The task of bowdlerising the tales was continued in the 1950s, when most of the RFC stories were republished by the Thames Publishing Company. It was decided that lovemaking might be included in the stories, but that swearing and drinking must be banned. 'My gosh! What a mess!' exclaims Biggles, as his windscreen is shot to pieces. When he sees a Camel pilot heading for disaster, he cries: 'Great Scott! What's he doing?' Thirsty airmen develop an astonishing taste for lemonade – the crowning absurdity occurring when Biggles and his friend Wilks vie with each other to obtain some bottles of lemonade from a French hotelier, that had been specially imported for an Englishman before the war; the lemonade, in the original story, was pre-war whisky. However, on one occasion Biggles is permitted to recommend a medicinal brandy — the original text favours 'a damn good double Scotch!'

Johns bemoaned these restrictions on the part of his publishers when talking to Robert Pitman of the *Sunday Express* in 1958. He complained that he was not allowed to include sex, hard liquor or strong expletives by his editors. 'Just think of the things I am not allowed. No sex. No hard liquor. The only time I made my chaps drink anything stronger than orange juice my sales fell by ten per cent. Then think of swear words. One publisher wouldn't let me use any expletives at all at first. But he relented and agreed to 'Oh dear' and 'Good gracious'. For stories about the Air Force, mind you! Imagine a chap messing up a landing, finishing up in a damned tree and then simply saying — Good gracious! Well, it's not lifelike, is it?'[16]

The RFC tales that Johns wrote for *Popular Flying* were for an adult readership. The ones that first appeared in *The Modern Boy* are more juvenile in tone and style, but as a whole the first Biggles stories are arguably the best works of fiction Johns ever produced. They have power and accuracy; no one knew better than he how to impart a feeling of immediacy to a scene of swift action. In the first story of all, Biggles is fighting an air duel with an enemy machine, a white Fokker. The British Sopwith Camel and the German aircraft circle each other, not a hundred yards apart, the Fokker gradually gaining in height. Biggles knows that the enemy will soon escape. If he pulls out of the circle the Fokker will be on his tail and get a shot at him. Whatever he does, he will not be able to shake the German off; if he rolls, the Fokker will roll, if he spins, it will spin, too, always maintaining its position.

> ... if he shot out of the circle he might get a lead of three hundred feet, and if he could loop fast enough he might get the Fokker from the top of his loop as it passed underneath his wake. If he was too quick they would collide; no matter, they would go to Kingdom Come together. A feeling of fierce exultation swept over him.
>
> 'Come on, you devil!' he cried. 'I'll take your lead,' and shot out of the circle. He shoved his stick forward savagely as something smashed through the root of the nearest centre-section strut, and then he pulled it

back in a swift zoom. A fleeting glance over his shoulder showed the Fokker three hundred feet behind. He pulled the stick right back into his stomach in a flick loop, and his eyes sought the sights as he pressed his triggers. Blue sky – blue sky – the horizon – green fields – where was the Fokker? Ah! There he was, flying straight into his stream of tracer. He saw the pilot slump forward in his seat. He held the loop a moment longer and then flung the Camel over on to an even keel, looking swiftly for the Fokker as he did so. It was rocketing like a hard-hit pheasant. It stalled; its nose whipped over in an almost vertical dive. Biggles saw the top-plane fold back, and then he looked away feeling suddenly limp and very tired ...[17]

As well as plenty of air duels and dogfights, the RFC Biggles stories contain direct practical advice. Biggles briefs new recruits to his flight from his own hard-won experience: 'Watch the sun', 'It's no use flying if you can't shoot'; 'keep your eyes peeled', 'never go down after a Hun'; and 'If you want to commit suicide do it here, because then someone else can have your bus' ...

In his foreword to *Biggles of the Camel Squadron* in 1934, Johns expressed a hope:

> ... that something may be learned from the 'combat tactics' employed by Biggles and his friends, by those who may one day find themselves in the cockpit of a fighting aeroplane, carrying on the glorious traditions of the flying service ...

It must have been a source of satisfaction when Johns had evidence that many of the pilots who fought the Battle of Britain in their Spitfires and Hurricanes had learnt their combat tactics by reading Biggles books in their youth.[18]

Meanwhile, however, in the early 1930s Europe was at peace and an RFC hero was already an anachronism. Quick to see the potential of the forceful character he had created, Johns swiftly followed *The Camels Are Coming* with *The Cruise of the Condor*, published by John Hamilton in August 1933. In this adventure yarn, Biggles and Algy Lacey, his cousin and fellow pilot from No. 266 Squadron, find themselves at a loose end after the war, until they meet Biggles' explorer uncle. Taking with them Flight Sergeant Smyth, Biggles' wartime mechanic, the airmen fly with the explorer to South America on a perilous quest. The chapter headings are eloquent: 'Indians', 'A Night of Horror' and 'The

Ants'. At last, 'in the savage heart of a savage continent', they reach their goal, a secret chamber piled high with countless objects made of pure gold – the treasure of the Incas. As Flight Sergeant Smyth says, 'It looks like money for jam'. However, an earthquake destroys 'the last stronghold of a mighty empire and the treasure of its mighty king', and Biggles and his friends escape with their lives only. Still, they have had a highly satisfactory adventure – although, as one of the characters remarks, 'you are going to find it hard to believe this story'.

A month before the publication of *The Cruise of the Condor*, a tale had appeared in *Popular Flying* about Biggles, Algy and the ubiquitous Flight Sergeant Smyth and their attempt to make ends meet after the war by flying a Vickers Vandal amphibian for hire. Ten more stories followed in *Popular Flying* and, together with two more, the series came out as a book, *Biggles Flies Again*, published by John Hamilton in August 1934. Like the original RFC Biggles tales, these stories are adult, even sophisticated, in style and plot. Successful as they were, however, Johns did not repeat the formula. It was *The Cruise of the Condor* that set the pattern for the fast, racy, wildly improbable and highly enjoyable adventure yarns about Biggles that appeared for the rest of the decade. Each subsequent Biggles book was serialised in *The Modern Boy*, but the airman never flew again in *Popular Flying*.

Not that the Biggles books of this period were all alike. Even the RFC stories, that continued to appear, as well as the postwar tales, changed somewhat in character. *Biggles Flies East*, published by Oxford University Press in August 1935 is a full-length First World War espionage drama, and *The Rescue Flight*, Oxford University Press, May 1939, is a complete novel set on the Western Front, with a young RFC pilot as hero and Biggles rather in the background. The age of his famous character presented Johns with a problem in his 'ripping yarns' – by the 1930s Biggles and Algy were in their thirties, getting rather long in the tooth for the principal roles in boys' stories. Johns' solution was a shrewd one: he introduced a new character in *The Black Peril*, Oxford University Press, March 1935, a bright teenage lad called Ginger. Now the young reader could identify with Ginger and also join him in his undisguised admiration for Biggles. In subsequent Biggles books Ginger was to play an important role.

Once Johns had established his permanent team – Biggles, the leader, Algy, the faithful friend, Ginger, the whizz kid, and Flight Sergeant Smyth to keep the aeroplanes flying – the series went from strength to strength. *The Black Peril*, about the threat of a surprise Soviet air attack on Britain, was followed by *Biggles Hits the Trail*, in August 1935. This far-flung adventure has some unforgettable moments, although a strong science fiction element in the story does not mix well with the realism of Johns' characters. The author did not make this mistake again, and in his next book played a masterstroke. In *Biggles Flies East* he had created an archetypal villain in the sauve, monocled Hauptmann Erich von Stalhein, the most brilliant and ruthless agent in the German Intelligence Service. At the end of the book he had imprudently killed him off, but, like Conan Doyle's notorious Moriarty, von Stalhein was too valuable an asset to be destroyed. Biggles thought that he had seen the last of his archenemy in 1918, but in *Biggles & Co.*, Oxford University Press, April 1936, he had the most violent shock of his life as he found himself staring at the face 'of a man who, he thought, was buried deep in the arid sand of Palestine ...' Von Stalhein was not only alive and well but destined to continue his deadly duels with Biggles for another twenty years, fighting gamely on, in spite of the fact that he always lost.

Johns was a mature, tough, kind-hearted man with an invaluable quality for a writer of juvenile fiction – he had never lost the vision of childhood. He viewed the world with a candid eye and he had retained a fresh, infectious curiosity and enthusiasm for a wide range of subjects. His interests often happily coincided with those of his young readers. He did not write down to children; he shared his knowledge and his own genuine convictions with them, carrying them along with him through his own enjoyment and sense of humour. These gifts, combined with his skill as a storyteller, proved irresistible.

Johns' interest in wildlife is evident in *Biggles in Africa*, Oxford University Press, 1936, which becomes one glorious safari, with another series of promising chapter headings: 'Alone with a Lion', 'Crashed by a Rhino' and 'The Snake in the Grass'. In *Biggles – Air Commodore*, Oxford University Press, May 1937, he returned to the grim theme of international treachery and surprise attack, but followed this with the light-hearted *Biggles Flies West*, Oxford University Press, September 1937, a thrilling story of buccaneers and buried treasure. Johns was fascinated by pirates and knew a good deal about them – he was to write *The Modern Boy's Book of Pirates*, published in 1939.[19] The first edition of *Biggles Flies West* contains a photograph of two Spanish doubloons 'in the possession of the author', and an informative passage about them points out: 'It is more than likely that both these coins were handled by pirates ...' The editor of *The Modern Boy*, introducing the first instalment of the tale, described how Johns had enthusiastically shown him the doubloons when he came to deliver the typescript.[20] 'I carry them about with me so if any readers spot me in the street they can stop me and handle something that was probably carried in the pocket of a gory-handed pirate,' said Johns. The tale starts with a prologue telling the story of the death of a pirate captain, and in the main narrative Biggles and his friends meet the captain's skeleton. The grand finale of the adventure has the airmen, arrayed in pirate gear, fighting for their lives, using muskets and a swivel-gun loaded with grapeshot.

Ancient history was another of Johns' hobbies, and *Biggles Flies South*, Oxford University Press, May 1938, also starts with a prologue set in the past, this time in the sixth century BC in Upper Egypt, where the Persian army of Cambyses was lost without trace in the desert on its way to sack Jupiter Ammon. Biggles' team encounter the descendants of Cambyses' army at the Lost Oasis, and Biggles is very nearly sacrificed to their sacred crocodile. The last three pre-war Biggles books were just as varied as their predecessors: *Biggles Goes to War*, Oxford University Press, May 1938, is a delightful Ruritanian melodrama; *Biggles in Spain*, Oxford University Press, May 1939, is a harsher adventure with some insights into the nature of war; and *Biggles Flies North*, Oxford University Press, May 1939, is Johns' very creditable version of a Jack London Alaskan-style gold-rush tale.

However absurd the story, the Biggles books of the 1930s carry an air of conviction. This may be because the aeroplanes are all described accurately and the flying is factually correct, but more probably it is due to the character of Biggles. He remains the practical RFC officer, drawn from life, whether he is foiling dire plots against the Empire or struggling in the coils of a giant python. Johns' own experiences of violence and horror also undoubtedly lend an underlying sense of truth to the clichés of the adventure story. Some of the incidents in the books are actually based on his life. In *Biggles Goes to War*, Biggles and Algy, now officers in the Air Force of Maltovia, are tried by a so-called military court and sentenced to be shot by a firing squad for espionage. There seems to be an element of wish fulfilment in the passage where Biggles defiantly faces the illegal tribunal.

> Biggles' hostile gaze was fixed on one man, obviously the president of the court ...
> The general returned his stare. 'Is your name Bigglesworth?' he asked in a loud voice.
> Biggles' lip curled slightly. 'Why waste time asking fool questions?' he said harshly. 'You know it is.'
> 'Answer my question!'
> 'Let me ask you one. What is the meaning of this farce?'

And so on. Similar situations recur in other Biggles books.

Biggles Goes to War also provided Johns with a wicked opportunity to give vent to his cynicism about politicians. Biggles explains to one of the Maltovian leaders that although a state of war does not officially exist with the hostile country Lovitzna, he proposes to destroy the bridge that spans the river between the two states. 'They'll complain,' objects the Maltovian. Biggles replies:

> 'So will you. You will be most upset, and send them a note asking what the dickens they mean by destroying the bridge, pointing out that by severing commercial relations they are deliberately trying to cause trouble!'
> 'But they won't believe that.'
> 'Of course they won't; neither will anyone else, but that doesn't matter. My dear boy, that is what is called diplomacy ...'

Wish fulfilment creeps in again at the end of the book. In the ideal, imaginary world of Maltovia, the League of Nations – scornfully referred to by Johns, in a political article, as the 'League of Rabbits'[21] – actually works. The dispute between Maltovia and Lovitzna is settled by the League, Lovitzna justly having to pay Maltovia an indemnity. In real life, in the 1930s, Johns vainly urged the Government to build more aeroplanes; in the world he created, the indemnity money was allocated to the

Air Arm for the purchase of machines and for pilot-training schemes. Biggles was already busy organising the Maltovian Air Force on British lines.

The success of the Biggles series was phenomenal. The critics were full of praise, from the *Sunday Times* − 'all the right kinds of excitement' − to the *Daily Mirror* − 'you can't beat Biggles for fast-moving adventure'. The *Church Times* praised Johns' authenticity and called the stories 'fast, moving and exciting'. *Public Opinion* called him 'versatile', *The Scotsman* 'masterly', the *Times Literary Supplement* 'accomplished', and the *Quiver* admired his humour and the unexpected twists and surprises of the narratives. 'Anyone who likes a well-written thriller will like Biggles', wrote the *Western Mail*.[22] Writing of one of his own books of verses for children, A. A. Milne accounted for its success by pointing out that it was 'the work of a light verse writer taking his job seriously even though he is taking it into the nursery.'[23] Many thriller writers in the adult field could take tips from the exciting plots and swift pace of Johns' yarns for children.

During the 1930s the children themselves established Biggles as their favourite hero. When, in November 1938, Mr George Vale, borough librarian at Bethnal Green, asked children between the ages of eight and fourteen about the books they liked best, he found that the Biggles series topped the votes. According to George Vale:

Time was when the bulk of children's reading was confined to school stories. Now the interest has shifted to the air; airscrews, ailerons, pilots and crude oil are the new symbols of speed and conquest.[24]

Johns frequently made appearances at signing sessions in bookshops, and Marjorie Ellis recalls seeing an excited line of boys, clutching Biggles books, stretching all the way up the stairs of Harrod's to the book department.[25]

The RFC stories and adventure stories of the 1930s established Biggles' lasting popularity, and they have continued to be published side by side with the postwar Air Police Biggles books. That they continue to fascinate both boys and girls is evident from the following comment on *Biggles Flies West*, which first appeared in 1937. A ten-year-old girl wrote in 1979:

As the pages turn you slowly find yourself and Biggles becoming one.

Plotting each move and crowing with delight as Deutch (the villain) finally dies at the end of the book, trying to regain the treasure you feel that you have helped to bring to light.

At first when I was given a Biggles book I didn't give it a chance – I gave one glance at the cover and decided I wouldn't like it, so it was some time before I read it. It was evening time when I began it and unknown to both my parents at least 12 pm when I put it down! That's how Biggles gets me, there's something about him which causes me to want to go on to the next page and the next until after a few minutes I'm so hooked I can't put the book down until I've finished it ...[26]

There must have been many a torch burning under the bedclothes in the 1930s, too.

11

THE MILITANT PACIFIST

By the end of 1932 it seems that Johns had given himself a small promotion; from Flying Officer to Captain. It is, of course, as Captain W. E. Johns that he has become world famous. However, when he left the Royal Air Force he was a Flying Officer, the equivalent to the army rank of a full lieutenant. In later years, explaining why he was a captain when there was no such rank in the RAF, Johns told those who enquired that it was his old RFC rank. According to *Boys' Own Paper* editor Jack Cox, '... his rank of Captain was never an Army title but a Royal Flying Corps distinction and he was immensely proud of it. To this day he still uses it as much as ever. I would never dream of publishing a story or serial of his except under the by-line "Captain W. E. Johns".'[1] But when the Royal Flying Corps merged with the Royal Naval Air Service to become the Royal Air Force, Johns only held the rank of 2nd Lieutenant. It seems that Johns felt that the title Captain would have a more immediate appeal to his younger readers. It sounded more dignified, more assured, and his youthful audience would know what a Captain was, but might not be sure about a Flying Officer – a rank scarcely a decade old. Thus, the December 1932 issue of *Popular Flying* was able to advertise *The Camels Are Coming* (published by plain W. E. Johns) and *The Pictorial Flying Course* (published with the by-line Flying Officer W. E. Johns) as being by *Captain W. E. Johns*. No one seemed to notice the discrepancy. Throughout the 1930s, Johns used the by-line which was to become world-famous with a cheerful inconsistency. For his adult work, books as well as magazines, he used simply W. E. Johns, but for his juvenile markets, right up until the end of 1939, he wavered between the titles Flying Officer and Captain. The last book to appear carrying the by-line Flying Officer W. E. Johns came out in September 1939.[2]

The editorship of *Popular Flying* had brought Johns status and a welcome financial security. Now he and Doris were able to make trips abroad more frequently, sometimes hunting for alpine plants for the rock garden. Johns wrote feelingly of breaking his fingernails trying to dig Cyclamen balearic out of a limestone scree, and mentioned 'dragging' his wife, 'poor wretch', up the Puig Major, the highest mountain in Majorca, on a quest for specimens. Each year, together with Howard Leigh and more often than not several other friends, Doris and Bill Johns would go on a Continental tour, usually towards the south of France. Johns was fascinated by the Riviera. 'Ignore the blasé swaggerers who may tell you that the Riviera is spoilt. Maybe it is spoilt from their point of view because it is now possible for people like you and me to go there. Nothing can spoil the Riviera.'[3]

In September 1932, returning from one such holiday, Johns, with Doris and Howard, flew back from Paris in a Heracles. 'We ran into thick fog over the Channel which got worse as we neared the coast and Commander Perry put the machine down at Lympne. Believe it or not but the passengers nearly all started grousing at not being taken on to Croydon, in spite of the fact that we heard Croydon was fog bound.'[4] Coaches were laid on to transport the disgruntled passengers to Victoria where the airline's traffic manager, Mr Handover, arranged a dinner at the Grosvenor Hotel, with rooms and baths and anything else the passengers wanted.

Dash it all, he couldn't do more than that! It is a lot more than railway officials do when the boat train is late owing to fog. I, who have never missed a free meal in my life, made a bee-line for the Grosvenor, closely followed by my wife, Howard Leigh, the artist, and a young fellow who had travelled with us. Dinner had been specially laid for the sixteen passengers. We were the only four who sat down. The rest preferred to harangue a worried Traffic Manager; where they ultimately went I neither know nor care.[5]

Johns did not allow his editorship of *Popular Flying* to prevent him from pursuing a host of other writing activities in addition to his books. He was always on the look out for new outlets for his work, including the comparatively new medium of the wireless. He had met J. M. Rose-Tramp, the News Editor of the British Broadcasting Corporation, in September 1931, on a press outing to Paris. Through Rose-Tramp's help, Johns broadcast his first talk on 21 June 1933. The talk was on 'The Opening of the New Norwich Municipal Aerodrome' by the Prince of Wales, who had flown there in a Dragon Moth. Johns admitted being 'scared stiff' when he went to Broadcasting House and entered Studio B4.[6] 'On one side was a little desk with a powerful lamp over it. On the desk stood a sinister instrument like a badly bloated spider – the microphone ... I sank into a chair and fixed my fascinated eye on the red electric bulb like a rabbit staring at a snake about to strike.' Johns made another broadcast on 15 July; a talk on 'How Can I Fly?', giving advice to people who wanted to become pilots. But radio was apparently not his medium, for he made no more broadcasts until, as a famous author, he was invited to appear on radio and television chat shows in subsequent decades.

Busy as he was with authorship, journalism, his frequent holidays abroad and the claims of his garden, Johns found time to keep a keen eye on politics. His name became known in the 1930s for a series of devastating attacks on the Government launched from his editorial columns, for he was extremely concerned about the world situation. In 1932 President Doumer of France and Prime Minister Tsuyoshi of Japan were assassinated by right-wing extremists. The Japanese had launched a military attack against China, using the neutral international settlement at Shanghai as a basis for operations. The Chinese were defeated. There were ominous signs from Germany, where the Nazi Party, with 230 seats, became the largest single party in the German Reichstag; and Sir Oswald Moseley had formed a British Union of Fascists. In spite of the unpropitious signs around the world, the British Government was scaling down defence expenditure, especially spending on the Royal Air Force, and there were serious talks about disbanding the service. Although he hated war, Johns believed that if nations were weak then it was obvious that the proud and strong would oppress them. The only way to stop the threat of oppression was to be armed and ready. He believed that there was a wide distinction between being prepared for self-defence and courting injury at the hands of the wrong-doer by a policy of appeasement and weakness. His philosophy could be summed up as a militant pacifism.

As early as May 1933, Johns wrote in scathing terms on the Government's lagging air policy under the title 'Disarmament, Dementia and Economy'. He quoted a speech that Lieutenant

Colonel Moore Brabazon had made in the House of Commons on 14 March 1933: 'The enemy of the Air Force is not across the Channel, it is in Whitehall.' Johns himself was quite certain what should be done. Rearmament was the only means of maintaining peace.

If you have a stick in your hand the other fellow thinks twice before he pulls your nose. If you have a stick and a knife, he thinks harder. If you have a stick, a knife and a pistol, it is improbable that he will pull your nose. Add a rifle and a Mills bomb to your equipment and he steps off the pavement to let you pass. Start throwing your weapons away and he steps back again. That is just what the orators are going to do if they are not stopped.[7]

Prophetically, he wrote:

Presently somebody will pull our nose severely; one or two people have already made tentative gestures in that direction. What are we going to do? Step off the path? The orators might, but the rest will not. Then the trouble will start. There will be a wild rush to build aeroplanes, and what will be more difficult, to teach men to fly them. In the rush to 'launch' new pilots, they will kill ten men a day and with them write off ten machines costing from £1,000 to £25,000 apiece. Is *that* economy?[8]

In the same editorial, Johns once again unequivocally states his anti-war attitude.

War, a barbaric custom handed down through centuries of fear, will only be condemned to the limbo of such things as witchcraft, torture and feudal systems, when nations come to know each other better, for with mutual understanding will come confidence, goodwill and a toleration of each others' national characteristics; our hopes, our curses and blessings, our likes and dislikes, and our pleasures and antipathies.[9]

In civil aviation, Johns saw a method of getting more people to go abroad for their holidays. 'By becoming accustomed to foreign travel they will forsake the beaten paths so often sown with prejudice and suspicion and see the people of the country *as they are* and learn that the prospect of becoming bomb-fodder is as abhorrent to them as it is to us.' It is ironic that in later years Johns was to be fiercely attacked as someone sowing the seeds of racial prejudice by putting stereotypes of different nationalities into his books and portraying foreigners as suspicious characters.

In the *Popular Flying* issue of December 1933, Johns reported on the growing pessimism about a future war in Europe. 'This country, and indeed the whole of Europe – or what I have seen of it lately – is rotten with pessimism, dismal depression, melancholy moping, chronic croaking and what the French call *malade imaginaire*.' But Johns correctly forecasts that the international Disarmament Conference would 'go to pieces'. The League of Nations had condemned Japan's invasion of China, and Japan had showed the ineffectuality of the League by simply withdrawing. Hitler was now Chancellor of Germany and had suppressed first the Catholic and Social Democratic Parties, then the Communists: and concentration camps had been established. In an editorial in January 1934, Johns saw the potential source of conflict as being between Germany and France. For the time being, he thought, the war scare would come to nothing, for France and Germany were in a position of stalemate; but meanwhile neither of these countries knew which side Britain was on, because the British Government was courting both. The British people did not know either.

Feeling in this country runs the way the party in power at Westminster wants it to run, its wishes being conveyed to the public by means of carefully prepared propaganda in the newspapers ...[10]

Johns goes on to say that although Germany was not permitted to arm by the Treaty of Versailles, that 'she has not kept strictly to the letter of the disarmament clause is no secret.' He reported figures showing the growth of aviation in Germany. 'In the matter of personnel, Germany is a nation of flyers. Flying has become a national sport.'

This may be taking an alarmist view, but let us not deceive ourselves. Sooner or later, when the festering sores of Europe break out into open eruption, every aeroplane in the sky, no matter what its size, shape, range, speed, ceiling, accommodation or pay load, will become a lethal weapon. Every soul in this country should know that. As long as we have our share, and by that I mean parity, we shall come to no harm, but God help us if we haven't. The cost of a thousand aeroplanes today would be nothing to what failure to safeguard ourselves might cost.[11]

William Earl Johns with his parents and
younger brother, Russell, at Hertford,
about 1908
(courtesy of Mrs Kathleen King)

(left) Second Lieutenant W. E. Jo
Royal Flying Corps, 1917
(courtesy of Mrs Marjorie Ellis)

(below left) Johns outside No
Squadron office at Azelot after a
This snapshot was taken by 2nd Lieu
ant Gormley, who was shot dow
30 August 1918; the photograph
fell into the hands of the Ger
officer who interrogated Johns w
he was brought down behind en
lines in September 1918

(below right) The first three Big
books: *The Camels Are Coming* (19
The Cruise of the Condor (1933),
Biggles of the Camel Squadron (19
The frontispiece is the work of Ho
Leigh

t) Johns in August 1919, awaiting
statement in the RAF
rtesy of Mrs Kathleen King)

ow left) Johns' poster for the 1927
don Air Display, of which he was
of the organisers
rtesy of RAF Museum, Hendon)

ow right) Johns own early visualisa-
of his hero Biggles. The artist
ard Leigh is said to have modelled
t. The painting was published to
crate 'The Balloonatics' by William
e in the July 1932 issue of *Popular*
g
rtesy of Mrs Marjorie Ellis)

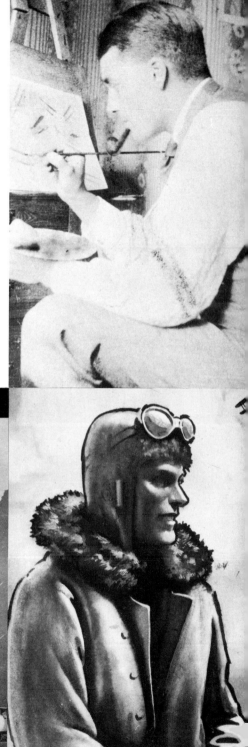

(left) Johns' son, Jack, shortly befor[e]
death in 1954
(courtesy of Mrs Sabena Johns)

(below) Doris and Bill Johns in [
House, Hampton Court
(courtesy of Mrs Marjorie Ellis)

In the March issue Johns harried the Government in support of the views of Brigadier-General P. R. C. Groves, CB, CMG, DSO put forward in his book *Behind the Smoke Screen*. In his editorial Johns accused the nation's leaders of betraying Britain through sheer muddling inefficiency and their policy of appeasement. Furthermore, they were betraying the RAF, by allowing it to be 'persecuted and bled by the two senior services, who visualize their own utility becoming dependent upon an upstart arm.'[12]

Johns' attacks did not go unanswered. Government personalities accused him in their turn of 'clamouring' for increased armaments and of warmongering; those sections of the press that supported the Government also abused him. In his July editorial he replied: 'I plead guilty to the clamouring but nothing more. Rightly or wrongly I hold the view that the more aeroplanes we have the more likely we are to avoid war. Our recent editorials, it seems, have led one or two people to believe that we, or I, personally want war. What utter nonsense. No one in his right mind wants war. Paradoxical though it may seem, it is my fear of war that makes me plead for more aeroplanes.' He insisted: 'Sooner or later there will be another European war; the people who should know, say so, and I believe them. If by making that admission I am an alarmist, then there are a good many alarmists in this country. Our only chance of keeping out of it is to have a ring of aerodromes around the coast. The more we bristle with aeroplanes, the longer people will think before they start anything. All we need is parity. When we have that I will turn my pen to more peaceful channels.'[13]

The Secretary of State for Air, Lord Londonderry, speaking at the Mechanics Institute, Darling, on 22 October 1934, reproved those 'crying out for a vast armament of aeroplanes'. Winston Churchill replied promptly by pointing out that 'Germany is arming secretly, illegally and rapidly. A reign of terror exists in Germany to keep secret the feverish and terrible preparations they are making.'[14]

That November Johns visited Barcelona and met Willy Heckel, a former pilot in Boelcke's Jadgstaffel. Heckel was 'full out for Hitler' and started to brag about the size of the growing Luftwaffe. According to Mrs Marjorie Ellis, Johns had also kept up a friendship and correspondence with the commandant of his last POW camp, Fort Orf, who was not a supporter of the Nazis and kept Johns informed of developments in Germany. Drawing on these sources, in the January 1935 issue of *Popular Flying* Johns published his most damning attack to date on the Government's policy in an editorial called 'The Mannock Spirit'.

A short time after, facts and figures of Germany's military build-up were published in the newspapers. They revealed an emphasis on the growth of the Luftwaffe. Johns could write with grim satisfaction:

Perhaps those readers who last year went off the deep end about certain of our editorials in connection with the re-equipment of German air squadrons, will, now that the Jagdstaffel Richthofen is once more on the wing, take back their impetuous accusations. 'Alarmist' and 'Scaremonger' were two popular ones. And will the two newspapers who mentioned me by name, at the same time uttering coarse guffaws, admit that they were wrong? They will not. A fat lot I care. We were the first to say it, but we should not have said it had we not been sure of our facts. We have our own sources of information and they are not the regular newspaper channels.[15]

On 8 August 1935 Doris and Bill Johns left England for another holiday in Monte Carlo.

Slowly and with considerable satisfaction I removed from my person the ridiculous garments imposed by civilization, and cast my sunstarved body into the sea. For a week I floated with ten fathoms of liquid turquoise below and a million azure miles above, crawling ashore from time to time for an *escalop*, a carafe of Bellet rosé, and fortywinks. Or it may have been fifty.[16]

But the holiday was far from idyllic. They went along the French-Italian border. Above La Bollene Johns stared at two great scars cut in the flanks of the mountain. Near at hand was a sign: 'Military zone. Photography forbidden under pain of arrest.' French soldiers were everywhere; in camps, digging in the hillside, widening the roads and throwing cable bridges across the ravines. On the other side of the border, Italian soldiers were doing the same thing.

As I sat brooding, three little white cloudlets appeared high up in the sky, very close together. Then three more. It's many a long year since I saw 'archie' but there was no mistaking him. And what 'archie'.

Spellbound, I watched, for I have never seen anything like it; nor did I believe it possible. Bursts of six and bursts of twelve appeared, incredibly close together. I could see no target. If there was one it was very far away but the grouping was unbelievable. It was a revelation. 'Archie', it seems, has kept pace with the times.

A dark-haired, low-browed woman came along the path with a basket of figs on her head and a child on her hip. 'What is it?' I asked, pointing. 'It is the guns at exercise,' she answered simply, and went on her way.

Thinking hard, I went on mine.[17]

In spite, or because, of Johns' controversial editorials, sales of *Popular Flying* had continued to increase, and by 1934 the circulation was 24,543 a month – the net sales figure had become higher than that of any other aviation magazine in the world.[18] Popular Flying Ltd, as a subsidiary of John Hamilton the book publishers was beginning to find it difficult to cope with such a grand-scale operation. In 1935 *Popular Flying* was sold to the magazine publishers C. Arthur Pearson, an associate company of George Newnes Ltd, who were eventually to take it into their stable. Pearson's began their publication of *Popular Flying* with the November 1935 issue. It was a tribute to Johns' editorship and his proven success formula for the magazine that the new owners asked him to stay as editor.

Johns' son, Jack, was now nineteen, and, inspired by his famous father, whom he could never acknowledge in public, he had begun to think of a career in journalism. Johns helped him in this respect and published his first article, signed Carmichael Earl, in the March 1935 issue of *Popular Flying*. Other articles followed, variously signed W. Carmichael Earle and J. Carmichael Earl. Jack also followed his father into the columns of *The Modern Boy* with an article about Johns, in which he had to change their relationship so that the article was entitled 'This Uncle of Mine!' When Howard Leigh edited his *New Book of the Air* for Oxford University Press in 1935 he included a piece by Jack on 'The Conquest of the Stratosphere'. Jack's first attempt at fiction – a short story entitled 'Liebe Garda' – appeared in *Popular Flying* in January 1937.

Under the new owners of *Popular Flying*, Johns' campaign for rearmament continued. He warned that Germany, still smarting from the punitive Versailles Treaty, would soon react.[19] He felt that the members of the Government were remaining silent rather than confessing

> ... their failure to grasp the greatest lesson of all history, the one unalterable basic quality of human nature. Which is this. However appalling war may be, and however remote the chance of success, a nation that can lay any claim to the title will always fight rather than suffer an intolerable peace.

Johns pointed out that this was what Germany was about to do. 'But, you might argue, why can't they take their losses like sportsmen? The answer is, they probably would if they could: but they can't. There are a lot of mouths at home to fill, and nothing to put in them. Can they be expected to starve?' Johns assured his readers that 'Germany will be next. She's nearly ready. What are we going to do? What can we do? The League [of Nations] doesn't work, so it looks as if we shall either have to play or hand back part of our winnings.' For Johns,

> There seems to be only one thing that we can do, and that is pick up the weapons we so foolishly laid aside when we went to Geneva, spit on our hands, and keep an eye on our property. Then, if anyone makes a pass at us, we can make two passes back. If no one does then we can stay at home and make the most of our winnings; but with our weapons within reach. Not forgetting that one of the greatest drawbacks of wealth is, that once having had it, it is so hard to do without it.[20]

As Johns prophesied, the Disarmament Conference finally collapsed. He commented: 'You will, I fear, feel your cheeks burn with shame, as mine did, when I heard the yell of derision go up from Europe (see foreign newspapers) on that fatal day in December when the British Empire took the nastiest smack in the eye of its long inspiring career ...'[21]

In February 1936 another trip with Doris to Majorca to see the almond trees in blossom and to climb Puig Major again, provided Johns with a temporary respite. 'The first sight of sheets of pale mauve clematis hanging over the grey faces of the rocks was a high-spot worth travelling far to enjoy' and when they had lunch on an alpine lawn at 4,500 feet, the countless millions of flowers around them were set 'in such a rock garden as no man could hope to make'. When they returned towards evening to Fornalutx far down the valley, 'through a world of purple shadows, we strode into the tavern feeling that the world was a pleasant place after all.'[22]

At home again, in May, Johns decided to reply to those who still attacked him as a 'warmonger' and 'sabre-rattler'. He wrote an editorial entitled 'On the Folly of War'.

These words are written in the hope that they will dispel any lingering suspicion that this magazine is a protagonist of the dreadful business of war. Why anyone should think so is more than I can say, but the Royal Commission on the Private Manufacture of, and Trading in, Arms evidently does think so, for in its report it has quoted certain statements that have been made on this page and endowed them with a meaning far from the one intended.

That I have supported armaments – or, rather, the policy of re-armament – is true, because it is my firm conviction that only by a fair balance of power can peace be maintained. Other nations, with disturbing deliberation, and unmistakable purpose, have armed themselves. They have talked of peace, of the limitation of weapons, and of total disarmament, but from behind their suave assurances has come the thud of hammers that were forging steel and the whirr of lathes that were turning it into forms unknown to husbandry. England alone allowed her machinery of war to fall into disrepair and obsolescence. The Disarmament Conference failed, and now they seek the reason. The reason was that England had lost her talking point. With three thousand more aeroplanes in the nation's hangars our 'friends' would have been more genuine in their anxiety to talk of peace. Surely it must be quite clear to anyone who has watched the march of events since 1918 that England, inadequately armed, was wasting her time by even attending conferences of any sort, where the men who have the guns have ever called the tune. Following the line of argument of the disarmament theorists we might as well disband the police force in the hope of ending crime.[23]

Johns went on to name the three nations who were arming for war and pursuing policies which would make war inevitable: Nazi Germany, Fascist Italy and the Japanese Empire, run by its semi-feudal warlords. Unlike many of his contemporaries, who agreed with the Fascist argument of a Communist menace, Johns did not see Russia as a threat. 'Russia doesn't want war, but she sees what is coming from the East, so she must get ready.' 'The East' was a reference to Japan who, says Johns, 'is driving fast for a war with Russia to acquire more territory. In the near future she will go to war with Russia ...' The following year, in fact, the Sino-Japanese War re-started with the Japanese aerial bombing of China. Johns noted that, at the same time, Japan was exporting gardening materials to England, and was a prominent exhibitor at the 1937 Chelsea Flower Show:

It seems a tragic thing, and one that I cannot regard without distress, that a country which can send out such delightfully worded bulb catalogues as does Japan, can at the same time unload an inferno of death and destruction on unhappy people, most of whom could not have been in the slightest degree responsible for the incident that provoked the outrage. How mimosa can go hand in hand with machine-guns and chrysanthemums with high explosive is something that I cannot understand ...[24]

Elsewhere in his work as a journalist at this time Johns expressed his feelings about peace. He had become very attracted to mountains and was now an alpine enthusiast. This enthusiasm started after reading the George Newnes monthly magazine *My Garden*, whose offices were next door to *Popular Flying*. 'It all began when I picked up casually one of the early copies of *My Garden* and found myself staring at plates showing some exclusive primulas.'[25] In seeking to answer what the attraction of mountains was, Johns wrote:

What is it about these harsh, bare rocks, so grim and stark, that calls us back, and back again. Is it the solitude, the joy of breaking away from the clutches of the monster we ourselves have made, the ogre called Civilization? Is it the relief of being able to gaze once more at an infinite distance, instead of a brick wall? Is it the silence, after the everlasting turmoil of the cities, or the purity of the air, after their poisonous vapours? Is it the freedom that we share with the eagles, soaring in the smokeless blue? I will tell you. It is all these things which together make that indefinable condition called peace. Not the mere peace of warring nations, but real peace, which is peace of mind, body and soul ...[26]

Johns' enthusiasm for gardening found a new outlet in May 1936, when he began to contribute articles to *My Garden*. The articles were to become a regular column, entitled 'The Passing Show', from January 1937, and were to run until the end of 1944. According to the editor of *My Garden*, Theo A. Stephens:

It happened in this way. The offices of *My Garden* were next door to those of *Popular Flying*, of which paper Captain Johns was, and still is, the editor. One day ... he came into my office and introduced himself. Thereafter we had many talks, though I was for the greater part merely an interested listener.

In the course of these talks I was so amused and at the same time edified that one day, scenting good 'copy' I asked Captain Johns whether he had ever written about any of his gardening experiences. He replied that he had not, but was so tired of writing articles and books on flying that it would be a relief and recreation to write on gardening. Commencing with a number of disconnected articles he, early this year, started a regular monthly feature under the title 'The Passing Show' which feature has proved so popular that I decided it was worthy of more permanent presentation ...[27]

The permanent presentation appeared in September 1937, in the form of a book entitled *The Passing Show*, an edited edition of his early articles with additional material. Howard Leigh illustrated it and it was published by *My Garden*. The reviews were enthusiastic. The *Church Times* asked:

Who is the happy gardener? ... We have small doubt that Captain Johns would serve as an example. Certainly he must have been in happy mood when he wrote this very light-hearted book. His pages bubble over with good spirits; we seem to hear between the lines his chuckles at his own jokes.[28]

The Guild Gardener said:

Captain Johns is a gardener first and last, one of the true brotherhood, and his book is humorous just because the joy of the earth fills him with a sense of mirth with which he infects his readers.[29]

Johns' gardening book certainly has a delightfully light touch. It is unique amongst Johns' writings in showing so clearly his love of beauty and his imagination at its gentlest. One day, he told his readers, he would make a 'Garden of Ghosts':

This bower will be bounded by sombre yews and cypresses, with a dark-leaved rhododendron here and there. From out of this sable background will creep white pinks, white stocks, and all the pale-faced people. Rising up from them will be spectral shapes, white foxgloves, lilies and the like, while from flower to flower will flit, on silent wings, white summer moths. Imagine what the perfume would be like on a warm June night! Imagine sitting in such a garden with someone playing softly the Sonata which he who wrote it called 'The Moonlight'. What more could one ask of life?

But the more familiar Johns was not far away. He continued:

What indeed! Yet someone would, I suppose, demand 'a spot of jazz'. I should keep a blunderbuss loaded with slugs and wire-worms for such people ...

Conscious of his new role as a gardening columnist, Johns attended the 1937 Chelsea Flower Show. Remarking on the wide range of nationalities present, he felt 'clearly, if there is one thing that makes the whole world kin, it is flowers.'[30] He described himself as 'a primula and meconopsis worshipper'. But Johns' critical eye was not lacking.

... I think the Society might provide better accommodation for the stand attendants, particularly in the matter of seating arrangements inside the marquees. After standing for ten hours or more in heat that would have collapsed a Singalese many of them were already feeling the strain, and I take my hat off to them for the way they stuck to their jobs.[31]

New war clouds were threatening now and claiming Johns' attention, this time from Spain, a country that he was very fond of and had frequently visited. At a general election in 1936 a Popular Front Coalition of the democratic political parties had come to power. The Falange, the Spanish Fascists, rebelled against them. The rebels were led by General Franco, who immediately set about obtaining military aid and supplies from Hitler and Mussolini in order to overthrow the democratically elected Government of the republic. Johns was bitter in his denunciation of the British Government for its policy of non-intervention. He felt that the democratic powers should have thrown their support against Fascism.

... I have an increasing suspicion that our so-called democracy is nothing like as democratic as it pretends to be. If it was — to take only one example – could it stand by unmoved and watch the cold-blooded murder of its friend in democracy – Spain? For do not be misled. The Spanish Government – by which I mean Republican Spain – is as democratic as a government can be. It was elected by the vote of the people. That it was a Left Wing government makes not the slightest difference. It was the will of the people, and the soul of democracy lies in the simple fact that 'the people are always right'. But our government, being Right Wing, does not hold that view. So it prefers to see Spain slaughtered by its own sworn enemies rather than lift a finger to save it. There you have the truth of the affair.

This is not a matter of politics. I have no politics myself because I believe that party politics belong to the past. It is a matter of right and wrong. I am concerned only with our preservation, and in the end only truth and justice can survive. If that is not so then our entire scheme of things, including religion, is awry.

Of all the foul and craven hypocrisy of which those in power in Britain have been guilty during the last decade – and nowhere in history will you find such a sequence of faint-hearted perfidiousness – this Spanish business is the worst. Regarding it today I can find only one crumb of comfort. We can sink no lower. We have touched the very bottom of the slough of baseness into which the short-sightedness and personal ambitions of our leaders have thrown us. For evermore, every Spaniard who survives this massacre, be he Franconian or Republican, will spit at the very name of England. And well he might. I could myself spit at this farce, this lie called non-intervention. What infamy! What does our Government of governesses think we are? A nation of fools? If this is the wages of democracy then let us for God's sake change our tune and be Fascist – Bolshevist – anything as long as we can be men again, instead of the mob of bleating sheep that the Government would have us be. What a different story it will be when we are getting what Barcelona is getting now.

Nothing we may do in the future will atone for the wrongs we have done since a parcel of imbeciles, or knaves (I don't know which), drew the Lion's teeth. When all the mediocrity and minor issues of this era have dropped away, and the events of today have become history, rising high out of the slime will be the brazen pyramids of Perfidious Albion. And their colour will be yellow. Have no doubt of that.[32]

However, at times, Johns seemed to have taken a contrary stand over the Spanish Civil War, probably swayed by contemporary propaganda. In an editorial in *Popular Flying*, September 1936 issue, he accused the Soviet Union of being

behind the war, in spite of the fact that it had been Franco, backed
by a few North African troops, who had raised military rebellion
against the Spanish Government. At first Franco had made no
headway against legitimate Spanish authority, until German and
Italian troops, supplied by Hitler and Mussolini, were sent to help
him. While berating the British Government for not going to the
aid of the Spanish Republic, paradoxically, Johns was attacking
the Soviet Union for doing just that. 'I wish the Russians would
keep their dirty work in their own country.'[33]

Johns now recalled his last trip to Spain in February and March
1936, when he had stood at the cathedral in Palma. Now, he
claimed, 'Bolshevik bombers from Catalonia have smashed it.
What folly! What criminal, insensate folly! ... Bolshevism
reminds me of a mad dog. It must bite somebody, even those who
have befriended it. There is only one thing to do with a mad dog.
Shoot it.'[34] Emotionally carried away, Johns must have repented
his hasty words when it was later shown that the bombing was
carried out by the Luftwaffe, whose Condor Legion was to carry
out devastating aerial attacks on Spanish cities and towns such as
Barcelona and Guernica, attacks which were primarily responsible for the crushing defeat of the Spanish Government forces.
The lessons learnt by the Luftwaffe in Spain were soon to be put
to use against British cities.

Reflecting on his last visit to Spain and Majorca in the light of
what was happening, Johns recalled that he had visited the great
cathedral at Palma and admired its imposing edifice, especially 'a
great rose coloured window [which] catches the midday sun and
floods the floor of the building with what seems to be molten
rubies.'[35] As he looked at this 'a queer feeling of depression swept
over me. Said I: what a ghastly thought it is, but one day some
fool may hit this building with a bomb.' On the ship to the
mainland his depression grew worse. In Barcelona he turned to
Doris and Howard Leigh, who were travelling with him, and
said: 'I am going to have a last look at the cathedral here, for it is,
without doubt, one of the most superb buildings erected, and I
have a feeling that something is going to happen to it. Now Palma
has been bombed ... and that lovely rose window, so I am told,
has been smashed.' The ship which took him to the Spanish
mainland, the *Ciudad de Barcelona*, was later sunk by a torpedo
and Barcelona was devastated by Franco's Luftwaffe mercenaries.

'It makes me sick to think of this. What fools men are, to be sure.'[36]

At Porto Cristo he had found a white geranium for his garden and he reflected that a battle had since been fought where the flower had grown.[37] He also reported that a customs man at Newhaven refused to allow him to bring a hibiscus into the country that he had bought in Barcelona, unless he could produce a certificate of health from its country of origin. He was unimpressed when Johns pointed out that 'the place of its origin was being swept by bullets when I left'. After this, he made sure he went abroad armed with a Ministry of Agriculture plant importation certificate.[38]

Johns said that he had two friends who had fought on opposing sides in the war. 'From what they told me,' he said, with his airman's dispassionate appraisal, 'I gather air fighting in Spain is nothing like so hot as it was in France in the Great War. Tactics seem to be more of the "hit and run" idea than the "fight to the finish" policy. It seems to me that they were both fed up with the whole business.'[39]

Johns was shocked to hear of the death of thirty-year-old Christopher St John Sprigg while fighting for the Republicans in 1937. He had known Sprigg since he was eighteen years old, and Sprigg had contributed articles to *The Modern Boy's Book of Aircraft*. Also under the name of Arthur Cave, he had written several flying adventure stories for *Popular Flying*. Under his own name, Sprigg had a growing reputation as a thriller writer and by his death had published seven thrillers, such as *Death of an Airman* (Hutchinson, 1934). Today Sprigg is still highly regarded by *aficionados* of the thriller genre and his books are eagerly collected. Johns commented: 'What a pity! What a tragedy! Above all, what waste. Heavens above, what waste!'[40]

In *Biggles in Spain*, which Johns sets in the Civil War, Johns included a character called Jock McLannoch, who flew a fighter for the Republicans. Johns' admiration of individual bravery and his conviction that war was tragic folly found expression when he wrote that Jock 'had abandoned his Highland home to fight in what he considered to be the cause of freedom and justice – a cause for which millions of men since the beginning of time have laid down their lives – usually in vain.'

In 1937 he and Doris were able to afford to move from the

cottage at Lingfield into a new house that had been built for them at Colley Chase, Reigate Hill, in Surrey. 'I am going to move my abode,' Johns told *My Garden* readers in April. Lingfield had become too small to accommodate all the visitors that used to call.[41] Also Johns was thinking of his future comfort.

For ten years I have lived in a house that was built six hundred (*sic*) years ago or thereabouts. Now I am going to a brand new house, so new that it is not yet finished, but it will be equipped with every modern device for comfort. When one is young such things as draughts and stone floors are a joke; cunningly concealed steps to trip one up, and beams to knock one down, are good fun ...[42]

The new house was being built through 1937. According to Mrs Marjorie Ellis, Johns took an active part in the building work.[43]

When I bought the land on which my house now stands, there stood the mansion of a noble lord ... in his spacious grounds, a part of which is now my garden, he built an *arc-de-triomphe* − some of the pillars filled the cellar when the house was demolished − the rest remain ...[44]

The 'noble lord's' house had fallen into decay and been demolished, but the basis for a garden remained. There were 'the yew hedges and the pines, the bushes and the climbers on the garden wall', and Johns hoped to incorporate them into his new scheme. Deep in the grass he came upon a marble slab incised with the words 'Here lies Flo, our Dog', and remembering that one of his own pets lay buried in the Lingfield garden he ordered that the stone should be untouched.[45] His plan to build his new home was interesting.

I am going to start with a clean sheet − I mean, a clean site. This orthodox practice of building a house and then making a garden round it is all wrong. Clearly, the thing to do is make your garden, then build your home in the middle of it.'[46]

Johns began the new garden − 'less than an acre of bare earth'[47] − by planting forget-me-nots. He loved blue flowers. 'To me pure blue is irresistible'. He found that he had problems with field mice and offered readers of *My Garden* advice as to how they might be caught. 'I discovered how to catch mice by accident when I was a small boy.' He found they loved buttered toast and birdseed – it seemed to work so far as he was concerned! He found that, as he put the emphasis, his work was interfering with his garden. On one occasion he was trying to build a wall when the telephone rang and he had to leave to attend a banquet.[48] However, he and Doris found time to take a sixteen-day trip to France during the August of 1937, journeying from Dieppe to the Rhone Valley from where he brought back some cypress trees and a rock for his rock garden.[49] He had pieces of rock and stone in his garden 'gathered from one end of Europe to the other. I would not part with these for worlds, they represent hours of my life ...'[50] They returned by way of Avignon and the Cevennes. 'It was so lovely I could have wept!'[51] At Chartres, near the cathedral – 'the like of which this world may never see again once a bomb has destroyed it' – he found a geranium and took a piece. War was still much on his mind and even in his gardening column he warns about it in the form of recounting a 'talk' with his herbaceous border. It is an amusing but significant piece of writing, in which the flowers demand gas masks, like the humans. Johns tells them that war is inevitable because 'all men are insane', and that war will come because of economic causes, industrialisation and the need to make money.[52]

It was on 12 January 1938 that he and Doris moved into their new house. It faced Reigate Heath[53] and had a terrace along its south side which was stone-flagged with a surrounding hollow wall. Johns' study led onto it.[54] On this terrace Johns was to feed the birds a great bowl of bread, cakes and rice with boiling water poured over it, every day during the cold winter of 1938–9.[55] They now had a maid called Edith and a gardener's boy called George.[56] Doris's mother, Mrs Florence Leigh, and her sister Marjorie, moved to Reigate with them. Marjorie was to become Johns' secretary, typing his manuscripts and helping him deal with the vast amount of correspondence he was now receiving.[57] Johns commented on Mrs Leigh during this period: 'My mother-in-law will stop to pluck up a fallen rose petal. She will also stop to pick up my cigarette ash when it falls on her carpet. But if she did not do this it is unlikely she would be such an excellent cook ...'[58] The other members of the Liegh family did not accompany Bill and Doris. Elsa was to marry Thomas Broom during the year of the move, while Howard Leigh had already married Olive Eldon at Lingfield parish church and had set up home at Lyme House Farm, Lingfield.

During the 1930s Johns' achievements had surpassed his wildest ambitions. Through his writing he had found fame and financial security; he was able to indulge his tastes for travel, for gardening and for entertaining in his new home. Only the gathering European war clouds threatened his idyllic existence.

12

VOICES PROPHESYING WAR

On 2 April 1938 George Newnes Ltd launched a sister paper to *Popular Flying*; a paper that would take some of the massive overspill of articles and stories which space precluded from inclusion in the monthly. It was called *Flying* and was a 3d weekly, published on Fridays. Johns was asked to take the editorial chair as well as continuing his role as editor of the monthly. In the April issue of *Popular Flying*, Johns explained:

> Without beating about the bush *Flying* contains the overflow from *Popular Flying*. Do not take that to mean the throw-out stuff. Oh no! Actually there will be little difference in the contents of the two papers, but the extra space – for that is what it amounts to – gives me a chance to deal with interesting stuff which would probably be pushed out of *Popular Flying* owing to lack of space.

Johns' output, always prodigious, was now astonishing: he was editor of a weekly magazine; editor of a monthly magazine; he wrote a regular monthly column for *My Garden*; and, from the 19 February 1938 issue of *The Modern Boy*, he was contracted to write a regular weekly column called 'Let's Look Around'. He also found time to contribute articles and stories to a host of other journals: from William Earle short stories in the *Daily Express* to a series of regular articles under his own name in *Men Only*, *Tit-bits* and *Answers*. In addition, he was still producing books at a breath-taking rate. In all, between 1931 and 1939, Johns produced forty titles: eighteen of these, plus an omnibus title, were Biggles books; six were a series devoted to his 'Raffles of the Air', Steeley; six were non-fiction; three were anthologies of various kinds; four were adult titles (three thrillers and one romance); one was a collection of his own short stories, *The Raid*, which John Hamilton published in April 1935; and one was a juvenile adventure tale about pirates entitled *Champions of the Main*, which Oxford University Press published in June 1938.

The Steeley books were written by Johns as adult thrillers and published as such. The first book, *Sky High*, was published by George Newnes in February 1936. A former RFC pilot, Steeley Delaroy, comes home after the war to the fabled 'land fit for heroes' only to find it not so. The British Government had betrayed their promises. Steeley sets about rectifying matters by robbing from the rich and distributing the money to impoverished ex-servicemen and their families. He is later joined by his ex-wartime companion Tubby Wilde and a young journalist, Bryan Ballantine. It was rather an astonishing theme for one now being accused of advocating a 'blind patriotism'. *Sky High* began serialisation in the new George Newnes aviation magazine *Air Stories* as 'Aerial Enemy No. 1'.[1] A second serialisation was almost immediately run in the Amalgamated Press crime magazine, *The Thriller*.[2] Subsequently, all the Steeley stories received their first serialisation in *The Thriller*.

The critics enjoyed *Sky High*. 'Thoroughly good crook stuff about an aerial bandit with a Robin Hood complex,' said *Pearson's Weekly*. 'Fast moving tale of a modern Raffles,' commented the *Hull Daily Mail*. *The Cambridge Daily News* felt 'there are many thrilling incidents in this brightly written story', and the *Glasgow Evening News* agreed that it was 'abounding in thrills'.[3]

The fourth title in the series, *The Murder at Castle Deeping*, 1938, was published by John Hamilton, while the other titles, with the exception of the sixth and last title, were published by George Newnes. The sixth story presents a mystery, for it has never been published in an English book version. It was, however, published in Norwegian, translated by Leif Borthen, as *Det Forsvunne Dagboksblad* ('The Missing Page') by Forlagshuset, Oslo, in 1939. 'The Missing Page', as a complete Steeley novelette, appeared in *The Thriller* for 16 October 1937. Johns might have been thinking of using 'The Missing Page' together with another Steeley novelette, 'Nazis in the New Forest', which appeared in *The War Thriller* for April 1940, to make another full-length Steeley book. However, he then cannibalised 'Nazis in the New Forest' for the first half of *Sinister Service*, published by Oxford University Press in June 1942. Steeley and Tubby become Lance and Rodney Lovell in this version.

At the end of the second book in the series, *Steeley Flies Again*, Johns decided to let his hero be 'won over' to work as a special agent for Colonel Raymond, the Assistant Commissioner at Scotland Yard – a character out of his Biggles books. This takes place much to the annoyance and suspicion of Steeley's archenemy, Detective Inspector Wayne. Of the third title, *Murder By Air*, the *Edinburgh Evening News* felt it was a 'thrilling tale of international intrigue ... Captain Johns can be depended on to write a good yarn, packed with action and excitement and this one leaves nothing to be desired.'[4] The *Hull Daily Mail* was quite rapturous: '*Murder by Air* ... is probably the greatest air thriller Captain Johns has ever written. Bristling with thrills and action all the way through ...'[5] However, for the *Torbay Express*, the fourth title, *The Murder at Castle Deeping*, 'is Captain Johns' best air thriller and entitles him to be popularly regarded as the Edgar Wallace of the air.'[6] At the beginning of the Second World War, Johns decided not to continue with his Steeley stories, presumably because the public was demanding modern tales of aerial warfare, featuring his more popular character, Biggles.

In 1936 Johns decided to attempt a romantic novel. The result was *Blue Blood Runs Red* by Jon Early, which Newnes published in December of that year. An 'anonymous reviewer' in the December issue of *Popular Flying* told how Johns came to write this atypical work.

At a dinner party several people were pulling WEJ's leg about his books. One lady asked why her sex did not figure more prominently. WEJ replied that he only wrote about things that interested him. This was followed by a challenge, the lady questioning WEJ's ability to write a novel. It was accepted with the observation that it was not necessary to know anything about romance in order to write a romantic novel.

WEJ shut himself up for a week and then reappeared with a bunch of papers in his hand. It was the manuscript of *Blue Blood Runs Red*. But when he handed it to his publishers they flatly refused to publish it under his own name, pointing out that the public learnt to expect a certain type of book from a particular author and it did not do to mislead them. WEJ struck out his name on the title page and wrote John Earlie (*sic*) instead. So now you know why.

Actually, the name on the book was Jon Early, not John Earlie, and 'W. E. Johns' was printed in brackets below it. The publishers described the book as a 'light romance sometimes achieving the frivolous gaiety of sheer farce and at others the crisp, observant dignity of good English prose. One might almost call it a musical comedy in book form without music.' The story is about a young Englishman, faced with financial ruin, who lets his ancestral home to an American for a year. He decides to get a job as a wine waiter in London, but somehow, in this role, he replaces his family butler at his former home – now occupied by a glamorous American heiress. The book has more than a touch of Dornford Yates, and can be classed as a pastiche of Yates at his most romantic – and ridiculous.

It was not a success, but Johns pressed on and followed this up with *Desert Night*, published under Johns' own name by John Hamilton in March 1938. The *Manchester Evening News* described it as 'love among the pyramids and every bit as romantic as a subject should be. A girl from America, a British agent, and a threat of tribal warfare. It is a struggle of duty and love makes the climax.'[7] The *Edinburgh Citizen* found it 'full of adventure and awkward turns, the story is very attractive'.[8]

In the summer of 1938 Johns went to lunch with the film producer and director Alexander Korda, who wanted advice on an aviation film he was producing for London Film Productions. It was called *Conquest of the Air* and the screenplay was by the American John Monk Saunders, who had written *Wings* in 1928 and *Dawn Patrol* in 1930; the music was by Sir Arthur Bliss. The film had been planned as early as 1934, but the project was constantly being shelved, and filming only started in 1936. At least five directors had worked on it. The story was intended to show the history of aviation from Lunarido (played by Laurence Olivier) to Wilbur Wright, and from Leonardo da Vinci to Count Zeppelin – but somehow it all refused to 'hang together'. Korda turned for advice to Johns, as editor of the country's top aviation magazine. As an adviser, Johns followed on good company, for in 1935 it had been announced that Winston Churchill was going to supervise some of the sequences. Whatever Johns' suggestions were, Korda finally decided to shelve the film for good. But late in 1939 the British director Charles Frend salvaged some footage, added a narration, and released it in May 1940 as a 71-minute feature for Key Films. In 1944 an edited 46-minute version of this was distributed.

Musing on his incursion into the motion picture industry, Johns wrote: 'One day I hope to get a film made of Biggles'.[9] Meanwhile, he had to be content with an amusing and accidental advertisement of the airman's name in the film *A Yank at Oxford*. This included a sequence with an Oxford bookshop in the background. A display of Biggles books and the names Biggles and Captain W. E. Johns could clearly be seen, and Johns received many letters telling him about this.[10]

As war in Europe became ever more imminent, Johns took a reflective look over his past editorials in *Popular Flying*. In January 1937 he had commented on the furore his pleas for rearmament had created. 'Astonishing how accurate some of our prophecies have been, isn't it?' he asked his readers.

I remember well the abusive letters that came in when, with nearly every newspaper in the land shouting about the magnificence of our air defences *Popular Flying* chipped in a small voice and protested that nothing would stop a determined bomber. Everyone admits that now.[11]

In the issue of July 1938 he quoted from some of the attacks he had made over the years about Government policies.

For writing that people called me a sabre-rattler, a warmonger! Who would deny the truth of it now? Our nose has been pulled and pulled severely. The rush to build aeroplanes has become a panic. Expedited flying training has cost far too many young pilots their lives. And that was the Government's idea of economy.[12]

Like most Britons, Johns was pleased when Prime Minister Chamberlain returned from his Munich talk with Hitler with the promise 'peace in our time'. But he was not as euphoric as other political commentators of the day. 'War may yet come,' he warned. 'As I write it has not started. Bearing that in mind, I would commend to readers this thought. But for Mr Chamberlain's trip to see Herr Hitler, war would have unquestionably started some time ago, which means that at this moment perhaps a hundred thousand human beings would be stretched out dead.'[13] Then the details of the Munich Pact were released to the public, and when Johns realised that Britain had betrayed the sovereignty of Czechoslovakia by allowing the Nazis to occupy the Sudetenland, in spite of its treaty obligations to the Czechs, he was very bitter.

When Mr Chamberlain first stepped into an aeroplane bound for Germany we were on the very brink of war. At the moment the Premier announced his intention of going, the feeling in well-informed quarters of the City was that war was inevitable within twelve hours. It may be, therefore, that Mr Chamberlain's action (made possible, curiously enough, by the very instrument that would have destroyed them) saved several million lives. That is how it appears from a superficial viewpoint, anyway, so the Premier deserves all the adulation that has been showered upon him by a Europe almost paralysed with fright, and now nearly hysterical with relief.

In plain, unvarnished fact, what really happened was this. Civilization was suddenly confronted by a new menace – an international gangster in a big way. That's all Hitler really is. Just an arch-gangster; a thug who points a machine-gun at a crowd of men, women and children and says: 'Give me what I want or I'll riddle the lot of you'.

In such circumstances there is only one thing to do – that is, if the crowd has any regard for life. Give the fellow what he wants. If the thing happens to belong to somebody else, the affair concludes to the satisfaction of all parties – except, of course, the poor wretch who has lost his wallet.

He adds:

The British Empire thanks Mr Chamberlain for saving the peace. America thanks President Roosevelt. Italy thanks Mussolini. Germany thanks Hitler. France thanks M. Daladier. Fine! But when the history of the period is written, the only country that will come out of the affair with its honour unsmirched is Czechoslovakia. She has no reason to thank anybody for anything. In fact, the courageous behaviour of that country was the only bright spot in a very dirty business. Future politicians might well set their clock by Prague.

And now, thanks to Mr Chamberlain, and by the gracious mercy of Herr Hitler, I'll go and plant my tulips.[14]

Johns' editorial in the December issue of *Popular Flying*, entitled 'On Peace in Our Time', reiterated his stance throughout and stated his belief yet again that only strength would save the day.

Were it not for the irritation the overworked phrase might provoke, I could dismiss the matter – justifiably, as old readers will agree – with those four hateful words 'I told you so'. Not that there is any credit to be claimed for this. The danger was there for all to see. Most people saw it. Unfortunately, those whose business it was to take the necessary precautions did not see it. Or if they did they buried their heads, ostrich-like in the sands of their commendable but out-of-date belief in British immunity from catastrophe.[15]

Johns attacked the 'succession of Air Ministers whose lack of vision will be a cause of speculation to future writers when dealing with this period of time'. He especially singled out Lord Londonderry. Johns, with prophetic accuracy, foresaw war within a year or two:

As far as one can judge there is only one way in which we as a nation, and as individuals, can save ourselves from this appalling ordeal. It is aeroplanes. Bombers, and still more bombers, with thousands of interceptors to guard our coasts. Parity is not enough. If Germany has five thousand bombers, then we must have ten thousand. For every blow that Hitler can strike we must be able to strike two in return. This is the only argument dictators understand.

Ruefully, Johns ends his editorial:

It is a pity that the demand for prophets has fizzled out, or I could hawk this round as a sort of testimonial as to my ability for a job in the Ministry of Prophecy.[16]

At this anxious time, Doris and Bill Johns decided to go to North Wales for the Christmas holidays. He wanted to see a famous garden, Bodnant, near Llandudno.[17] According to Johns 'the one country in Europe with the exception of Russia which I had not visited was Wales'.[18]

For about forty years people have been saying to me, on account of my name, 'You come from Wales' thus revealing that they know more about me than I do myself. There may be truth in it. I don't know, and I don't care. What my ancestors did or where they came from concerns me no more than it does you, so we need waste no time discussing it.

The trip was fairly eventful. The weather was bad and near Oxford Johns' car went into a skid. 'After the car had skidded backwards, and sideways farther than I thought it possible for a car to skid, a policeman came up to me and said, in a voice heavy with sarcasm "which way *do* you want to go, sir?" ' On the other side of Oxford another motorist slid sideways into Johns' car and both cars ended up in a snowdrift. To make matters worse the driver of the other car was hilariously drunk. Doris and Bill finally left him on the road, extricated their own car and drove on.

The Cotswolds were the devil. I tackled them with a careless laugh on my lips and terror in my heart. The snow got deeper and deeper but there was no going back.

In sight of Broadway the car burst into flames, due, I believe to the ignition being chafed to pieces by frozen snow.

I put the fire out with a soda-syphon. The syphon was, of course, an accessory to a bottle of whisky which I thought might save my life if I got frozen in somewhere. It was a Schweppes syphon; and if you think that Schweppes are going to keep me in free soda water because I mention their name you are wrong. The wise guy always puts Schweppes in his car because he can swop the empty syphon for a full one at any pub on the road for a few pence. Which is something you cannot do with a local syphon. Put that in your notebook and don't say I never give you a tip.

I must say that I felt very foolish as I squirted soda water on the fire; to an onlooker it would, I feel, have been an engaging spectacle.

To make a long story short, after two days' struggle with the elements – as they say in the papers –I reached Deganwy where, heavens be praised, I neither saw nor heard an aeroplane, so I was able to devote my undivided attention to matters of interior interest.[19]

They returned to London in early January to find his editorial attacks on the Government had upset several prominent politicians who were now bringing pressure to bear on George Newnes Ltd to have him removed from his editorships. Johns was unconcerned. In the March issue of *Popular Flying* he made another damning attack on the British Government for their non-intervention policy over Spain, accusing them of 'foul and craven hypocrisy' for letting Republican Spain fall into the clutches of the Fascists.[20] But by the time this editorial appeared, Johns had been removed from the editorship of the weekly *Flying* and given notice that the May issue of *Popular Flying* would be his last as editor. According to Mrs Marjorie Ellis: 'Captain Johns wrote an editorial attacking the Government and he was asked to go to the

Houses of Parliament to see someone about it. He received an awful rocket about it.'[21] According to information that Johns gave his publishers, Hodder and Stoughton: 'In 1939, as a result of criticism of the Government's lagging air policy, he was removed from the editorial chairs of both *Popular Flying* and *Flying*, but continued writing on air subjects for British and overseas journals'.[22] Johns' last signed editorial appeared in the weekly *Flying* on 21 January, and the 25 February issue carried a brief note: 'Will readers please note that I am no longer editor of *Flying*. Letters should therefore be addressed to the editor and not to me. WEJ.' No explanation for his dismissal was published at the time.

The only sign that his cavalier dismissal upset Johns was the fact that his doctor ordered him to go on holiday for a rest, ostensibly because of flu and 'a touch of fever'.[23]

While recovering from influenza, Johns found that his sister-in-law Marjorie had been watering his alpine plants with ice-cold water from the outside tank. Fortunately, his plants recovered and the corydalis 'threw up a fountain of fern-like foliage' within a week.[24] Johns, obeying his doctor's orders, took Doris down to the South of France in March. It was while they were exploring the mountains near the French-Italian border that Johns decided to take the opportunity to write his editorial for the April issue of *Popular Flying*.

So I sit here on the top of a mountain, the name of which I do not even know. A thousand feet below me the mediaeval town of St Agnes hangs like an eyrie on its pinnacle of rock. Far below again is Menton, which the Italians still call Mentone, and beyond that again, the blue Mediterranean. On my left, the sun-soaked Cote d'Azur, dappled with the yellow and pink of mimosa and almond blossom, which Signor Mussolini covets and says he will have. Well might he covet it.

'Behind me when I turn my head the azure sky is pierced by the gleaming minarets of the High Alps. So this is, as you will perceive, a pleasant place for contemplation. Lying on my stomach on a bed of aromatic thyme, by shading my eyes with my hands I can see, far below, many people. Some are working in their vineyards. Some, on the Italian side, move slowly along the lines of brilliant colour which I know are acres of carnations. Those who toil, toil pleasantly and easily. Which is toil as it should be. Far out on a turquoise sea a pink sail bends gently to the breeze as a fisherman from Ospedaletti or Ventimiglia makes his catch. Other people, although I cannot see them, are at play. A few, like me, are doing nothing, content to lie in the sun and bask.

But Johns was not merely contemplating the splendour of the scenery.

Yet when Mussolini strikes the gong, the heaven in which I am now lying will be shattered in an instant of time. For as I walked up here, on every side, I saw what appeared to be little matchstalks sticking out of the rocks. I can see them now, bristling from every hill that offers its profile. The little sticks are guns. Guns – guns – guns – everywhere guns. How very foolish it is. Think of the labour of making them. Think of the labour of dragging them up to where they now menace the pleasant scene. What an excellent thing it would be if I could stand up and roar to the happy labourers below to come and help me cast all these cannons into the sea. Why don't they do it, I wonder? The people on both my left and right would sleep and work and play the happier if they were not there; for one day those same guns are going to destroy the homes that have taken a lifetime to build. And to destroy *them*, too. Yet they dare not do it. It is very curious.[25]

Johns left the mountain to go to a tavern ran by an Italian, Mario, and his French wife, Narcisse. 'I shall drink a stoup of wine to the confusion of those who would turn this paradise into hell.'[26] When Doris and Bill Johns returned home, they found that one of their dogs had been run over and killed.[27] It was not until the end of the year that Johns bought a new Sealyham puppy, called Mitts, to replace the animal.[28]

The time had so come for him to write his last editorial for *Popular Flying*. Following its launch, he had built it up, after eight years as editor, into the world's leading aviation magazine. One could forgive the touch of bitterness that crept into his article.

It has been my fortunate fate – or unfortunate, as I sometimes think, to see from close range the 'moving finger writing' this unhappy passage of our history. Those of you who have read this paper from its inception must know the story fairly well, for I have referred to it in part more than once: indeed, I think I may be forgiven if I claim to have stated fairly accurately what the future held. If anyone questions that, let him read the Editorials of *Popular Flying* from number one up to last summer when, before a word of crisis had been mentioned, I hinted what was coming 'after the harvest was up'.[29]

However, Johns felt that he could lay down his editorial pen having at least succeeded in making the British public, even the reluctant Government, aware of the danger of appeasement, and of the need to rearm in the face of the Fascist threat.

For years past, inspired by heaven only knows what false information, most of the feature writers in the daily press had been belittling the bomber as a potent factor of warfare, and/or making groundless claims that our few antiquated interceptors could stop enemy bombers. And it was that as much as anything that drove me into incoherence on these pages. Oh, I had some raps over the knuckles for those Editorials, make no mistake about that. But I had a power behind me. It was Truth. And judging from my correspondence, most readers recognised it.

Well, that's the story. It's all over, I think, except for the final bang. We have nearly finished eating humble pie. If Hitler or his henchmen ever had the idea of breaking the British Empire, they've lost their chance. But the very fact that they might once have done it is not pleasant to contemplate.[30]

The magazines were now taken over by Oliver Stewart who took a non-controversial editorial line. They were not to survive the war years. There can be no doubting Johns' successful editorial capabilities, which made *Popular Flying* and *Flying* the most widely read aviation magazines in the world. A glimpse of Johns in his editorial chair comes from Robert Polendine, a contributor to *Popular Flying*. He had submitted a highly technical article on 'Thrust', and Johns told him, with disarming candour, that personally he was unable to judge whether it was accurate or not. Polendine assured him that it was, whereupon Johns promptly accepted it. As the piece appeared in *Popular Flying* in June 1939, this must have been one of his last editorial decisions.[31]

Free from the constraint of his office job, Johns celebrated by taking Doris on another holiday to see the Bodnant Gardens, near Llandudno in North Wales. They spent Whitsun there.[32] The loss of income from his enforced resignation did not worry him unduly. He was not particularly interested in riches. 'The quest of wealth is like chasing a rainbow,' he once wrote. 'I have hunted a rainbow in an aeroplane but always in the end it was just grey mist ...'[33] However, he still had his regular features in *The*

Modern Boy and *My Garden*, and *Pearson's Magazine* now asked him to start a regular monthly column for them too, to be called 'What Men Are Talking About'. The amazing quantity of short stories, articles and serials which he produced for a wide variety of magazines, together with his books, made financial worries of little consequence.

Now he could live at Reigate without having to make daily trips to London, which suited him very well. He hated London. Apart from the hours spent in his office there, the only time he enjoyed 'in the bedlam which is called London'[34] was lunch-time, when he could potter round flower or bulb stores or delve among old books among the shops in Charing Cross Road, searching for out-of-print gardening prints and books. Mrs Marjorie Ellis believes: 'Had it not been for Doris he would probably have ended up as a gamekeeper, just living in the country, doing his painting and that kind of thing.'[35] Whatever might have been, however, by 1939 the names of Biggles and Captain W. E. Johns, his creator, were household words. Johns' journalism, his outspoken advocacy of rearmament and his other books had all helped to make him well known, but it was his airman hero who brought him fame, transcending national barriers. Ironically, *The Camels Are Coming* had been published in Germany in 1936 as *Feindlich Flieger in Sicht* (*Enemy Flyer in Sight*), translated by Hans Herdegen, and published by Goldmann Verlag in Munich. Johns was proud of this fact.[36] Translation rights from Norwegian and Swedish companies were also being accepted. Biggles had already become a byword, and when, in 1939, Johns went aboard an airliner, the young airline pilot greeted him with 'How's Biggles?'[37] After the outbreak of war, the Biggles series was to take on a new significance and earn a place in history. Meanwhile, in that uneasy summer, Johns could no longer attack the Government from the 'Editor's Cockpit'. However, thanks to Chamberlain's efforts at Munich, there was still time to cultivate his garden.

13

FOR THE DURATION

The eve of war found Johns in Monte Carlo 'hoping for the best'.[1] Johns had been a visitor to the casino for several years, but he had never seen such vast amounts being gambled as in the last days of peace. Doris and Bill Johns had gone to the South of France for another trip in August, and Johns spent some time, 'collecting seeds in the Alpes Maritimes'.[2] When the news came that Britain was on the verge of war and had delivered an ultimatum to Germany concerning her invasion of Poland, 'I drank of a little wine quickly to restore my composure to that tranquil mien which seems to be expected of the British in times of stress, and made my way briskly to the station in time to insinuate myself into the tail-end of the great homeward trek ...'[3] He was in London when the official declaration of war was made.

'September 3, 1939, will surely go down in history as the occasion of the world's greatest anti-climax,' he observed. Following the Prime Minister's declaration, 'the sirens wailed their warning and the whole world held their [sic] breath, waiting for the crack of doom which would announce the beginning of the end.'[4]

But nothing happened. The sun continued shining; the birds went on singing; cattle browsed unmoved, and bees went about their business with undiminished activity. Soft music continued to emanate from the radio.

An hour passed – two hours. The sun continued shining; the birds went on singing; cattle browsed unmoved, and the bees went about their business unmoved.

The day passed. The moon rose as usual; the waves still fretted on the shore; the stars twinkled as usual; a ripple spread over the face of the waters and the poplars stirred as the world breathed again. People opened their doors and stared at the sky as if finding it hard to believe that it was still there. Little dogs ran out and trotted from pillar to post with more than usual alacrity.

I don't think there has ever been, or will ever again be, a more extraordinary week than that which followed – at any rate in London.

Johns spent the days loafing round his clubs, the Royal Aero Club in Piccadilly and the Royal Aeronautical Club, listening to the gossip.

At one famous club in Waterloo Place an army of men were feverishly piling sandbags as if the enemy were already at our gates. In another, next to it, there was not a sandbag to be seen; instead, painters were carefully repairing the frieze in the lounge as leisurely as if the War were no more than a bickering between two remote tribes.[5]

In another club Johns found a small but cheerful party engaged in manufacturing rumours. 'Even while I was there a man came in who claimed to have met a man who had actually witnessed an incident which had been concocted in that very room less than an hour before.'

The Phoney War was to continue for some months – the short uneasy interlude before Göring's Luftwaffe began the blitz bombing of London and other large cities, a bombing which Johns had foreseen years before. It must have been with some irony that he considered his enforced resignation from *Popular Flying* and *Flying* for warning against the very thing that had now come to pass.

At the outbreak of war, Johns, in common with many of his contemporaries, thought in terms of getting back into uniform. There would be no leaping on his mare and galloping away to the battlefront the second time round, but he hoped that his RAF experience would stand him in good stead. According to Jack Cox: 'Johns' first reaction was to go back to flying on active service. But he was forty-six and the Air Ministry had other plans for such a useful person.'[6] Mrs Marjorie Ellis remembers that Johns was offered a post of some kind at the Air Ministry in London, but he preferred to offer his services to help the Air Defence Cadet Corps, a junior branch of the RAF, which trained boys still at school. The Corps had been in existence since 1938, although as early as 1929 there had been a British Young Airman's League. Leonard Taylor, editing the *Air Defence Cadet Corps Gazette* in August 1940 was able to report:

We have been fortunate in securing the collaboration of Captain W. E. Johns, well-known to all of you as the editor of *Popular Flying* and author of many thrilling books of air stories. In this issue he writes an interesting article on the qualities that make up an air 'ace'.

Johns became a lecturer to the Air Defence Cadet Corps, and when it became the Air Training Corps in April 1941 he continued with the work. Jack Cox wrote:

The Air Ministry used him as a lecturer and he talked all over Britain on every possible subject concerned with flying from 'Combat Tactics in the Air' to 'Escaping from PoW Camps'. Air Cadets liked his breezy manner and the countless personal anecdotes which livened his talks.[7]

Johns also said that he 'wrote specialised books on air subjects for the Air Ministry and the Ministry of Information'.[8] Such books did not carry a by-line and so are now, unfortunately, impossible to trace. Johns supplemented the information he was passing on to young Air Cadets when he started a regular column in *The Boys' Own Paper* entitled 'Skyways: Jottings from My Log-Book' with the September 1941 issue. The column was almost entirely devoted to the activities of the ATC. A month later, in October, Johns started a similar column in *The Girls' Own Paper* on matters concerning the Women's Auxiliary Air Force (WAAF). However, after the March 1942 issue of both these publications, the column came to be signed simply by 'The Pilot', a practice which continued until June 1945 in the case of *The Boys' Own Paper*, and November 1942 in *The Girls' Own Paper*. In addition to these activities, Johns joined the Air Raid Precaution (ARP) at Reigate Heath.

But Johns' chief contribution to the war effort had already been made during the 1930s. Alan Morris wrote:

I cannot express the Nation's debt to his Biggles books, which encouraged thousands to join the Auxiliary Air Force and RAF Volunteer Reserve or to acquire an A licence in time for September 1939. These, together with his mid-30's advocacy ... of an appropriate strategic bomber force can never be properly rewarded.[9]

Johns' books continued to have a marked influence throughout the war. Jack Cox reported that:

The Air Ministry woke up to the fact that during the black-out, Biggles became an established boys' hero and was a most valuable recruiting aid for the RAF.

Johns was persuaded to produce a new female counter-part for girls and soon Worrals of the WAAF was diving in and out of adventures of all kinds. The War Office decided that they must not be left behind in this popular method of recruiting young people. Soon a remarkable commando officer made his mark on the world of boys' fiction. His name was Gimlet.[10]

More important, however, than these new ventures was the enduring effect of the Royal Flying Corps Biggles books that Johns had written in the pre-war period. In 1934 he had prefaced a collection of the tales with the hope that the pilots of the future would learn something about the tactics of war flying from them. Now he received many letters from readers who had read Biggles' First World War flying adventures, telling him how much they owed to the stories. During the war the Sunday newspaper *Reynolds News* interviewed a leading British fighter pilot and asked him to what he owed his success. The pilot answered, 'Biggles'. According to Johns: 'The reporter naively headed his article "Who is Biggles?" I gather a lot of people answered his question.'[11] Talking to the *Sunday Express* reporter Robert Pitman, Johns recalled, 'I also had a visit from an RAF officer who said he had escaped from a PoW camp by deliberately employing methods he had learned from Biggles.'[12]

Biggles' widespread influence was not confined to Britain. After the war two Norwegian boys hitchhiked to England to have their photographs taken with Johns, their favourite author. They told him that during the wartime occupation of their country by the Germans they had frequently smuggled themselves over the Swedish border to buy the latest Biggles books, which, naturally, had been banned by the Germans. Only one Johns' title had been published in Norway before the Occupation and no more were to come out until after the war. However, in neutral Sweden, two publishers, B. Walhström and Bonniers, vied with each other in bringing out new Johns' books in translation. Walhström had brought out the first Swedish Biggles book *Biggles Stridsflygaren* (*Biggles of the Camel Squadron*) in 1940, and the same company still publishes the series, which remains immensely popular.

In turning his attention to his garden in the early days of the war, Johns' first thought was to build an air-raid shelter. 'In 1918 I little thought that the day would come when I should build a dug-out in my own garden. But this I have done. It isn't exactly a dug-out, but a formidable stockade of timber, sand and rocks. This is flanked with stone troughs ...'[13] Another sign of the times was the call up of George, his gardener's boy, into the army. Johns felt 'strangely moved' by the event. 'He was so gentle – his thoughts all on his work with the soil'. Johns reflected that 'he has nothing to gain and all to lose in this senseless slaughter ...'[14] But Johns was quite contemptuous of a lady neighbour who was upset because her cook had been called up and who, looking at her ration books 'in a kind of daze', complained she could not manage.[15] Johns immediately got to work in his garden and bought more land for £250, including within his boundary a 'fine upstanding Scotch fir' in order to preserve it.[16] A few years later this fir was to be shattered by a bomb.[17] He had now cleared his flower beds and was working hard 'to make my soil produce the maximum crop of food'. He had finally found a use for white dress gloves, items of apparel he had always disliked – he found they made strong and pliable gardening gloves.[18] By March 1941 he was able to report, 'I have practically the whole garden, including the lawn, under vegetables.'[19]

A welcome piece of family news brightened the early days of the war, when Johns' son, Jack, married Sabena Hammond, a nurse who had been looking after his mother. The marriage took place in Norwich on 3 October 1939. Neither Johns nor Maude was able to attend the wedding. At the time, Maude Johns was in the process of having her knee pinned, to try to relieve the terrible pain she suffered from arthritis. Jack, unable to join up because of his ill-health, was now making a career for himself in local journalism. Johns' first grandchild, Perdita, was born on 19 September 1940, to be followed by her sister, Faith, born on 15 June 1943. Although Johns did not see his son's family often, father and son seemed to get on well and the granddaughters liked and admired their famous grandfather.[20]

With the period of the Phoney War over, war came to Reigate Hill with a vengeance. In August 1940 a bomb fell five miles away and broke two panes of glass in Johns' greenhouse. He was able to boast: 'I'm far more scared of crossing a main road than I am of being hit by a bomb'.[21] However, on 4 September the Luftwaffe mounted a raid on the light industry complexes around Reigate. According to Johns, the local police reported 137 bombs falling in the area.[22] When the air raid started, Johns went to get Mrs Florence Leigh to go to the air-raid shelter. 'My ultra Victorian mother-in-law, knitting under the apple tree, did not stop knitting — when I called her attention to what was going on she merely said: 'nonsense!'[23] The raid was the first of many in the vicinity. A few weeks later Johns was in his bathroom and saw that 'some two hundred enemy aircraft were intercepted over the house'. He noticed that his neighbour's gardener, an old man, went on digging his potatoes undismayed by the battle raging above.[24] There were some near misses, too.

> The other night incendiary bombs set fire to the yew hedge in two places. It burnt briskly. I made the discovery that bombs in a yew hedge are difficult to get at ... A score of bombs fell in and around the garden. As six of the fifteen houses of which I am warden received direct hits, to say nothing of a garage and a fowl house, we had an engaging twenty minutes. At the end of that time we had everything under control, because everybody knew just what to do.[25]

In spite of his lecturing, fire-watching with the ARP, and allied activities, Johns continued to write at his usual phenomenal pace, although he confessed that he was now doing all his writing work during the evenings.[26] Soon after the war started, he found that several of his regular markets were folding, owing to the paper shortage, especially of newsprint. Sadly, one of the first to go was the weekly which had established Johns in the juvenile field, *The Modern Boy*, which folded with the issue of 14 October 1939. In this last issue Johns told the young readers of his 'Let's Look Around' column:

> ... by the time you read this we shall have been at war with Germany for some weeks.
> I don't often preach, as you must admit, but in the circumstances I can't help saying that I hope you will all 'do your bit', in other words, play the game by doing what you are told. War makes things quite difficult enough without unnecessary irritations.

The Modern Boy readers were told to turn to *The Gem*, where a

Biggles serial continued, but this paper was also doomed and had to be amalgamated with *The Triumph* on 30 December 1939, which in turn merged with *The Champion* on 25 May 1940. Readers were told:

... owing to the war in Norway, there is a great shortage of supplies of paper pulp from the country. Consequently it has been found necessary to reduce the number of periodicals published in Great Britain.[27]

Pearson's Magazine, which had been running a monthly column by Johns entitled 'What Men Are Talking About', as well as publishing William Earle short stories, also folded with the November 1939 issue. For the time being, the only regular feature Johns had left was his monthly gardening column, 'The Passing Show'. He now decided to concentrate more on his fiction work.

In September 1939 the first book by Johns to appear after the declaration of war was *The Modern Boy's Book of Pirates*. Written by Johns in its entirety, it was the last of his works to carry his real rank, with the by-line 'specially written by Flying Officer W. E. Johns'. Then in January 1940 his final book published by John Hamilton appeared, *The Unknown Quantity*. This was an adult thriller, concerning a man who took the law into his own hands to avenge the murder of his brother by a London crime syndicate. In 1941 John Hamilton ceased to publish after, it seems, being bombed out of business. That year the company was put into the hands of the receivers, who tried to assess the damage caused by fire to the company's warehouses. The company, however, though not engaged in publishing, remained in existence on paper until 2 April 1968, when it was renamed Petty Business Forms Ltd, part of the British Printing Corporation. In its sixteen years' existence as a publishing house, John Hamilton had been the leading aviation publishers and founder-publishers of *Popular Flying*, and later of *Wings* magazine. Its name will always be linked with Johns' early work.

Three Biggles books were scheduled to be published by Oxford University Press in 1940. Two of these were pre-war adventures: *Biggles — Secret Agent*, a tale featuring Biggles' archenemy, von Stalhein, which was serialised in *The Modern Boy* from 12 August to 14 October 1939; *Biggles in the South Seas*, a highly coloured, tropical extravaganza, serialised in *The Gem* from 14 October to 9 December 1939; and lastly, *Biggles in the Baltic*, serialised in *The War Thriller* from 9 March – it was the first story of the series to have a Second World War setting. There was no Phoney War in Biggles' world. The book begins with the dramatic words of Chamberlain – 'England is now, therefore, in a state of war with Germany' – coming over the radio, and Biggles scarcely has time to murmur, 'It looks as if we are in for another spot of war flying', before the telephone rings. He is summoned, together with Algy and Ginger, to report immediately to the Air Ministry, where a thrilling assignment awaits them.

In 1941 two more Biggles books with wartime backgrounds were published by Oxford University Press. In *Biggles Defies the Swastika*, the airman and his comrades defy the German invasion of Norway and have another brush with von Stalhein. In *Biggles Sees it Through*, the heroes lend their help to Finland against the Soviet invasion of 1939–40, and defeat von Stalhein yet again. These tales, like *Biggles in the Baltic*, in spite of their contemporary settings, followed the familiar pattern of the adventure yarns of the previous decade, and Johns realised that he must become more up to date. His readers expected Biggles to play his part in the Battle of Britain and engage in the kind of dogfights that they read about in the newspapers or actually saw for themselves in the skies overhead. *Spitfire Parade* was Johns' attempt to satisfy this demand, but he confessed that he did not know much about modern aerial combat, nor did he know contemporary RAF slang. In the earlier Second World War Biggles books, Johns' hero was still referring to 'archie' instead of 'flak' or 'ack-ack' and making other blatant errors, and his pilots seemed curiously reluctant to use r/t (radio/transmitters) with which all modern RAF aircraft were fitted. Johns finally consulted Squadron Leader 'Teddy' Ellis, who was soon to marry Doris's sister, Marjorie. The Squadron Leader supplied him with a list of current RAF slang.

But Johns still needed authentic flying background for his new tales of war flying and he took the easy way out. He simply went back to the Royal Flying Corps stories that had first appeared in *Biggles in France* in November 1935 and updated many of them, chopping them about and adding new material where necessary. He also added a First World War tale which had appeared in *The*

Modern Boy's Annual for 1937. Some of the original description of Biggles from the very first story – 'The White Fokker' – also reappears; his 'deep-set hazel eyes' were still restless with a strange fire in them, and his hands remained 'as small and delicate as those of a girl', but now 'his bearing was that of a man of experience'. *Spitfire Parade* has an uneasy quality about it, readily understandable in the light of its history. One Sopwith Camel plus 200 mph does not really amount to a Spitfire.

There is a probably unconscious irony in Johns' dedication of the book of reworked stories: 'To all those boys who knew Biggles in the early days ...'

In fact, in his efforts to provide his readers with contemporary aerial warfare stories, Johns became an amazing self-plagiarist. In the March 1940 issue of *Air Stories* there appeared a tale called 'Sausage and Mash' by 'Old Timer'. This is clearly Johns, and an uncollected short story called 'Spitfire Parade', unrelated to his book, appears under his own name in the same issue. A close reading of 'Sausage and Mash' reveals it to be none other than 'The Trap' from *Biggles of the Camel Squadron*. Johns' attempt to update it to a Second World War setting is, quite frankly, terrible. In using the same story sequences and merely changing the names of the machines, Johns has a modern Blenheim bomber flying in figures of eight, while signalling to artillery men on the ground the position where their shot is falling. The story, which was based on the fact that the machines of 1918 were slow and unarmoured, becomes patently ridiculous when these are replaced by the more sophisticated aircraft of the Second World War.

A boost to Biggles' prestige came in November 1941, when *Biggles Flies Again* was issued as Penguin Book No. 348. As early as the mid-30s, the popularity of Biggles had caused Allen Lane, who had recently started the paperback firm, to contact Johns and explain he was looking for popular authors for his new lists. He was interested in publishing an early Biggles book, one that would suit the adult market. Johns invited him to dine at his home. At that time he was still at the cottage in Lingfield.[28] The project was not pursued until the early war years when Allen Lane decided that *Biggles Flies Again* provided exactly what he was looking for.

In May 1942 Oxford University Press published a pre-war

Biggles adventure with a tropical setting, *Biggles in the Jungle*, and in 1943 they brought out their last two Biggles titles. *Biggles Charter Pilot*, a series of pre-war adventures told in a wartime RAF mess by Ginger, was a collection of near science fiction short stories, which had started serialisation in *The Boys' Own Paper* in October 1941. *Biggles in Borneo* was a tale of Biggles and his squadron with the Japanese as the enemy.

For some considerable time Doris had been worried about Johns' rather unprofessional dealings with his publishers and the fact that he had sold most of his early books, including the Biggles series, outright. Marjorie Ellis remembers how Johns would put on his beret and set off to London on the Bluebell Line bus, taking his manuscripts with him. Doris knew that he should not dispose of his work in this summary fashion and sometimes she would ask a friend, John Townsend, to waylay Johns before he could get to the publishers.[29] Doris felt that he needed an agent to safeguard his interests, and in 1940 she finally persuaded him to employ one. Johns went to see Peter Watt, of A. P. Watt, a firm which had established itself in the late nineteenth century as Britain's first literary agency, handling such figures as H. Rider Haggard, Rudyard Kipling, Anthony Hope, Dornford Yates, Edgar Wallace, and a host of other popular authors. Watt agreed to take Johns on and sort out his business problems.

A. P. Watt's first move was to persuade Oxford University Press to change their contract and give Johns royalty payments instead of an outright sum for each book. According to Frank Eyre, who worked in OUP's Juvenile Department as assistant editor at this time, Johns had originally asked OUP 'for a regular payment so that he would have no worries about whether or not the books would sell and there would be no royalties. From memory the figure was £250 a book and we agreed to take two books a year, so he was drawing a regular income which was quite a lot for a children's writer in those days (we are talking about the Thirties). What I can remember very clearly is that the books did not sell well for a long time and it took some years for us to write off those payments. It wasn't until after the war that their phenomenal sales began.'[30] Frank Eyre also recalls that: 'Captain Johns appointed an agent, Watts, and was then persuaded to demand very high royalties from Oxford. We preferred to let the books go and they were taken over by Hodder and Stoughton.' In fact, Oxford University Press did not let their Johns' titles go until the mid-1950s, and were still reprinting them until that time.

According to Charles Hadfield, who took over the Juvenile Department of Oxford University Press on 1 April 1939:

In pre-war days, an outright payment to an author was normal for juvenile books of a kind that Captain Johns wrote – we called them 'rewards' (ie. they were used in their most expensive first published form – usually 5s. – as school prizes before being put into cheaper editions). Indeed, many adult books were also then paid for outright. The saving to the publisher of having to keep royalty accounts was considerable, while the author had a guaranteed return irrespective of sales.

As I remember, under the original agreement Captain Johns made with my predecessor, Mr L'Estrange, Johns received a fixed sum for each book delivered. Soon after I took over the department, I remember that we sold the Swedish translation rights of one or two of his books. Such sales had not been envisaged when the Johns' agreement was first made and I recollect that we decided to make Johns an ex-gratia payment to him of part of the proceeds.[31]

Charles Hadfield went into the services but returned to Oxford University Press at the end of the war. 'During the war (when every juvenile book printed sold every copy for which paper could be provided) Captain Johns realised that he ought to revise his agreement and had gone to a literary agent. The latter had advised him to ask sums OUP were not prepared to pay ...' According to another OUP editor, John Bell, although OUP were not prepared to alter their outright payment agreement for any new Johns title, 'after the war, first Frank Eyre, and later I, offered to pay either a further fee or a small royalty to Captain Johns in the light of the continuing success of the volumes'.[32] In the late 1950s Oxford University Press ceased to reprint the twenty-two Johns titles they had bought and allowed the rights to revert to Johns. Most of the titles immediately sold in new hardcover editions with Brockhampton's Hampton Library series and in children's popular paperback editions.

Johns had never considered himself solely as a children's writer, although he was now being labelled as such and had continued popularity with stories in *The Boys' Own Paper* and *The Girls' Own Paper*. He still wrote adult short stories, and with growing success. Before the war his short stories had appeared in the *Daily Express*, *Pearson's Magazine*, *Britannia and Eve*, and other journals. Now he was finding markets in *Woman's Journal*, *Woman's Magazine* and *The Strand*. He was also going further afield, with contributions to *Colliers* and *Extension* in the USA, and *Macleans* in Canada. One story, 'Wine with a Lady', was first broadcast on the BBC Home Service short story spot and later published in the *Kit Book of Best Short Stories* of the Year in America.

It was not until after the war that Johns gathered two selections of his adult stories to be published by Latimer House as *Short Stories* in May 1950, and *Sky Fever* in June 1953. Another book of related short stories, concerning a scientist counterspy, and called *Dr Vane Answers the Call*, was published by Latimer in November 1950. These tales had started serialisation in *Pearson's Magazine* in October 1939. The books were not successful in spite of a warm critical reception. Johns was too firmly categorised as a children's writer and they did not achieve sufficient sales among adult readers, while juvenile readers were annoyed by tales of romance. However, the *Daily Telegraph* observed: 'The versatility of the author is reflected in the variety of his topics and his skill as a writer in their attractive treatment.' Lionel Gamlin, of the BBC, said of *Short Sorties*: 'I suggest you start with two stories entitled "Potpourri" and "Wine with a Lady". If you do, you'll go on to read the other eighteen right off the reel.' 'Written with the enviable fluency of a first-class story-teller, it combines clarity and brevity with an unaffected style,' commented the *Liverpool Evening Express*. 'His character drawing is very much on the beam,' said the *Royal Aero Club Gazette*. 'Altogether this book contains in its 200 odd pages stories which, combining ingenuity of plot and sensible dialogue, are some of the most factual fiction ever written about flying.'[33]

Still thinking in terms of adult markets, Johns decided to attempt a new medium in 1942 and turned to radio drama. Working with G. Rodney Ranier, who had experience in radio scriptwriting, he interested the BBC in a projected crime series to be called 'Room 215'. Each episode would be a complete tale. The first of the episodes was to be called 'The Machine Which Disappeared', and it was produced as a pilot episode by Fred O'Donovan and broadcast on the Home Service on 19 June 1942.

According to the BBC Archives: 'for reasons of programme space, however, the idea was not pursued'.[34] But a second episode in the series, 'The Charming Mrs Nayther' — originally entitled 'Birds of a Feather' — was produced by Hugh Stewart and broadcast on 15 August 1942. In 1943 the BBC had to obtain Johns' permission for the script of 'The Charming Mrs Nayther' to be sent, at the request of ENSA, to 'the ship's company of a destroyer' for private entertainment purposes.[35]

It was in September 1941 that Johns' second most famous character appeared in *Worrals of the WAAF*, the book Johns was asked to write by the Air Ministry to aid recruitment to the Women's Auxiliary Air Force. It was published by Lutterworth. 'A worthy sister to Biggles,' greeted the *Daily Mail*. 'Another celebrated character of Captain Johns' invention,' commented the *Scotsman*. 'The kind of grand stuff which the schoolgirl of today will jump at,' said the *Western Mail*. The *Daily Telegraph* called her 'That intrepid yet amazingly unspoilt WAAF'. While *The British Weekly* said she had 'a personality you can't help liking'.[36]

The tale featured Flight Officer Joan Worralson ('Worrals' of the WAAF) and her chum, Section Officer Betty 'Frecks' Lovell. Both girls are qualified pilots, whose job it is to ferry machines from manufacturers to fighting squadrons. It was a job that Johns had prophesied women pilots would be doing back in the early 1930s. Hodder and Stoughton, who were to publish the second Worrals book, *Worrals Flies Again*, in September 1942, commented in their publicity: 'Captain Johns, alive to every phase of RAF history, was not likely to overlook the part women are playing in this new historic age. So he created *Worrals of the WAAF* and now *Worrals Flies Again* with an even more exciting job of work this time than ferrying fighter aircraft. She has a mission to accomplish in France under the very nose of the Gestapo and she carries it off with a courage, resource and dash that rivals Biggles' own'.[37] Johns himself wrote of his 'intrepid young woman' later: 'She undertook some remarkable missions but none (although for security reasons this couldn't be divulged at the time) more desperate than were actually being made by girls in the same Service ...'[38]

Even Johns' recent critics Don Aitkin of Macquarie University and Sue Elderton of Sydney have admitted:

Given Johns' ready acceptance of the prevailing values of his time, it is surprising to find that he does, in one respect challenge traditional conceptions of the capabilities of women and of their proper place in society. His heroine Worrals operates in a man's world, and sounds at times like an embryonic feminist. She is fond of emphasising the contribution women have made to the war effort and is quick to resent any paternalistic behaviour on the part of her male colleagues.[39]

As an example of this, Aitkin and Elderton quote a typical passage taken from *Worrals of the Islands*, which Hodder and Stoughton published in October 1945:

'What does he think I am – one of the Babes in the Wood?' she inquired coldly. 'He's got two flights up topsides, but does he worry about them? No. Why not? Because they're being coaxed through the cumulus by pilots in pants. Men! They can take care of themselves, but we're poor little lambs who can't be trusted to find a way home unless the sun is shining. Fiddlesticks to him.'

Certainly Worrals, in every book, is scornful of male prejudice and paternalism towards women. Having, quite rightly, paid tribute to Johns' very pro-feminist line in the Worrals books, Aitkin and Elderton then claim that 'Johns' championship of women's rights was half-hearted'. To support this claim they can turn only to the last Worrals book, *Worrals Investigates*, published by Lutterworth in 1950. In this tale her task is to rescue a group of women who have been kidnapped by a mentally deranged millionairess, Amelia Haddington, who tries to establish an all-female society on a desert island, based on the Amazonian model. From this tale, which admittedly is not one of Johns' best, Aitkin and Elderton deduce that Johns 'is opposed to the notion of women choosing to live without men', a rather sweeping assertion, in support of which they make an edited quotation from the book.

Another idea was, the country ought to be run by women. She actually started a sort of society to put this over, and with all her money you can imagine the sort of females, spongers and hangers-on, this brought to her house. Some of them may have been genuine, and really thought, like Hitler, they'd been born to run the world. I don't know. Naturally this scheme only made Amelia a laughing-stock, and seeing she wasn't getting anywhere she got an even crazier brain-wave. If

England didn't want her she would start a little kingdom of her own, run by women. No men on the premises at all. In that way she could satisfy both the bugs in her brain – her hatred of men and her belief that she was born to be a queen.

From this quotation Aitkin and Elderton are able to assert that 'it is likely that Johns' enthusiasm for women's capabilities was a product of the contribution of women to war-production. With the war over Johns found no niche for Worrals and in 1950, or thereabouts, he retired her (presumably to contribute to the postwar baby boom)'. Had they been a little more thorough in their researches they would have discovered that Johns' enthusiasm for women's capabilities went back long before the war. He had been in favour of women's participation in the air services as early as 1934. In an editorial, 'Women and Wings', he forecast: 'They are going to fly ... make no mistake about it, the average girl flies as well as the average man.'[40] He not only foresaw women as delivery pilots but asked why there should not be a 'lady ace' filling out her combat report. He clearly and accurately saw that 'women pilots will take the air in a national emergency ... they will want to fly and there is no sane reason why they should not. As far as club-trained women pilots are concerned, time will show that the taxpayers' money has not been wasted.' At this time Johns was an admirer of and friendly with many famous pioneer airwomen such as Amy Johnson, with whom he sometimes lunched.[41]

Aitkin and Elderton have seized on a rather weak example on which to base their criticisms of Johns' alleged attitudes. After all, his villain Amelia Haddington is a megalomaniac, setting herself up as a dictator and supported by some nasty henchmen (henchwomen?) with guns, who keep the majority of women captives in slave-like conditions. Johns clearly explains why Amelia has come to hate men. The only daughter of a multi-millionaire who indulged his child's every whim, Amelia is thoroughly spoilt. She wanted to marry a man who rejected her for someone else. She had a nervous breakdown and spent several years in a home for the mentally disordered. Thereafter she develops the notion of establishing a society, ruled by her as a dictator, in which no men would be allowed. Worrals' and Frecks' rescue of her unwilling slaves can surely not – unless one is hopelessly pedantic – be seriously interpreted as Johns being 'opposed to the notion of women choosing to live without men'.

Another critic of Johns' books, Bob Dixon, writing in *Catching Them Young*[42], paid Worrals an unintentional compliment by calling her 'a kind of female Biggles'. Why shouldn't she be? A host of little girls would be delighted if they earned this description. But Dixon obviously expects women to be the opposite of Biggles – that is, cowardly, feeble and impractical – for he goes on, with unconscious male chauvinism, 'though she's woman enough to faint briefly at the end of *Worrals of the WAAF*'.

For thousands of girls growing up during the 1940s and 1950s, it can be said that the Worrals books influenced them in challenging the old sexist assumptions.

The Worrals series went to eleven titles, six of which were published by Lutterworth Press and five by Hodder and Stoughton. Six of the books had wartime settings, while the other five pursued the adventures of Worrals and Frecks after the war. Aitkin and Elderton are again wrong, therefore, in saying: 'With the war over Johns found no niche for Worrals and in 1950, or thereabouts, he retired her (presumably to contribute to the postwar baby boom)'. Johns ceased to write Worrals stories not because he could find no postwar niche for his heroine – he had plenty of ideas, as demonstrated in the five postwar books that were published. Also, there are some Worrals tales of this period which appeared in magazine form in *The Girls' Own Paper*, but which were never collected into book form.[43] The reason why Johns dropped Worrals was because the demand for Biggles had become overwhelming. And during the 1950s, with the advent of a new interest in space travel due to the successful German wartime rocket experiments, Johns was beginning to toy with the idea of a science fiction series.

The War Office, observing the recruiting strength of Biggles and Worrals to the air services, approached Johns to invent a soldier hero. The result was the appearance in October 1943 of Johns' commando hero, Captain Lorrington King DSO, known as 'Gimlet' King of the Commandos. The first book of what was to prove a popular series was *King of the Commandos* and Gimlet was no carbon copy of Biggles – he was altogether more formidable, tougher and more ruthless, and somewhat lacking in humour. Johns drew attention to the differences between the two characters:

A word of warning. His methods are not always as gentlemanly as Biggles. When things get rough he's apt to get tough. Which is why, of course, he was given a bunch of wildcats to command. After all, kid gloves are about as useful to a commando on his job as roller skates would be to a steeple jack.[44]

King of the Commandos was published by the University of London Press, a subsidiary of Hodder and Stoughton. The *Times Educational Supplement's* review was typical of those which greeted the start of the new series: 'Captain Johns has four attractive characters in Captain "Gimlet" King and three men from his old unit, and it is to be hoped that there will be many more books about them ... Everything they do is made to seem plausible, possible and at the same time exciting'.[45]

The second of Gimlet's adventures – *Gimlet Goes Again* – appeared in February 1944. These were the only two Gimlet books with wartime settings, but Johns kept Gimlet going for a further eight adventures, ending with *Gimlet Takes a Job* in 1954. The ten books continued their popularity even into the 1960s and were reprinted as Armada children's paperbacks.

After A. P. Watt's failure to secure a better contract deal with Oxford University Press, who had been sole publishers of the Biggles stories since 1935, Hodder and Stoughton took over the new books in the series. The company had published their first Johns' book, *Worrals Flies Again*, in September 1942. In November they produced their first Biggles tale, *Biggles Sweeps the Desert*. This was followed by *Biggles 'Fails to Return'* in August 1943, *Biggles in the Orient* in April 1945, and *Biggles Delivers the Goods* in April 1946, which completed Biggles' wartime adventures. Johns had found a new and acceptable formula for his Second World War stories after the dubious expedient he had employed in *Spitfire Parade*. The tale as a whole would be about all the members of Biggles' Squadron (No. 666), but the chief adventure would still befall Biggles, Algy and Ginger, with the addition of one newcomer to the old pre-war team, Flight Lieutenant Lord 'Bertie' Lissie. The only exception to this pattern was *Biggles 'Fails to Return'*, an adventure for the four main characters only, a book remarkable for containing an account of Ginger's love affair, and for portraying Biggles' decidedly warm admiration for a lovely princess. Johns was to remain with Hodder and Stoughton, and its subsidiary Brockhampton, for the rest of his life. His works were now being illustrated by Leslie Stead, one of the top children's book illustrators, whose name has now become firmly linked with Biggles illustrations.

Of the many reviews that the Biggles books received during this period, Johns was particularly pleased by an unsolicited testimonial from D. K. Armstrong, the headmaster of Ealing College Lower School. According to Mr Armstrong's colleague P. W. J. Westermann, formerly headmaster of the Ealing College Upper School, Armstrong, who died in 1963, 'thought very highly of the Biggles books as providing excellent entertainment for his pupils'.[46] Armstrong wrote to Johns:

May I presume to congratulate you upon your stories of Biggles and Worrals? They are a fine type of story for the boys and girls of the modern age. My gratitude and admiration for the author of good healthy stories for our young people. We have a complete set of books in our libraries and they are indeed very popular.[47]

The letter, with permission from Mr Armstrong, was subsequently printed in part on the jackets of Johns' books.

Soon after, Johns received another testimonial from the English master of a secondary modern school who wrote:

Boys will find in these books all the thrills and excitement they seek for in their reading, and having learned that reading can be a pleasurable occupation, they will be led to explore further among books.[48]

The war years brought one personal tragedy to Johns and the Leigh family. Howard Leigh was discovered to be suffering from malignant cancer. He died from cardiac failure brought about by his condition on 6 February 1942, at the age of thirty-two, in the Sackville Nursing Home, Clayton Road, Newcastle-upon-Tyne. His mother, Mrs Florence Leigh, was at his bedside. He was buried four days later at St Peter's in Lingfield. During the war years, Howard had been living with his wife, Olive, at Lyme House Farm, Lingfield. As well as continuing his aviation illustrative work, he had enlisted in the National Fire Service 'for the duration' and, at the time of his death, was a Senior Company Officer. His death was a great shock and loss. In his short life Howard had already established himself as one of the foremost British aviation artists. He will always be associated with the illustrations for the early Biggles books, especially his graceful and accurate colour frontispieces for the John Hamilton and Oxford University Press titles.

Johns continued to be devoted to his garden, growing vegetable crops, although he longed to get back to flower cultivation. 'My gardener went to war: I could not get another; vegetables had to come first, grass cutting second, and the borders round the house third ...'[49] He had abandoned his rock garden, a particular pride and joy, which had been thirty-five yards long and some five to six yards wide, to its fate. He had found a good use for his old typewriter ribbons.

String for tying plants may soon be difficult to get. I have for years used my old typewriter ribbons. For soft stemmed plants these are better than anything you can buy, being broad, of fine substance, yet of gentle strength. For tomatoes the ribbon is ideal. I loop my old ribbons over the branch of a tree so that the rain can wash the ink off, otherwise the ribbon is dirty to handle.[50]

The January 1943 issue of *My Garden* contains an article by Johns at his humorous best relating how he pulled a mandrake up, finding the plant growing 'out of a ramp of sandbags on the terrace'. Relating the superstition about mandrakes, he said, 'I own freely that had it shrieked, or even moaned, I should have fled gibbering from the spot'. In August 1941 he had symbolically spaded in an oak sapling into the border of his garden. It was to be his victory oak which, in the days to come, would be a reminder of 'an heroic era'.[51] He continued to be extremely concerned with nature conservation and was angry when he found that scores of conifers on Reigate Heath were having their heads cut off by people cashing in on the seasonal market for Christmas trees.

I cannot see that it is much use talking about a new world until people have been taught to take care of what they already have ... While this lust for destruction persists, it is clear that to hand the country over to the 'people' (as some demand) would merely be to deliver it to fire and axe. There would not be left a flower in the field, a fish in the rivers, or a bird in the woods ...[52]

There were still frequent visitors to Johns' Reigate Hill home, including his son, his mother and his brother, Russell.

My brother, who lives in London and is rather a clever scientist, came to see me the other day. 'I say,' he cried, looking at my delphiniums, 'what lovely lupins.' Shortly afterwards, in five minutes, he corrected a fault in my radiogram which I have been trying to locate for weeks. One can't have it both ways.[53]

When, in the summer of 1943, a friend arrived from abroad, he brought two lemons and gave one to Doris and Bill Johns. Lemons were impossible to get at this time and Johns reflected on the items of luxury food that people were now used to being without. 'What fun it will be rediscovering those lost luxuries. And how soon, alas! shall we become accustomed to them.'[54] One luxury Johns found almost impossible to do without was tobacco. Like Biggles, Johns was a heavy smoker, and Doris, too, smoked. The shortage of tobacco made him contemplate the idea of growing it, but he later discovered that it was illegal.[55] Illegalities did not prevent a neighbour from growing hemp (*Cannabis sativa*) but Johns felt no urge to augment his tobacco supply from this source. He admitted having once had hashish, but it had brought on delusions and left him with 'a violent headache' and his 'tongue cemented to the roof of his mouth'.[56] Another luxury Johns tried not to deny himself was wine. During his lonely hours of fire-watching as an ARP warden, Johns longed for his favourite pre-war vintages. He went so far as to plant vines in his garden.[57] His favourite wine, a rosé of St Romain Bellet, was often in his thoughts. 'In lonely spells of fire-watching I remember it with ecstasy and sorrow in my heart ...'

On the Cote d'Azur with my almonds I drink a rosé of St. Romain Bellet, a wine of such incredible colour that it has to be seen to be believed. In fact that was how I – or rather my wife – discovered it. She saw a priest drinking it, and the colour so excited us that we went over and asked what it was. He told us, whereupon we drank a litre of it together – or it may have been two litres – I forget; it seems so long ago.[58]

Johns had laid in a stock of pre-war wine; a few years later he reported that he had built a new terrace on his house underneath which he had laid five years' accumulation of empty wine bottles – 'the glassy companions of many a merry firewatch, which alone would have been a dreary affair'.[59]

Johns certainly liked his tipple and made no bones that he had little time for teetotallers who 'sneered at the alcohol habit'. In 1944 he recalled, 'At 3 am the other morning, standing on my terrace watching the sky being scissored into sections by searchlight beams', he was interrupted by a neighbour, whom he slightingly calls 'Groglace'. Johns offered him 'a glass of the amber nectar', but the man made clear his views on alcohol and people that drank it.

'Groglace,' said I sadly, 'this may be neither the time nor place for philosophy, but you've asked for it. Now I'll have my say. At twenty a man plunges into the dawn-mist of the future without a care for what is behind. At forty, through fog that is beginning to lift, without pausing in his stride, he may snatch an occasional glance over his shoulder. But at fifty, suddenly aware that the distance he has covered is greater than that which lies before him, that the summit of the peak he hoped to scale is still as far away and that his strength is now failing, he stops, perhaps to sit, to look back along a trail now clear in the light of the setting sun, to ponder on the things that were to be, the things that have been, and – with a wistful sigh, perhaps – on the things that might have been. It is then, after that first poignant heart-search, when he resumes his march with sobered step, he notices the flowers beside the way, and, remembering those he crushed beneath his feet, if he loiters to pick a few who shall blame him?'

While 'Groglace' was considering his answer the 'All Clear' went – he went home. I made a thoughtful reconnaissance of my garden in the moonlight – a practice much to be recommended for the good of the soul – and went to bed.[60]

The war had, of course, stopped any question of holidays abroad; indeed, it was difficult to go on a holiday at all. In the autumn of 1942 Johns, presumably with Doris, went on 'a week's hike round the pleasant rural country where I spent my youth'.[61] He found that Hertfordshire had changed very little. 'On the whole, the country looked very well; little gardens gay with flowers, the birds singing, trout rising, people cheerful, watermills grinding and horses clip-clopping on the roads as in the good old days'.[62] Johns had apparently revived his boyhood enthusiasm for fishing, and autumn fishing trips in Hertfordshire seem to have become the norm for an annual holiday. Johns wrote of one trip in the autumn of 1943:

> In the hall of the tavern which nestles beside the stream wherein dwell the fish I aspire one day to see upon my table, there hangs a barometer. The other morning, being in some doubt as to the weather, I tapped it, whereupon, with a sharp, decisive movement, it performed the function for which it was designed. It indicated, by what is called going back (as opposed to going up) that it was going to rain. I donned my macintosh. Leaving the tavern I encountered the Oldest Inhabitant, who chuckled when, after an appraising glance, he saw me, thus accoutred. 'You won't need that,' said he. 'It aint a-going to rain'. Of this he was quite sure, and, indeed, convinced me, for, as he said, he had lived there (man and boy) for eighty-three years. So I discarded my macintosh. An hour later I was wet to the skin. Somehow I feel there is a moral in this story.[63]

In April 1944 a friend named MacNiven of Tomintoul, Banff, Scotland, invited Johns to go on a fishing holiday there, 'whither I took myself in April to match my wits against those of the Avon salmon'.[64] Scotland impressed Johns very much, although, when MacNiven told him he had lost his entire potato crop during the previous July because of frost, Johns commented: 'I do not think I could garden in a climate capable of producing a killing frost in July'. But Johns was growing dissatisfied with gardening and his enthusiasm had paled considerably. By the end of 1943 he reflected:

> Too much of anything in the end becomes a burden on the soul, and over the past four years I have had such a surfeit of gardening that I am weary of it ... I am conscious of only one thing – my hands. I can do nothing properly. Writing becomes a labour. When my grimy fingers fall on smooth piano keys I recoil with a shudder ...[65]

In May of the following year he was complaining:

> My left arm is out of commission. What has happened to it I do not know, but it won't work. So now I must garden with one hand, which does not make it any easier. Serve me right, my grandmother would say, for grumbling about not having a gardener ...[66]

The bombing was also getting on his nerves. From the first heavy raid on the light industries in the Reigate area on 4 September 1940, the area was a frequent target for Luftwaffe attacks. That month of May 1944, 'a near bomb the other night shook several panes of glass out of the greenhouse'. But they fell on soft cinders and there were no breakages. By June, with the Allied landings in Normandy, Johns – together with most British people – was hoping that the war would be over by the autumn. 'I am persuading myself – although it may well turn out that I am deluding myself – that the war will end in the late autumn ...'[67] Instead came the period of Germany's 'terror weapons' – the 'doodlebugs' (V1s) and the rocket bombs (V2s). That summer, Doris and Bill Johns, with the Leigh family, went on a fishing holiday to the Grantown-on-Spey area of Morayshire. Johns had fallen deeply in love with the peace and serenity of the Strathspey countryside. Readers of *My Garden* were puzzled when the September 1944 issue carried no article by Johns for the first time since 1936. Then, in the October issue, Johns revealed that he had decided to establish his home in Scotland.

Enemy action at last forced me to abandon my home. What has happened and what is happening to the garden, I do not know. Nor do I care particularly. No one, I imagine, can garden with enthusiasm in a sort of minor Hades, with an occasional shower of bricks and mortar. It seemed to me that if I was to go away I might as well remove myself as far as possible from the clamour which I have endured for nearly five years. So, to the serene heart of the Highlands of Scotland I took myself, [to] a remote glen where no man goes from one year to another ...[68]

From the local laird, Grant of Grantown-on-Spey, Johns rented a large house called Pitchroy Lodge, just outside of the town, which looked out to the Cairngorm Mountains. In Scotland he found the peace and tranquillity to be able to relax and recover from the pressures and anxieties of sleepless nights, constant bombing and the hazards of war.

Seated on Ben Avon, in a *cirque* of purple heather flowing almost crimson against the deep blue of the Cairngorms, with cloud shadows chasing each other round the contours, I found myself wondering, not so much that overseas Scots pine for home, as why they ever leave it ...[69]

14

THE YEARS OF FAME

For two years the readers of *My Garden* heard no more from
Johns and no explanation was given for his sudden disappearance
from the magazine to which he had been a regular contributor
since 1936. Then, in the February 1947 issue, under the title 'The
Show Has Passed', Johns wrote a final article to explain his
departure.

The longer I live the more clearly I perceive what tremendous
consequences can result from an incident so trivial in itself that not by
any stretch of the imagination could the effect have been foreseen. Three
years ago, it was a chance meeting with a man whom I had not seen
since we were at school together that threw the hammer into the gears
which controlled the well-oiled cycle of my daily round. He was going to
a place of which I had sometimes heard but, curiously enough, had
never seen, a place called Scotland, where, so I had been misinformed,
the staples were oatcakes and haggis, a diet which a man of my age
could hardly be expected to contemplate with enthusiasm. It was not the
fascination of swinging kilts or skirling pipes that took me to a climate
where – again I had been misinformed – the hardiest of plants could not
without disorder endure the brutal lash of winter. It was – I admit it
freely – the thought of the fish that were alleged to dwell in rivers that
still ran in their natural beds, rivers unpolluted by the effluence of a
misguided civilisation.

I went, I saw and was conquered – aye, conquered by a spell cast
upon me by the simple virtue of people unspoiled by laws that breed
corruption, laws which, if they persist, will surely bring mankind to the
rottenness of a last year's marrow on a manure heap. Here, on my very
doorstep, so to speak, was the thing I had long been looking for but dare
not hope to find; a place where a man could, without bribery, without
whispering over a counter, without any of those miserable subterfuges
which lower a man to the level of a worm but which he must employ if
he would live, demand those things to which he is entitled.

It was, believe you me, refreshing to renew contact with such things
as healthy independence and honest self-respect, with hospitality and
generosity untainted by ulterior motive – the reward of those who live

close to the soil. So I stayed. My garden, the garden on which I had lavished so much care, could go hang. What need to toil when I could live in a mighty natural garden which flourished without any help from me, where flowers grew in countless millions, as they always do, presumably, when they find a spot they like and where they can go about their business undisturbed. Yes, I stayed.

Johns told his readers that at his home in Scotland he would make another garden. 'That would happen were I domiciled at one of the Poles or in the Sahara'. If he made a noteworthy discovery he would return to the pages of *My Garden* to tell his readers about it. But he never did. He wrote only once more for the magazine and that was in the December 1951 issue, when *My Garden* folded up. His tribute was brief but warm:

'Nothing is so difficult as beginning ... unless perhaps the end'. Thus wrote Byron, and none who knows life will dispute his melancholy muse.

Well I remember the beginning of *My Garden* which, starting as the seed of an idea, grew swiftly into a sturdy plant that was to bear, through the years, some memorable flowers ... Let Mr Stephens and his staff take comfort from this. The seeds sown by *My Garden* have fallen on fertile soil in many lands, where they will bloom again to bring back happy memories of the parent plant from which they sprang.

From the time he moved to Scotland, in the autumn of 1944, the gardening world lost Bill Johns. Only Doris went with him to their new home in Morayshire. Her mother, Mrs Florence Leigh, preferred to remain at Reigate Hill while her sister Marjorie, who had been Johns' secretary, also remained behind to marry Squadron Leader Teddy Ellis and set up her own home. For Johns, the years spent at Pitchroy Lodge were an ideal existence. He could even view the political scene with a more benign yet still cynical eye. As he told *My Garden* readers in 1947:

Sitting on my distant hill I watch without concern the pageant of frenzied politicians streaming across the face of the earth, bickering, jostling and arguing, in frantic search of what their multitudes demand – peace. Harnessed to their cities, their committees and conventions, they seek in vain. I could show them where it is.

In Scotland, Johns could not only work in peace and solitude but he could also pursue his favourite sports – shooting and fishing. As an ardent country conservationist, he had decided views on the way game should be preserved and a shoot conducted. In many ways he regretted the number of wild animals which were killed by gamekeepers to preserve game for sport. 'Slaughter,' he wrote at one time, 'slaughter – yet we call this civilization'.[1] He loved living in the country and, when the war finally ended with the unconditional surrender of Germany on 8 May 1945, a few months after his move from Reigate Hill, he had no wish to return. Explaining his new lifestyle, Johns wrote:

When one lives in the Highlands of Scotland, far from a town, it is not always a matter of what one would like to do, but what is possible. There can be no going out if a blizzard is raging, or even afterwards if it has filled the road with snow. Once I was cut off from the world for five weeks – no papers, no mail, nothing. Terrible? Not a bit. It was refreshing ...[2]

In normal conditions, from February to June, Johns would get up at 4 am and go straight into his dressing room where tea had been laid overnight. He would switch on the electric kettle and then examine the sky, choosing what clothes he would put on. If the mountains were painted pink by the rising sun it was generally a sign of good weather. Johns felt that this early dawn period was the best time of the day.

Perceive what a lovely place is the world if only people would leave it alone. Notice a little less snow on Ben Rinnes, which means that the river will be growing and fresh fish running. Turn my spy glass on the river. A silver gleam and a splash of spray tells me all I want to know. Drink a cuppa, slowly, with the first cigarette of the day. All is quiet. Ideas come easily. On with the dressing-gown and down to the study. Pen fairly flies over paper getting down the one or two chapters thought out the previous day.[3]

At 8.30 am Johns took a cup of tea to Doris and sat chatting about plans for the day. Then he would have a bath and dress, listening to the 9.00 am weather report. Pitchroy Lodge had several domestic and estate staff, and after breakfast he would go out to give the estate workers instructions for the day and hear the local gossip, which seldom moved far away from salmon, grouse, deer, poachers and whisky. At 10.00 am Doris would come out with a lunch basket.

Rods stand ready on the rail. Important discussions now as to the size and pattern of the fly for the day. Into waders and into river. If the fish are taking well I think of nothing else. If they are 'stiff' my mind wanders to the story I am writing. I can fish, keep an eye on the wild birds and beasts around me, and work out dialogue at the same time. With sparkling water swirling round my waist and all nature singing, ideas seem to come naturally. This goes on until the line sliding through my fingers tells me that I'm onto a fish, or a yell behind warns me to clear the way for my wife who is coming down the river with a big 'un.[4]

Doris and Bill Johns would lunch on the river bank and finally pack up at 6.00 pm. The fish they caught would be sorted, weighed, noted in a game book and then despatched to various places. Some would go to Aberdeen to be smoked, some would go to friends and relatives. Johns would return home to read his mail and the newspapers, and have a drink before dinner. If there were no guests to be entertained, after dinner he would listen to some music and then go back to his study to jot down ideas he had thought out during the day. When he was tired, any time from 10.30 pm to 1.00 am, he would go to bed.

On 1 July a typist would arrive from London, and Johns would present his handwritten manuscripts to her for typing. He always wrote out his manuscripts with a fountain pen; invariably they were written in a neat, orderly and easily readable style with hardly any grammatical, spelling or other mistakes. As Marjorie Leigh was no longer his secretary, Johns employed an agency typist.

When August came the landscape would change. The talk was then of heather, high ground and birds, and there would be great activity in Pitchroy Lodge as preparations were made for the bevy of guests who would arrive to spend the shooting season there. Doris and Bill Johns loved entertaining, not only relatives but friends and acquaintances. At one time, Mrs Marjorie Ellis remembers Doris and Bill sitting down to dinner with four duchesses at the table.[5] 'Great business every morning of packing parcels of game for the south,' wrote Johns. 'I tick off names on the list in the game larder as parcels go off'.[6] His writing routine did not vary. He would be up early, write until 8.30 am, and then go off shooting, traversing sometimes ten and sometimes twenty miles a day. Doris, who was not only an excellent fisherwoman, proved herself a great dog handler and was always in the party.

With the coming of October or November, Doris and Bill would pack their cases and head for London, to spend a week or so with relatives and in order that Johns might see his literary agent and editors. Then on to Paris, a combination of business and pleasure, for Johns had become very friendly with Sven Nielsen, owner of Les Presses de la Cité, who was now publishing Johns' works in translation. Nielsen and his wife often invited them to their estate in the Sologne area of France. Johns was intrigued and stimulated by this countryside and its history, and it was there, in 1955, that he wrote *Biggles Takes Charge*. He dedicated the book to the Nielsens: 'to Monsieur and Madame N, who introduced me to that fascinating land of lake, forest, sunshine and shadow, which but for them I might never have seen – La Sologne'. He also included a five-page preface praising the beauties of the area, and mentioning the tremendous part played by the local Maquis during the war years. He also turned to the setting in his adult thriller *No Motive For Murder*, published in 1958. Sometimes, as guests of the Nielsens, Doris and Bill Johns would spend fishing or shooting holidays there. 'In the autumn hunting season La Sologne is the Mecca of sportsmen, for game abounds – pheasant, partridge, woodcock, snipe, wild duck, and the like. There are fish, too, in the lakes – enough to satisfy the most ambitious angler'.[7] Johns loved the isolation of the area.

But unless the voyager has some specific reason for going there, or happens to find himself on the great highway known as Route Nationale 20, it is unlikely that he will hear of La Sologne. Even in that event he will little suspect what lies on either side of the road, for hundreds of square miles of forest, swamp and jungle, are not what he would expect to find in the heart of a country wherein agriculture is a basic industry.

To paint a pen portrait of this strange land of nearly a million and a half acres will not be easy, but we must try, for the reader should know something of it from the outset. Apart from being a land of moods, La Sologne takes care that you do not see all her face at one time. At every turn the scene is different, yet there is no particular view to remember. Indeed, from La Ferté St Aubin in the north (on the map you will find it about twenty-five miles south of Orleans) to Vierzon in the south, a matter of roughly forty miles, the traveller by road may think the countryside monotonous. Actually, it is one of the wildest, and for that reason for some people one of the most fascinating, stretches of country in Western Europe.

For the most part La Sologne is true forest, with strands of oak, chestnut, birch, fir and pine. The ground underfoot may be arid, supporting a tangle of heather, sometimes waist high, or it may be a reedy swamp extending for miles. There are jungles of scrub and undergrowth that are literally impenetrable. Everywhere trailing brambles drag on the feet. Scattered over the whole area are lakes, large and small, more than a thousand of them, dark, solitary, tranquil, fed by furtive-looking streams that glide mysterious courses through the labyrinth. Over all hangs a brooding silence that seems to fall from the sky, and at sunset creates a haunting often sinister, atmosphere.

This is not to say that so vast a tract of land is uninhabitable. On the main road that cuts through it like a knife from north to south there are one or two small towns and villages, and on either side of it you will find an occasional farmer scratching a living in a clearing; for the soil is poor, and in recent years a great many of these homesteads have been abandoned. Apart from the diehards fighting their losing battle with nature, the only man you might meet, except in the shooting season, would be a forester or a gamekeeper. The visitor might walk all day long, as has the writer, without seeing a living soul or hearing the sound of one. A man seeking solitude will certainly find it here.[8]

Sometimes, after a stay in Paris, Doris and Bill Johns would move straight on to their favourite spot – the Riviera – 'to give my skin a sunbath and spring clean the brain ready for new ideas'.[9] In February he would be back in Scotland again. 'Taking it all round it is a strenuous life,' he reflected, 'and may not be your cup of tea; but it's a healthy mixture of work and play that keeps us fit and fully occupied – for the time being, anyhow. There will be time, I hope, to sit around in cities when the old muscles begin to creak'.[10]

In 1951 he told a *Daily Mail* reporter:

I do about two months' work. Then, when the fishing starts in February, I fish. After that, I shoot from August 12 until the first week in November. Then I pack a few notebooks and round off the year with a tour of European countries into whose languages my books are translated and return in February for the salmon and more work.

My wife likes Scotland as much as I do. We both find life a bit easier here than in London.[11]

A few weeks later the same newspaper reported that Johns was off to tour France, Belgium, Spain and Italy. 'I'll be back by mid-March when the fish should be running nicely in the Spey'.[12] When he returned, the *Daily Mail* reported that he had brought back some amusing impressions of Europe. Gambling at Monte Carlo was on a far bigger scale than anything he had seen in the last thirty years:

Americans alone are bothering about the possibility of a war with Russia. France is quite gay, irresponsibly happy and squandering money. Captain Johns' visit to his Italian publisher in Turin was marked by a series of real life adventure stories – in the flooded Po Valley.[13]

After the war Johns kept a firm attachment to *The Boys' Own Paper*, in which many of his later books were serialised. The new editor of the paper was Jack Cox, who, after service in the Royal Engineers during the war, had joined the Lutterworth Press, which had published several Worrals books. Cox recalled that the Lutterworth editor Margaret Stewart was a great friend of Johns. He met Johns soon after the war at Lutterworth's office at Doran Court, Redhill. 'I am sure that Johns and Mrs Johns were visitors that year (1947)'.[14] In September 1948 Lutterworth returned to their pre-war offices in Bouverie Street, where Johns became a regular visitor. Then Cox became editor of *The Boys' Own Paper*.

I published Biggles stories in serial form before [book] publication ... [Johns] was in Scotland a great deal fishing and shooting in the far north-east. We never lunched much as I recall; he liked to come in the afternoon and drink lots of tea before catching an evening train north. 'Phones off the hook. Mrs Johns was always very pleasant. She often went shopping and left him with me. He always seemed to like what I wrote about him and hated the rough handling he sometimes got from people who did not know him. He was a very good 'pro' and we got on well but he was no Press Club-man![15]

The Boys' Own Paper was holding its own, but the number of juvenile publications had decreased markedly since pre-war days. However, Johns still sold serial rights to various newspapers and magazines, and he found another market in the vast number of children's annuals and 'one off' books being published. He wrote a great number of short stories, mainly Biggles tales, which were often compiled into book form later. So prolific and diverse were the stories and outlets that it is impossible to track down all the Johns stories which appeared. John Beal, when editor of the *Daily Mail Annual* in the 1950s, made a point of commissioning an original Biggles tale from Johns and many other editors followed suit.

The nine years spent in Scotland were happy ones and the countryside provided many settings for Biggles stories, as well as a background for the adult thriller *The Man Who Lost His Way*. But, at the age of sixty, as Johns had foreseen — 'there will be a time, I hope, to sit around in cities when the old muscles begin to creak' — the time had come to leave Scotland. The idyll ended in 1953, when Doris and Bill Johns planned to return to the London area to live, to be nearer their family and roots. Johns decided to buy a large Queen Anne mansion in the busy Hampton Court Road — Park House, Hampton Court. It had belonged to Lord Marchwood, who, as Johns told Robert Pitman, had installed a Queen Anne cupboard which, at the flick of a switch, became a cocktail cabinet.[16] When *Woman* correspondent Jeanne Heal went to interview him, she was surprised to find that the house was next door to the one in which she had grown up as a child.[17] The large garden was beautifully kept, for Johns had returned, with new enthusiasm, to his love for gardening. According to Frank Entwistle of the *Evening Standard*:

You are in a different world when you enter this big Queen Anne house behind a high wall off the busy Hampton Court Road. And it is not just the white pillared drawing room, or the panelled walls, or the carved fire-places, or the subtler proportions of another century that gives this impression. There are, for instance, the pictures in the study of the author, Captain W. E. Johns. A painting of a 1914–18 War air fight with the Boche getting the worst of it from a dashing DH4. The portrait of a young man (Biggles) in flying helmet and goggles grinning healthily before a Hurricane. The colours are those of boys' book illustrations between the wars. Romantic. Nostalgic.[18]

When Robert Pitman, of the *Sunday Express*, went to see Johns:

Captain Johns took me upstairs to his study. A field lay below the window. Johns pointed: 'That's the Royal Paddock. I often see the

Queen there with her children and the Queen Mother, right below this window. I hear some fascinating things, I can tell you.

'One day the children were nearly kicked by a horse, and you should have heard the Queen Mother ticking off her daughter about it.[19]

The only drawback to the house at Hampton Court must have been the heavy traffic passing on one side of it, although the high walls cushioned some of the effect, and to ears accustomed to aero engines the sound was, perhaps, negligible.

A year after his return from Scotland, Johns suffered a tragic bereavement with the death of his only son. Jack had been ill for many years with diabetes, and, after the war, tuberculosis developed. He spent two years in a sanatorium in Davos, Switzerland. Johns saw him occasionally during this period, and frequently sent him fish from Pitchroy Lodge. After Jack returned home, he worked for a while on the *East Grinstead Courier*, living with his wife and children at Dormansland, not far from his father's old home, Lingfield. Then it was discovered that he was a victim of multiple sclerosis and this, combined with his diabetes and his weakness from tuberculosis, proved fatal. He died on 15 March 1954, aged thirty-eight. His wife, Sabena, recalled: 'In later years when my husband came home from the sanatorium, he [Captain Johns] visited us frequently.'[20] According to Mrs Marjorie Ellis, Johns used to pay regular sums of money to his son and it was he who paid for Jack's stay in the sanatorium at Davos.[21]

Jack's mother, Maude Johns, was not to die until 1 April 1961, at the age of seventy-nine. She died at the Resthaven nursing home in Thorpe St Andrew's, Norfolk, and was described, on her death certificate, as 'wife of William Earl Johns − a journalist'. Naturally, at that time, Doris and Bill Johns discussed the possibility of marriage but decided against it. If they married now, and the news became public knowledge, it could be extremely damaging to Johns' image. Children's writers, above all others, were supposed to live lives of exemplary morality. It was only too likely that reporters would have a field day if one of Britain's leading juvenile writers − whose books were generally acknowledged to teach conventional morals − was discovered to have lived with someone for forty years while still legally married to someone else. Johns himself was very much aware of the standards set by his imaginary airman. In the foreword to *The First Biggles Omnibus*. published by Hodder and Stoughton in 1953, he wrote somewhat uneasily:

> What would Biggles say (and what would you say) if I were caught in some unlawful enterprise? Would you trust me after that? Would he? You see what I mean when I say that I must bow to that stern code which I once set for Biggles – and he now sets for me?

After their devoted partnership for almost forty years, no couple could have a stronger claim than Doris and Bill Johns to be man and wife in every way that mattered, but their lack of legal status still made them vulnerable to press scandal. According to Maude's sister Mrs Kathleen King, it was their father, Reverend Hunt, who had stopped any question of a divorce previously. 'After father died in 1941 my sister informed Captain Johns he could proceed with a divorce. He did not take up the offer as he said it would cause too much scandal and the publicity would be ruination to his literary work.'[22] However, Mrs Marjorie Ellis believed that Maude's attitude to a divorce remained the chief obstacle.[23]

The immediate postwar years brought a new financial prosperity to Johns. Many European countries, freed from the restrictions of war and occupation, were looking for escapist literature, not only for adults but, also in juvenile fields. Johns had been published in Sweden throughout the war years. Oxford University Press had sold most of their titles to Bonniers, but they had to share Johns with Walhströms, who also started publishing his work in 1940 and who are still producing four or five titles a year. Forlagshuset of Oslo, who had only published one title before the German occupation, now eagerly sought his work, publishing not only Biggles but Worrals and Gimlet tales as well. In France, Johns had a false start with Editions Arthaud, but then Les Presses de la Cité, Nielsen's company, took over producing practically all of Johns' work, including his adult fiction. During the 1950s Johns became the fourth bestselling writer in France.

In Italy, Chiantore, La Sorgente and Celi vied with one another for translation rights. Luis Caralt of Barcelona was also making Biggles popular in Spain, although several Biggles books were produced by Ediciones Daimon and Ediciones Ayma.

Spanish–American editions were produced by Zig-Zag of Chile. In Portugal, Ediciones Confluencia began publishing Biggles, and Biggles even appeared in Hungarian translation from Singer and Wolfner. In Holland, Uitgevenj Het Spectrum were to become his main publishers in Dutch, but De Telg had produced the first Biggles book in 1947, to be followed by a whole series from Born during the early 1950s. Three of Johns' Biggles books were produced by Meulenhoff's English Library, with annotations, for Dutch schools and students of English. Flemish translations of Biggles, Gimlet and Johns' pre-war hero Steeley, were published by De Ster of Antwerp. In Finland, Kirjayhtymä Oy had started producing Finnish translations in 1948, and Tammi took the series over in 1958. In 1947 Branner og Korch began to publish Biggles and Worrals in Danish translation, and the Biggles series was then taken over from 1952 by Grafisk Forlag. In Iceland, in 1948, Norori started Icelandic translations of Biggles, finding the name so difficult that they decided to call him Benni. Logi, and more recently Hagprent, in Iceland, also published many Johns' titles. Even in the east, Eastern Universities Press in Singapore have been publishing Biggles books in Bahasa Malaysian, in which they are extremely popular. Most impressive of all was Biggles' postwar popularity in Germany. One Biggles book, *The Camels Are Coming*, had been published in pre-war Germany, in 1936. In 1948 Komet Verlag of Dusseldorf went ahead with a pre-war *Biggles in the South Seas*. Then, from the early 1950s, Hallweg began to produce other Biggles titles. Johns could now bask in the glow of world fame. In 1964 the first UNESCO Statistical Yearbook reported that Biggles books had been placed 29th on a list of the most translated books in the world and that Biggles was the most popular juvenile hero in the world.[24] Emphasising this great expansion in the demand for Johns' works, from 1941 onwards no less than thirty-seven of his books appeared in Braille editions. Johns freely donated all the rights for them to the National Association for the Blind.

The only black spot, upon which Johns several times reflected, was America. Although no less than fifty-nine of his books had appeared in North American, mainly Canadian, editions, sales on the North American continent were depressingly low. Biggles, it seemed, was considered 'too British' to make any impact with American readers. Outside Britain, Johns was most popular in

Australia, France, Holland and the Scandinavian countries.

From the late 1940s broadcasting was to make Biggles even more popular in Britain. The BBC's Home Service 'Children's Hour' programme began to broadcast dramatised versions of the Biggles books. From 11 March 1948, through the month, *Biggles Flies West* enthralled young listeners so much that a repeat was demanded in the October 'Request Week'. On 26 November 1948 *Biggles Flies North* was dramatised, and listeners demanded a repeat of that also. *Biggles in the Jungle* was broadcast through June 1949, and once again listeners demanded a repeat in November. The BBC then asked Johns to write some original Biggles short stories which could be read on the Home Service 'Twelve Noon' story spot, and in August and September of 1949 three Biggles tales were read. Audiences in Britain could not get enough of Biggles, it seemed. *Biggles Hunts Big Game* was dramatised in October 1950; *Biggles in the Blue* was broadcast in November 1953; *Biggles and the Pirate Treasure* was dramatised in September and October 1955; and *Biggles' Chinese Puzzle* and *Biggles of the Interpol* were broadcast in August and September 1957. Finally, *Biggles Presses On* was broadcast in May 1959.

But it was in Australia that Biggles, as a radio personality, was to become an institution. Australian Amalgamated Wireless went ahead in 1949 with a series of fiteen-minute radio episodes based on the Biggles series. The radio series soon had to be expanded to half-an-hour episodes and was to remain a popular radio feature until 1955. The first 208 episodes were produced in Adelaide before Amalgamated Wireless moved its studios to Sydney where the subsequent series were recorded. Biggles was played firstly by Moray Powell, while Brian Wright and Harry Howlett, experts at cliffhanger serialisations, wrote the scripts alternately. The programme was produced by Maurice Chapman.

An executive producer of the series recalls that early negotiations with Captain Johns proved rather difficult mainly because he lacked a basic understanding of radio techniques. For instance, Captain Johns frequently created situations where his characters were alone and indulged in soliloquy. This is all very well in a novel but totally unacceptable in a radio script. Our people had great difficulty in convincing Johns that radio dramatisations had no use for reflective soliloquies.[25]

The series proved so successful that Amalgamated Wireless sold and distributed the programmes to the South African Broadcasting Corporation as well as New Zealand and other Pacific countries. The programmes greatly enhanced Johns' sales and reputation in Australia. However, reminiscing about the series, Johns recalled a problem that was not of his own making. 'Suddenly I got a sack of mail from Australian kids. The broadcasting people had run out of my stories. They'd made Biggles take up with a blonde. The boys said, "Has Biggles gone soft?" I had to stop that of course. It wasn't Biggles. He wouldn't behave like that'.[26]

According to Keith A. MacDonald, who took over the role of Biggles and also produced some of the later programmes, the show came off because it was unable to compete with new developments in children's television.[27] Looking back on his career in acting, Keith MacDonald had a fond remembrance of playing the part of Biggles. 'He was an entirely healthy hero. All four series in which I played Biggles were about the war, but violence was certainly not overdone. Biggles was anti the enemy but that was all right.'[28]

Johns' popularity in Australia allowed him to sell serial rights of thirteen postwar Biggles books to Australian Consolidated Magazines; serial rights of other books to Australian Associated News Service, to the *Melbourne Herald* and the *Sydney Morning Herald*, and *The Silver Jacket* magazine, published by Beaconsfield Productions Pty, Sydney, whose first issue of October 1953, began the serialisation of *Biggles Works it Out*. So popular was Biggles in Australia that Action Comics Pty, Sydney, launched a Biggles comic at this time. A British edition, published by Strato Publications Ltd, London, was also successful.

Johns' world-wide fame was commented on by Graham Greene, who, in an article about Kenya, in the *Sunday Times* reported: 'A missionary told me that the works of Shakespeare and of the author of the Biggles books were the only form of imaginative literature to which he found his pupils attracted'.[29]

Such success inevitably brought with it disadvantages. According to Robert Pitman:

... even the bad things which happen to the man behind Biggles are the calamities of success.

Such as the time when he was ill a few years back ('some devilish bug I'd picked up on holiday in North Africa'). Lying weak, unable to work, Johns was handed in a demand for his previous year's taxes. The figure on the bill was £16,000.[30]

In fact, Johns admitted that he usually made £10,000 on each Biggles book published.[31] A fellow writer who knew him, Eric Leyland, recalled:

I remember that he was eternally worried about income tax! (Who isn't?) You see he made a great deal of money in the first year of his success and spent it all. The next year he had to write even more books in order not only to live but to pay the tax due on the previous year's earnings. So it went on for many years. It was an eternal worry to him.[32]

The answer to the problem was to form a public company, like many another successful author before him, and W. E. Johns (Publications) Ltd came into being on 30 November 1953. At first Johns was the sole active director and paid himself a salary which alleviated the high rate of income tax he had to pay. At one time during the mid-1950s he had complained to reporters that he was only being left one shilling in the pound. His solicitor, C. E. Morier, became a director and from 1963 Doris was also a director.

With the end of the war a new role had had to be found for Biggles. *Sergeant Bigglesworth CID* appeared in August 1947. Biggles and some of the characters from No. 666 Squadron go to work for Air Commodore Raymond who has returned to his old pre-war job as a Police Commissioner at Scotland Yard. His brief is to set up a special Air Police Force. This was not an original Johns' idea. The writer John Templer had written a series of Air Police tales in the 1930s featuring Flight Lieutenant L. Jayson DFC, AFC, known as Jaggers, and his comrade, Flying Officer Winkles. In fact, the first tale, *Jaggers of the Air Police*, was serialised in *The Modern Boy* in 1936. However, it was Johns who popularised the idea and made the Air Police Branch of Scotland Yard sound not only credible but necessary. M. André Bossard, the real-life Secretary-General of Interpol, remarked in an interview in November 1980: 'You cannot take a bicycle to run after people who hijack aeroplanes. Policemen must also use aeroplanes ...'[33]

Sergeant Bigglesworth CID and *Biggles' Second Case* were considered a cut above ordinary juvenile crime fiction and were both issued in 1954 in the Hodder Yellow Jacket series – a series devoted to adult crime fiction. As early as September 1942, Johns' First World War espionage novel, *Biggles Flies East*, had also appeared in the Yellow Jacket format. These tales stand up very well in the adult category.

With the fourth of the Air Police tales, Biggles' former wartime companions fall away, leaving the familiar team of Biggles, Algy and Ginger, plus one newcomer, Lord Bertie Lissie. Flight Sergeant Smith, indefatigably servicing Biggles' aircraft throughout the Second World War was on the strength of the Air Police in its early days, but is not mentioned after *Biggles of the Special Air Police* in 1953.

In Britain serialisations of the Biggles Air Police tales appeared regularly in *The Boys' Own Paper*, but new juvenile publications such as *The Eagle*, *Junior Mirror* and *Express Weekly* were also demanding their share of serial rights. Even daily newspapers, such as the *Liverpool Daily Post*, the London *Evening News* and the *Daily Mail* were publishing Biggles stories. Sweden had become the second biggest market for newspaper and periodical serialisations of the books, with France running a close third. A new venture was a Biggles card game, manufactured by Pepys and brought out in 1954. All the cards bore illustrations by Stead, drawn from eight different Biggles books, with either jungle or desert settings. The 'good' cards showed incidents which helped Biggles, and the 'bad' cards pictured setbacks. Designed as a duel between two players only, it was very well worked out, ingenious, fast and ruthless.

With the start of the 1960s, Biggles made a further increase in popularity when Granada Television launched a series featuring the airman hero. Theatre manager Bert Ray and film producer Caris Carter had formed themselves into a company to find ideas and stories for television. Their first success was in selling Granada the idea of a Biggles series. The *Evening News* commented that the programme would be a refreshing change from cowboys.[34] The series was launched on Friday, 1 April 1960, at peak children's viewing time, 6.30 pm. Ken Bailey of *The People* reported: 'I have to reveal a deadly plot against the hypnotic powers of Cliff Michelmore and BBC's "Tonight" team.

On at least one evening a week they are in danger of being shot down in flames by an ITV counter attraction. Every Friday at 6.30 Captain W. E. Johns sends Biggles out to sabotage the Michelmore spell.'[35]

The scripts for the series were written by several writers, including Tony Warren who was to create Granada's famous soap opera – 'Coronation Street'. Biggles appeared in his role of Inspector of Air Police. Nevil Whiting played the part of Biggles, with John Leyton as Ginger, David Drummond as Bertie, and Carl Duering as the archvillain, von Stalhein. Algy was dropped from the stories. Each story consisted of three episodes. At first the episodes were shown weekly, but so successful were they that ITV decided to screen them twice weekly after the first fourteen weeks. They were shown on Wednesdays and Fridays and ended with the forty-fourth episode on 12 October 1960. Towards the end of the run, *TV Times* carried an article and photograph headed 'Beauty for Biggles'; the photograph was of a seventeen-year-old bikini-clad bathing beauty, Jackie Goddard.[36] It was stated that Miss Goddard, who had been Singapore's 'Goddess of Love' and had won several other beauty contests, was to 'get involved in the start of the new Biggles' adventures' when they were screened the following year. Whether Johns stepped in, in view of his insistence that Biggles' fans did not like women getting involved with the hero, is not known. Certainly there was no further mention of Miss Goddard's involvement with either the series or Biggles – and Biggles did not return to the television screen, in spite of the success of the series and a kindly reception by television critics. The *Daily Mirror* critic had commented that the series was 'a welcome addition to early evening television'.[37] That there were plans to extend the series was plain from the *TV Times* article. According to Mrs Marjorie Ellis, Johns did not like the programme.[38] He felt the characterisation of his hero had been betrayed. It is more than likely that he stopped any further adaptations.

It was in 1954 that Johns embarked on a new venture, making the first of his sorties into the world of science fiction. He was very enthusiastic about the series, which ran to ten titles, the last one being published in 1963. He contributed a foreword to each book, giving a scientific basis to the story. Mrs Margaret Collins, Johns' niece, said that Johns' brother, Russell, gave him a good deal of scientific advice and background for the stories. Ironically, in view of the developments of the late 1960s and 1970s, Johns was to write: 'It is unlikely that a rocket will answer the question of space flight, for although it has taught us much its limitations are apparent'.[39] The books feature Group Captain 'Tiger' Clinton and his son, Rex, who come upon Professor Lucius Braine, who has invented a flying saucer. With his servant Judkins, they join the professor in space exploration. Various other characters were added as time went on, including 'Toby' Paul, an ex-RAF friend of Clinton, and Vargo Lentos, an officer in the Martian Remote Survey Fleet.

Surprisingly, the critics were more than kind to the series. Of the first title, *Kings of Space*, the *Guardian* commented: 'A fine yarn of interplanetary exploration'. The *Daily Mirror* felt: 'Captain Johns' first space adventure book is a winner'. *The Scout* observed: 'The famous creator of Biggles and Gimlet can write as good a space story as the next man. You can't put down a Johns' book'. Of the second title, *Return to Mars*, 1955, *Time and Tide* felt it was 'Another of Captain Johns' superbly exciting space stories with enough probability to appeal to any scientifically minded boy or girl'. The *Church Times* felt it was 'honest, unashamed science fiction rattlingly well told, as one would expect from this writer's practised hand. The theme is adventure on Mars and its surrounding satellites and planetoids ... young readers will be glued to it'. As for the third volume, *Now to the Stars*, 1956, the *Manchester Evening News* found it 'very exciting and with sufficient deference to scientific fact to make it plausible'. The fourth title, *To Outer Space*, 1957, has 'just the right science fiction mixture; a combination of scientific facts and imaginative conception that brings the perils and excitements of space travel into realistic perspective', said the *Nottingham Evening Post*. When the fifth title, *The Edge of Beyond*, was published in 1958, the *Times Literary Supplement* joined in the praise for the series by saying: 'Captain Johns writes as imaginatively of the perils and pleasures of flight to the "edge of beyond" as ever he did of the chartered airs of Earth. This is a good tale, well told'. Of the seventh title, *To Worlds Unknown*, *Books and Bookmen* said: 'Captain Johns ... claims the object is to show the younger generation what the future has in store, so that events can be followed intelligently. The new volume succeeds admirably in this object ... and combines fact and imagination in the right proportions'.[40]

However, according to Donald H. Tuck, Johns' 'science fiction is not as notable as the juvenile fiction of writers predominantly in the SF field'.[41] Read today, the stories seem extremely dated and unbelievable, although they were republished by Piccolo in paperback form in 1980 with remarkable success. However, they certainly lack the zest and appeal of his best work. According to Geoffrey Trease: 'In his later years, as space exploration seized the juvenile imagination, he made a spirited effort to enter that market too. There was a wide gulf, however, between the early Biggles adventures, set in a milieu he really knew, and these interplanetary romances for which he had not the technical background of his younger and more inspired competitors'.[42]

In 1948 Johns had tried his hand at a juvenile western, *The Rustlers of Rattlesnake Valley*, which was certainly not among his best works. Two related adventure tales, *Adventure Bound* and *Adventure Unlimited*, followed in 1955 and 1957. Then he wrote a tale set in Scotland, *Where the Golden Eagle Soars*, 1960. It was not so much an adventure but, as a subtitle on the book put it, 'a story for lovers of nature about wild life in the Highlands of Scotland'. Also in 1960 came *Adventures of the Junior Detection Club*, a feeble book about some schoolboy sleuths and their efforts to solve various mysteries.

Johns' attempts to establish himself in the adult field and his inability to do so because of the label 'juvenile writer', seemed to rankle a little. In 1954 he wrote:

The writer of books for children soon carries the tab 'juvenile' in the trade. It can only be shaken off by a change of name. You can go from adult to juvenile, but you can't go back without causing confusion in the bookshops and in the minds of your friends, the boys and girls who have taught you to write good, plain, honest English.[43]

In the 1930s he had written several adult fiction books and, of course, Biggles had made his debut in the adult fiction market. During the 1940s Johns' adult short stories had found a large market, and were finally brought out in book form in the early 1950s by Latimer, who also reprinted the Steeley series. But the stories were not as successful as Johns had hoped they would be.

In 1958 Johns persuaded Hodder and Stoughton to publish an adult thriller of his, *No Motive for Murder*. Its setting – La Sologne – may have helped to sell the French translation rights; the novel was published as *Motif d'enquête* by Les Presses de la Cité in 1959. The book was not a success and reviewers hardly noticed its existence, but Johns did not give up. He made a further attempt with *The Man Who Lost His Way*, which was published by Macdonald's in February 1960. Macdonald's explained, perhaps hopefully, to readers of the book: 'The name of W. E. Johns is one of almost legendary fame with members of the younger generations, but he is equally skilled at writing thrillers for older readers as well. *The Man Who Lost His Way* is his latest venture in the genre and a most exciting story from beginning to end'. But it was no good; while it sold to America, and a French edition appeared, the tale had no more impact on critics than *No Motive For Murder*. These two thrillers were Johns' final efforts to enter the adult market; he returned to the world of juvenile fiction for good, and more specifically, to the world of Biggles.

Biggles was certainly his mainstay, and during the 1950s and 1960s every Biggles book also came out in a Children's Book Club edition, and paperback editions were being printed by Knight Books and Armada. After 1963 Johns wrote only Biggles books.

15

SUCCESSFUL JUVENILE FICTION

With Johns' phenomenal success as a children's writer, several critics and interviewers began to ask what the secret of that success was; what ingredient contributed to making a bestselling writer of juvenile fiction? In 1947 the author Geoffrey Trease had corresponded with Johns for material for a survey of children's fiction which he was writing and which appeared in 1949 as *Tales Out of School*.[1] Trease did not preserve the original letter from Johns, but, with his permission, quoted parts of it in his book.[2] According to Trease: 'Johns and I differed greatly in our views, and I think our subsequent lunch-time encounter may have found us both a bit wary'. The year *Tales Out of School* was published, Trease and Johns served together on an authors' brains trust, at the *Sunday Times* National Book Exhibition. Other leading children's writers Richmal Crompton, John Keir Cross, Mary Dunn, and Josephine Pullein-Thompson were also on the panel.

When Geoffrey Trease asked Johns by what yardstick a book for children could be judged good or bad, Johns had replied with apparent cynicism: 'There is only one criterion, and that is the number it sells'. In later interviews with reporters in the 1950s his comments on his work indicates that this remark should not have been taken seriously. Johns' humour, sometimes cynical and frequently perverse, was often a cause of misunderstanding among his critics.

In reply to a question about how he approached the technique of writing for children, Johns responded that the work 'demands a peculiar technique based on an understanding of the juvenile mind which, unless one is born with it, or retains it from childhood is not easy to develop'. The reply is rather pretentious and one can agree with Trease's comment:

I am not clear how one can be born with an understanding of the juvenile mind – it seems a precocious piece of equipment – but if there is such a person as 'a born teacher' he too presumably possesses it. On the whole, though, I think Captain Johns is closer to the truth when he speaks of retaining it from childhood. I doubt if it is so much 'an understanding of the juvenile mind' as a vivid retention of one's own thoughts, feelings and interests, all those years ago.[3]

In this remark, Trease is absolutely right. Johns had never lost his vision of childhood. As we have previously remarked, he viewed the world with a candid eye and he had retained a fresh, infectious curiosity and enthusiasm for a wide range of subjects. He did not write down to children – he shared his knowledge and his own genuine convictions with them, carrying them along with him through his own enjoyment and sense of humour. When forced into the position of evaluating his work – something no author should be allowed to do – Johns swings from humour to an uncomfortable, self-conscious pretentiousness. Many of his statements, not only to Geoffrey Trease but also to later interviewers, are far from an accurate reflection of his work. They merely express platitudes, as can be seen from Johns' reply to Trease when the latter asked him why he wrote for children:

First of all for the entertainment of my reader. That is, I give boys what they want, not what their elders and betters think they ought to read. I teach at the same time, under a camouflage. Juveniles are keen to learn, but the educational aspect must not be too obvious or they become suspicious of its intention. I teach a boy to be a man, for without that essential qualification he will never be anything. I teach sportsmanship according to the British idea. One doesn't need blood and thunder to do that. In more than forty novels about my hero Biggles, he has only once struck a man, and that was a matter of life and death. I teach that decent behaviour wins in the end as a natural order of things. I teach the spirit of team work, loyalty to the Crown, the Empire, and to rightful authority.[4]

If one thing is taught in the Biggles books, leaving aside the example of Johns' other works, it is a cynicism for 'authority' be it politicians or 'brass hats'. Johns' own anarchic cynicism towards governments and 'rightful authority' pervades practically every book and, rather than preaching unquestioning loyalty, he fosters a healthy scepticism, leaving it for his readers to judge what is right and wrong, rather than letting 'their betters' simply tell them. In many books, ranging from *Biggles in the South Seas*, (1940) to *Biggles and the Leopards of Zinn* (1960), the dubious benefits of empire for native peoples, as well as the morality of empire, are called into question.

In explaining his views further, Johns says:

Today, more than ever, the training of the juvenile mind is important. The adult author has little hope of changing the outlook, politics, or way of life of his reader, whose ideas are fixed. The brain of a boy is flexible, still able to absorb. It can be twisted in any direction. A born hero-worshipper, he adores his heroes, and what they do he will do, so upon the actions of his heroes will his own character be formed. I know from my fan mail how true this is. Upon us, who cater for him at the most impressionable age of his life, rests a responsibility which has been perceived by at least one political party. To them I must give credit for working out that in four or five years' time these readers will be voters. Biggles, therefore, may have some bearing on the future of the country. But he will remain Biggles. He isn't interested in politics. He stands for something higher. Boys who read of his exploits may be able to tell you what it is.[5]

(We shall return to this passage in the following chapter as selected sentences from it were used as a basis for an attack on Johns' work by Bridget Harris, of Teachers Against Racism.)

Talking to Hunter Davies of the *Sunday Times* some years later, Johns amplified his statement that 'at least one political party' observed how Biggles books could influence the political persuasions of children as they grew to adulthood. Johns said: 'After the war, a member of the Labour Government came up to see me at my house in Scotland. They were impressed by the hold Biggles had on young minds, minds which in another five years would be voting. Couldn't I possibly give Biggles a few Socialist tendencies? It would be worth my while. Of course, I refused. Point blank. Biggles has no politics.'[6]

Certainly party politics as such play no part in the Biggles series, but, with the start of the Cold War in the late 1940s, Communists became the enemy and the Communist philosophy was explained to Johns' readers as merely envy felt by those who had not for those who had. *Gimlet Bores In* (1950) contains a typical passage:

'Listen,' said Gimlet distinctly. 'These men are Bolsheviks. How can they look anything but sour-faced when their minds are warped by envy — hatred of anyone better off than themselves? They go through life scheming how they can get by force, or by talking, what other people get by working. That's how it is here. They boss the country. Now you know why it is as you see it. No country can thrive under a parcel of tyrants.

This simplistic look at Communist ideology is echoed again in *The Man Who Lost His Way* (1960):

'As I said just now, you never know what a Communist will do. As an intelligence officer in Malaya I had to interrogate some of them. Their minds don't work like ours. They can't. They've been so warped and poisoned by propaganda, that their only real faculty is hate. It's easy to persuade the masses that the good things of this world are unequally divided particularly as it happens to be true; wherefore you have only to plant the seed of envy to watch it grow to Communism.'

It is typical of Johns' disarming honesty and candour that he can make such a damaging admission: 'It's easy to persuade the masses that the good things of this world are unequally divided *particularly as it happens to be true* ...' Incidentally, in this book there is also an echo of Johns' anti-war feelings when, in commenting on those who are considered the great men of history, he points out that they are all military men, conquerors and soldiers. People who take life are respected more than people who give it. 'Penicillin must have saved millions of lives but you don't hear of Fleming the Great. Nor, it seems, can artists, musicians, writers and philosophers and others who have given the world something, qualify for the title'. Johns' choice of Communists as villains was merely reflective of public opinion; even Biggles' archenemy, Erich von Stalhein, goes over to the Soviet bloc. Naturally, during this period most villains in popular Western fiction were Soviet agents, and in this Johns in no way differed from his contemporaries. Popular writers such as Dennis Wheatley were virulently anti-Communist and, compared with them, Johns' anti-Communism is almost refreshingly mild.

In considering Johns' account of teaching 'under a camouflage', Geoffrey Trease commented:

It is to be hoped that even the adults reading this paragraph have still sufficiently absorbent brains to take in its highly interesting implications.

Meanwhile, let us adopt the suggestion in the final sentence. What can the boys tell us? Paul Harlen speaking, fourteen years old, in *Junior Bookshelf*: 'Biggles seems to me a true Britisher. He always fights for right against might ... Biggles is a born leader of men, a man to look up to with admiration. He is, in fact, the type of man that I would like to be. The supporting characters, Ginger and Algy, back Biggles up in everything he does and do not argue too much. Their chief virtue is that they hero-worship Biggles ... The villains are entirely different. It is easy to hate them.' There could hardly be a more eloquent tribute to a writer's success in achieving a desired effect.[7]

Some years after Trease published these questions, answers and comments, Johns made a further attempt to analyse his motivation in *The Writer*.

The backbone of my stories is the urge which is still the dominant driving force in the young human male. Adventure. It may last all his life. If his environment forbids active expression he will satisfy the craving secondhand by reading. Subconsciously, perhaps, a boy sees himself doing what his hero is doing, and hopes to do it himself one day. Security, which is the offspring of fear, is not yet for him.

Remember, you are catering for brains that are fresh, eager, receptive; brains not yet warped by the ugly side of life or political propaganda; brains not yet disillusioned; clean, healthy youth that still believes in the basic principles of decent behaviour – courage, loyalty, fair play, knight-errantry. All boys, of every race, colour and creed, believe in these things – or so I judge, as my books sell as well in the Orient as in Iceland. And you must believe in them too, or shatter the confidence of your reader should your insincerity be exposed.[8]

Reflecting on the new generations reading his books during the 1950s, Johns commented:

For better or worse, the boy of today is not the boy of yesterday. Born into an age of wonders that he accepts as a matter of course, he keeps pace with the times more easily than his elders. He sees what's going on around him, and more often than not knows more about technical and scientific developments than his parents. He is a well-informed and unforgiving critic. Let the author make one boob and his fan mail may shock him. I once took a chance and made an aircraft fly 200 miles farther than its official endurance range allowed. In poured letters from outraged readers demanding to be told how this miracle had been achieved. You may gloss over mechanical details with adults but not with youngsters.

Again, the adult author, accustomed to having everything at his command to punch into his thrills, suspense and climax (sex, hard liquor, blasphemous expletives, for example) must now get his effects without those proven instruments. These, even today, will keep a book out of many homes, out of serials, and certainly out of schoolreaders and rewards, both at home and abroad. English is taught in most European schools, and Biggles is published in dual languages, for school use in several countries.[9]

To a *Daily Express* reporter Johns said that there were four cardinal rules which he had adopted during the 1950s when writing juvenile fiction for boys. Firstly, no girls or love interest, although this did not prevent him from bringing back Biggles' great love, Marie Janis, in *Biggles Looks Back* in 1965. Secondly, absolute accuracy. 'Modern children are astoundingly well informed and if they think you don't know your facts – you are out'.[10] He illustrated this point to an *Evening News* reporter: 'The modern child ... checks his facts. In one of my books I mentioned a Mauser.32. Next thing I get a letter from a child telling me that Mausers never made a .32. Quite right, too.'[11] The third rule was plenty of action. 'Action is really all that matters'.[12] Fourthly, no descriptions. 'In a grown-up's novel you can write that the scarlet sun was sinking in the West and go on about it for hours. But a schoolboy knows what the sun looks like when it is sinking; he knows that it is red, that it is sinking, and that it is in the West – so shut up about it.'

As Johns had little respect for rules, one is once more drawn to the conclusion that he was merely stating what he felt was expected of him. Speaking to a *Sunday Despatch* reporter, who asked him about rules, he contrarily replied: 'Rules? Well, the way to write for children is, of course, not to write for children. Tell your story, work in plenty of action, and end up with a strong finale'.[13] To Frank Entwistle of the *Evening Standard* Johns described his hero Biggles as 'a quiet unassuming fellow. Wasn't much good at school or sport. Not even given to bashing people on the jaw. He's the reverse of the material for most thriller heroes. No sex. No hard liquor. No violence. No coarse expletives'.[14] But to Robert Pitman, of the *Sunday Express*,

Johns bemoaned that it was his editors who forbade sex, liquor and strong expletives in the Biggles books.[15] The first Biggles book had contained all three.

It is an undeniable fact that Biggles, now considered an archetypal British hero, had a quality that appealed to children of every nationality. Letters from Biggles' admirers came from all over the world. According to Frank Entwistle: 'Among the fanmail on his desk this week, Captain W. E. Johns found the following sentence. "Dear Sir ... I am a Chinese boy and I want to grow up like Biggles ..." And ... "I am a Pakistan girl. I am 14. I live in Lahore. And I am in love with Biggles. What can I do about it?" '[16] When Robert Pitman saw Johns some years earlier, Johns showed him a similar letter from an Estonian girl living in Switzerland. 'You can have no idea how much Biggles has meant to me. I was passionately in love with him.'[17]

In the *TV Times* Johns was asked to write an article – 'What is the secret of Biggles?' In this he sought to answer the question 'What is the quality, the universal factor, that causes a man to be regarded with admiration and affection in every country of the world, no matter of what race, colour or creed? What, in this context, has the Scandinavian in common with the Latin, the Asiatic with the African?'[18] According to Johns:

In the great multitude of ordinary people throughout the world, good, bad or indifferent in their way of life, there has developed through the ages an acceptance of the dividing line between right and wrong, good and evil; a belief, whether practised or not, in the fundamental virtues without which the human race could not have survived.

It could hardly be otherwise, for these have been extolled by the founders of every religion since the earliest civilisations.

Biggles may not be particularly virtuous, but at least he represents right versus wrong, law against disorder, which is something most people appreciate.

He does the right thing. It is expected of him, and those who know him well would be shocked if he did anything else. Yet he has the faculty of seeing the other fellow's point of view. If he hates anything it is tyranny.

Thus, for years, his most dangerous opponent was a Prussian secret agent who had also been a soldier and an air pilot. But that to Biggles did not make him a villain.

His code of ruthless efficiency was different, but he recognised in him a man who, in his own way, was doing for his side what he, Biggles, was trying to do for his. He could make excuses for him.

The enemy was, of course, Erich von Stalhein and their enmity is finally reconciled in *Biggles Buries a Hatchet* (1958) when Biggles rescues von Stalhein from a Soviet prison camp and they become the best of friends.

There is no doubt that whatever the secret of successful writing for the juvenile market was, Johns knew it — perhaps unconsciously rather than consciously. According to Geoffrey Trease, in a later assessment of Johns, 'The entertainment value of his fiction is beyond dispute'.[19] However, Trease goes on to say:

He made no difficult demands on his readers, whose requirements and reactions he felt that he completely understood. Plot and situation were straightforward, characterization was black and white, values were those conventionally accepted at the time, and settings though tirelessly varied and sometimes exotic, were the scenic stereotypes that any cinema-going youth could instantly recognise.

Furthermore, Trease felt:

Johns wrote in a mediocre style. His characters communicate in long, often slangy and facetious dialogues, their remarks being 'snapped', 'groaned', 'averred', 'opined' or otherwise conveyed. John Rowe Townsend has suggested that these books leave 'no residual legacy' in the young reader's mind. They have, however, been fiercely attacked by other critics on ideological grounds. Certainly, they often express chauvinistic sentiments and an aggressive conviction of British and white superiority which are unacceptable in most quarters today. It may well be that in years to come they will be read chiefly by half-incredulous research students, investigating the social values prevalent in children's fiction during the second quarter of the 20th Century.[20]

The pace of this indictment almost carries all before it, but its sweeping statements contain so many half-truths that it is worth considering some of them individually. Certainly, Johns did not make 'difficult demands upon his readers'; as a writer of thrilling adventure stories for children he was quite right not to do so. However, although he told an exciting story with clarity and gusto, his vocabulary was not simple, nor were his ideas. Some of the values in the books make very real demands on young readers, and were not just 'those conventionally accepted at the time'. War was seen as anything but glorious, and patriotism was not an unquestioned virtue. Even the dilemma of whether your friends or your country should come first was sometimes posed and left for the reader to answer. In *Biggles in Spain*, Ginger wrestled with the agonising question:

Would he be justified in handing the letter, vital to his own country's interests (of that he had no doubt) to a potential enemy in order to save the lives of his best friends, friends who meant more to him than the rest of the world? Either way the remorse would be dreadful; he could see that clearly. So the more he contemplated the sacrifice which such a bargain would inevitably entail – his country on one hand or his friends on the other – the more he quailed before it ...

Geoffrey Trease is right again when he says that in Johns' books 'plot and situation were straightforward', but this was only because the author's skill as a storyteller made his tales easy to follow. Some of his plots, as in *Worrals of the WAAF* and *Worrals Flies Again* are ingenious, and his situations can be charged with varied emotions. The scene where Biggles rescues von Stalhein from the convict camp in *Biggles Buries a Hatchet* is a case in point. Biggles, hiding near the quarry where von Stalhein is working under the eyes of armed guards:

... did make one more remark, and he did so because not by the flicker of an eyelid had von Stalhein indicated that he had heard the instructions. Biggles knew all about his old enemy's ice-cold imperturbability, but even so he was a little worried and wanted to make sure that von Stalhein had grasped the plan. Moreover, an awful doubt had assailed him that von Stalhein had no intention of taking orders from him. It would be in keeping with his stubborn character.
    Had Fritz [von Stalhein's nephew] not been there he might even have supposed that von Stalhein intended to betray him for the sheer satisfaction of seeing him in the slave gang, so that their careers would end together as had more than once been prophesied. But Biggles dismissed this as an unworthy thought. Anyway, the presence of Fritz ruled that out. However much von Stalhein might hate him, Biggles, he would hardly condemn his nephew to a living death.
    Anyway, as von Stalhein went past the next time, Biggles said: 'Do you understand?'

Von Stalhein spoke for the first and only time. And he did not waste words. 'Yes,' he answered, succinctly.

That was all. He passed on.

Biggles began to count the minutes ...

The imperturbable German is a good example of a character who is not just 'black' or 'white'. He has a complex personality that develops over the years, and Biggles never hides his admiration for some of his qualities. Johns' heroes are not merely 'good' characters either; they can be terrified, lose control, doubt themselves and go to pieces. However, Geoffrey Trease is right in that many minor characters, as in most successful adventure stories, are not drawn in depth.

It is most surprising that Geoffrey Trease thinks that the settings of Johns' stories are manufactured in Hollywood. Actually, the author often wrote of places he knew well; Scotland for instance, or parts of France. His intimate knowledge of Monte Carlo and the surrounding area lends a vivid realism to *Biggles 'Fails to Return'*; the bleak setting of the limestone mountains of Causse Méjean, in central France, in *Worrals on the Warpath*, is most evocative, as well as the gloomy forests of La Sologne which make *Biggles Takes Charge* one of the most haunting of the Air Police stories. Johns was careful not to be 'over-descriptive' and risk boring his young readers, who knew that the setting sun was red, but his descriptions of the earth or the sky as seen from the cockpit of an aeroplane are always particularly effective. For example:

Biggles looked over the side [of his Sopwith Camel] and caught his breath sharply as he found himself gazing into a hole in the clouds, a vast cavity that would have been impossible to imagine. It reminded him vaguely of the crater of a volcano of incredible proportions. Straight down for a sheer eight thousand feet the walls of opaque mist dropped, turning from yellow to brown, brown to mauve, and mauve to indigo at the basin-like depression in the remote bottom. The precipitous sides looked so solid that it seemed as if a man might try to climb down them, or rest on one of the shelves that jutted out at intervals ...[21]

One wonders if the 'cinema-going youth' would 'instantly recognise' this 'exotic' setting. Even Johns' most obvious backgrounds for his yarns, deserts or jungles, have the touch of authenticity.

The most serious charge that Trease makes, concerning Johns' ideology, will be considered in the next chapter. But there remains the question of his style. To say that this was 'mediocre' is not only wide of the mark but also to ignore the striking differences between the author's earlier and his later writing. Johns' juvenile fiction written in the 1930s and 1940s is highly stylised in language and expression, and the stories swing along at a breathless pace, almost mesmerising in its effect. In the postwar books the old exuberance has been replaced by a fairly sober realism. The tales have slowed down and the style is factual and workmanlike, well adjusted to the content. In the Air Police tales, Biggles and his team still have enthralling adventures, but now they would never discover all the treasure of the Incas, or save entire nations from disaster. Fortunately, Lord Bertie Lissie, Johns' monocled, 'silly-ass' character straight out of P. G. Wodehouse, is much in evidence to lend a touch of defiant colour. 'Amazing what a little red, white and blue can still do, By Jove!' murmurs Bertie, in *Biggles Hunts Big Game*. Although some of Johns' later books are frankly weak, others rank amongst his best work, and when his interest seems to be truly engaged the writing improves dramatically.

The style of the first books of the Biggles series is exactly right for their subject matter. It is only 'mediocre' if the style of the best stories by Frank Richards, P. G. Wodehouse or Damon Runyon is mediocre. Billy Bunter's famous 'Yaroo!' finds an equivalent in Biggles' bitter expletive 'perishing!' In the 'long, often slangy and facetious dialogues' of which Geoffrey Trease complains, Johns makes the avoidance of a simple 'said' into his own form of art. As well as 'snapping' or 'groaning' his characters often 'grate' or 'growl', or, as in *Biggles, Secret Agent*:

'You seem to know all about it,' said Algy, with more than a suspicion of a sneer in his voice.
'It is my business to know,' purred von Stalhein.

Only villains *purr*.

Admittedly, sometimes the dialogue does have a schoolboy facetiousness; but after all, it was written for schoolboys. In

Biggles and Co., Biggles has just descended an improvised rope into a moat, as he escapes from a castle, and Ginger is anxious:

'My goodness, what a shocking noise you made!' he muttered apprehensively, as he held out his hand and hauled Biggles up the wall. 'The people inside will think a walrus has drifted in.'

'They can think I'm a school of whales if they like,' snarled Biggles, unwinding coils of slimy weed from his neck and body. 'I'm nothing for this Jack Sheppard business; it's too unnerving. Besides, I'm wet through ...'

While he was about it, it is odd that Geoffrey Trease did not castigate Johns' fondness for clichés, favourite descriptions of his own devising. These too contribute unique elements to his inimitable style; many an aeroplane under fire 'twists and turns like a startled snipe'; many a stricken machine 'rockets like a wounded pheasant', and practically all crashing aircraft 'spread' themselves 'over the landscape'.

One wonders what sort of 'residual legacy' John Rowe Townsend expected Johns' books to leave in the young reader's mind? Admittedly, the Biggles series does not describe the world of childhood with its timeless discoveries – the works of Edgar Wallace, in his day, or of Agatha Christie or Frederick Forsyth probably do not leave much of a 'residual legacy' either. Johns' juvenile fiction is excellent entertainment and his adventure stories must be evaluated as the accomplished thrillers that they are. But, to give them their due, the books do leave a legacy in the young reader's mind – ideas about the horrors of war, about courage, about fear, about friendship, about the hypocrisy of politicians, the doubtful blessings of civilisation, the frequent incompetence of 'authority', and about fate.

No popular writer can expect to remain popular for ever. For example, who recalls the once magical name of Talbot Mundy today, except, perhaps a small bookish élite? Yet during the 1920s and 1930s the British-born Mundy was the highest-paid bestselling author of adventure fiction, with followings in Britain and America; his works were compared to H. Rider Haggard and Rudyard Kipling. Popularity is transient – a popular writer just gives countless readers pleasure in his own time. In this Johns was truly successful and his hero, Biggles, has outlived even that limitation. Perhaps one day Biggles will be totally forgotten, and not even rediscovered by the 'half-incredulous research students' that Geoffrey Trease imagines 'investigating the social values prevalent in children's fiction' in the 20th Century. But if such students ever do find Biggles again, in the opinion of the present authors, they will thoroughly enjoy their researches, and if they are businessmen as well as scholars, they will start a Johns' revival.

16

THE ATTACKS

Adverse criticism of Johns' books, attacking their attitude to racialism, sexism and violence, came late in his life. He was never able to understand what the fuss was about. The first broadside was fired in 1963 when William A. Taylor, the borough librarian of St Pancras, London, was reported by newspapers as having 'banned' Biggles books, along with Richmal Crompton's William stories and Enid Blyton's books. Mr Taylor, however, explained to the press that the books had not been banned, but they had been taken from the library shelves and were no longer being bought by the libraries in the borough. It was revealed that seven other public libraries had followed suit.

Speaking particularly of Biggles, Mr Taylor told the *Evening Standard*: 'His attitude to coloured people reflects an outmoded Kipling approach which many people these days consider bad for children'.[1] He added that when children specifically asked for Biggles or Worrals books, his librarians 'would recommend other books we consider better. The children go away quite happy'. The *Standard* asked Johns for a comment. 'I am completely non-political and non-racial in my books,' he said in wonder. 'They are published everywhere this side of the Iron Curtain. But there has to be a villain; sometimes it's an Englishman, sometimes a foreigner – even a coloured man'.

During the following year, an *Evening News* reporter rang up Johns to report that a librarian in Canberra, Australia, had taken Biggles books off the shelves 'because better books were available'.[2] Johns replied: 'Can't understand it. Australia is one of my best markets.' However, a few months later, in November, he was mollified by the Statistical Yearbook of UNESCO which reported that Biggles was the most popular hero in the world to schoolboys. Biggles books had been placed 29th in a list of the world's most translated books.[3]

In 1965, when Hunter Davies interviewed Johns for the

Sunday Times, Davies raised the subject of racialism with Johns, and quoted him as saying:

> The villains have always caused a bit of trouble. One London library has banned Biggles because they say he has a colour prejudice. This is nonsense. I've had as many white villains as coloured. I take great care with villains. If I make him Spanish, my Spanish sales slump. If he's a Communist, they won't buy it in East Germany.[4]

It was only after Johns' death that the attacks became more persistent. In 1970 Peter Grosvenor of the *Daily Express* reported that Ipswich's chief librarian, Miss Dorothy White, had removed Biggles from the shelves of her library and placed them in the reserved category with sex books. Biggles, it was claimed, was a 'fascist'. Peter Grosvenor wryly commented: 'The extraordinary thing about children's books is that the more popular they are with children the less popular they are with librarians'.[5]

In March 1973 Bridget Harris, organising secretary of Teachers Against Racism, launched an attack on Biggles as an archetypal racist.[6] She quoted passages from *Biggles in the Underworld* and *Biggles and the Black Raider* to demonstrate her contention that Johns was creating a distrust of people who were not British or did not conform to British standards. Furthermore, Miss Harris contended that Johns was doing this knowingly and purposefully. In proof of this she quoted selected sentences from the letter Johns wrote to Geoffrey Trease, published in *Tales Out of School*, and in her selection cast a more sinister interpretation on the sense.

> I teach under a camouflage ... Juveniles are keen to learn but the education aspect must not be too obvious or they become suspicious of the contents. I teach sportsmanship, according to the British idea ... I teach the spirit of teamwork, loyalty to the Crown, Empire and to rightful authority.[7]

Compare this with the full text in the previous chapter.

Jane Osborne, Johns' editor at Hodder and Stoughton, commented that Miss Harris was 'making a mountain out of a molehill', and the following week the *Sunday Times* was inundated with letters defending Johns' work. Under the headline 'Biggles was not a Racist', the paper reported:

Young and old have raced to the rescue of their hero, Biggles, and his author-creator, Captain Johns, who, as revealed ... in last week's *Sunday Times* have been accused of racialism by the Teachers Against Racism group.[8]

A selection of letters followed, including an outspoken contribution from John de Waal:

I am aged eleven and a great reader of Biggles, but not once has the idea that Biggles is a racist occurred to me.

Biggles has as many foreign friends as enemies. Teachers against Racialism [*sic*] don't know what they are talking about.

Another reader, Michael Hall, aged thirteen, was equally unconvinced by his elders, and could write with authority:

I have read 77 Biggles books ... and in none have I thought that they were against foreigners. Teachers Against Racism ... are bringing to the notice of children something which they would not think of themselves by just reading the books.

But in November 1975 the adult offensive was resumed. At the Library Association Conference, the senior Merseyside race relations officer Dorothy Kuya launched what the *Daily Mail* described as the 'fiercest attack yet' on Biggles books, calling them chauvinistic and racialist, and urging all public libraries to destroy them, along with all books for children that had wrong attitudes to women's liberation, racism and the working class.[9] Her speech provoked an immediate comment from Eric Clough, then past president of the Library Association and a fellow of the Polytechnic of North London, who said: 'We would not be in favour of destroying books that are already on the shelves, and librarians would not exercise censorship over the books they buy'. Bill Johnson, then president of the 50,000 strong Assistant Masters Association, defended Biggles books by saying: 'I read Biggles when I was young and I thought they were rattling good adventure stories. They never instilled me with feelings of hate against foreigners'.[10]

In March 1976 it was the turn of Nicholas Tucker, of Sussex University, to join in the debate. Dismissing the fact that Biggles books were still selling half a million copies a year, he wondered 'whether these books are really popular with children'.[11] He considered that 'Captain Johns obviously held the uncomplicated anti-black prejudices common to his age'. Again, it was Hodder and Stoughton editor Jane Osborne who replied to the criticism: 'Biggles was never racist. He loved all people providing they were honest and not wicked ...'[12]

The next year a further attack on Johns and Biggles was made by Bob Dixon, an English lecturer at Stockwell College, in a two-volume study called *Catching Them Young*.[13] He regarded the Biggles series as racist and jingoistic in the extreme, and considered that 'Johns' fixation on race is quite abnormal'. In 1979 the Education Institute of Scotland dismissed all Johns' books as racialist.[14]

The best informed of recent attacks on the Biggles books was a dissertation to the Australia Political Studies Association's 20th Annual Conference at Adelaide, 30 August–2 September, 1978, when Don Aitkin, Professor of Politics at Macquarie University, Sydney, and his wife, Sue Elderton, of the University of Sydney, delivered a paper entitled 'Revisiting Heroes: a study of series fiction'. The dissertation was widely reported, and it was then discovered that the New South Wales State Library had been banning Biggles books for the last twenty years on the grounds that they were racist and violent. It was also revealed that the books were not available in school libraries. These revelations and the criticisms made by Aitkin and Elderton aroused a heated controversy in Australia and, as in England, Biggles did not lack defenders. Keith MacDonald, who had played the part of Biggles in the radio series of the 1940s, said:

All this criticism is to no account at all. Describing him as racist and violent is completely foreign to my thinking about Biggles.[15]

John Kirby, in an article in the *Sunday Mail*, quoted the opinion of an Australian schoolboy 'authority', thirteen-year-old Darren Pine:

Biggles is not really violent at all. The books often have a bad German guy in them, but there are bad guys in every country.[16]

Kirby himself wrote:

After rereading some Biggles books, I was impressed by the lack of violence in Johns' narratives, especially those set in wartime.

There would be far more violence and racism in standard classics that are considered essential reading for children.

Meanwhile, the question of the banned Biggles books reached Parliament. In the New South Wales State Assembly a member asked the Minister for Education, Dr Hopgood, if he would institute an investigation to discover whether the libraries were actually enforcing a ban on the Biggles series. Dr Hopgood replied that what should and what should not be stocked was a matter of judgement for librarians.[17] The *Advertiser* asked the state librarian in Sydney, R. Doust, about the situation, and he responded that personally he was not impressed by the arguments stating that Biggles was a racist. However, the ban seemed to operate in municipal libraries over which he had no control. The controversy caused a South Australian 'Hands Off Biggles' society to be proposed, while in Melbourne a Biggles Appreciation Society was inaugurated at a dinner.[18]

The British as well as the Australian press reported and commented on these events with evident enjoyment. In 1977 a 'Spectrum' article in the *Sunday Times* referring to Bob Dixon's attack on Biggles had been illustrated by a picture of an aeroplane, with the observer asking the pilot: 'Whose side are we really on, Biggles old chap?'[19] Now the same spirit inspired the headline 'Biggles in a Tight Corner' in the *Daily Telegraph*,[20] and an article 'On your guard chaps – it's a plot by the frightful foe' in the *Daily Mail*.[21] In Australia, the *Advertiser* had 'Biggles gets a broadside',[22] and an article by Professor Aitkin himself, subsequent to the famous dissertation, was headed 'Taking some flak over the perils of Biggles'.[23]

Now that the flak has died down, it is time to take another look at the charges levelled against Johns' books for children and the Biggles series in particular. The question of sexism has been considered in earlier chapters and it seems impossible that any informed critic could argue seriously that the stories are too violent or that they glorify war. Johns never dwelt unnecessarily on bloodthirsty details. As a point of fact, though, his own careless statement to Geoffrey Trease, made in 1947, that 'in more than forty novels about my hero, Biggles has only once struck a man, and that was a matter of life and death', was true in spirit but not in letter. Biggles knocked a man down on several occasions, but only when he had to. When Biggles was fighting the Russians on behalf of Finland in *Biggles Sees it Through* (1941), he had to dispose of an enemy soldier, an orderly cook:

> There was a thud as the butt of his pistol struck the Russian's head. With a grunt the man fell across his own fire. Biggles dragged him clear and returned to Ginger.
> 'I hate doing that sort of thing, it's so primitive', he said disgustedly, 'but there was nothing else for it!'

In *Biggles, Secret Agent* (1940) it was plain that he didn't like shooting people in cold blood either:

> 'I'm sorry I had to shoot your man, von Stalhein', he said. 'He shouldn't have gone for his gun when he saw that I had mine already covering him ...'

It is the question of Johns' racism that is crucial, and it must be admitted at once that scattered through the ninety-six Biggles books there are some racist remarks and comments – but they are scattered pretty thinly. A handful of books are the culprits; in most of the tales there is nothing to object to at all. The critics who have judged the series adversely seem to have done so on very little reading and highly selective quotations. If Johns' work is to be assessed responsibly, it should be remembered that the books were written over a period of thirty-six years, times of tremendous political and social changes. Johns' stories should be seen in relation to the events of the day and the attitudes prevalent when they were written. Furthermore, 'objectionable' passages themselves should be considered in their contexts.

In the earliest Biggles tales, set in the First World War, there is no racism at all. The Germans are the enemy as a matter of historical fact, but Biggles feels no contempt for them personally, unless an individual breaks the unwritten code of behaviour honoured by airmen on both sides. The Germans are fellow pilots and the spirit of the Royal Flying Corps stories is the spirit which in real life caused RFC officers to drop a wreath on Douai aerodrome to honour in death their greatest enemy, the German ace Baron von Richthofen. In the books Johns wrote during the

Second World War, a similar spirit lingers on, but Nazis and Gestapo agents are condemned for their brutality, especially in books such as the first Gimlet tale, *King of the Commandos*, where the action takes place in occupied France. The Japanese, in some of the Second World War stories, are portrayed as callous and sadistic,and here Johns was reflecting public opinion in Britain at the time. Yet compared with those of other popular writers of the period, Johns' characterisations of the Japanese are surprisingly restrained. Typical of many contemporary writers' descriptions are those of Edgar Rice Burroughs (creator of *Tarzan of the Apes*). Burroughs could write quite unabashedly of the Japanese as 'monkey men' and, whenever Japanese characters talk, they always 'jabber'.[24]

Of the fifteen Biggles adventure yarns set in the period between the two wars, and published from 1933 to 1942, a few contain passages where the British airmen encounter other nationalities which are depicted as 'lesser breeds', but the evidence is often contradictory. The Indians in South America in *The Cruise of the Condor* and the Malayan Dyaks in *Biggles – Air Commodore* are shown as extremely primitive with no redeeming features, and the Chinese villains in the science fiction book *Biggles Hits the Trail* are treated as less than human – but as they are able to make themselves invisible they do seem less – or more – than human. *Biggles in Africa* contains a sequence, almost obligatory in a boys' adventure story of the period set in the Dark Continent, when the heroes face death at the hands of a bunch of savage natives, led by their grotesque witch doctor. Those who have called Johns a chauvinist might point to the following words spoken by Algy, as the airmen await their fate: 'Why pretend? Let us face our end with the cold, calm philosophy of our race' – but the passage goes on – 'as they say in books,' he continued sarcastically. 'Frankly, if they take us to that crocodile pool, I shall scream my head off ...' Johns' impish humour is never far away. In *Biggles Flies Again* there is the suave Chinese with the Oxford accent who makes complete fools of Biggles and Algy, and ends up the victor in the story in which he appears. In *Biggles in the South Seas*, one of the last of the vintage adventures, the brave and graceful Polynesians are painted in glowing colours, and Ginger clearly loses his heart to a lovely local girl called Full Moon. Ginger, Full Moon and a Polynesian boy called Shellbreaker, are affectionately referred to by Biggles as 'the kids'. It is in *Biggles in the South Seas* that we also get a reminder of the disastrous effects of empire upon the native peoples of the islands.

Johns certainly made his amends to 'primitive' peoples, including the formerly despised Malayan Dyaks, in later books. In *Biggles Delivers the Goods* the Dyaks lend their aid to Biggles and his squadron, proving invaluable, if bloodthirsty, allies against the Japanese. One of the toughest of them is an ardent film fan: after he has just killed two Japanese sailors with his *parang* (a heavy curved sword), he wipes his weapon on his sarong and says with a grin: 'Hit 'em. Like Clark Gable ...' Li Chi, the Chinese who is an Oxford graduate, is there to underline the moral. When Biggles remarks that the Dyak's method of fighting is 'messy':

'War is always a messy business, my friend, no matter where it is; the *parang* is no more barbarous than the bomb, the tank or the flame thrower, such as the civilised peoples of Europe use,' said Li Chi stiffly, with emphasis on the word civilised ...

The same point is made in *Biggles in Borneo*. Biggles' squadron has established a secret base in the jungle, aided by a local British prospector, Rex Larrymore. The Punan warriors of the region are of great assistance, but after an encounter with the enemy:

They nearly all carried burdens that made Ginger back away in horror. They were Japanese heads.

'Must they do that?' gasped Ginger, feeling sick.

'Take no notice,' said Rex quietly. 'Heads are merely souvenirs to them. Our chaps collect German helmets – there really isn't very much difference ...'

In the postwar Air Police stories, Johns' attitude moved with the times, and there are several condemnations by Biggles of the imperial role, especially in Africa. In *Biggles and the Leopards of Zinn* the airman decides to conceal the fact that the area in Africa where a simple tribe lived is rich in bauxite.

'Do you realize what would happen if one of the big metal operating companies knew what we know? Armies of workmen and engineers would arrive at Lake Jumu. The place would become a maze of factories and chimneys covered in red dust. The bowels would be torn out of the ground. Engines and cranes would thump and thunder day and night. A railway would appear. The lake would be polluted. The fish would die, and so would the poor old hippos. The Zinns, instead of living quiet, peaceful lives in a little world of their own, far from the scares of hydrogen bombs and other horrors civilisation is producing, would be wiped out, or what would be even worse, find themselves slaves, digging holes in the ground for stuff that's no use to them for purposes they couldn't begin to understand. Why should we inflict that on them? I say let's leave them alone, happy and content with their fishing ...'

There may still be an element of paternalism in this passage, but Biggles' concern with the life style of another people and his disillusionment with Western civilisation faithfully reflect ideas current when the book was written. One of Johns' own deeply held convictions is apparent in a late story, *Biggles and the Deep Blue Sea* (1968). In this tale the airman continues to reject materialistic values and envies an Englishman who has chosen to live alone on a tropical island: 'peace and quiet is what half the world is looking for ...'

In the attacks which claim Johns expressed chauvinistic and racialist attitudes, the nationalities of his villains have been dwelt on. It has been stated that many of Johns' villains are 'half-castes' and, moreover, that he has an abnormal fixation on race. Without counting stories with wartime backgrounds, it is true that the majority of the villains in the Biggles series are foreigners. This is hardly surprising in the fifteen adventure yarns set in the period between the wars, because all but one of these tales have foreign settings. The exception is *Biggles and Co.*, in which the action takes place in both England and Germany, the villain being von Stalhein. However, in the postwar Air Police stories, more adventures occur in England, and it is interesting that although there are still plenty of foreign villains, including ex-Nazis, Communists and American gangsters, there is a marked increase in the number of Britons taking to crime – including ex-RAF officers and men. Foreigners are numbered among their victims; a former Flight Lieutenant of the RAF tries to rob a young Indian prince in a tale included in *Biggles Takes the Case* (1952), and another ex-RAF officer murders an Arab Sheikh in a short story in the collection *Biggles of the Interpol* (1957). However, perhaps the most surprising villain in the whole series is the murderer in

'The Case of the Missing Constable' from *Biggles' Chinese Puzzle* (1955). The man who ruthlessly shoots a young policeman is the popular rector of a village in Hertfordshire and the fingerprints that help to convict him are taken from his own pulpit!

The charge that Johns includes large numbers of half-caste villains in his books is, to put it mildly, exaggerated. The actual facts are as follows. In the fifteen adventure yarns published in the 1930s or early 1940s 6 half-castes feature as either principal or memorable villains; in the fifty-two Air Police adventures published between 1947 and 1970 the number of chief villains who are half-castes is 8, plus 2 Eurasians and 3 very dubious Eastern types. It may be worth recording that these rogues are matched by 13 prominent British villains in the Air Police books, who include in their ranks a peer of the realm and his brother (ex-RAF), and 6 more ex-RAF characters. Other chief villains are drawn from at least 17 different nationalities, with Germans, Americans and Russians predominant.

A similar pattern emerges in the nine collections of Air Police short stories published in the 1950s and 1960s. A countdown of the principal villains reveals that in eighty-two tales there are 31 British, 17 of whom are ex-RAF; 12 Germans; 11 Americans; 33 miscreants of assorted origins; and 2 half-castes! Our figures are based on a detailed study of every Biggles book Johns wrote, and we feel that no comment on them is needed – except to promise that we do not intend to develop a theory that Johns was prejudiced against RAF personnel.

It may also be noted that the texts of the ninety-six Biggles books have yielded few passages on the evils of mixed parentage; three short accounts seem to be the sum total. How sad that *Biggles Does Some Homework*, the tale that Johns was working on when he died, was never published, for in it a 'half-caste Indian' becomes Biggles' friend and successor-designate as head of the Air Police.

Turning to some of the comments made by individual critics, it is difficult to counter Bob Dixon's remarks on Johns' books in *Catching Them Young* because he seems to have missed the point altogether. It is fatal to approach Johns without a sense of humour, or, indeed, any literature from a doctrinaire point of view. Dixon's disapproval extends to many other popular writers for children; even E. Nesbit, that ardent socialist, is suspect because the boys and girls in her stories are middle class. However, a few specific points may be made. *Biggles and the Black Raider* (1953) is singled out for special attack: the Raider himself, whom Biggles is asked to track down, is described variously as 'a scoundrel', a 'black devil', 'a fiend' and a 'self-appointed Lord of Africa'. Dixon objects to these terms, but in the context of the story they are justified. The Raider is a game-poacher, specialising in elephant tusks and rhino horns, and he is also a mass murderer, killing Africans, Indians and whites alike, razing their houses, destroying their crops and stealing their cattle. Unless no African can ever be a poacher or a gangster, there is nothing racialist about the words used to describe him. As for his ambition to be Lord of Africa, it is obvious why Dixon omitted to quote the following passage:

'Some believe he was born in Kenya and was brought up at a Mission School there. But as I say, nobody knows for certain, although from the fact that he speaks English well we may assume that he was once in contact with white men.' The Air Commodore smiled wryly. 'Maybe it was from them that he got the dictator idea ...'

Referring to *Biggles of the Camel Squadron*, Dixon writes disparagingly:

... we find that war is still a 'game' with Biggles and a German air ace each refusing to take what was considered an unfair advantage of the other ...

The incident in question occurs in the moving story 'The Great Arena'. Biggles' guns jam at a crucial moment in aerial combat, and the enemy pilot, seeing this, waves cheerfully instead of firing at him, and turns to fly by his side:

For some minutes they flew thus, smiling at each other across the void, and then the enemy pilot, with another wave that was half a salute, turned slowly and glided away towards his own Lines ...

It is hard to understand why Dixon feels the incident worthy of criticism. In real life, Major Maclaren, the Canadian ace, had an almost exactly similar experience. Johns was reporting how pilots actually behaved in the First World War, not putting forward an opinion.

Don Aitkin and Sue Elderton, in their paper on series fiction, make a number of interesting points about Biggles, but numerous factual errors and small slips in their general survey of the stories somewhat undermine the credibility of their findings. They are not even aware of how many books there are. 'In all, the Biggles saga issued in several dozen short stories and probably 60 novels; we have not read them all, and we are not even sure that we know them all ...'[25] They also acted on the astonishingly naive assumption that 'one Biggles book is like any other'.[26] Still, in spite of these drawbacks, they make some valid points, about the way Johns emphasises the idea of 'fair play', team spirit and loyalty. However, when they quote from *Biggles – Secret Agent*, 'the British Government looks after those who serve it', they take Johns' sarcasm seriously and fail to note that in the same book Biggles points out to his friends that if they are caught by the enemy on the secret mission that lies ahead of them 'in no circumstances whatever would the British Government come to our assistance'. In several other stories, Biggles is angered by the behaviour of those in authority, and in two tales he rescues British agents himself after they have been callously abandoned by his senior officers. 'The Carrier' in *The Camels Are Coming* is one such example. Aitkin and Elderton are totally wrong in saying that Biggles puts over the concept that 'the British dislike spying and that this sort of work comes more naturally to foreigners'.[27] It is true that Biggles disliked espionage work, but when asked to do it he does it very well, and in fact, on one occasion, he expresses his admiration for spies. In *The Camels Are Coming* a spy, with 'an educated English voice', posing as a Belgian peasant, comes to Biggles' rescue when he lands on the wrong side of the lines in a fog, and earns the airman's heartfelt thanks and admiration: 'God! What jobs some people have to do. I wouldn't have that fellow's job for a million a year and a thousand VC's ...' Aitkin and Elderton's idea of what they believed Johns thought about spies is flatly contradicted by the following passage in *Biggles Looks Back*. He and von Stalhein are reminiscing about their former enmity and the Prussian says:

'... So we were all spies. Let us congratulate ourselves on being members of an honourable profession.'

'Honourable? Who said it was honourable?'

'Your own King, George V. He said: 'In my opinion the spy is the greatest of soldiers. If he is detested it is because he is the most feared.' And Napoleon once remarked that one spy in the right place was worth 20,000 men in the field. Armies can't do without spies.'

Aitkin and Elderton are correct in stating 'the social origins of the Biggles team make it a lop-sided microcosm of English society'. They refer, of course, to the four-man team adopted by Johns in the Air Police stories dating from 1947. There is certainly no denying that Algy (Algernon Montgomery Lacey) is an 'Honourable' – although the fact is not referred to after *The Camels Are Coming*; Biggles (James C. Bigglesworth) is his cousin and presumably of the same social origins; Bertie (Lord Lissie) is an aristocrat; only Ginger Hebblethwaite's origins are working class (when he makes his debut, it is as Ginger Habblethwaite – see *The Black Peril*). However, is it really obligatory for the heroes of adventure stories to provide a 'microcosm of society'? The important factor is that Biggles and his friends do not behave in a snobbish or class-conscious way. In *Biggles and the Noble Lord* the Air Police become suspicious of the activities of Lord Malboise and his brother, Clarence, but Biggles decides not to tell his chief, Air Commodore Raymond, about their investigations for the time being. 'He's a bit old-fashioned where titles are concerned,' Biggles grinned. 'Fortunately, we're not ...' Later in the story, Clarence Malboise, who has been a squadron leader in the RAF, protests angrily:

'You have the brass face to call *me* a crook. It's the government you work for who are the crooks. During the war I risked my life a hundred times. What did I get for it? My brother and I were taxed until we hadn't a penny to put our property in order. Look at the state this place is in. Now you know why. Well we've thought of a way to get over our difficulty, and you're not going to stop us. Don't you call *me* a crook.'

'Have you ever thought of working for a living?' snapped back Ginger ...

Aitkin and Elderton go on to make the familiar charges of racism. However, in his disarming article 'Taking some flak over the perils of Biggles', Don Aitkin puts the affair into perspective. His article begins with a clever Johns pastiche. Air Commodore Raymond tells Biggles that a new deadly menace has arisen:

Biggles whistled slowly. 'Has von Stalhein joined the Americans?'

'No, it's not that.' The Air Commodore passed his hand wearily across his brow. 'It's something bigger, and stranger, too. Tell me, Bigglesworth, have you ever heard of academics?'[28]

Assuring the reader that he and his wife were 'as sorry as the next person' that Biggles had been banned from libraries, Aitkin wrote:

As old Biggles fans, we would be the first to point out that Johns teaches some worthwhile things too. He himself saw his role as a teacher, putting forward his values under 'camouflage' (his word). He was, among other things, for teamwork, loyalty to the group, personal courage, sportsmanship, self-sacrifice, and 'decent behaviour' ...

But Aitkin contended, if all those who sprang to Biggles' defence went back to the books for a quiet read, he thought they would discover that 'not everything between the covers is applaudable'. With this moderate judgement we must, of course, agree.

The heart of the matter is the overall effect of the Biggles books. It is easy to counter quotation with quotation and to show that the children for whom the tales were actually written love them and can find no fault with them. There is no question that Biggles and his friends are always courageously on the side of right against might. However, if the series promotes chauvinism and racism it is harmful − on the other hand, if it advocates friendship and equality amongst all men of goodwill, then it is a force for good. Johns' readers of all ages will make up their minds on this issue themselves − the present authors merely record their belief that the airman's credo in *Biggles Delivers the Goods* truly indicates the attitude that pervades the world of Biggles.

'I know you have some queer friends scattered up and down the globe −'

'While men are decent to me I've tried to be decent to them, regardless of race, colour, politics, creed or anything else,' asserted Biggles curtly. 'I've travelled a bit, and taking the world by and large, it's my experience that with a few exceptions there's nothing wrong with the people on it, if only they were left alone to live as they want to live.'

'All right − all right,' said the Air Commodore soothingly ...

BIGGLES LIVES!

The last fifteen years of Bill Johns' life were spent fairly quietly. Still keeping rigidly to his work routine, writing only between dawn and 8.30 am, he was able to keep up an output of three, four and sometimes five books a year. However, the length of his books had been reduced by a third compared to his pre-1955 titles. He remained always the professional; meeting his deadlines, writing to the required wordage, and providing what his editors wanted, when they wanted it. He made fewer public appearances at school prize-givings and lectures, but he always welcomed newspaper and magazine interviewers to Park House. Johns loved talking, he loved an audience, for he was a born raconteur. When Johns started to tell a story, people stopped to listen.

Mrs Marjorie Ellis remembers an occasion when Johns was on holiday in Cornwall in the early 1960s. When he started to tell, in the hotel bar, a yarn about flying, he soon collected a crowd round him to enjoy his tale and his company.[1]

Johns was a man of great personal charm. In any group he was a distinctive figure, with his bright, hazel eyes, his trim hairstyle with the centre parting, and his sturdy figure, grown stouter over the years, irradiating good fellowship and self-confidence. Some people found him overconfident, but perhaps they missed one of the keynotes of his character, his tremendous sense of humour. He loved to poke fun at things, especially at himself and his own alleged prejudices. In his writing he took an impish delight in 'sending himself up', and many critics have rushed headlong into the trap of taking him seriously. He was not a serious person. His wit is wry, Puckish, his sarcasm subtle, and his style deliberately laconic − conveying that attitude to fate, his own and other people's, born of the exigencies of war. Johns' books are rich with underlying humour, a wry smile at life as he saw it. His adult short stories contain some of the best examples of his amusing but telling irony.

After he had settled at Park House, he returned to being 'the happy gardener' as the *Church Times* had dubbed him in 1937. At the time the reviewer had noted:

Not only does he talk to his plants, but he tries to form an idea how they would like to express themselves if they could speak. He is not the only gardener to believe that they are sympathetic to the touch of some people's hands, and will recoil from those of others.[2]

It was forty years before scientific experiments were made into the response of plants to atmospheric vibrations, as described in *The Secret Life of Plants* by Peter Tomkins and Christopher Bird, published five years after Johns' death. Johns' garden at Park House, filled with roses, was living proof of the success of his sympathetic approach.

As well as gardening, Doris and Bill Johns still enjoyed their annual travels, usually heading for their favourite spot, the Riviera, via Paris or La Sologne to see the Nielsens. In his later years Johns disliked driving a car. The novelist Mary Boughey, who knew him, recalled he had a small car and hired a chauffeur to drive long distances.[3] Also, a shock to many Biggles fans, he developed a dislike of flying and would always travel by ship to the Continent. Sometimes Doris and Bill Johns went off by themselves, more often than not they would make up a party with friends and relations.

The few public appearances he made on radio and television in his last years were mainly concerned with the art of writing for children. He was one of a panel on the BBC Home Service programme considering contemporary children's books on 6 June 1957. On 16 July the same year, he was interviewed by Cliff Michelmore in the television 'Tonight' programme. On 7 October 1962 he was interviewed on the BBC Home Service 'On Writing for Children', giving the same views he had expressed in his article in *The Writer* in 1954. His final appearance was on the BBC radio programme 'The World at One' on 11 January 1967. This last interview was on the death of *The Boys' Own Paper*, which folded with its February 1967 issue. It had been published since 18 January 1879, first as a weekly and then as a monthly, and Johns had been associated with it since the early 1940s.

On 21 June 1968 Johns rose at his usual early hour, made his tea, and then went down to his study. He was working on *Biggles Does Some Homework*. At 8.30 am he finished writing page 8 of chapter 12 of the manuscript and then put it aside in mid-sentence when he noticed the time. He made some more tea for Doris and himself, taking it up to their bedroom. Handing Doris her cup, Johns went to sit in the piece of furniture always known as 'Bill's chair'. As was customary, he was planning the day with Doris, talking happily and normally, when, without any warning, he suddenly slumped down in his seat. Shocked, Doris got out of bed and felt for his pulse. He was dead.[4] Doris called Doctor A. J. Dix Perkin who later certified that Johns had suffered a coronary thrombosis brought on by chronic coronary artery disease and lachaemic mycarditis.[5]

The Times recorded:

Bill Johns was a popular figure both in Service circles and in the book world. His stocky, bulky figure, with his well groomed iron-grey hair and friendly smile was always greeted with chaff and enthusiasm by his wide range of friends. Professionally he was a first class craftsman. His work was delivered on time to editors to the exact length asked for: it was always checked and rechecked for accuracy in detail.[6]

The *Sunday Express* stated:

Captain Johns was, by any test, a significant writer. His name has been a magic one for generations of schoolboys all over the world.

He believed that 'all boys are at heart the same in their admiration of the fundamental virtues in a man'.

And Biggles seems to prove him right. The brave airman is one of the most fantastically popular characters in all juvenile fiction.

For those of us who grew up on sweet rations and margarine during the last war, Biggles is a potent name, a thunderclap in words guaranteeing thrills and just-about-plausible adventure.[7]

According to the *Evening Standard*:

Schoolboys – and girls – all over the world will be saddened today by the news that Captain W. E. Johns – creator of the internationally famous air hero Biggles, has died at the age of 75.[8]

The *Daily Mail* pointed out:

Many real life escapes from prisoner-of-war camps in the Second World War were based on the adventures of Biggles whose creator Captain W. E. Johns died yesterday, aged 75.[9]

The *Illustrated London News*, in whose columns Johns had begun his short career as an aviation illustrator, also paid tribute.[10]

Air Pictorial said:

Johns was writing right up to his death, and his hand, imagination and the meticulous precision of his working schedule were as sure as ever. Like Biggles himself, he changed very little over the years in his style and outlook. Like Biggles, too, he made only the most necessary concessions to the modern way of life and modern thought. Yet this is undoubtedly the secret of his appeal now to what is the third generation of his readers. His plots are ingenious, always exciting. His rare personal appearances during the last decade inevitably ended in his being mobbed. Nor is his reputation confined to Britain ...

The writer added:

Some, too, may remember hearing of the newspaper reporter who, on asking Battle of Britain pilots to what they attributed their success, frequently received the cryptic reply: 'Biggles'. Anyone of that generation brought up on Biggles books would certainly have known the basic elements of aerial combat – a tribute indeed to an author who, in his own way, has done as much to promote an interest in aviation as many official bodies.[11]

His publishers, Hodder and Stoughton, felt, 'He is a colossus, spanning the Second World War in a way which only Geoffrey Trease, Arthur Ransome, and a handful of other pre-war writers have done in esteem with children, outdoing all of them in the number and fanaticism of his devotees.'[12]

Johns left an estate of £27,602. Apart from small bequests to his brother, Russell, Sabena Johns (his son Jack's widow) and Mrs Kathleen King, the estate went to Doris.[13] Doris now became the sole beneficiary of W. E. Johns (Publications) Ltd, the company which Johns had formed in 1953, and Michael I. Horniman, of A. P. Watt Ltd, Johns' literary agents, was appointed to the board and became his literary executor. On the death of Doris, Michael Horniman was to become chairman of the company, with Doris's sisters Mrs M. Ellis and Mrs S. Kane, and nephews J. C. Broom and T. P. Broom being elected directors, as they had become shareholders of the company under the will.[14] The company continues to be as active as ever, for Johns' books go on selling well at home and abroad.

A few years before Johns died, a group of schoolgirls had written to him. They had looked up his age in *Who's Who* and were concerned lest Johns died and the adventures of their hero, Biggles, might come to an abrupt end. 'Dear Sir,' they had written. 'We are sorry to see that you are getting old. Will you please write lots more books so that we can continue to read them after you are dead ...'[15] Johns was amused by the letter and told a reporter: 'I shall probably retire Biggles eventually. Death would be too cruel.'[16] Ironically, he had been working on a book about Biggles' approaching retirement when he died. Johns never made any bones about the fact that Biggles was aging with the times, as a careful reading of the books shows. He did not, as many superficial critics have thought, allow Biggles' age to remain constant. 'He must be nearly 70 now,' Johns told an *Evening Standard* reporter. 'But the boys accept him as immortal.'[17] Johns had left behind him four Biggles manuscripts, which were to be published posthumously, and the unfinished manuscript of *Biggles Does Some Homework*. Within a month there was a rumour that Kingsley Amis would finish the manuscript, although Anthony Kamm, the editor at Brockhampton, the children's book division of Hodder and Stoughton, commented: 'It is a very interesting suggestion. But I don't think it is very likely'.[18] The book has remained unfinished and unpublished, on the direct instructions of Johns' literary agent, in whose view it is 'untypical' of Johns' work. Among his notes, Johns also left behind an outline for a new omnibus volume to be called *The Best of Biggles* in which he had listed the stories and excerpts he wanted to see in the volume. It was announced that Kingsley Amis would write an introduction and edit the book which would appear in 1969.[19] The book did not appear, however, due, it was stated, to copyright difficulties.

Since the posthumous publication of Johns' own manuscripts, the only 'new' Biggles titles to appear have been an anthology of First World War tales entitled *Biggles of the RFC*, edited from the original sources and introduced by Piers Williams in 1978, and four Biggles comic books, written and drawn by Bjorn Karlstrom (which were translated by Peter James and published by Hodder and Stoughton).[20] A *Biggles Annual* was launched by the World International Publishing Company in August 1980. Sadly, as it proved for most Biggles devotees, *Biggles – The Authorised Biography* by John Pearson made its appearance from Sidgwick & Jackson on 15 January 1979. Pearson had previously written an entertaining 'spoof' biography of Ian Fleming's fictional hero, James Bond, based on Fleming's fourteen books and the Bond sequel *Colonel Sun*, written by Kingsley Amis under the pseudonym of Robert Markham. But, in turning his attention to Biggles, Pearson fell sadly short of the standards he had set in *James Bond: The Authorised Biography*, published by Sidgwick & Jackson in 1973. Unfortunately, Pearson merely produced what appears to be a quickly written hodgepodge of popular misconceptions about Johns' hero. He had clearly made no attempt to study the Biggles canon in detail, preferring instead to invent some new tales of his own about the airman and his friends, including their hitherto unrevealed sexual adventures. He did, though, take up Johns' own story about Biggles and Marie Janis, the beautiful spy the hero loved and lost in 1918. Pearson made her the mistress of the archvillain von Stalhein and described how she was killed in 1944 in an air raid carried out by Biggles' own squadron. It was a pity that this meant Pearson had to ignore Johns' own very different sequel to the story, for in *Biggles Looks Back*, published in 1965, Johns at last gave the love affair a happy ending when Biggles rescues Marie from behind the Iron Curtain. After the First World War, Pearson treated *Biggles and Co.* as the next book in chronological order, although *The Cruise of the Condor* predated it and was specifically introduced by Johns as Biggles' first adventure after being demobbed in 1919. *Biggles: The Authorised Biography* was an extremely disappointing book, bearing little relation to the Biggles of Johns' ninety-six books.

As early as 1938 Johns had expressed his wish that a film of Biggles be made. At the time of writing this biography, his wish has not yet been fulfilled. In 1969 the film rights of *Biggles Flies East* were sold to World Wide Film Services and there was talk of James Fox playing the air hero.[21] A screenplay was produced entitled 'Biggles Sweeps the Skies' by Allan Scott and Chris

Bryant. The story was 'loosely' based on the book, with the writers producing a characterisation of Biggles that was certainly not as Johns envisaged him.[22] However, the film did not get to the shooting stage and the rights reverted. Then, in 1976, film rights on all the books were sold to producer Peter James.[23] Again, the project did not reach the shooting stage and the rights were subsequently passed on to Yellowbill Productions Ltd, run by Adrian Scrope and Kent Walwyn, who announced their intention of producing a story set in the 1930s, starring the comic-actor Dudley Moore as Biggles.[24] Late in 1980 Yellowbill signed a contract with Walt Disney Inc. to finance a screenplay. Shooting was scheduled for mid-September 1981 and a production company called Biggles Ltd was formed.

Interest in Biggles is still widespread, even in the hallowed halls of Cambridge University, where, on 7 December 1980, Malcolm Pratt of the library staff of St John's College, held a symposium for the Cambridge Old Boys' Book Club on the Biggles books, giving a dissertation on the complexities of English first editions.[25]

A year after Johns' death, Doris put an in memoriam in the *Daily Telegraph*.

In Memoriam:
Johns, Capt. W. E. RFC (Retd). Author. – From his desolate wife Doris Mary. June 21, 1968.
And time remembered is grief forgotten –
And frosts are slain and flowers begotten
And in green underwood and cover
Blossom by blossom, the Spring begins.[26]

A few months later Doris Johns was dead. She died on 26 September 1969, at Weybridge Hospital. The cause of her death was cancer. According to her sister, Marjorie: 'Bill and Doris lived for each other. She was his inspiration. When he died she really did not want to go on living.'[27]

And now, twelve years after Johns' death, Biggles is still alive and performing deeds of derring-do, breathlessly followed by the children of many countries. Biggles has become a byword, part of the English language. Over the years he has triumphantly overcome all his enemies and survived every kind of danger. He is still alive after being condemned to death by a firing squad on five occasions and hanging on two. He has eluded the bullets of the Germans and Japanese in wartime, and a variety of gangsters in peacetime; he has escaped the jaws of crocodiles, the tentacles of octopuses and the outcries of critics. The books live on in spite of calls to ban and burn them and the librarians who relegate them to the darkened vaults below their libraries. In trying to analyse the secret of his immortality, and thereby Johns' immortality, we can only return to the admirable summing up by *Guardian* critic Stanley Reynolds:

Beyond the ... thrills a boy gets from the 'what's going to happen next?' plots, the appeal is that Biggles is a flier and Captain Johns writes wondrously well about flying. Even diving through that old cliché, a hole in a cloud, comes alive in an amazing fashion. The writing is so vivid that it sticks in your mind and years after you remember it, but forget where you read it.

It comes as a surprise to remember that it was only in Biggles. Only in Biggles? By Jove![28]

SOURCE NOTES

1 'W. E. Johns' Philosophy'. First printed as 'The Airman's Philosophy' in *The Modern Boy's Book of Aircraft*, 1931, and subsequently printed as 'Biggles' Philosophy' in *Spitfire Parade*, 1941

Introduction

 1 *Daily Mirror*, 18 September 1980
 2 31 July 1979
 3 18 August 1979
 4 4 June 1976, and 11 June 1976
 5 *Flying*, 13 August 1938
 6 *Popular Flying*, November 1937
 7 *Popular Flying*, July 1934
 8 *Popular Flying*, May 1936
 9 *Popular Flying*, May 1933
10 *Biggles Looks Back* 1965
11 *Popular Flying*, May 1933

1
An Ambition to be a Soldier

 1 'Don't Be Depressed', an apparently unpublished article by W. E. Johns, in the possession of Mrs Marjorie Ellis
 2 *Books and Bookmen*, December 1957
 3 Mrs Margaret Collins, letter to authors, 27 April 1979
 4 *My Garden*, August 1938
 5 *My Garden*, September 1941
 6 *My Garden*, December 1937
 7 Now the Richard Hale School, Hertford
 8 D. F. Jack, letter to authors, 28 June 1979

9 *Books and Bookmen*, December 1957
10 'Don't Be Depressed' (see above)
11 Ibid.
12 *The Modern Boy*, 10 December 1938
13 'This Uncle of Mine', published in *The Modern Boy*, 1 December 1934. Jack has to pretend, for the sake of Johns' public image, to be his nephew and not his son.
14 *The Modern Boy*, 10 December 1938
15 *The Modern Boy*, 1 December 1934
16 *The Modern Boy*, 3 September 1938
17 *The Modern Boy*, 26 November 1938
18 *The Modern Boy*, 10 December 1938
19 *The Modern Boy*, 12 November 1939
20 *The Modern Boy*, 1 February 1939
21 *My Garden*, August 1938
22 'Don't Be Depressed' (see above)
23 Ibid.
24 Mrs Margaret Collins, letter to authors, 27 April 1979
25 Mrs Kathleen King, letter to authors, 6 March 1979
26 *Crockford's Clerical Directory*, 1913
27 'Don't Be Depressed' (see above)

2

In The Trenches

1 *Flying*, 13 August 1938
2 Ibid.
3 *Popular Flying*, October 1938
4 *Men Only*, March 1940
5 Letter dated Tuesday, 12 September 1916. Copy with authors
6 *Books and Bookmen*, December 1957
7 *My Garden*, January 1940
8 *The Modern Boy*, 18 June 1938
9 *My Garden*, February 1940
10 Ibid.
11 *The Modern Boy*, 7 May 1938
12 *The Modern Boy*, 15 October 1938
13 *Flying*, 13 August 1938
14 *Popular Flying*, October 1935
15 *Macedonian Memories* by H. C. Day, Cranton, London, 1930
16 Ibid.
17 *Popular Flying*, October 1938. In another version of the tale given by

Johns in *Popular Flying*, July 1933, the name of the soldier is given as Jimmy Clay. As Johns seemed fond of giving pseudonyms to several former comrades, neither name should be considered accurate.

18 Ibid.
19 *The Passing Show*, 1937
20 *Popular Flying*, October 1938

3
The Flying Instructor

1 *The Modern Boy*, 26 December 1931
2 'Planes I Have Crashed', *The Modern Boy's Annual*, 1937
3 'Adventures in the Air', *The Modern Boy's Annual*, 1934
4 *The Modern Boy*, 26 December 1931
5 *Popular Flying*, October 1938
6 'Planes I Have Crashed' (see above)
7 Ibid.
8 'Runaway Planes', *The Modern Boy's Book of Aircraft*, 1931
9 *The Modern Boy*, 24 September 1932
10 Ibid.
11 *The Modern Boy*, 19 February 1938
12 *The Modern Boy*, 9 April 1938
13 *Flying*, 30 April 1938
14 *The Modern Boy*, 9 April 1938
15 Ibid.
16 *Popular Flying*, August 1937
17 'Runaway Planes' (see above)
18 Ibid.
19 *Popular Flying*, December 1932
20 'Planes I Have Crashed' (see above)
21 Ibid.
22 *The Modern Boy*, 28 February 1931
23 *The Modern Boy*, 19 September 1931
24 *The Modern Boy*, 20 February 1932
25 RAF Museum, letter to authors, 9 July 1979
26 'Forced Landings', *The Modern Boy's Book of Aircraft*, 1931
27 Ibid.
28 'Planes I Have Crashed' (see above)
29 *The Modern Boy*, 30 January 1932
30 *The Modern Boy*, 20 February 1932
31 *The Modern Boy*, 26 December 1931

32 *The Modern Boy*, 10 January 1931
33 Ibid.
34 *The Modern Boy*, 28 February 1931
35 Ibid.
36 'Forced Landings' (see above)
37 *The Modern Boy*, 19 March 1938
38 *The Modern Boy*, 23 July 1938
39 *Popular Flying*, May 1933
40 *Popular Flying*, May 1935

4
No. 55 Squadron, France

1 *Popular Flying*, May 1935
2 Ibid.
3 Ibid.
4 Record of Service, RAF Officers' Record Department, Gloucester. It
   has been impossible to establish the exact date that Johns joined
   No. 55 Squadron. In his various accounts Johns made it clear that it
   was towards the end of July 1918. Thorough cross-checking with
   Bomb Raid reports and Reconnaissance Patrol accounts at the Public
   Record Office have been unfruitful. The staffs of the Public Record
   Office and the RAF Museum have pointed out that such records that
   remain from combat squadrons during those hectic days are not fully
   trustworthy and have often shown themselves to be inaccurate. Of
   course, one has to bear in mind the conditions of the time and the
   circumstances in which these records were made. Johns' method of
   posting himself to No. 55 without Air House orders, by no means
   unheard of, is an example of the total confusion in paperwork during
   the period. Official records, for example, have only corroborated five
   of Johns' combat missions.
5 'The Day's Work', *Wings: A Book of Flying Adventures*, 1931
6 *Popular Flying*, September 1934
7 Public Record Office, Air 1/480/15/312/245
8 *The Modern Boy*, 5 December 1931
9 'Adventures in the Air', *The Modern Boy's Annual*, 1934
10 'Forced Landings', *The Modern Boy's Book of Aircraft*, 1931
11 *Popular Flying*, May 1935
12 Ibid.
13 Ibid.
14 Public Record Office, Air 1/1750/204/139/9
15 Ibid.

16 *Popular Flying*, May 1935
17 Public Record Office, Air 1/1750/204/139/9
18 *The Modern Boy*, 30 April 1938
19 *Popular Flying*, May 1935
20 The following account is compiled from Johns' own version of the patrol as published in 'The Day's Work' (see above), from which all quoted speech is taken.
21 *Popular Flying*, November 1936
22 Ibid.
23 Ibid. Johns also relates this story, in variant form, in *Popular Flying*, May 1935.
24 *Flying*, 14 January 1939
25 *Popular Flying*, May 1935
26 Ibid.
27 Ibid.
28 Ibid.
29 Public Record Office, Air 1/1750/204/139/4
30 *Popular Flying*, May 1935
31 Public Record Office, Air 1/480/15/312/245
32 *Popular Flying*, October 1936
33 *Popular Flying*, May 1932
34 Ibid.
35 *Biggles of the Camel Squadron*, 1934

5

War Flying

1 Public Record Office, Air 1/480/15/312/241
2 *The Modern Boy*, 28 February 1931
3 Public Record Office, Air 1/1750/204/139/9
4 'Planes I Have Crashed', *The Modern Boy's Annual*, 1937. The article which also recounts this incident and gives the correct target as Buhl and not Stuttgart is 'A Long Distance Raid', *The Modern Boy's Book of Aircraft*, 1931.
5 Public Record Office, Air 1/480/15/312/241
6 Introduction to *The Camels Are Coming*, 1932
7 *Popular Flying*, May 1938
8 'The Last Show', *The Camels Are Coming*, 1932. It was Johns' publishers Thames Publishing Co. who deleted references to whisky from the story when they republished it in an edition entitled *Biggles – Pioneer Airfighter*, in 1954.
9 'Adventures in the Air', *The Modern Boy's Annual*, 1934

10 Ibid.
11 Public Record Office, Air 1/480/15/312/241
12 *Popular Flying*, May 1935
13 'A Long Distance Raid', *The Modern Boy's Book of the Air*, 1931
14 Ibid.
15 Ibid.
16 Ibid.
17 Johns' memory is apparently at fault here for the observer in number 5 aircraft on this mission was in fact 2nd Lieutenant H. R. Burnett.
18 'A Long Distance Raid' (see above)
19 Ibid.
20 Ibid.
21 Ibid.
22 This cannot be accurate for Johns has already seen Waterous, flying Rayment's aircraft, dive for home. The only pilots credited with bringing down enemy machines on this mission were Attwood and Silly.
23 'A Long Distance Raid' (see above)
24 Public Record Office, Air 1/480/15/312/241
25 Ibid.

6
Johns 'Fails to Return'

1 *Popular Flying*, October 1936. The following account is based on Johns' own description, from which all quoted speech is taken.
2 Ibid.
3 Ibid.
4 Ibid.
5 Public Record Office, Air 1/1750/204/139/9. It is interesting to note the German version of the raid contained in the Munich War Ministry file (Mkr. 13 927) – Bayerisches Hauptstaatsarchiv – of a telegram from the 6th Brigade, dated 17 September 1918: 'Landau 16.9.18. Between 1400 hrs and 1500 hrs this afternoon Mannheim-Ludwigshafen was attacked by a larger number of enemy bombers, coming in three waves. Anti-aircraft guns and fighter-planes interfered, and they had to drop their bombs indiscriminately on the city and its surroundings. Nine persons were injured, one of them seriously. The damage caused is, on the whole, slight. Two enemy aircraft were shot down.' Johns was officially listed as 'missing in action' in *The Times*, 30 September 1918.
6 *Popular Flying*, June 1936. Johns told this story in three other articles; 'Shot Down from 20,000 Feet!', *The Modern Boy*, 2

February 1931; 'My Most Thrilling Flight', *Popular Flying*, June 1932; 'Why I Am Still Alive!', *Answers*, 11 August 1934. Yet another, but rather inaccurate account appeared in *The First of Many : The Story of the Independent Air Force, RAF* by Alan Morris, Jarrolds, London, 1968.
7 *The Modern Boy*, 14 February 1931
8 *Popular Flying*, June 1936
9 Ibid.
10 'VCs Won in the Air', *Wings*, Vol. II, No. 4
11 *The Modern Boy's Book of the Air*, 1932
12 *Popular Flying*, June 1936
13 Ibid.

7

Prisoner of War

1 *Popular Flying*, June 1936
2 Ibid.
3 *Popular Flying*, July 1937
4 *Evening Standard*, 2 April 1960
5 *The Times*, 22 June 1968
6 *Ace of the Black Cross* by Ernst Udet, trs. Kenneth Kirkness, George Newnes, London, 1931; and *Eva and Adolf* by Glenn Infield, New English Library, London, 1974
7 *Popular Flying*, June 1936
8 *The First of Many : The Story of the Independent Air Force, RAF* by Alan Morris, Jarrolds, London, 1968
9 *Popular Flying*, June 1936
10 'Air Intelligence' by Vigilant, *Wings*, Vol. I, No. 1, Summer 1934
11 Dr Heyl, letter to authors, 19 March 1979
12 *The Modern Boy*, 10 December 1932
13 *The Modern Boy*, 10 December 1938
14 *Popular Flying*, June 1936
15 Ibid.
16 *The Modern Boy*, 4 February 1939
17 *Popular Flying*, June 1936
18 *The Modern Boy*, 4 February 1939
19 *The Modern Boy*, 13 May 1939
20 *The Modern Boy*, 14 April 1934
21 Ibid.
22 Foreword to *The Camels Are Coming*, 1932
23 Ibid.

24 *Popular Flying*, June 1936. Unfortunately, Johns gives no details of exactly how he effected his escape.

25 *Sunday Express*, 26 April 1958

26 *Popular Flying*, June 1936. Johns makes another reference to this escape attempt in *My Garden*, April 1943: 'In 1918 I escaped from a German prison camp and put this business of living on the land seriously to the test. Even though I stole garden produce and ate wheat in the fields, hunger was soon gnawing at my vitals. Before a week was out I was so hungry, so weary and so utterly miserable, that I didn't care much whether I lived or died. Consequently, it was almost a relief when, one October dawn, I was interrupted at a breakfast of raw apples by a Bavarian farmer who made certain suggestions to me, and backed them up with a twelve-bore ...'

27 *The Modern Boy*, 4 February 1939

28 In the Bayerisches Haupstaatsarchiv (Kriegsarchiv), *Prisoner-of-War Ingolstadt*, Vol. XVIII, quoted in letter to authors, 6 June 1979

29 *The Modern Boy*, 3 December 1938

30 *The Modern Boy*, 12 November 1938

31 *The Modern Boy*, 2 February 1935

8
The Recruitment Officer

1 'Planes I Have Crashed', *The Modern Boy's Book of Aircraft*, 1931

2 *The Modern Boy*, 16 April 1938

3 *The Modern Boy*, 1 December 1934

4 *My Garden*, May 1941

5 *Flying*, 20 August 1938

6 Ibid.

7 *Sky High*, 1936

8 *Flying*, 20 August 1938

9 *Popular Flying*, July 1935

10 *The Mint* by T. E. Lawrence, Jonathan Cape, London, 1955

11 *Popular Flying*, July 1935

12 Ibid.

13 Ibid.

14 *Sunday Times*, 5 April 1951

15 Ibid.

16 *Popular Flying*, July 1935

17 *The Secret Lives of Lawrence of Arabia* by Phillip Knightly and Colin Simpson, Nelson, London, 1969

18 *Flying*, 27 August 1938

19 Ibid.
20 *Flying*, 20 August 1938
21 Ibid.
22 *Flying*, 27 August 1938
23 *The Modern Boy*, 27 June 1931
24 'Planes I Have Crashed' (see above)
25 RAF Records (Gloucester), letter to authors, 5 September 1979
26 *The Modern Boy*, 8 October 1932
27 *The Modern Boy*, 4 April 1931
28 *The Modern Boy*, June 13 1931
29 *The Modern Boy*, 5 December 1931
30 *The Modern Boy*, 2 July 1938
31 *My Garden*, November 1937
32 *My Garden*, March 1941. Johns makes two further references to this
    posting in *My Garden*; in the August 1943 issue, he wrote: 'I recall
    once, after a long march across the desert with my Arab orderly, we
    came suddenly on our objective. It was an oasis – not the thing you
    read of in books of fiction but a real one. That is to say, there was a
    muddy pool set about with generations of camel dung ...' In the
    issue of *My Garden*, February 1944, he refers to the fact that during
    this time he had an Arab servant named Ali.
33 *Wings*, Vol. I. No. 2, Autumn 1934
34 *Flying*, 27 August 1938
35 Mrs Kathleen King, letter to authors, 6 March 1979
36 Mrs Marjorie Ellis, in interview with authors, 29 May 1979
37 *The Modern Boy*, 31 December 1932
38 Mrs Marjorie Ellis, in interview with authors (see above)
39 Foreword to *Planes of the Great War* by Howard Leigh, John
    Hamilton, London, 1934

9

Artist to Editor

1 *The Modern Boy*, 1 November 1938
2 Howard Leigh also illustrated and edited *The Aircraft Modeller's
   Guide* for John Hamilton, published in December 1933. This was so
   popular that it was reprinted in April 1934. A second series volume
   was also produced in December 1934, but the third series volume
   was edited by the artist Stanley Orton Bradshaw. Howard Leigh was
   also author of *Planes of the Great War*, with a foreword by Johns,
   published by Hamilton in June 1934, and *The New Book of the Air*,
   Oxford University Press, 1935.

3 *My Garden*, January 1940
4 *The Passing Show*, 1937
5 *The Modern Boy*, 1 December 1934
6 *The Passing Show*, 1937
7 *My Garden*, April 1944
8 *My Garden*, February 1938
9 *The Modern Boy*, 26 September 1931
10 Quoted in John Hamilton's catalogues
11 Ibid.
12 Mrs Marjorie Ellis, in interview with authors, 29 May 1979
13 *Popular Flying*, May 1935
14 *Popular Flying*, May 1932
15 *Popular Flying*, May 1932
16 *Popular Flying*, July 1932
17 Ibid.
18 *Popular Flying*, August 1932
19 *Reach for the Sky*, by Paul Brickhill, William Collins, London, 1955
20 *Popular Flying*, November 1932
21 *Popular Flying*, October 1932

10
Biggles is Born

1 Foreword to *The First Biggles Omnibus*, 1953
2 *Radio Times*, 26 August 1949
3 Foreword to *Biggles of the Camel Squadron*, 1934
4 'The Story of Biggles' by Captain W. E. Johns, undated manuscript, in possession of Mrs Marjorie Ellis
5 *Radio Times*, 26 August 1949. Not all pilots who had fought in the 1914–18 war appreciated Johns' efforts. The poet V. M. Yeates, who had flown 248 hours in Sopwith Camels on the Western Front, crashing four times and being shot down twice, wrote to his friend the author Henry Williamson: 'I read an awful book the other day called The Camels Are Coming; it was about Camels in the War and it was superbunk'. Williamson quoted this letter in writing an introduction to Yeates' book about his flying experiences – *Winged Victory*, Jonathan Cape, London, 1935. *Winged Victory* is considered a classic of aerial warfare, but Yeates did not live to see its publication. He died on 15 December 1934, aged thirty-seven, from tuberculosis due to war strain, technically known as 'flying sickness D' – 'D' for debility.
6 *TV Times*, 27 March 1960

7 *The Camels Are Coming*, 1932
8 *The Courage of the Early Morning* by W. Arthur Bishop, William Heinemann, London, 1966
9 *The Modern Boy*, 14 April 1934
10 *Biggles Learns to Fly*, 1935
11 *Biggles of the Camel Squadron*, 1934
12 *Radio Times*, 26 August 1949
13 Mrs Marjorie Ellis, in interview with authors, 29 May 1979
14 *Radio Times*, 26 August 1949
15 *News Chronicle*, 17 November 1938
16 *Sunday Express*, 26 April 1958
17 'The White Fokker', *Popular Flying*, April 1932
18 See chapter 13 'For the Duration'
19 As well as *The Modern Boy's Book of Aircraft* and *The Modern Boy's Book of Pirates*, Johns − in a rough list of his publications drawn up by him on 1 September 1959 − claimed to have edited *The Modern Boy's Book of Highwaymen* for Amalgamated Press, about 1930. No record of such a title can be traced. Johns' dating on this list is inaccurate; for example, he gives the following as publication dates: *Mossyface*, 1921; *Muder at Castle Deeping*, 1931; *Desert Night*, 1932; *Sky High*, 1933; *Rustlers of Rattlesnake Valley*, 1938, etc. Compare these dates with the bibliography. It must be noted that Amalgamated Press did publish *The Modern Boy's New Book of Aircraft* (September 1936), but no editor's name appears and there are no signed articles by Johns, although there is one Johns' illustration.
20 *The Modern Boy*, 26 June 1937
21 *Popular Flying*, June 1936
22 Hodder and Stoughton publicity material
23 *It's Too Late Now* by A. A. Milne, Methuen, London, 1939
24 *News Chronicle*, 17 November 1938
25 Mrs Marjorie Ellis, in interview with authors (see above)
26 School essay written by Catriona Cardiff, 1979, in possession of authors

11

The Militant Pacifist

1 *Books and Bookmen*, December 1957
2 *The Modern Boy's Book of Pirates*, 1939
3 *Popular Flying*, April 1935
4 *Popular Flying*, March 1937

5 Ibid.
6 *The Modern Boy*, 7 October 1937
7 *Popular Flying*, May 1933
8 Ibid.
9 Ibid.
10 *Popular Flying*, January 1934
11 Ibid.
12 *Popular Flying*, March 1934
13 *Popular Flying*, July 1934
14 *Daily Express*, 1 November 1934
15 *Popular Flying*, May 1935
16 *Popular Flying*, November 1935
17 Ibid.
18 *Popular Flying*, March 1936
19 *Popular Flying*, December 1935
20 Ibid.
21 *Popular Flying*, February 1936
22 *My Garden*, May 1936
23 *Popular Flying*, May 1936
24 *My Garden*, October 1937
25 *My Garden*, July 1936
26 *The Passing Show*, 1937
27 Foreword to *The Passing Show*, 1937
28 *Church Times*, 31 December 1937
29 *The Guild Gardener*, February 1938. Other reviews can be found in *Amateur Gardener*, 6 November 1937; *Bystander*, 17 November 1937; *Poole Herald*, 25 November 1937; *The Times*, 4 December 1937; *Public Opinion*, 14 January 1938; *Derbyshire Advertiser*, 10 February 1938; and *Men Only*, June 1938
30 *My Garden*, July 1937
31 Ibid.
32 *Popular Flying*, March 1939
33 *Popular Flying*, January 1937
34 Ibid.
35 *The Modern Boy*, 3 March 1938
36 Ibid.
37 *The Modern Boy*, 9 April 1938
38 *The Passing Show* (see above)
39 *The Modern Boy*, 3 March 1938
40 *Popular Flying*, May 1937
41 *My Garden*, May 1941
42 *My Garden*, December 1937
43 Mrs Marjorie Ellis, in an interview with authors, 29 May 1979
44 *My Garden*, January 1939

45 *My Garden*, December 1938
46 *My Garden*, April 1937
47 *My Garden*, January 1938
48 *My Garden*, April 1938
49 *My Garden*, November 1937
50 *My Garden*, December 1937
51 *My Garden*, November 1937
52 *My Garden*, September 1937
53 *My Garden*, September 1938
54 *My Garden*, June 1938
55 *My Garden*, January 1939
56 *My Garden*, June 1938
57 Mrs Marjorie Ellis, in an interview with authors (see above)
58 *My Garden*, April 1939

12
Voices Prophesying War

 1 *Air Stories*, January–March, 1936
 2 *The Thriller*, 8–15 August 1936
 3 Publisher's publicity material on jacket of *Blue Blood Runs Red*,
    1936
 4 *Edinburgh Evening News*, 18 September 1937
 5 *Hull Daily Mail*, 15 October 1937. Other reviews: *Cambridge Daily
    News*, 22 September 1937; *Bristol Evening Post*, 22 September 1937
 6 *Torbay Express*, 13 January 1938. See also *Evening News*, 24 May
    1938; *Sunday Times*, 15 May 1938; *Observer*, 29 May 1938;
    Current Literature, May 1938; *Manchester Evening News*, 6 June
    1938; *Northern Echo*, 25 May 1938; *Liverpool Daily Post*, 10 May
    1938; *Montrose Standard*, 13 May 1938
 7 *Manchester Evening News*, 11 April 1938
 8 *Edinburgh Citizen*, 22 April 1938
 9 *The Modern Boy*, 3 September 1938
10 *The Modern Boy*, 5 November 1938
11 *Popular Flying*, January 1937
12 *Popular Flying*, July 1938
13 *Flying*, 22 October 1938
14 *Flying*, 29 October 1938
15 *Popular Flying*, December 1938
16 Ibid.
17 *My Garden*, February 1939
18 *Popular Flying*, February 1939

19 Ibid.
20 *Popular Flying*, March 1939
21 Mrs Marjorie Ellis, in interview with authors, 29 May 1979
22 Publisher's publicity material on jacket of *No Motive for Murder*
23 *My Garden*, April 1939
24 *My Garden*, June 1939
25 *Popular Flying*, April 1939
26 Ibid.
27 *My Garden*, November 1938
28 *My Garden*, January 1940
29 *Popular Flying*, May 1939
30 Ibid.
31 Robert Polendine, in conversation with authors
32 *My Garden*, July 1939
33 *My Garden*, December 1937
34 *My Garden*, March 1939
35 Mrs Marjorie Ellis, in interview with authors (see above)
36 *The Modern Boy*, 17 December 1938
37 *The Modern Boy*, 5 August 1938

13
For the Duration

1 *Pearson's Magazine*, November 1939
2 *My Garden*, November 1939
3 Ibid.
4 *Pearson's Magazine*, November 1939
5 Ibid.
6 *Books and Bookmen*, December 1957
7 Ibid.
8 Publisher's publicity material on jacket of *No Motive for Murder*
9 *The First of Many: The Story of the Independent Force, RAF* by Alan
   Morris, Jarrolds, London, 1968. This opinion is echoed by Brian
   Doyle, compiler and editor of *The Who's Who of Children's
   Literature*, Hughes Evelyn, London, 1968: 'It was said he did more
   for Service recruiting than a million posters'.
10 *Books and Bookmen*, December 1957
11 Foreword to *Biggles of the Camel Squadron*, Thames Publishing
   edition of 1954. Johns also told the story, naming *Reynolds News*, in
   a *Reynolds News* interview, 10 August 1958, and gave the date of the
   piece as being in 1944. However, the authors have not been able to
   find this article.

12 *Sunday Express*, 26 April 1958
13 *My Garden*, November 1939
14 Ibid.
15 *My Garden*, April 1942
16 *My Garden*, December 1939
17 *My Garden*, May 1942
18 *My Garden*, June 1940
19 *My Garden*, March 1941
20 Mrs Sabena Johns, letter to authors, 13 July 1979
21 *My Garden*, September 1940
22 *My Garden*, August 1941
23 Ibid.
24 *My Garden*, November 1940
25 *My Garden*, July 1941
26 *My Garden*, June 1940
27 *The Champion*, 25 May 1940
28 Mrs Marjorie Ellis, in interview with authors, 29 May 1979
29 Ibid.
30 Frank Eyre, letter to authors, 17 January 1979
31 Charles Hadfield, letter to authors, 10 January 1979
32 John Bell, letter to authors, 2 January 1979
33 Publisher's publicity material on jacket of *Sky Fever*
34 BBC Archives, letter to authors, 3 July 1979
35 Ibid.
36 Publisher's publicity material on jacket of *Worrals Goes East*
37 Publisher's publicity material on jacket of *Worrals Flies Again*
38 Preface to *The First Biggles Omnibus*, 1953
39 *Revisiting Heroes: a study of series fiction* by Don Aitkin and Sue Elderton, Address to Australia Political Studies Association, 20th Annual Conference, Adelaide, 30 August–2 September 1978
40 *Popular Flying*, June 1934
41 *The Modern Boy*, 7 May 1938
42 *Catching Them Young* by Bob Dixon, Pluto Press, London, 1977
43 See entry under Short Stories in Bibliography
44 Publisher's publicity material on jacket of *Gimlet Goes Again*
45 Publisher's publicity material on 1950s book jackets
46 P. W. J. Westermann, letter to authors, 29 July 1979
47 Publisher's publicity material on 1950s book jackets
48 Ibid.
49 *My Garden*, September 1943
50 *My Garden*, September 1942
51 *My Garden*, September 1941
52 *My Garden*, February 1943
53 *My Garden*, September 1941

54 *My Garden*, June 1943
55 *My Garden*, December 1940
56 *My Garden*, November 1943
57 *My Garden*, August 1942
58 Ibid.
59 *My Garden*, February 1944
60 *My Garden*, June 1944
61 *My Garden*, November 1942
62 Ibid.
63 *My Garden*, November 1943
64 *My Garden*, July 1944
65 *My Garden*, January 1944
66 *My Garden*, May 1944
67 *My Garden*, June 1944
68 *My Garden*, October 1944
69 Ibid.

14

The Years of Fame

1 *My Garden*, September 1938
2 'My Week', an apparently unpublished article, undated, in the possession of Mrs Marjorie Ellis
3 Ibid.
4 Ibid.
5 Mrs Marjorie Ellis, in interview with authors, 29 May 1979
6 'My Week' (see above)
7 *Biggles Takes Charge*, 1956
8 Ibid.
9 'My Week' (see above)
10 Ibid.
11 *Daily Mail*, 4 October 1951
12 *Daily Mail*, 8 November 1951
13 *Daily Mail*, 10 March 1951
14 Jack Cox, letter to authors, 24 April 1979
15 Ibid.
16 *Sunday Express*, 25 March 1958
17 *Woman*, undated article, clipping in Hodder and Stoughton publicity file
18 *Evening Standard*, 2 April 1960
19 *Sunday Express*, 25 March 1960
20 Mrs Sabena Johns, letter to authors, 13 July 1979

21 Mrs Marjorie Ellis, in interview with authors (see above)
22 Mrs Kathleen King, letter to authors, 30 March 1979
23 Mrs Marjorie Ellis, in interview with authors (see above)
24 *Evening Standard*, 11 November 1964
25 Amalgamated Wireless, letter to authors, 19 July 1979
26 *Evening Standard*, 2 April 1960
27 Keith A. MacDonald, letter to authors, 4 April 1980
28 *Sunday Mail*, Australia, 10 September 1979
29 *Sunday Times*, 4 October 1953
30 *Sunday Express*, 25 March 1958
31 *Daily Express*, 24 May 1954, and *Evening Standard*, 3 April 1960
32 Eric Leyland, letter to authors, 23 May 1980
33 *Sunday Telegraph Magazine*, 23 November 1980
34 *Evening News*, 15 February 1960
35 *The People*, 13 April 1960
36 *TV Times*, 11–17 September 1960
37 *Daily Mirror*, 2 April 1960
38 Mrs Marjorie Ellis, in interview with authors (see above)
39 Foreword to *Kings of Space*, 1954
40 Publisher's publicity material on jackets of Johns' science fiction series
41 *The Encyclopedia of Science Fiction and Fantasy* (3 vols) compiled by Donald H. Tuck, Advent Publishers Inc., Chicago, USA, 1974, 1978 and 1981
42 *Twentieth Century Children's Writers* by Geoffrey Trease, Macmillan, London, 1978
43 *The Writer*, January 1954

15

Successful Juvenile Fiction

1 *Tales Out of School* by Geoffrey Trease, Heinemann, London, 1949
2 Geoffrey Trease, letter to authors, 2 February 1979
3 *Tales Out of School* (see above)
4 Ibid.
5 Ibid.
6 *Sunday Times*, 4 July 1965
7 *Tales Out of School* (see above)
8 *The Writer*, January 1954
9 Ibid.
10 *Daily Express*, 24 May 1954
11 *Evening News*, 17 August 1964

12 *Daily Express*, 24 May 1954
13 *Sunday Despatch*, 1 December 1957
14 *Evening Standard*, 12 April 1966
15 *Sunday Express*, 26 April 1958
16 *Evening Standard*, 12 April 1966
17 *Sunday Express*, 26 April 1958
18 *TV Times*, 27 March 1960
19 *Twentieth Century Children's Writers* by Geoffrey Trease, Macmillan, London, 1978
20 Ibid.
21 *Biggles Learns to Fly*, 1935

16

The Attacks

1 *Evening Standard*, 5 April 1963
2 *Evening News*, 17 August 1964
3 *Evening Standard*, 11 November 1964
4 *Sunday Times*, 4 July 1965
5 *Daily Express*, 14 February 1970
6 *Sunday Times*, 4 March 1973
7 Ibid.
8 *Sunday Times*, 11 March 1973
9 *Daily Mail*, 14 November 1975; see also *The Scotsman* and *The Morning Star*, 14 November 1975
10 Ibid.
11 *Daily Express*, 6 March 1976; also *Where?*, March 1976
12 Ibid.
13 *Catching Them Young* by Bob Dixon, Pluto Press, London, 1977
14 *Daily Mirror*, 11 April 1979
15 *Sunday Mail*, Sydney, 10 September 1978
16 Ibid.
17 *Advertiser*, Sydney, 13 September 1978
18 *The National Times*, Sydney, 30 September 1978
19 *Sunday Times*, 12 June 1977
20 *Daily Telegraph*, 12 September 1978
21 *Daily Mail*, 15 September 1978
22 *Advertiser*, Sydney, 1 September 1978
23 *The National Times*, Sydney, 30 September 1978
24 *Tarzan and the Foreign Legion* by Edgar Rice Burroughs, Burroughs Inc., USA, 1947
25 *Revisiting Heroes: a study of series fiction* by Don Aitkin and Sue

Elderton, Address to Australia Political Studies Association, 20th Annual Conference, Adelaide, 30 August–2 September 1978

26 *The National Times*, Sydney, 30 September 1978

27 *Revisiting Heroes* (see above). Johns mentions his admiration for the work spies do in *The Modern Boy*, 22 April 1938: 'It takes a lot of nerve to be a spy.'

28 *The National Times*, Sydney, 30 September 1978

17
Biggles Lives!

1 Mrs Marjorie Ellis, in interview with authors, 29 May 1979

2 *Church Times*, 31 December 1937

3 Recounted by Mrs Elizabeth A. Lewisohn, letter to authors, 17 October 1980

4 Mrs Marjorie Ellis, in interview with authors (see above)

5 Johns' death certificate (St Catherine's House, London)

6 *The Times*, 22 June 1968

7 *Sunday Express*, 24 June 1968

8 *Evening Standard*, 22 June 1968

9 *Daily Mail*, 22 June 1968

10 *Illustrated London News*, 27 June 1968

11 *Air Pictorial*, August 1968. An obituary also appears in *Cross and Cockade*, (USA) Vol. 9, No. 3, Autumn, 1968

12 Hodder and Stoughton obituary statement, from their files

13 The sums were: £500 to his brother: £200 to Mrs Kathleen King and £100 to Mrs Sabena Johns. Taken from copy of will (Somerset House). Also published in the *Daily Telegraph*, 7 September 1968, and the *Evening Standard*, 6 September 1968

14 J. W. Bell, letter to authors, 3 June 1980

15 *Surrey Comet*, 29 June 1968

16 Ibid.

17 *Evening Standard*, 11 November 1964

18 *Daily Mail*, 7 July 1968

19 Ibid.

20 See bibliography

21 *Evening Standard*, 30 January 1969

22 'Biggles Sweeps the Skies', screenplay script in private collection of Christopher Lowder

23 *Sunday Times*, 5 February 1976

24 *Observer Colour Magazine*, 2 November 1980. See also *Portsmouth Evening News*, 4 November 1980

25 *Collector's Digest*, January 1981
26 *Daily Telegraph*, 21 June 1969
27 Mrs Marjorie Ellis, in interview with authors (see above)
28 *Guardian*, 6 January 1979

BIBLIOGRAPHY

The Works of W. E. Johns

There is, at the moment, no complete bibliography of the works of W. E. Johns although, in the course of our researches, we have compiled a fairly extensive bibliography. The prolific nature of Johns' short-story writing and journalism, the many serialisations of his books and the number of foreign languages in which his work has been published, both in magazine and book form, make the task of compiling a comprehensive bibliography of his writings an extremely difficult one. Even making a check-list of books presents certain pitfalls. In 1939, for example, the *British Catalogue* and *Whitaker's* (against which all titles have been checked) show that Oxford University Press issued three Biggles titles in May. This is a highly unusual practice for a publisher and, indeed, a contemporary publication says one of these titles was actually issued in October. Catalogue dates for OUP titles may therefore be suspect. Similarly, in the period 1960–2, many Johns' titles are not even noticed by the *British Catalogue* or *Whitaker's* and no month of publication can be provided. The following list contains a chronological record of first editions and, where possible, first serialisations. The author's name appears against titles listed below only when the by-line was other than Captain W. E. Johns.

Books and Serialisations

1 *Wings: A Book of Flying Adventures* edited by W. E. Johns, Ace series, John Hamilton Ltd, London, August 1931
2 *The Modern Boy's Book of Aircraft* edited by W. E. Johns, Amalgamated Press, London, August 1931
3 *Mossyface* by William Earle, Mellifont Press, Dublin and London, 1932

4 *The Pictorial Flying Course* by Flt. Lt. Harry M. Schofield and F/O W. E. Johns, illustrated by W. E. Johns, John Hamilton Ltd, London, May 1932

5 *The Camels Are Coming* by W. E. Johns (William Earle), illustrated by W. E. Johns, John Hamilton Ltd, London, August 1932

   Serialisation: seventeen stories comprise the book. Seven of these stories first appeared under the pseudonym of William Earle in *Popular Flying* from April to October 1932. Fourteen of the stories then appeared under the by-line of Flying Officer W. E. Johns in *The Modern Boy* between 14 January 1933 and 15 April 1933. Two of the remaining three stories then appeared in the 14 and 21 October issues of the magazine.

   Stories from this title reappeared in a slightly amended form in *Biggles of the Special Air Police* (1953) and *Biggles – Pioneer Airfighter* (1954).

6 *Fighting Planes and Aces*, illustrated by Howard Leigh, John Hamilton Ltd, London, November 1932

7 *The Spy Flyers*, illustrated by Howard Leigh, Ace series, John Hamilton Ltd, London, August 1933

8 *The Cruise of the Condor*, illustrated by Howard Leigh, Ace series, John Hamilton Ltd, London, August 1933

   Serialisation: Published as 'Wings of Fortune', *The Modern Boy*, 11 August to 22 September 1934.

9 *Biggles of the Camel Squadron*, illustrated by Howard Leigh, Ace series, John Hamilton Ltd, London, March 1934

   Serialisation: The book comprises thirteen stories of which five appeared in *Popular Flying* From January to May 1933, and ten appeared in *The Modern Boy*, from 15 July to 16 September 1933. This title was also republished as *Biggles Goes to War* in The Boys' Friend Library, No. 610, February 1938, which must not be confused with the Oxford University Press title *Biggles Goes to War*.

10 *Biggles Flies Again*, illustrated by Howard Leigh, Ace series, John Hamilton Ltd, London, August 1934

   Serialisation: Of the thirteen stories that comprise the book, eleven of them appeared in *Popular Flying* between July 1933 and May 1934. Some of them were then republished in *The Modern Boy* between 27 April and 15 June 1935.

11 *Biggles Learns to Fly*, The Boys' Friend Library, No. 469, London, March 1935

   Serialisation: The stories appeared in *The Modern Boy* from 14 April 1934 to 30 June 1934.

   A revised edition was first published in hardback by Brockhampton Press, 11 July 1951. An abridged version was issued on cassette recording, read by Simon Ward, produced by Ivan Berg Associates (Audio Publishing) Ltd, London, March 1977.

12 *The Black Peril*, John Hamilton Ltd, London, March 1935
Serialisation: Published as 'Winged Menace' in *The Modern Boy*, 9 February to 13 April 1935.
This title was also issued as *Biggles Flies East* by The Boys' Friend Library, No. 621, May 1938, which must not be confused with the Oxford University Press title *Biggles Flies East*.

13 *The Air VCs*, John Hamilton Ltd, London, March 1935
Serialisation: The book was based on articles published in *Popular Flying* 1932–4.

14 *The Raid*, Ace series, John Hamilton Ltd, London, April 1935
Serialisation: Of the five stories that comprise this book only one seems to have appeared elsewhere before book publication: 'The Raid' (*Wings*, Vol. 1, No. 2, Autumn 1935); 'All's Fair'; 'Strange Freight' (*Wings*, Vol. 1, No. 3, Winter 1935); 'Old Soldiers Never Die'; 'The Ace of Spades – A Biggles Tale' (*The Cockpit*, John Hamilton Ltd, August 1934).

15 *Thrilling Flights*, illustrated by Howard Leigh, John Hamilton Ltd, London, June 1936
Serialisation: The book was based on articles published in *Popular Flying*.

16 *Some Milestones of Aviation*, John Hamilton Ltd, London, June 1935.

17 *Biggles Flies East*, illustrated by Howard Leigh and Alfred Sindall, Oxford University Press, London, August 1935
Serialisation: *The Modern Boy*, 28 September to 28 December 1935.

18 *Biggles Hits the Trail*, illustrated by Howard Leigh and Alfred Sindall, Oxford University Press, London, August 1935
Serialisation: 'The Mountain of Light', *The Modern Boy*, 22 June to 24 August 1935.

19 *Biggles in France*, The Boys' Friend Library, No. 501, November 1935
Serialisation: *The Modern Boy*, 7 July 1934 to 19 January 1935. The stories in this book were used as a basis for *Spitfire Parade* (1941). Six stories were rewritten as Second World War Tales; the rest were reprinted in *Biggles of 266* (1955).

20 *Sky High*, George Newnes, London, February 1936
Serialisation: 'Aerial Enemy No. 1', *Air Stories*, January to March 1936. Also as 'Calling All Cars' and 'Steeley Muscles In', *The Thriller*, 8 and 15 August 1936.

21 *Biggles & Co.*, illustrated by Howard Leigh and Alfred Sindall, Oxford University Press, London, April 1936

Serialisation: 'The Gold Flyers', *The Modern Boy*, 4 January to 7 March 1936.

22 *Steeley Flies Again*, George Newnes, London, June 1936
Serialisation: 'The Kidnapping of Virginia Marven' and 'Steeley in the Gangster's Stronghold', *The Thriller*, 10 and 17 October 1936.

23 *Biggles in Africa*, illustrated by Howard Leigh and Alfred Sindall, Oxford University Press, London, August 1936
Serialisation: *The Modern Boy*, 1 August to 26 September 1936.

24 *Blue Blood Runs Red* by Jon Early, George Newnes, London, December 1936

25 *Biggles – Air Commodore*, illustrated by Howard Leigh and Alfred Sindall, Oxford University Press, London, May 1937
Serialisation: *The Modern Boy*, 3 October to 5 December 1936.

26 *Murder By Air*, George Newnes, London, August 1937
Serialisation: 'Prisoner of the Dope Ring' and 'The Dope Smugglers', *The Thriller*, 16 and 21 January 1937. Also serialised in *Flying*, 2 April to 28 May 1938.

27 *The Passing Show: a garden diary by an amateur gardener*, illustrated by Howard Leigh, *My Garden*, George Newnes, London, September 1937
Serialisation: The book comprises nine articles published in *My Garden* between May 1936 and August 1937, with additional material.

28 *Biggles Flies West*, illustrated by Howard Leigh and Alfred Sindall, Oxford University Press, London, September 1937
Serialisation: *The Modern Boy*, 26 June to 11 September 1937.

29 *Desert Night*, John Hamilton Ltd, London, March 1938

30 *Biggles Flies South*, illustrated by Howard Leigh and Jack Nicolle, Oxford University Press, London, May 1938
Serialisation: *The Modern Boy*, 19 February to 9 April 1938.

31 *Biggles Goes to War*, illustrated by Howard Leigh and Martin Tyas, Oxford University Press, London, 1938
Serialisation: *The Modern Boy*, 25 September to 4 December 1937.

32 *The Biggles Omnibus* (consisting of *Biggles Flies East*, *Biggles Hits the Trail* and *Biggles & Co.*) Oxford University Press, London, May 1938

33 *The Murder at Castle Deeping*, John Hamilton Ltd, London, May 1938
Serialisation: 'Scandal at Castle Deeping' and 'The Counterfeiters' *The Thriller*, 10 and 17 June 1937.

34 *Champion of the Main*, illustrated by H. Gooderman, Oxford University Press, London, June 1938

Serialisation: *The Modern Boy*, 28 May to 23 July 1938.

35 *Wings of Romance*, George Newnes, London, February 1939
Serialisation: *The Thriller*, 27 September to 30 October 1937.
Also as 'Wings of Rebellion' in *Flying*, 4 June to 16 July 1938.

36 *The Rescue Flight*, illustrated by Howard Leigh and Alfred Sindall,
Oxford University Press, London, May 1939
Serialisation: 'Biggles' Rescue Flight', *The Modern Boy*, 1
October to 3 December 1938.

37 *Biggles in Spain*, illustrated by Howard Leigh and J. Abbey, Oxford
University Press, London, May 1939
Serialisation: 'Wings Over Spain', *The Modern Boy*, 21 January
to 1 April 1939.

38 *Biggles Flies North*, illustrated by Howard Leigh and Will
Narraway, Oxford University Press, London, May 1939
Serialisation: *The Modern Boy*, 23 July to 17 September 1938.

39 *The Modern Boy's Book of Pirates* ('specially written by Flying
Officer W. E. Johns') Amalgamated Press, London, September
1939
Serialisation: From articles 'They Flew the Jolly Roger' in *The
Modern Boy*, 6 August to 21 September 1938.

40 *Det Forsvunne Dagboksblad* (The Missing Page), translated by Leif
Borthen, Forlagshuset, Olso, Norway, 1939
This title is listed because it is a first world edition and the only
book publication of the Steeley story 'The Missing Page', which
appeared in *The Thriller*, 16 October 1937. There is no English
edition of this intriguing tale.

41 *The Unknown Quantity*, John Hamilton Ltd, London, January 1940

42 *Biggles – Secret Agent*, illustrated by Howard Leigh and Alfred
Sindall, Oxford University Press, London, May 1940
Serialisation: 'Castle Sinister', *The Modern Boy*, 12 August to 14
October 1939.

43 *The Biggles Flying Omnibus* (consisting of *Biggles Flies North*,
Biggles Flies South and *Biggles Flies West*), Oxford University
Press, London, June 1940

44 *Biggles in the Baltic*, illustrated by Howard Leigh and Alfred
Sindall, Oxford University Press, London, June 1940
Serialisation: 'Storm Troops of the Baltic Skies' in *The War
Thriller*, 9 to 18 March 1940.

45 *Biggles in the South Seas*, illustrated by Norman Howard, Oxford
University Press, London, September 1940
Serialisation: 'Biggles' South Seas Adventure', *The Gem*, 14
October to 9 December 1939.

46 *Biggles Defies the Swastika*, illustrated by Howard Leigh and Alfred
Sindall, Oxford University Press, London, August 1941

47 *Biggles Sees it Through*, illustrated by Howard Leigh and Alfred Sindall, Oxford University Press, London, August 1941

48 *Spitfire Parade – Stories of Biggles in War*, illustrated by Ratcliffe Wilson, Oxford University Press, London, August 1941

These stories were mainly rewritten from *Biggles in France* (1935), plus an uncollected tale 'Biggles' Exciting Night' (*Modern Boys' Annual*, 1937) which was rewritten as 'The Fortunes of War' and 'Bertie Picks the Lock'. Interestingly, Johns' short story 'Spitfire Parade' (*Air Stories*, March 1940) is not included.

49 *The Third Biggles Omnibus* (consisting of *Biggles in Spain*, *Biggles Goes to War* and *Biggles in the Baltic*), Oxford University Press, London, August 1941

50 *Worrals of the WAAF* Lutterworth Press, London, September 1941

51 *Biggles in the Jungle*, illustrated by Terence Cuneo, Oxford University Press, London, May 1942

52 *Sinister Service*, illustrated by Stuart Tresillian, Oxford University Press, London, June 1942
The first half of this book was rewritten from a Steeley story which appeared as 'Nazis in the New Forest' in *The War Thriller*, 27 April 1940. In this version Steeley becomes Lance Lovell and Tubby Wilde becomes Rodney Lovell.

53 *Worrals Flies Again*, illustrated by Leslie Stead, Hodder and Stoughton, London, September 1942
Serialisation: *Girls' Own Paper*, October to February 1942–3.

54 *Worrals Carries On*, illustrated by Stead, Lutterworth Press, London, October 1942
Serialisation: *Girls' Own Paper*, October 1941 to September 1942.

55 *Biggles Sweeps the Desert*, illustrated by Leslie Stead, Hodder and Stoughton, London, November 1942

56 *Worrals on the Warpath*, illustrated by Stead, Hodder and Stoughton, London, July 1943

57 *Biggles, Charter Pilot*, illustrated by Mendoza, Oxford University Press, London, July 1943
Most of the stories comprising this collection appeared in *Boys' Own Paper* from October 1941, through to January 1944.

58 *Biggles in Borneo*, illustrated by Stuart Tresillian, Oxford University Press, London, July 1943

59 *Biggles 'Fails to Return'*, illustrated by Stead, Hodder and Stoughton, London, August 1943

60 *King of the Commandos*, illustrated by Stead, University of London Press, London, October 1943

61 *Gimlet Goes Again*, illustrated by Stead, University of London Press, London, February 1944

62 *Worrals Goes East*, illustrated by Stead, Hodder and Stoughton, London, May 1944

63 *Biggles in the Orient*, illustrated by Stead, Hodder and Stoughton, London, April 1945

64 *Biggles Delivers the Goods*, illustrated by Stead, Hodder and Stoughton, London, April 1946

65 *Gimlet Comes Home*, illustrated by Stead, University of London Press, London, December 1946

66 *Comrades in Arms*, illustrated by Stead, Hodder and Stoughton, London, August 1947
The book comprises six stories, three of which concern Biggles, Worrals and Gimlet respectively. The first tale 'An Oriental Adventure' (a Gimlet tale) appeared as 'Seeds of Trouble' in *Boys' Own Paper*, July to September 1945. The others have not been traced, though it is obvious they appeared in other publications.

67 *Gimlet Mops Up*, illustrated by Stead, Brockhampton Press, Leicester, August 1947

68 *Sergeant Bigglesworth CID*, illustrated by Stead, Hodder and Stoughton, London, August 1947

69 *Worrals in the Wilds*, illustrated by Stead, Hodder and Stoughton, London, November 1947
Serialisation: *Girls' Own Paper*, November 1945 to November 1946.

70 *The Rustlers of Rattlesnake Valley*, Thomas Nelson, London, July 1948

71 *Biggles' Second Case*, illustrated by Stead, Hodder and Stoughton, London, August 1948
Serialisation: *The Boys' Own Paper*, January to September 1946.

72 *Biggles Hunts Big Game*, illustrated by Stead, Hodder and Stoughton, London, August 1948

73 *Gimlet's Oriental Quest*, illustrated by Stead, Brockhampton Press, Leicester, 1948

74 *Worrals Down Under*, illustrated by Stead, Lutterworth Press, Leicester, 1948
Serialisation: *Girls' Own Paper*, October 1946 to July 1947.

75 *Biggles Takes a Holiday*, illustrated by Stead, Hodder and Stoughton, London, June 1949

76 *Biggles Breaks the Silence*, illustrated by Stead, Hodder and Stoughton, London, August 1949
Serialisation: *Liverpool Daily Post* (according to agents' files). This book was later retitled *Biggles in the Antarctic* (Armada, London, 1970).

77 *Worrals Goes Afoot*, illustrated by Stead, Lutterworth Press, London, September 1949

78 *Gimlet Lends a Hand*, illustrated by Stead, Brockhampton Press, London, October 1949

79 *Worrals in the Wastelands*, illustrated by Stead, Lutterworth Press, London, 1949

80 *Short Sorties*, Latimer House, London, May 1950
The adult short stories in this collection began to appear in a wide variety of journals from the 1930s, but most were published in the 1940s — for example, in *Britannia & Eve*, *Woman's Journal*, *Woman's Magazine*, *Colliers* (USA), *Extension* (USA), *Macleans* (Canada). Some were also adapted and broadcast on BBC Radio.

81 *Biggles Gets His Men*, illustrated by Stead, Hodder and Stoughton, London, July 1950

82 *Worrals Investigates*, illustrated by Stead, Lutterworth Press, London, 1950

83 *Gimlet Bores In*, illustrated by Stead, Brockhampton Press, Leicester, September, 1950

84 *Dr Vane Answers the Call*, Latimer House, London, November 1950
These stories began to appear in *Pearson's Magazine* (as adult fiction) in October 1939. However, with the November 1939 issue the magazine folded. While Johns indicates that the other eight tales in this ten-story collection appeared elsewhere, it has, so far, not been possible to trace them.

85 *Another Job for Biggles*, illustrated by Stead, Hodder and Stoughton, London, February 1951

86 *Biggles Goes to School*, illustrated by Stead, Hodder and Stoughton, London, June 1951
Serialisation: 'Biggles At School', *Boys' Own Paper*, October 1950 to March 1951.

87 *Biggles Works It Out*, illustrated by Stead, Hodder and Stoughton, London, October 1951
Serialisation: *Boys' Own Paper*, April to September 1951.

88 *Gimlet Off the Map*, illustrated by Stead, Brockhampton Press, Leicester, 1951

89 *Biggles Takes the Case*, illustrated by Stead, Hodder and Stoughton, London, March 1952
The nine short stories that comprise this collection are to be found in a wide variety of annuals and books such as *Boys' Book of Adventure*, 1950; *Wonder Book of Comics*; *Children's Jolly Book*; *Every Boy's Annual*, etc. One story, 'The Renegade' appeared weekly in the *Daily Mail* from 19 August 1950 to 30 October 1950. Another story, 'The Case of the Mysterious Gunshots', was first

presented to the public on BBC Radio, 5 September 1949, on the 12.00 noon 'Hello Children' programme. Interestingly, the last story in the collection, 'The Hare and the Tortoise', a Second World War tale which appeared in *Every Boy's Annual* 1952, is a rewritten First World War tale which originally appeared as 'The Fledgling' in the *New Book of the Air*, edited by Howard Leigh, Oxford University Press, London, 1935, and subsequently as 'Biggles' Fledgling' in *The Modern Boy*, 7 June 1939. According to agents' files, the serial rights on *Biggles Takes the Case* were sold to the *Liverpool Daily Post*.

90 *Biggles Follows On*, illustrated by Stead, Hodder and Stoughton, London, 14 June 1952
　　Serialisation: *Boys' Own Paper*, April to September 1952.

91 *Biggles, Air Detective*, Marks & Spencer, London, 7 July 1952
　　Serialisation: Agents' files state the *Melbourne Herald* bought serial rights. These stories also seem to have appeared in annuals, and one of them was broadcast on BBC Radio, on 29 August 1949, on the 12.00 noon 'Hello Children' programme.

92 *Gimlet Gets the Answer*, illustrated by Stead, Brockhampton Press, Leicester, 8 September 1952

93 *Biggles and the Black Raider*, illustrated by Stead, Hodder and Stoughton, London, 5 March 1953

94 *Sky Fever and Other Stories*, Latimer House, 22 June, 1953
These adult short stories are a collection of stories published in magazines mainly during the 1940s, though some, such as 'The Tourist' appeared under the Johns pseudonym of William Earle as early as October 1939 in *Pearson's Magazine*.

95 *Biggles in the Blue*, illustrated by Stead, Brockhampton Press, Leicester, 20 July 1953
　　Serialisation: *The Eagle*.

96 *The First Biggles Omnibus*, (consisting of *Biggles Sweeps the Desert*, *Biggles in the Orient*, *Biggles Delivers the Goods* and *Biggles 'Fails to Return'*) Hodder and Stoughton, London, 24 September 1953
Mistitled in view of the fact that Oxford University Press had already produced three omnibus volumes.

97 *Biggles in the Gobi*, illustrated by Stead, Hodder and Stoughton, London, 8 October 1953
　　Serialisation: *The Eagle*.

98 *Biggles of the Special Air Police*, Kingston Library, Thames Publishing Co., London, (undated) 1953
Red boards first issue, blue boards subsequent issues.
The contents are six Air Police tales, the first six stories from *The Camels Are Coming* (1932), plus 'The Ace of Spades'.

99 *Biggles Cuts it Fine*, illustrated by Stead, Hodder and Stoughton,

London, 4 March 1954

Serialisation: According to agents' files *The Liverpool Daily Post.*

100 *Kings of Space*, illustrated by Stead, Hodder and Stoughton, London, 13 May 1954

101 *Gimlet Takes a Job*, illustrated by Stead, Brockhampton Press, Leicester, 21 June 1954

102 *Biggles and the Pirate Treasure*, illustrated by Stead, Brockhampton Press, Leicester, 19 July 1954

Serialisation: These eleven stories appeared in a wide variety of publications such as the *Daily Mail Annual* 1952, and *Boys' Own Paper*, etc.

103 *Biggles, Foreign Legionnaire*, illustrated by Stead, Hodder and Stoughton, London, 23 September 1953

Serialisation: According to agents' files, the *Liverpool Daily Post.*

104 *Biggles Pioneer Airfighter*, Kingston Library, Thames Publishing Co., London, (undated) 1954

This volume contains the rest of the stories from *The Camels Are Coming* not included in *Biggles of the Special Air Police*, plus two stories – 'The Thought Reader' and 'Biggles Finds His Feet' – from the 1934 edition of *Biggles of the Camel Squadron*, which were then left out of the 1954 Kingston Library reprint of the book.

105 *Biggles in Australia*, illustrated by Studio Stead, Hodder and Stoughton, London, 31 March 1955

Serialisation: *The Junior Mirror.*

106 *Adventure Bound*, illustrated by Douglas Relf, Thomas Nelson, London, 14 April 1955

107 *Biggles' Chinese Puzzle*, illustrated by Stead, Brockhampton Press, Leicester, 9 May 1955

These eight short stories appeared in journals and annuals such as *The Boys' Own Paper*, *The Boys' Own Companion*, *Treasure Book of Comics*, etc.

108 *Return to Mars*, illustrated by Stead, Hodder and Stoughton, London, 8 September 1955

109 *Biggles of 266*, Kingston Library, Thames Publishing Co., London (undated) 1955

These stories were taken from *Biggles in France* (1935), including 'Under Open Arrest' and 'The Laugh's With Us', which appeared as 'One Good Turn' in *Spitfire Parade* and here appears in its original form as 'Reprisals'. Also included are two stories from the 1935 edition of *Biggles Learns to Fly* which then had to be omitted from the 1955 Brockhampton edition of the book.

110 *Biggles Air Detective Omnibus* (consisting of *Sergeant Bigglesworth CID*, *Biggles' Second Case*, *Another Job for Biggles* and *Biggles Works It Out*), Hodder and Stoughton, London, 15 March 1956

111 *No Rest for Biggles*, illustrated by Studio Stead, Hodder and Stoughton, London, 15 March 1956
   Serialisation: *The Junior Mirror.*
112 *Biggles Takes Charge*, illustrated by Stead, Brockhampton Press, Leicester, 1956
113 *Now to the Stars*, illustrated by Stead, Hodder and Stoughton, London, 16 August 1956
114 *Adventure Unlimited*, illustrated by Douglas Relf, Thomas Nelson, 25 January 1957
115 *Biggles Makes Ends Meet*, illustrated by Stead, Hodder and Stoughton, London, 7 February 1957
116 *Biggles of the Interpol*, illustrated by Stead, Brockhampton Press, Leicester, 23 May 1957
   Serialisation: *The Evening News* 12–17 June 1954.
117 *Biggles on the Home Front*, illustrated by Stead, Hodder and Stoughton, London, August 1957
118 *To Outer Space*, illustrated by Stead, Hodder and Stoughton, London, 12 September 1957
119 *Biggles Presses On*, illustrated by Stead, Brockhampton Press, Leicester, 20 January 1958
   The eleven stories appeared in annuals such as the *Daily Mail Annuals* 1956–7, the *News Chronicle I-Spy Annual* 1956, etc.
120 *No Motive For Murder*, Hodder and Stoughton, London, 23 January 1958
121 *The Edge of Beyond*, illustrated by Stead, Hodder and Stoughton, London, 20 March 1958
122 *Biggles on Mystery Island*, illustrated by Stead, Hodder and Stoughton, London, 3 July 1958
123 *Biggles Buries a Hatchet*, illustrated by Stead, Brockhampton Press, Leicester, 8 September 1958
   Serialisation: *Boys' Own Paper*, March to September 1958.
124 *Biggles in Mexico*, illustrated by Stead, Brockhampton Press, Leicester, 19 January 1959
125 *Biggles' Combined Operation*, illustrated by Stead, Hodder and Stoughton, London, 1959
126 *The Biggles Book of Heroes*, Max Parrish, London, 1959
127 *Biggles at the World's End*, illustrated by Stead, Brockhampton Press, Leicester, 1959
128 *The Death Rays of Ardilla*, illustrated by Stead, Hodder and Stoughton, London, 5 March 1959
129 *The Man Who Lost His Way*, Macdonald, London, 1 February 1960
130 *Biggles and the Leopards of Zinn*, illustrated by Stead, Brockhampton Press, Leicester, 11 April 1960

131 *Biggles Goes Home*, illustrated by Stead, Hodder and Stoughton, London, 8 September 1960
Serialisation: *Express Weekly*.

132 *Where the Golden Eagle Soars*, illustrated by Colin Gibson, Hodder and Stoughton, London, 1960

133 *To Worlds Unknown*, illustrated by Stead, Hodder and Stoughton, London, 1960

134 *Adventures of the Junior Detection Club*, Max Parrish, London, 1960

135 *The Quest for the Perfect Planet*, illustrated by Stead, Hodder and Stoughton, 22 March 1961

136 *Biggles and the Poor Rich Boy*, illustrated by Stead, Brockhampton Press, Leicester, 1961

137 *Biggles Forms a Syndicate*, illustrated by Stead, Hodder and Stoughton, London, 6 July 1961
Serialisation: *Express Weekly*, starting on 30 January 1960.

138 *Biggles and the Missing Millionaire*, illustrated by Stead, Brockhampton Press, Leicester, 1961

139 *Biggles Goes Alone*, illustrated by Stead, Hodder and Stoughton, London, 11 January 1962

140 *Orchids for Biggles*, illustrated by Stead, Brockhampton Press, Leicester, 1962

141 *Biggles Sets A Trap*, illustrated by Stead, Hodder and Stoughton, London, 1962

142 *The Biggles' Book of Treasure Hunting*, illustrated by William Randell, Max Parrish, London, 1962

143 *Worlds of Wonder*, illustrated by Stead, Hodder and Stoughton, London, 22 March 1962

144 *Biggles Takes it Rough*, illustrated by Stead, Brockhampton Press, Leicester, 10 February, 1963

145 *Biggles Takes a Hand*, illustrated by Stead, Hodder and Stoughton, London, 6 May 1963

146 *Biggles' Special Case*, illustrated by Stead, Brockhampton Press, Leicester, 22 July 1963

147 *Biggles and the Plane that Disappeared*, illustrated by Stead, Hodder and Stoughton, London, 30 September 1963

148 *Biggles Flies to Work*, Dean and Son, London, 1963
A collection of eleven short stories collected from *Boys' Own Paper* and various annuals such as the *Daily Mail Annual, Stirring Stories for Boys* 1960, etc.

149 *The Man Who Vanished Into Space*, illustrated by Stead, Hodder and Stoughton, London, 3 November 1963

150 *Biggles and the Lost Sovereigns*, illustrated by Stead, Brockhampton Press, Leicester, 24 February 1964

Retitled *Biggles and the Lost Treasure* (Knight Books, Leicester, 1978).

151 *Biggles and the Black Mask*, illustrated by Stead, Hodder and Stoughton, London, 22 June 1964

152 *Biggles Investigates*, illustrated by Stead, Brockhampton Press, Leicester, October 1964
A collection of eight stories, previous publication of which is untraceable.

153 *Biggles Looks Back*, illustrated by Studio Stead, Hodder and Stoughton, London, 26 February 1965

154 *Biggles and the Plot That Failed*, illustrated by Stead, Brockhampton Press, Leicester, 20 April 1965

155 *Biggles and the Blue Moon*, illustrated by Stead, Brockhampton Press, Leicester, May 1965

156 *Biggles Adventure Omnibus* (consisting of *Biggles Gets His Men*, *No Rest for Biggles* and *Biggles Takes a Holiday*), Hodder and Stoughton, London, 9 August 1965

157 *Biggles Scores a Bull*, illustrated by Stead, Hodder and Stoughton, London, 23 August 1965

158 *Biggles in the Terai*, illustrated by Stead, Brockhampton Press, Leicester, February 1966

159 *Biggles and the Gun Runners*, illustrated by Stead, Brockhampton Press, Leicester, September 1966

160 *Biggles Sorts it Out*, illustrated by Stead, Brockhampton Press, Leicester, February 1967

161 *Biggles and the Dark Intruder*, Knight Books, Leicester, April 1967
This title is unique as it is the only Johns title (apart from The Boys' Friend Library issues of *Biggles Learns To Fly* and *Biggles in France*, both 1935), to appear in paperback first, Knight Books being a division of Brockhampton Press Ltd. The first hardcover was issued by Brockhampton in February 1970.

162 *Biggles and the Penitent Thief*, illustrated by Stead, Brockhampton Press, Leicester, September 1967

163 *Biggles and the Deep Blue Sea*, illustrated by Stead, Brockhampton Press, Leicester, February 1968

164 *The Boy Biggles*, Dean & Son Ltd, London, March 1968

165 *Biggles in the Underworld*, illustrated by Stead, Brockhampton Press, Leicester, September 1968

166 *Biggles and the Little Green God*, illustrated by Stead, Brockhampton Press, Leicester, March 1969

167 *Biggles and the Noble Lord*, illustrated by Stead, Brockhampton Press, Leicester, August 1969

168 *Biggles Sees Too Much*, illustrated by Stead, Brockhampton Press, Leicester, July 1970

169 *Biggles of the Royal Flying Corps*, introduced and edited by Piers
Williams, Purnell, Maidenhead, September 1978
Ten stories from *The Camels Are Coming* and *Biggles Learns to Fly*,
edited in their original form.

Note: Biggles Does Some Homework: Johns had completed twelve
chapters and made notes of this, the last Biggles' book, at the time of
his death. We list it with the fond hope that W. E. Johns
(Publications) Ltd may one day allow it to be finished and published
for the enjoyment of the countless Biggles' devotees.

W. E. Johns' works listed by series and category

'Biggles'

1 *The Camels are Coming*, 1932
2 *The Cruise of the Condor*, 1933
3 *Biggles of the Camel Squadron*, 1934
4 *Biggles Flies Again*, 1934
5 *Biggles Learns to Fly*, 1935
6 *The Black Peril*, 1935
7 *Biggles Flies East*, 1935
8 *Biggles Hits the Trail*, 1935
9 *Biggles in France*, 1935
10 *Biggles & Co.*, 1936
11 *Biggles in Africa*, 1936
12 *Biggles – Air Commodore*, 1937
13 *Biggles Flies West*, 1937
14 *Biggles Flies South*, 1938
15 *Biggles Goes to War*, 1938
16 *The Biggles Omnibus*, 1938
17 *The Rescue Flight*, 1939
18 *Biggles in Spain*, 1939
19 *Biggles Flies North*, 1939
20 *Biggles – Secret Agent*, 1940
21 *The Biggles Flying Omnibus*, 1940
22 *Biggles in the Baltic*, 1940
23 *Biggles in the South Seas*, 1940
24 *Biggles Defies the Swastika*, 1941

25 *Biggles Sees it Through*, 1941
26 *Spitfire Parade*, 1941
27 *The Third Biggles Omnibus*, 1941
28 *Biggles in the Jungle*, 1942
29 *Biggles Sweeps the Desert*, 1942
30 *Biggles – Charter Pilot*, 1943
31 *Biggles in Borneo*, 1943
32 *Biggles 'Fails to Return'*, 1943
33 *Biggles in the Orient*, 1945
34 *Biggles Delivers the Goods*, 1946
35 *Sergeant Bigglesworth CID*, 1947
36 *Biggles' Second Case*, 1948
37 *Biggles Hunts Big Game*, 1948
38 *Biggles Takes a Holiday*, 1948
39 *Biggles Breaks the Silence*, 1949
40 *Biggles Gets His Men*, 1950
41 *Another Job for Biggles*, 1951
42 *Biggles Goes to School*, 1951
43 *Biggles Works it Out*, 1952
44 *Biggles Takes the Case*, 1952
45 *Biggles Follows On*, 1952
46 *Biggles – Air Detective*, 1952
47 *Biggles and the Black Raider*, 1953
48 *Biggles in the Blue*, 1953
49 *The First Biggles Omnibus*, 1953
50 *Biggles in the Gobi*, 1953
51 *Biggles of the Special Air Police*, 1953
52 *Biggles Cuts it Fine*, 1954
53 *Biggles and the Pirate Treasure*, 1954
54 *Biggles Foreign Legionnaire*, 1954
55 *Biggles Pioneer Airfighter*, 1954
56 *Biggles in Australia*, 1955
57 *Biggles' Chinese Puzzle*, 1955
58 *Biggles of 266*, 1955
59 *Biggles Air Detective Omnibus*, 1956
60 *No Rest for Biggles*, 1956
61 *Biggles Takes Charge*, 1956
62 *Biggles Makes Ends Meet*, 1957
63 *Biggles of the Interpol*, 1957
64 *Biggles on the Home Front*, 1957

65 *Biggles Presses On*, 1958
66 *Biggles On Mystery Island*, 1958
67 *Biggles Buries a Hatchet*, 1958
68 *Biggles in Mexico*, 1959
69 *Biggles' Combined Operation*, 1959
70 *Biggles at the World's End*, 1959
71 *Biggles and the Leopards of Zinn*, 1960
72 *Biggles Goes Home*, 1960
73 *Biggles and the Poor Rich Boy*, 1960
74 *Biggles Forms A Syndicate*, 1961
75 *Biggles and the Missing Millionaire*, 1961
76 *Biggles Goes Alone*, 1962
77 *Orchids for Biggles*, 1962
78 *Biggles Sets a Trap*, 1962
79 *Biggles Takes it Rough*, 1963
80 *Biggles Takes a Hand*, 1963
81 *Biggles' Special Case*, 1963
82 *Biggles and the Plane that Disappeared*, 1963
83 *Biggles Flies to Work*, 1963
84 *Biggles and the Lost Soveriegns*, 1964
85 *Biggles and the Black Mask*, 1964
86 *Biggles Investigates*, 1964
87 *Biggles Looks Back*, 1965
88 *Biggles and the Plot that Failed*, 1965
89 *Biggles and the Blue Moon*, 1965
90 *Biggles Adventure Omnibus*, 1965
91 *Biggles Scores a Bull*, 1965
92 *Biggles in the Terai*, 1966
93 *Biggles and the Gun Runners*, 1966
94 *Biggles Sorts it Out*, 1967
95 *Biggles and the Dark Intruder*, 1967
96 *Biggles and the Penitent Thief*, 1967
97 *Biggles and the Deep Blue Sea*, 1967
98 *The Boy Biggles*, 1968
99 *Biggles in the Underworld*, 1968
100 *Biggles and the Little Green God*, 1969
101 *Biggles and the Noble Lord*, 1969
102 *Biggles Sees Too Much*, 1970

'Worrals'

 1 *Worrals of the WAAF*, 1941
 2 *Worrals Flies Again*, 1942
 3 *Worrals Carries On*, 1942
 4 *Worrals on The Warpath*, 1943
 5 *Worrals Goes East*, 1944
 6 *Worrals of the Islands*, 1945
 7 *Worrals in the Wilds*, 1947
 8 *Worrals Down Under*, 1948
 9 *Worrals Goes Afoot*, 1949
10 *Worrals in the Wastelands*, 1949
11 *Worrals Investigates*, 1950

'Gimlet'

 1 *King of the Commandos*, 1943
 2 *Gimlet Goes Again*, 1944
 3 *Gimlet Comes Home*, 1946
 4 *Gimlet Mops Up*, 1947
 5 *Gimlet's Oriental Quest*, 1948
 6 *Gimlet Lends a Hand*, 1949
 7 *Gimlet Bores In*, 1950
 8 *Gimlet Off the Map*, 1951
 9 *Gimlet Gets the Answer*, 1952
10 *Gimlet Takes a Job*, 1954

'Steeley'

1 *Sky High*, 1936
2 *Steeley Flies Again*, 1936
3 *Murder by Air*, 1937
4 *The Murder at Castle Deeping*, 1938
5 *Wings of Romance*, 1939
6 *Det Forsvunne Bagboksblad (The Missing Page)*, 1939

Science fiction series

1 *Kings of Space*, 1954
2 *Return to Mars*, 1955
3 *Now to the Stars*, 1956

4 *To Outer Space*, 1957
5 *The Edge of Beyond*, 1958
6 *The Death Rays of Ardilla*, 1959
7 *To Worlds Unknown*, 1960
8 *The Quest for the Perfect Planet*, 1961
9 *Worlds of Wonder*, 1962
10 *The Man Who Vanished in Space*, 1963

Miscellaneous juvenile titles

1 *Champion of the Main*, 1938
2 *Sinister Service*, 1942
3 *Comrades in Arms*, 1947
4 *The Rustlers of Rattlesnake Valley*, 1948
5 *Adventure Bound*, 1955
6 *Adventure Unlimited*, 1957
7 *Where the Golden Eagle Soars*, 1960
8 *Adventures of the Junior Detection Club*, 1960

Adult thrillers and romances

1 *Mossyface (William Earle)*, 1932
2 *The Spy Flyers*, 1933
3 *The Raid*, 1935
4 *Blue Blood Runs Red (Jon Early)*, 1936
5 *Desert Night*, 1938
6 *The Unknown Quantity*, 1940
7 *Short Sorties*, 1940
8 *Dr Vane Answers the Call*, 1950
9 *Sky Fever*, 1953
10 *No Motive for Murder*, 1958
11 *The Man Who Lost His Way*, 1960

Anthologies edited

1 *Wings: A Book of Flying Adventures*, 1931
2 *The Modern Boy's Book of Aircraft*, 1931
3 *Thrilling Flights*, 1935

Non-Fiction

1 *The Pictorial Flying Course (with Flt. Lt. H. Schofield)*, 1932
2 *Fighting Planes and Aces*, 1932
3 *The Air VCs*, 1935
4 *Some Milestones in Aviation*, 1935
5 *The Passing Show*, 1937
6 *The Modern Boy's Book of Pirates*, 1939
7 *The Biggles Book of Heroes*, 1959
8 *The Biggles Book of Treasure Hunting*, 1962

Uncollected short stories

It would be futile to attempt to list all the adult short stories written by Johns, either under his own name or his pseudonym of William Earle. It must be remembered that the very first Biggles stories were written for adults under this pseudonym, and he was soon using it for other adult tales, such as 'A Flying Start' in *Popular Flying*, November 1932. His output became prolific.

In listing some of the publications from which the stories contained in the volume *Short Sorties* (1950) derived, Johns said, 'some were written for the American magazines after our own short story market had almost died for lack of paper ... after the Liberation made it possible some were published on the Continent'. That there are numerous uncollected Johns' adult short stories about is evidenced by the many discovered by the authors. For example: 'Coffee for Two' (*Daily Express*, 4 January 1934); 'Encounter' (*Daily Express*, 17 February 1934); 'Winged Justice' (William Earle) (*The New Book of the Air*, 1935); 'The Badge' (*Strand Magazine*, January 1950).

A similar difficulty arises in attempting to list juvenile short stories. What we have listed below are uncollected Biggles' tales, all of which have First World War settings:

'Biggles' Xmas Box', *The Modern Boy*, 15 December 1934
'Biggles' Christmas Tree, *The Modern Boy*, 22 December 1934
'Biggles and the Joker', *The Modern Boy*, 2 February 1935
'Biggles' Night Out', *The Modern Boy*, 31 August 1935
'Biggles on the Spot', *The Modern Boy's Book of Adventure Stories*, 1936
'Biggles Takes the Bait', *The Modern Boy's Annual*, 1937

We should also list:
'Biggles' Exciting Night', *The Modern Boy's Annual*, 1937
'The Fledgling', *The New Book of the Air*, edited by Howard Leigh, Oxford University Press, London, 1935 (which also appears as 'Biggles' Fledgling' in *The Modern Boy*, 7 June 1939)

The above two tales have never appeared in book edition in their original form. 'Biggles' Exciting Night' was rewritten as two stories – 'The Fortunes of War' and 'Bertie Picks the Lock' in *Spitfire Parade* (1941) – while 'The Fledgling' was rewritten, again with a Second World War setting, as 'The Hare and the Tortoise' in *Biggles Takes the Case* (1952). In this respect, Johns' self-plagiarism leads to many a trap for the unwary bibliographer. 'Sausage and Mash', which appeared in *Air Stories*, March 1940 credited to 'Old Timer' is blatantly a Johns' story. On close examination, it turns out to be 'The Trap' from *Biggles of the Camel Squadron*, rewritten as a Second World War tale, in which Biggles becomes Flight Lieutenant 'Porky' Bacon, and some of the original passages are deleted.

The only Worrals uncollected short story discovered is 'Worrals Works it Out', *Girls' Own Paper*, September 1947. But, on a list of 'stories not yet used in book form' made by Johns in November 1954 (copy in the authors' possession), he lists 'Worrals on the Home Front' and 'Worrals takes a hand', but the authors have been unable to trace these. The list also includes stories entitled 'A matter of observation' and 'The Dingo trail' – also untraceable.

Anthologies

For obvious reasons, Johns' work in anthology form is difficult to list, so diverse were his markets in this field. Books of flying tales, such as *Flying Thrills*, *Flying Stories* and *Flying Adventures*, edited under the by-line 'Flight Lieutenant', all contain Johns' stories and articles. Oxford University Press also issued anthologies, such as *The New Book of the Air* (1935), which contain a number of Johns' stories, some never collected in any other book form. Also, during the 1930s Johns' stories were included in some of Faber and Faber's 'My Best Story' anthologies. Starting with *The Modern Boy's Annual* in the

1930s, Johns' juvenile stores were published in a very varied number of children's annuals, especially during the 1950s.

Journalism

Johns' prolific output in fiction was matched by an equally large output of articles, regular columns and other pieces in an equally wide variety of publications. His most prolific period in journalism was the 1930s, yet even as late as 1960 articles by him were cropping up in publications such as the *Daily Mail*, on such topics as the walking craze – two Britons had just completed a walk across America and Dr Barbara Moore was in the headlines – (18 June 1960), and on etiquette ('Why Lift Your Hat', 20 August 1960). The following is not a complete list, but gives details of columns Johns wrote on a regular basis:

The Modern Boy:	'What Plane Was That?' 27 December 1930 to 13 March 1932
	'Let's Look Around', 19 February 1938 to 14 October 1939
Popular Flying:	Editorials (as editor) from April 1932 to May 1939
Flying:	Editorials (as editor) from 2 April 1938 to 19 January 1939
My Garden:	'The Passing Show' May 1936 to October 1944
Pearson's Magazine:	'What Men Are Talking About' June 1939 to November 1939
ATC Gazette.	August 1940–1941
Boys' Own Paper:	'Skyways – Jottings from My Logbook' September 1941 to March 1942
Girls' Own Paper:	'The World On Wings' October 1941 to March 1942

Biggles in comic strip form

Biggles enjoyed considerable popularity in comic strip form during the 1950s. Pat Williams' full-colour strip adaptation of *The Cruise of the Condor* was published in book form in May

1955 by Juvenile Productions Ltd. During the late 1950s and early 1960s, the *Express Weekly* published regular strip adventures of Biggles. With Biggles' immense popularity in Australia in the early 1950s, Action Comic Pty, of Sydney launched a Biggles comic entitled 'The Adventures of Biggles', which ran to 68 pages and was priced one shilling. The strips were drawn by A. Devine and John Dixon. An English edition of the comic was published by Strato Publications Ltd of London. The authors have only seen Nos. 1 to 9 of the series. As well as Biggles strips, issues 8 and 9 contained Gimlet adventures.

Biggles on commercial recording

An abridged version of *Biggles Learns to Fly* was issued on cassette recording by Ivan Berg Associates (Audio Publishing) Ltd of London, in March 1977, price £1.84 plus VAT. The stories were read by actor Simon Ward. Music was by Major Records. The abridged stories were: 'First Time Up'; 'Landed – but Lost'; 'The Boat to France and Battle'; 'Pilots and Planes and Late for Dinner'; 'A Daring Stunt'; 'Eyes of the Guns'; 'The Camera and the Yellow Hun'; and 'The Dawn Patrol'.

Broadcasting (radio)

Plays:

The Machine That Disappeared (co-authored with G. R. Rainier)
  Produced by Fred O'Donovan, BBC Home Service, Friday, 19 June 1942

The Charming Mrs Nayther (co-authored with G. R. Rainier)
  Produced by Hugh Stewart, BBC Home Service, Saturday, 15 August 1942

Stories:

Johns says that several of his short stories, such as 'Wine With A Lady', were first broadcast on BBC Radio in the late 1940s. These have been impossible to trace.

Biggles radio dramatisations:
'Biggles Flies West'
  BBC Home Service, 'Children's Hour', 1948
    11 March: The Doubloon
    18 March: The Eventful Journey
    25 March: Pirates All
    1 April: Louis Dakeyn's Secret

    6 October: Repeat 'Request Week' edition

'Biggles Flies North'
  BBC Home Service, 'Children's Hour', 1948
    26 November: Fort Beaver
    3 December: Grim Encounter
    10 December: McBain Strikes
    17 December: Life or Death

    8 April 1949: Repeat 'Request Week' edition

'Biggles in the Jungle'
  BBC Home Service, 'Children's Hour', June 1949
  Weekly from 3 June to 10 June

    11 November 1949: Repeat 'Request Week' edition

BBC Home Service 'Hello Children'
  12.00 noon short story reading, 1949
    29 August 'The Case of the Stolen Aircraft'
    5 September 'The Case of the Mysterious Gunshots'
    12 September 'The Case of the Lump of Metal'

'Biggles Hunts Big Game'
  BBC Home Service, 'Children's Hour', 1950
    8 October: An Assignment with the Counterfeiter
    13 October: Tight Corner

'Biggles in the Blue'
  BBC Home Service, 'Children's Hour', 1953
    18 November: An Ill-Timed Meeting
    25 November: An Egg Makes a Mystery
    2 December: The Secret of Inague

'Biggles and the Pirate Treasure'
  BBC Home Service, 'Children's Hour', 1955
    30 September: Biggles and the Pirate Treasure
    7 October: Biggles and the Case of the Obliging Tourist
    14 October: Biggles and the Unknown Diamonds
    21 October: Final Instalment

    22 April 1958: repeat of 'Biggles and the Case of the Obliging Tourist'

'Biggles' Chinese Puzzle' and 'Biggles of the Interpol'
  BBC Home Service, 'Children's Hour'
    14 August 1957 weekly to 18 September 1957: Adaptations of six stories from the above two books
'Biggles Presses On'
  BBC Home Service, 'Children's Hour', 1959
    8 May: The Case of the Ambitious Fishmonger
    15 May: Fishy Business

Amalgamated Wireless (Australia) Ltd
Amalgamated Wireless bought broadcasting rights on twelve Biggles books and began to broadcast a series of fifteen-minute episodes from Adelaide in 1949. After the first 208 episodes Amalgamated Wireless moved to Sydney. The series became very popular and was expanded to thirty minutes and ran until 1955, broadcast from Station 5AO. New Zealand and South African broadcasting stations secured rights to broadcast the series, which was produced by Maurice Chapman. The part of Biggles, first played by Moray Powell, was later played by Keith MacDonald.

Broadcasting (television)

'Biggles'
  Granada Television Network Production
Friday, 1 April 1960, at 6.30 pm, weekly until episode 14; then the series was shown on Wednesdays and Fridays until episode 44, Wednesday, 12 October 1960.
  The series did not consist of adaptations of Johns' stories, but of stories about Biggles and the Air Police written by the screenwriters, who included H. V. Kershaw, Alick Hayes,

Thomas Clarke, Tony Warren (creator of 'Coronation Street'), Rex Howard Arundel and Edward Luckarift. Each story, which consisted of three episodes, had a different producer.

Biggles was played by Nevil Whiting; Bertie by David Drummond; Ginger by John Leyton; and von Stalhein by Carl Duering.

Other related books

(a)   *Biggles: The Authorised Biography* by John Pearson, Sidgwick & Jackson, London, 15 January 1979

(b)   *Biggles and the Sargasso Triangle*, written and drawn by Bjorn Karlstrom, translated by Peter James, Hodder and Stoughton, London, 1978

(c)   *Biggles and the Golden Bird*, written and drawn by Bjorn Karlstrom, translated by Peter James, Hodder and Stoughton, London, 1978

(d)   *Biggles and the Tiger*, written and drawn by Bjorn Karlstrom, translated by Peter James, Hodder and Stoughton, London 1981

(e)   *Biggles and the Menace from Space*, written and drawn by Bjorn Karlstrom, translated by Peter James, Hodder and Stoughton, London 1981

(f)   *Biggles Annual*, World International Publishing Ltd, Manchester, August 1980
The first-ever annual, this contains an abridgement of *Biggles and the Plane That Disappeared* by W. E. Johns.

(g)   *Biggles i Sverige – en pilote-studie. Innerhåll, spridning och kritik av W. E. Johns Bigglesböcker* (Biggles in Sweden: a pilot study of the content and influence, with criticism, of W. E. Johns' Biggles books) Stefan Mählqvist, Bonniers Förlag, Sweden 1982

INDEX

Abbasieh, SS 21
Air Defence Cadet Corps Gazette 176, 177
Air Pictorial 247
Air Police Stories 237–9, 242
Air Stories magazine 164, 183
Air Training Corps 177
Aitkin, Professor Don 187–90, 233, 234, 241–3
Alexandria 24
Amalgamated Press 124, 164
Amey, 2nd Lt A. E. 77, 79, 82, 86, 87, 90–3
Ashton, Captain 33, 34
Attwood, 2nd Lt J. T. L. 55, 81, 82
Australia 208, 209, 229, 233
Azelot 52, 60, 61, 63, 64, 72, 74–8, 81, 83-6, 94, 128

Bader, Douglas 129
Ball, Captain Albert 49
Behind the Smoke Screen (Groves) 149
Bell, Captain J. R. 53, 56, 57, 67, 69, 72
Bengeo, Hertford 11, 12
Biggles stories *passim*
Bishop, Billy 48, 49, 129, 133, 134
Boys' Own Paper, The 11, 144, 177, 184, 185, 204, 212, 245
Brabazon, Lt Col Moore 147
Brockhampton Press 133, 191
Brownhill, Lt E. A. 57

Buhl aerodrome 72, 73, 74

Carter (RNAS Officer) 99, 100
Catching Them Young (Dixon) 190, 233, 239
Chamberlain, Prime Minister Neville 167, 168
Champion, Major 44, 49
Champion, The 181
China 4, 146, 148
Churchill, Sir Winston 24, 149, 166
Church Times 142, 155, 214, 245
Cobham, Sir Alan 122
Coley Park aerodrome 33, 34, 37, 38
Collins, Mrs Margaret (niece of W. E. Johns) 11, 213
Conquest of the Air (film) 166
Constantine of Greece, King 26
Cox, Jack 11, 13, 144, 176, 177, 204
Coxhill, 2nd Lt F. N. 55, 59–65, 72, 73, 86
Cranwell 104, 105
Cunningham, 2nd Lt P. J. 69
Cutson, 2nd Lt C. W. 57

Daily Express 163, 186, 222, 231
Daily Mail 2, 187, 203, 204, 232, 234, 246
Daily Mail Annual 205
Daily Mirror 2, 142, 214
Daily Telegraph 2, 186, 187, 234

David, Lt   42
Davies, Hunter   219, 230
Dawn Patrol (Saunders)   166
Day, Captain H. C.   29–31
Death of an Airman (Sprigg)   159
Dixon, Bob   190, 234, 239, 240
Doehler, 2nd Lt H. H.   69
Dombasle, Lt Col G. C. St P. de   33
Doumer, President   146
Dowswell, 2nd Lt S. L.   69
Dunn, 2nd Lt J. B.   57, 67, 77
Dymond, 2nd Lt G. P.   77

Eagle, The   212
Earle, William (pseudonym of W. E. Johns)   117, 124, 131, 151, 163, 180
Early, Jon (pseudonym of W. E. Johns)   165
Edinburgh Citizen   166
Edinburgh Evening News   64
Elderton, Sue   187–90, 233, 241, 242
Ellis, Mrs Marjorie (née Leigh, sister of Doris Leigh)   126, 134, 135, 142, 149, 160, 170, 174, 176, 184, 201, 206, 207, 213, 244, 248; *see also* Leigh, Marjorie
Ellis, Squadron Leader 'Teddy'   182, 199
Entwistle, Frank   92, 205, 222, 223
Ettendorf   91–3, 95
Evans, Major Lloyd   65, 66
Evening Standard   92, 205, 222, 230, 246, 248
Express Weekly   212
Eyre, Frank   184, 185

Farmer, Arch   38, 39
Field, The   126
film rights (on W. E. Johns'

books)   2, 249, 250
Flying   3, 163, 170, 171, 173, 176
Flying Aces   131
Fox, Captain   54, 86
Franco, General   156, 158
Frend, Charles   166
Fryatts, Captain   95

Gallipoli   4, 21, 22, 24
Gamlin, Lionel   186
Gee, Sgt Major   109
Gem, The   180, 182
George Newnes Ltd   151, 154, 163, 164, 170
Germany   146, 148, 150–3
'Gimlet' stories   44, 190, 191
Girls' Own Paper, The   177, 185, 190
Glasgow Evening News   164
Goddard, Jackie   213
Gompertz, 2nd Lt H. G. T.   54, 69, 70, 80, 81
Göring, Hermann   92, 93, 128
Gormley, 2nd Lt A. J. G.   69, 94
Gorrill, 2nd Lt G.   86
Graham, Miss Glenda   126
Graphic, The   122
Gray, Major Alec, MC   52, 53, 64, 66, 68, 73, 74, 76, 129
Greece   26, 27
Greene, Graham   210
Grosvenor, Peter   231
Groves, Brigadier General P. R. C.   149
Guardian, The   10, 213, 251
Guild Gardener, The   155
G-2 Battle Aces   131

Hadfield, Charles   185
Hamilton, General Sir Ian   24
Hamilton, John (publisher)   120, 124–9, 131, 137, 138, 151, 163, 164, 166, 181, 193

Hammond, Sabena   179; *see also* Johns, Sabena

Harley (South African pilot)   96, 98

Harmey, Grafton   45

Harris, Bridget   219, 232

Heal, Jeane   205

Heckel, Willy   149

Hendon Air Display   112, 129

Hertford   11

Hertford Grammar School   13, 15

Hicks, 2nd Lt R. I. A.   46, 69

Hitler, Adolf   93, 148, 156, 158, 167–9, 173

Hobson's Choice (Miller)   125

Hodder and Stoughton (publishers)   171, 187, 188, 190–2, 207, 216, 231, 247, 248

Hodgson, Brigadier H. W.   22

Hollywood   128, 226

Hopgood Dr   234

Horniman, Michael I.   247

Hull Daily Mail   164, 165

Hunt, Rev. John   17, 20, 102, 116, 207

Hunt, Kathleen   116, 117; *see also* King, Kathleen

Hunt, Maude Penelope   17, 20, 25; *see also* Johns, Maude

Illustrated London News   115, 117, 118, 122, 247

India   113–15

Ingram, Captain Bruce S., OBE, MC   117

Iraq   113–15

Jagdstaffel 4   92, 93

Jaggers of the Air Police (Templer)   211

Japan   146, 148, 153

Janes' Aircraft   95

Johns, Doris   *see* Leigh, Doris

Johns, Elizabeth (née Earl, mother of W. E. Johns)   11, 17

Johns, Faith (grand-daughter of W. E. Johns)   179

Johns, Maude (née Hunt, wife of W. E. Johns)   24, 25, 38, 105, 106; marriage 20; leaves husband 116; ill health 117, 179; death 206

Johns, Perdita (grand-daughter of W. E. Johns)   179

Johns, Richard   12

Johns, Richard Eastman (father of W. E. Johns)   11, 12, 17

Johns, Russell Ernest (brother of W. E. Johns)   11, 17, 20, 194, 213, 247

Johns, Sabena (née Hammond)   206, 247

Johns, William   11

Johns, William Earl   ancestors and parents 11, 12; birth 11; schooldays 13–16; in cadet corps 13, 14; ambition to be soldier 15, 16; articled as surveyor 16; studies music 16, 17; appointed sanitary inspector at Swaffham 16; death of father 17; joins Territorial Army 18; serves in First World War 19–103; marriage 20; serves at Gallipoli 21–4; birth of son 24; joins Machine Gun Corps 24; promoted lance corporal 25; serves in Salonika 26–32; learns to fly 33; posted to No. 25 Flying Training School, Thetford 38; appointed flying instructor 38; promoted 2nd Lieutenant 49; serves in France 50–89; taken prisoner 90; interrogated 93–6; attempts escape 97; in solitary confinement, 98, 101; escapes and is recaptured 100; demobilised 102; marriage breaks down 105; rejoins RAF as recruiting officer 106; serves in Iraq and India 113, 114; transferred to Birmingham 115; meets Doris Leigh 116; posted to Newcastle 117; sets up home with Doris 117; posted to Record Office, Ruislip 117; begins to paint and write 117; transferred to HQ Air Defence 117; transferred to RAF Reserve 119; edits *Popular Flying* 126; writes first Biggles stories 126; begins to write on gardening 155; moves to Reigate 160; removed from editorship of *Flying* and *Popular Flying* 170; returns to London on outbreak of war 175; joins Air Defence Cadet Corps 176; writes for radio 186; moves to Pitchroy Lodge, Scotland 197; moves to Hampton Court 205; death of son 206; death of wife 206; works published abroad 207–12; works televised 212, 213; death 246

appearance 244; sense of humour 7, 244; on imperialism 8; on politics 3, 141, 146, 157, 219; on war 3–5, 19, 28, 29, 70, 71, 134, 147–9, 153, 167, 220; love of gardening 12, 121, 154–6, 160, 161, 193, 196, 205, 245; love of mountains 154; love of sport 200, 202; love of wine 194, 195; dislike of London 174; method of writing 200, 201, 222; assessment and criticism of his works 2, 10, 139, 224–43

Johns, William Earl Carmichael ('Jack', son of W. E. Johns) 14, 15, 38, 105, 106, 116, 117, 121, 151; birth 24; marriage 179; death 206

Johns W. E. (Publications) Ltd 247

Johnson, Amy 6, 189

Johnson, 'Navvy' 115

Jones, 2nd Lt T. A. 69

Junior Mirror 212

Keyes, 2nd Lt A. C. 77

King, Mrs Kathleen (née Hunt) 17, 207, 247

King's Own Royal Regiment (Norfolk Yeomanry) 18, 19

Kinkead, Ft Lt S. M. 120

Kinman, Major G. W. 13, 14

Kit Book of Best Short Stories 186

Knightly, Phillip 110

Korda, Alexander 166

Landshut, POW camp 98–101

Lane, Allen 183

La Sologne 202, 203, 216, 245

Latimer House (publishers) 186

Lawrence, T. E. 107–11

Lee, 2nd Lt J. A. 67

Leigh, Doris meets W. E. Johns and sets up home with him 116–119; moves to Lingfield 120, 121; moves to Reigate 159; persuades Johns to have agent 184; moves to Scotland 199–201; moves to Hampton Court 205; after death of Johns' wife 206, 207; becomes director of W. E. Johns (Publications) Ltd 211; death of Johns 246, 247; death 250

travels with Johns 123, 145, 150, 152, 158, 161, 169, 171–3, 175, 197, 202, 245

Leigh family   116, 161, 192, 197
Leigh, Mrs Florence Beatrice
    (mother of Doris)   116, 161,
    180, 192, 199
Leigh, Howard (brother of
    Doris)   joins Johns' studio as
    artist 120; success as aviation
    illustrator 124, 126, 128, 193;
    travels with Johns 145, 158, as
    editor and illustrator 151, 155;
    marriage 162; death 192, 193
Leigh, Marjorie (sister of
    Doris)   161, 171, 182, 199,
    201, 250; see also Ellis,
    Marjorie
Leigh, Mrs Olive (née Eldon, wife
    of Howard Leigh)   192
Leyland, Eric   211
Liégeois, Hotel, Nancy   82, 83
Lindbergh, Charles   120
Lingfield, Sussex   119–121, 125,
    160, 162, 183, 192
Little Dunham, Norfolk   17, 24,
    25, 38, 43, 102, 105, 116
Liverpool Daily Post   212
Liverpool Evening Express   186
Llandudno   169, 173
London, Jack   7
Londonderry   149, 169
London Evening News   212, 222
London Gazette   32
Luftwaffe   149, 150, 158, 176,
    180, 197
Lutterworth Press   188, 190, 203
Lympne, Kent   50, 145

McClure, Major S.   33
McCudden, Major James T. B.,
    VC   48, 49, 129
Macdonald, Keith A.   210, 234
Machine Gun Corps   24
Mackay, Captain D. R. G.
    ('Jock')   53, 54, 56, 57, 67,
    72–4, 77, 86, 87

MacLaren, 'Don'   48
MacNiven (friend of W. E. Johns)
    196
Manchester Evening News   166,
    214
Manley, Pat   100
Mannock, 'Mick'   48, 49, 134
Manston, Rev A. C.   20
Marcelle (French girl)   85, 86
Marske-on-Sea   44, 47
Melbourne Herald   210
Mellifont Press Ltd   124, 125
Men Only   163
Michelmore, Cliff   212, 213, 245
Miller, Esther   125
Milne, A. A.   142
Milne, General Sir George   27
Mint, The (T. E. Lawrence)   107,
    108
Mitchell, Brigadier General 'Billy'
    76
Modern Boy, The   122, 124, 125,
    130, 133, 135, 136, 138, 140,
    151, 163, 180, 181, 211
Modern Boy's Annual   183
Monro, General Sir Charles   24
Monte Carlo   175, 204
Morning Post   126
Morris, Alan   177
Morse, Lt Col A. F.   18, 21
Moseley, Sir Oswald   146
Mussolini, Benito   156, 158
My Garden   12, 154, 155, 160,
    163, 174, 193, 197–9
Myring, 2nd Lt T. F. L.   56, 69

Nancy, France   52, 58–60, 70,
    76, 82, 83, 102
Narborough, Norfolk   38, 39,
    41–3
Nelson, Ft Lt   110
New Book of the Air   151
New Statesman   2
Nielsen, Sven   202, 207, 245

Norfolk 16, 17
Norfolk Yeomanry 21, 22, 24
Norwich Municipal
  Aerodrome 146
Nottingham Evening Post 214
No. 1 School of Aeronautics,
  Reading 33, 38
No. 2 School of Air Fighting,
  Marske-on-Sea 44. 46
No. 5 Reserve Squadron 52
No. 25 Flying Training School,
  Thetford 38, 41
No. 34 Squadron 52
No. 41 Wing 66
No. 43 Squadron 95
No. 55 (Day) Bombing
  Squadron 50, 52–8, 64, 67,
  68, 70, 72, 74, 76–80, 82, 86, 91
  104
No. 59 Training Squadron 104
No. 99 Squadron 52, 62, 73
No. 104 Squadron 52, 63, 64, 68

O'Donovan, Fred 186
Olympic, SS 21
Osborne, Jane 231, 233
Oxford School for Officer Cadets
  33
Oxford University Press 134,
  138–40, 151, 163, 181–5, 191,
  193, 207

Pace, Lt W. J., DFC 56, 57, 72
Papworth, 2nd Lt A. S. 57, 69
Paris 202, 203
Parke, Lt J. 72
Patey, 2nd Lt, DFC 70, 76
Pattinson, Major L. A. 52
Pearson, C. Arthur 151
Pearson, John 249
Pearson's Magazine 174, 181,
  186
Pearsons's Weekly 164

People, The 212
Perry, Commander 145
Pershing, General John 76
Pitchroy Lodge 199, 200, 201
Pitman, Robert 100, 136, 178,
  205, 210, 222, 223
Polendine, Robert 174
Popular Flying launched by
  John Hamilton 126–8, 181;
  editorship of W. E. Johns 70,
  75, 130, 144, 151, 154, 155,
  157, 167, 168; contributions by
  W. E. Johns 130–3, 135, 136,
  148–51; sold to C. A. Pearson
  151; contributions by Jack
  Johns 151; contributions by C.
  Sprigg 159; launch of sister
  paper, *Flying* 163; reviews *Blue
  Blood Runs Red* 165; W. E.
  Johns removed from editorship
  and writes last editorial 170–3,
  176.
Public Opinion 142
Punch 2
Python, Monty 2

Quinnell, Major J. C. 52, 64
Quiver 142
Ranger 124
Ranier, G. Rodney 185
Rayment, 2nd Lt C. L. 'Pip' 67,
  68, 70, 72, 81
Reading 33, 38
Record Office, Ruislip 117
Reigate 174, 179, 180, 194, 197
Reigate Hill 160, 199, 200
Rendlesham Park, Suffolk 20
Reynolds News 178
Reynolds, Stanley 10, 251
Richthofen, Baron Manfred von
  ('Red Baron') 29, 92, 128, 235
Riefenstahl, Leni 93
Riviera 145, 203
Rose-Tramp, J. M. 145

Ross (*see* Lawrence, T. E.)
107–11
Royal Aero Club Gazette 186
Royal Air Force 19, 44, 182
Royal Flying Corps 19, 32, 44,
131–43, 235
Royal Naval Air Force 44
Russia 153, 154
Ryder, Charles 123
R101 (airship) 120

St Mihiel Salient 76, 77
Salonika 26–31
Sanders, General Otto Liman von
21
Sarrail, General Maurice 26
Saunders, John Monk 166
Savage, Major 118
Schneider Trophy 120, 125
Schofield, Harry 120, 125
Scotland 196, 197, 199–205
Scotsman, The 142, 187
Scout, The 214
Secret Life of Plants, The
(Tompkins & Bird) 245
Secret Lives of Lawrence of Arabia
(Knightley & Simpson) 110
Sedgeford, Norfolk 42
Silly, Captain B. J. 53, 55–7, 65,
76–82
Silver Jacket, The 210
Simpson, Colin 110
Sky Birds 131
Smell, 'Smasher' 45
Smithson (pilot) 66
Spain 155–8, 169
Spooner, Winifred 127
Spooner, Captain Hugh 'Tony'
127
Sprigg, Christopher St John 124,
159
Stead, Leslie 192
Steeley books 164, 215
Stephens, Theo A. 154

Steward, Lt D. W. 56, 57, 72
Stewart, 2nd Lt E. R., DFC 57
Stewart, Hugh 187
Stewart, Margaret 204
Stewart, Oliver 173
Strand, The 186
Suez Canal 24
Sullivan, Sgt 117
Sunday Despatch 222
Sunday Express 100, 136, 178,
205, 222, 246
Sunday Times 142, 210, 217,
219, 231, 232, 234
Swaffham, Norfolk 16, 17
Swann, Air Vice-Marshal Sir
Oliver 111
Swayze (Canadian soldier) 100
Sweden 207, 212
Sydney Morning Herald 210

Tales Out of School (Trease) 217,
231
Taylor, Leonard 176
Taylor, William A. 230
Teachers Against Racism 219,
231, 232
Templer, John 211
Thames Publishing Company
134, 135
Thetford, Norfolk 38, 40, 43
Thriller, The 164
Time and Tide 214
Times, The 92, 246
Times Educational Supplement,
The 191
Times Literary Supplement 142,
214
Tit-bits 163
Torbay Express 165
Townsend, John Rowe 184, 228
Trease, Geoffrey 215, 217, 218,
220, 221, 224–9, 231, 234, 247
Trenchard, General H. ('Boomer')
52, 56, 72, 111

Triumph, The 181
Tsuyoshi, Prime Minister 146
Tuck, Donald H. 215
Turner, Lt C. 81, 82
TV Times 213, 223

Udet, Ernst 92, 93

Vale, Mr George 142
Valerie, Squadron Leader 110
Venizelos, Eleutherios 26

War Birds 131
Ward, Simon 2
Warren, Tony 213
War Thriller, The 164, 182
Waterous, 2nd Lt Don J. 67, 68, 72–4, 81
Watt, A. P. Ltd 191, 247
Watt, Peter 184
Watts, Roy 2

W. E. Johns (Publications) Ltd 247
Welchman, Lt P. E. 72, 76
Westerman, Percy F. 124
Westermann, P. W. J. 192
Western Mail 142, 187
Wigglesworth, Air Commodore C. G. 135
Wings (Saunders) 57, 114, 166, 181
Woman 205
Woman's Journal 186
Woman's Magazine 185
Women's Auxiliary Air Force (WAAF) 177
Worrals books 6, 187–91
Writer, The 221, 245

Xaffervilliers 51

Yank at Oxford, A (film) 167